ARNHEM
BLACK TUESDAY

ARNHEM
BLACK TUESDAY

AL MURRAY

bantam

TRANSWORLD PUBLISHERS
Penguin Random House, One Embassy Gardens,
8 Viaduct Gardens, London SW11 7BW
www.penguin.co.uk

Transworld is part of the Penguin Random House group of companies
whose addresses can be found at global.penguinrandomhouse.com

Penguin
Random House
UK

First published in Great Britain in 2024 by Bantam
an imprint of Transworld Publishers

A CIP catalogue record for this book
is available from the British Library.

ISBNs
9780857506566 hb
9780857506573 tpb

Typeset in 11/15.5pt ITC Giovanni Std by Jouve (UK), Milton Keynes
Printed and bound in Great Britain by Clays Ltd, Elcograf S.p.A.

The authorized representative in the EEA is Penguin Random House Ireland,
Morrison Chambers, 32 Nassau Street, Dublin D02 YH68.

Penguin Random House is committed to a sustainable future
for our business, our readers and our planet. This book is made
from Forest Stewardship Council® certified paper.

MIX
Paper | Supporting
responsible forestry
FSC® C018179

To Jim, for walking and talking the ground

CONTENTS

TIMELINE

	THE BRIDGE	THE TOWN
0000HRS	**1. THE BESIEGED:** Lt. Col. Frost assesses state of play: buildings on fire, ammunition will need to be conserved.	**5. THE GENERAL:** Maj. Gen. Urquhart stuck in the loft of 14 Zwarteweg.
0100HRS		**2. THE EMBATTLED:** Attacks into the Town called off for now. Remnants of 1st Para Bn out of touch with 3rd Para Bn. 2nd Bn South Staffs and 11th Para Bn are moving into Town to join effort to reach Bridge.
0200HRS	Enemy attack the school: knocking everyone out with a 'bazooka'.	**8. THE COLONELS ON THE RIVER ROAD:** Decision to attack. 1st Para on the lower River Road, 2nd South Staffs along the Higher Road towards The Monastery, 11th Para Bn on South Staffs' left flank and in reserve.
0245HRS		3rd Para Bn, unknown to the others in the Town, attack along River Road.
0300HRS	Germans surround the school. Mackay and his men repulse this attack.	
0330HRS		
0400HRS		1st Para Bn as they attack meet 3rd Para Bn retreating along River Road: Dorrien-Smith 'not bloody likely'.
0430HRS		Hand-to-hand combat along the River Road, German armour in evidence.
0500HRS		
0600HRS		2nd South Staffs push on up the Higher Road to The Monastery, despite German armour making an appearance.

THE VILLAGE	THE WOODS
3. A QUIET NIGHT?: Div. HQ under Brig. Hicks trying to make sense of what to do in Maj. Gen. Urquhart's absence. Rumour is the Bridge has fallen.	**4. WAITING FOR TOMORROW:** 4th Parachute Brigade successfully clear of its DZs. Brig. Hackett unhappy with the situation as he finds out about it. Decides to visit Divisional HQ.
6. DIVISIONAL HEADQUARTERS – THE BRIGADIERS: Brig. Hackett argues with Hicks in Maj. Gen. Urquhart's absence about what to do. Returns to his HQ having 'written himself some orders' to attack in the Woods.	7th Bn KOSB move to Johanna Hoeve area to protect the LZ for the arrival of the Poles. They encounter the enemy east of the LZ and decide not to engage.
7. THE GUNS. 1ST LIGHT AIRLANDING REGIMENT, RA: 1st Airborne's firepower – is it up to the job?	
	156 Bn are ready to attack in the Woods, towards the high ground to the east. With them glider pilots, including Louis Hagen. 10th Para Bn also moving up to make their attack on the Amsterdamseweg.

	THE BRIDGE		THE TOWN
0600HRS	**9. TOTTERING ABOVE THE BOILING TIDE**		**10. THE DOCTOR:** Capt. Stuart Mawson prepares his aid post.
0630HRS			
0700HRS	German attacks intensify.		Maj. Gen. Urquhart sprung from his loft by passing South Staffs. Sets off back to Divisional HQ. Meets Capt. Mawson at aid post.
0730HRS			**11. THE BATTALION:** 11th Bn faces the problems of fighting in a built-up area.
0745HRS			**12. THE MONASTERY:** 2nd Bn South Staffs make it to The Monastery and dig into the hollow there.
0800HRS			
0830HRS			
0900HRS			
0930HRS			
1000HRS	Radio contact made with 2nd Army, who promise relief today once they've got across the river at Nijmegen.		
1100HRS			Fighting at The Monastery ends. Remnants of 2nd South Staffs withdraw to the Bottleneck.
1130HRS			
1200HRS	**17. NO RELIEF**		**16. ON THE BRINK:** 11th Bn and the South Staffs attempt to take the high ground at Den Brink. Both battalions caught in the open – 11th Bn overwhelmed, Staffs also. Retreat.
1300HRS			

THE VILLAGE	THE WOODS
Light Regiment engaging targets in support of the attacks in the Town.	**15. THE BRIGADE:** Brig. Hackett's 4th Parachute Brigade prepare to attack in the Woods.
	156 Bn attack goes in, initial 'anti-climax', seems the enemy are not present.
	10th Bn moves up to the Amsterdamseweg. Timings uncertain – there is no War Diary for the 10th Bn.
13. DIVISIONAL HQ AND ELSEWHERE: Padre Pare witnesses return of Maj. Gen. Urquhart to Div. HQ: 'an air of confidence'. Then sets off to bury Generalmajor Kussin.	
14. ALARUMS AND EXCURSIONS IN THE WEST: 1st Bn the Border Regiment hold the line at the Landing Zones.	A Coy of 156 Bn meets extremely heavy resistance.
	Hackett visits 156 Bn HQ: unaware of how badly it's going.
	156's HQ joins the attack. Things going wrong.
	18. DISENGAGE: With his attacks having failed in the Woods, Hackett tries to extract his Brigade from contact with the enemy.
	Crowds of men retreat to the railway line. 4th Squadron RE discover the tunnel under the railway line.

	THE BRIDGE	THE TOWN
1400HRS		
1430HRS		
1500HRS	MkIII Panzer attacks.	**19. 1500 HRS: SKIES OVER ARNHEM:** The Supply Lift arrives, followed at 1530 by the Poles in their gliders.
1530HRS	Focke-Wulf Fw 190 hits the church tower. Rejoicing.	
1600HRS		
1700HRS		
1800HRS	**26. ALL AFIRE:** Systematic in their tactics, the Germans seek to burn out Frost's men building by building.	
1900HRS	Three Tiger tanks attack, firing AP rounds directly into the buildings around the Bridge.	
2000HRS	Padre Egan wounded.	
2100HRS	Capt. Mackay considers holding on to be almost impossible.	
2200HRS		
2300HRS		

THE VILLAGE	THE WOODS
	Capt. Queripel covers his men's withdrawal.
22. THE CHURCH: Lt. Col. Thompson saves the Division from being cut off at the river, organizing the men retreating from the Town into a defensive posture.	**20. ENGLAND AND THE WOODS: THE POLES:** Fog-bound, Sosabowski and his men wait to leave for Arnhem; his heavy equipment goes anyway.
21. CRUMBS OF COMFORT?: Major Powell discovers supplies in the Woods. In the Village Capt. Kavanagh tries to recover supplies.	
23. LIFE AND DEATH AT THE CROSSROADS	
	Remnants of 4th Parachute Brigade start to assemble, 10th Bn south of the Wolfheze level crossing, 156 Bn further east in the woods south of the railway line.
25. LAST BATTALION LEFT: 1st Bn the Border Regiment, who have had a relatively quiet day, repel a probing attack in the west. A taste of things to come?	
	24. FINAL DECISION: Brig. Hackett decides to dig in for the night and only move into the Divisional area in the morning.

Gliders on Landing Zone 'L' around Wolfheze. A vast fleet of 320 gliders had set off for Arnhem on Sunday, 17 September: these large fields were ideal for a massed glider landing. Visible are the gliders' detached tails, each one a story of a crew trying to unload their glider and get off the LZ as quickly as possible.

MAPS

OPERATION MARKET GARDEN
Campaign at 17 September.
Countdown: 48 hours to Black Tuesday

North Sea

Utrecht

The Hague

Lek Nederrijn

Rotterdam

Geldermalse

Waal

Dordrech

S-Hertogenbosch

Moerdijk

Vught

Breda

Tilburg

Bergen op
Zoom

Western Scheldt

BELGIUM

FRONT LINE 17 SEPTEMBER

Antwerp

Albert Canal

Kempisch Canal

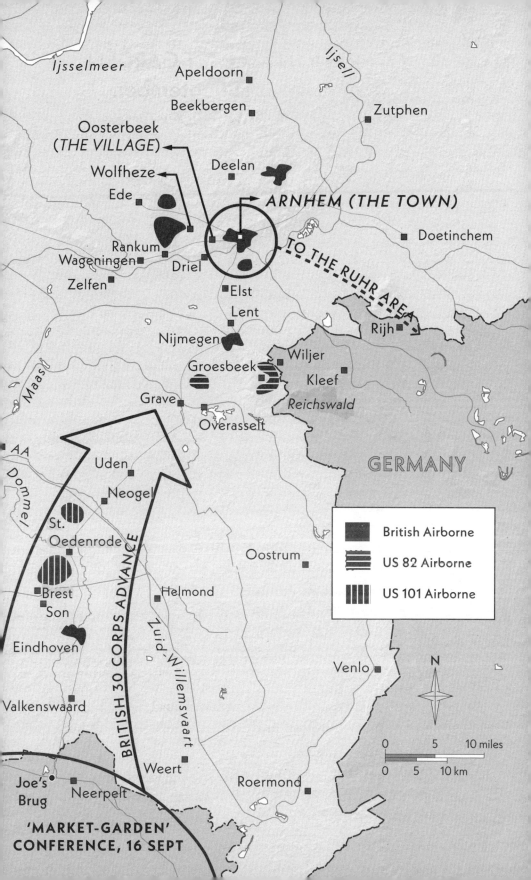

Ijsselmeer

Apeldoorn

Beekbergen

Zutphen

Ijsell

Oosterbeek
(*THE VILLAGE*)

Deelan

Wolfheze

Ede

ARNHEM (*THE TOWN*)

Doetinchem

Rankum

Wageningen

Driel

Zelfen

TO THE RUHR AREA

Elst

Lent

Rijh

Nijmegen

Wiljer

Groesbeek

Kleef

Grave

Reichswald

Maas

Overasselt

GERMANY

AA

Uden

Dommel

Neogel

St.
Oedenrode

Oostrum

Brest

Helmond

Son

Zuid-Willemsvaart

Eindhoven

Venlo

N

Valkenswaard

Weert

Roermond

	British Airborne
	US 82 Airborne
	US 101 Airborne

BRITISH 30 CORPS ADVANCE

0   5   10 miles

0   5   10 km

Joe's
Brug

Neerpelt

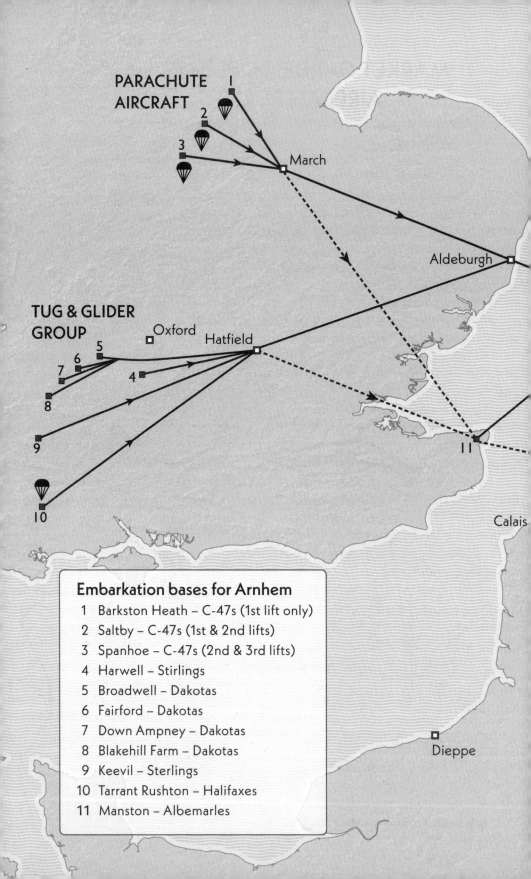

PARACHUTE
AIRCRAFT

1

2

3

March

Aldeburgh

TUG & GLIDER
GROUP

Oxford

Hatfield

5

6

7

4

8

9

11

10

Calais

Dieppe

Embarkation bases for Arnhem

1   Barkston Heath – C-47s (1st lift only)
2   Saltby – C-47s (1st & 2nd lifts)
3   Spanhoe – C-47s (2nd & 3rd lifts)
4   Harwell – Stirlings
5   Broadwell – Dakotas
6   Fairford – Dakotas
7   Down Ampney – Dakotas
8   Blakehill Farm – Dakotas
9   Keevil – Sterlings
10 Tarrant Rushton – Halifaxes
11 Manston – Albemarles

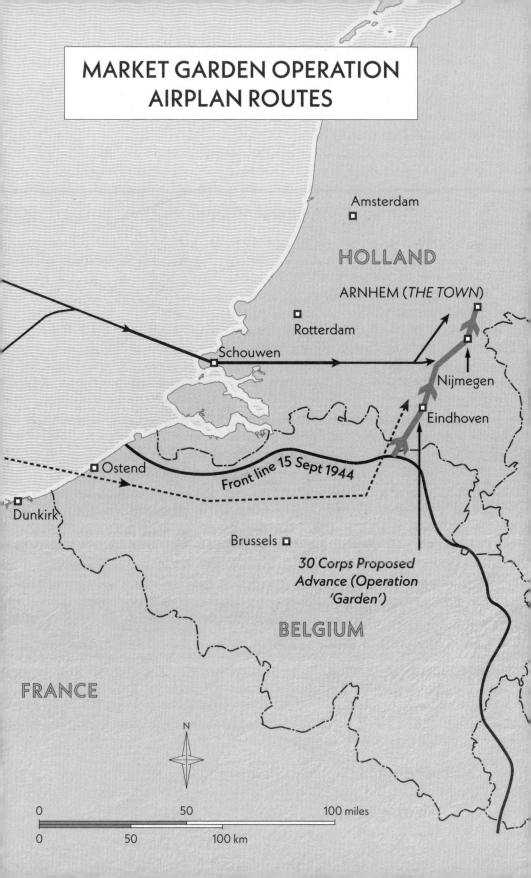

MARKET GARDEN OPERATION AIRPLAN ROUTES

Amsterdam

HOLLAND

ARNHEM (*THE TOWN*)

Rotterdam

Schouwen

Nijmegen

Eindhoven

Ostend

Front line 15 Sept 1944

Dunkirk

Brussels

30 Corps Proposed Advance (Operation 'Garden')

BELGIUM

FRANCE

N

| 0 | 50 | 100 miles |

| 0 | 50 | 100 km |

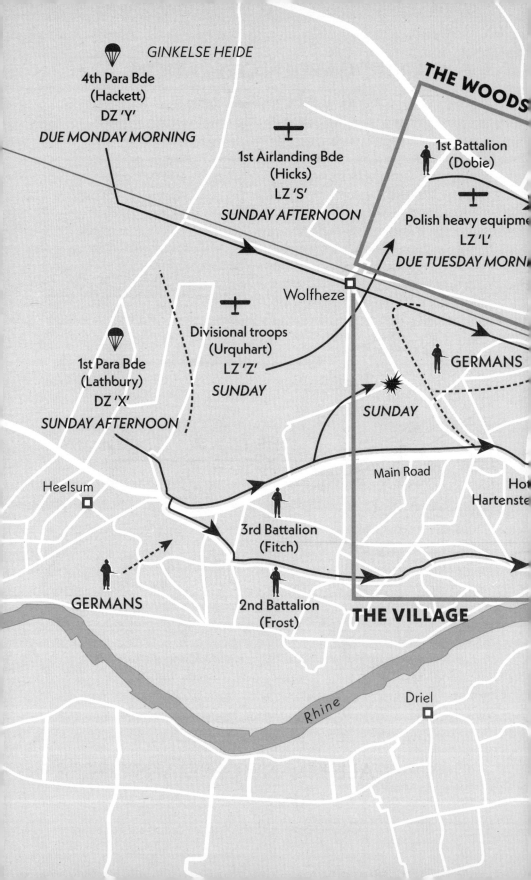

GINKELSE HEIDE

4th Para Bde
(Hackett)
DZ 'Y'
DUE MONDAY MORNING

THE WOODS

1st Airlanding Bde
(Hicks)
LZ 'S'
SUNDAY AFTERNOON

1st Battalion
(Dobie)

Polish heavy equipme
LZ 'L'
DUE TUESDAY MORN

Wolfheze

Divisional troops
(Urquhart)
LZ 'Z'
SUNDAY

GERMANS

1st Para Bde
(Lathbury)
DZ 'X'
SUNDAY AFTERNOON

SUNDAY

Main Road

Ho
Hartenste

Heelsum

3rd Battalion
(Fitch)

GERMANS

2nd Battalion
(Frost)

THE VILLAGE

Rhine

Driel

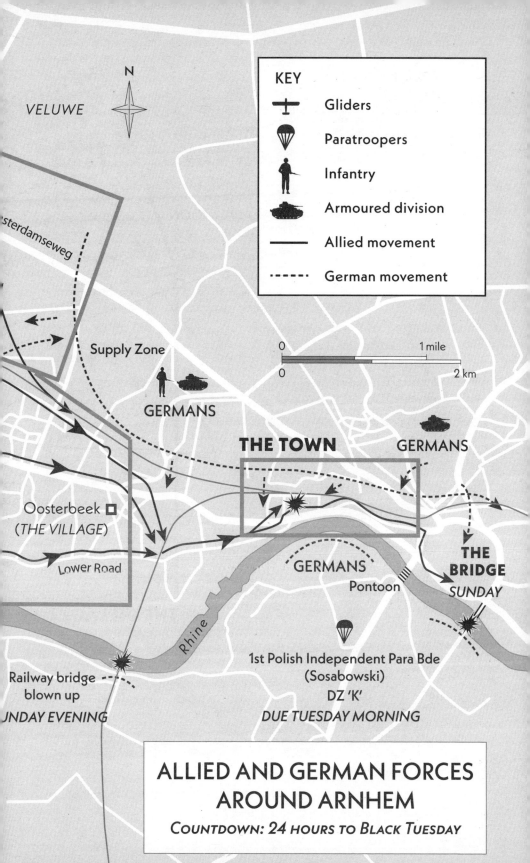

VELUWE

N

KEY

✈ Gliders

☂ Paratroopers

👤 Infantry

🛡 Armoured division

— Allied movement

- - - German movement

...sterdamseweg

Supply Zone

0 ——— 1 mile
0 ——— 2 km

GERMANS

THE TOWN

GERMANS

Oosterbeek □
(*THE VILLAGE*)

Lower Road

GERMANS

Pontoon

**THE
BRIDGE**
SUNDAY

Rhine

Railway bridge
blown up
...UNDAY EVENING

1st Polish Independent Para Bde
(Sosabowski)
DZ 'K'
DUE TUESDAY MORNING

ALLIED AND GERMAN FORCES
AROUND ARNHEM

COUNTDOWN: 24 HOURS TO BLACK TUESDAY

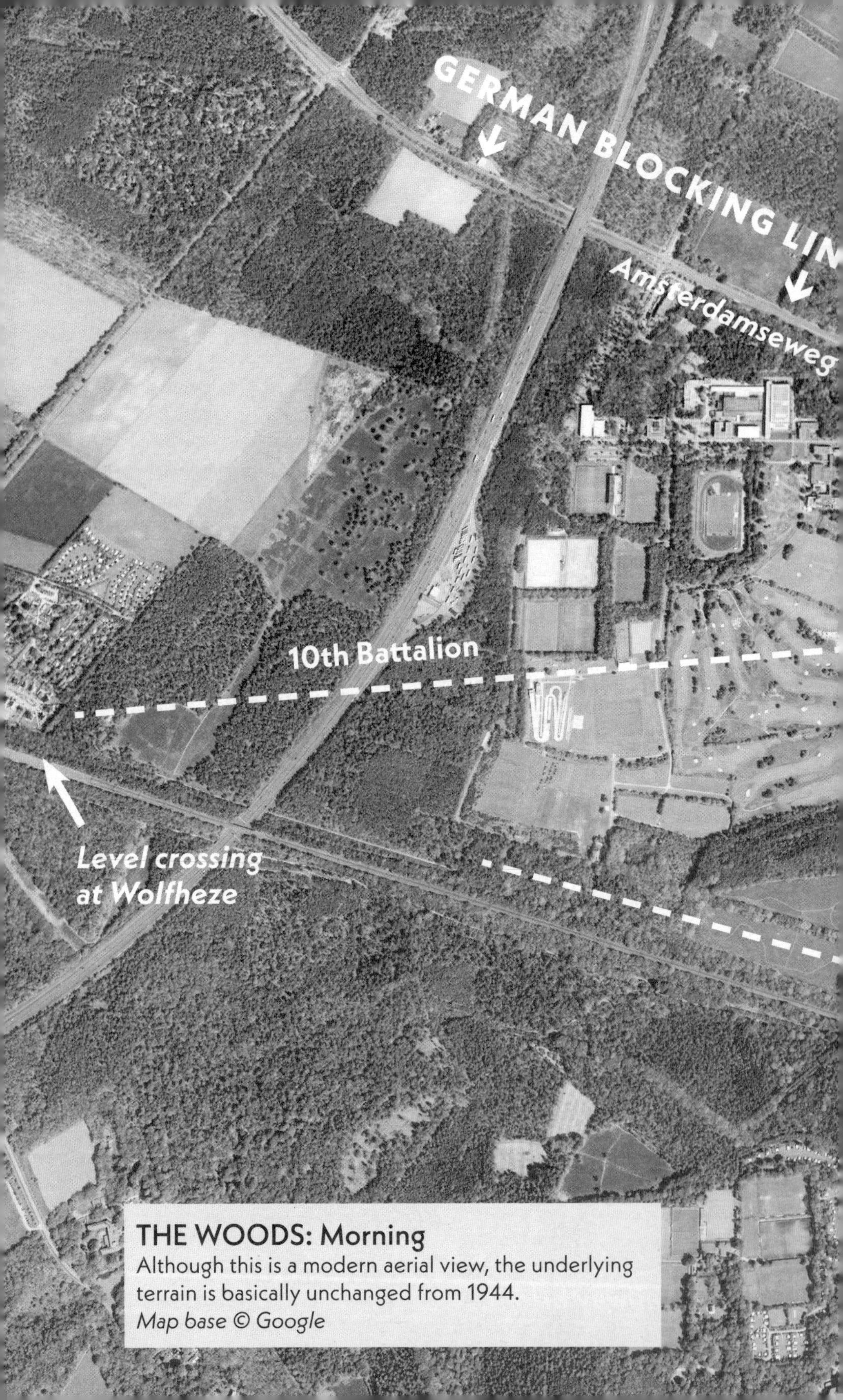

GERMAN BLOCKING LINE

Amsterdamseweg

10th Battalion

Level crossing
at Wolfheze

THE WOODS: Morning
Although this is a modern aerial view, the underlying
terrain is basically unchanged from 1944.
Map base © Google

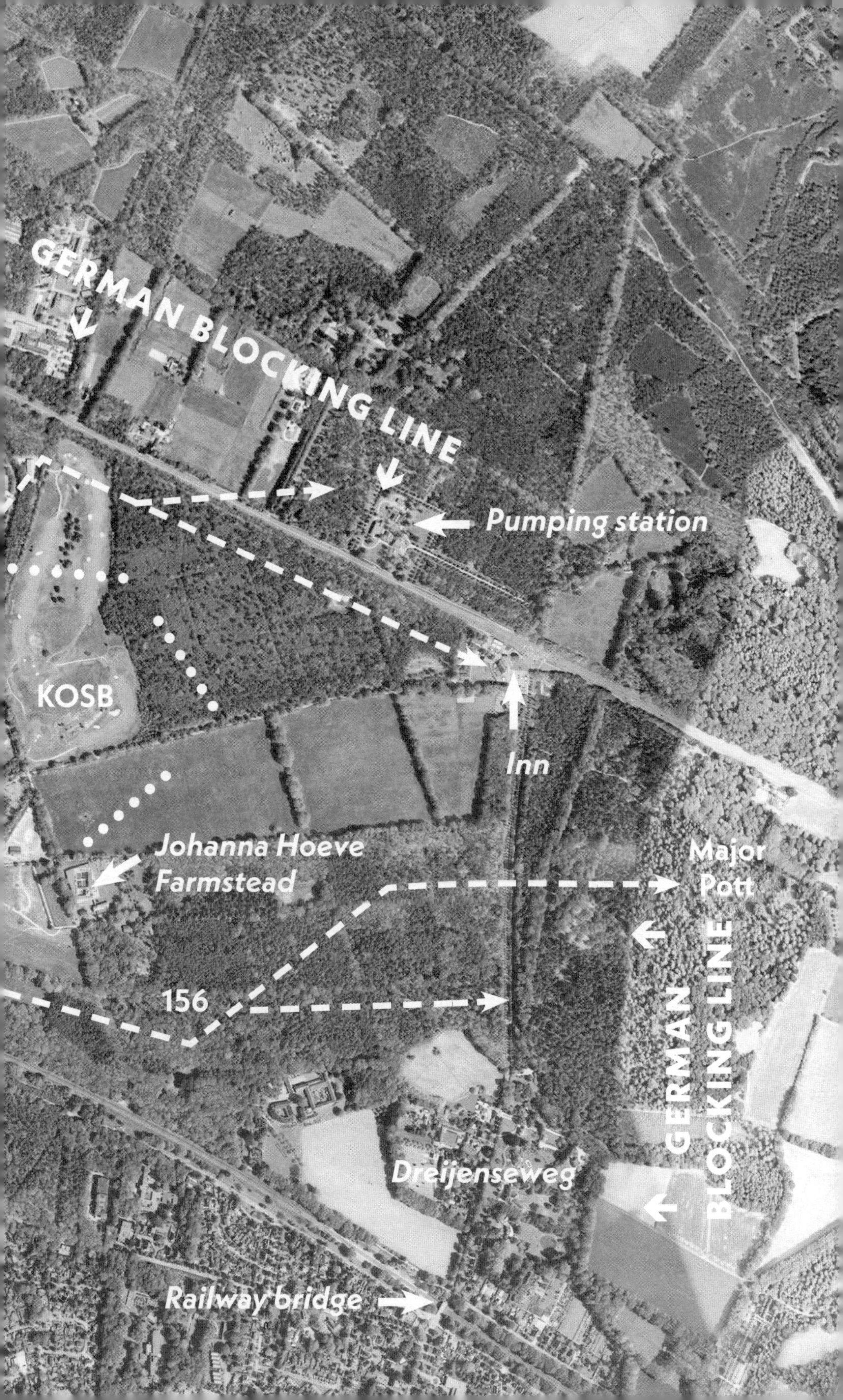

GERMAN BLOCKING LINE

Pumping station

KOSB

Inn

Johanna Hoeve
Farmstead

Major
Pott

156

GERMAN BLOCKING LINE

Dreijenseweg

Railway bridge

GERMAN ATTACKS

THE PRISON

THE LOFT

← 5) 11th Battalion and South Staffs overwhelmed

← 6) Survivors retreat

THE TOWN AND THE BOTTLENECK
Although this is a modern aerial view, the underlying terrain is basically unchanged from 1944.
Map base © Google

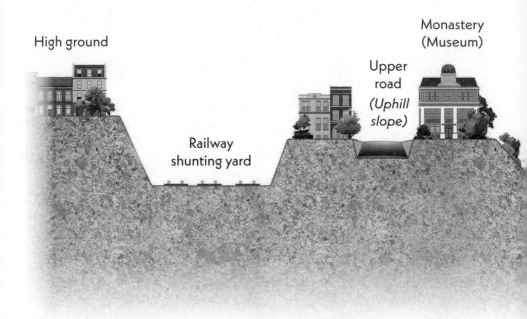

High ground

Monastery
(Museum)

Upper
road
(Uphill
slope)

Railway
shunting yard

Below: German troops close in on The Monastery, the airborne men inside having no option but to surrender. Being captured was something few men had considered.

CROSS SECTION OF THE TERRAIN IN THE TOWN
[DIAGRAM NOT TO SCALE]

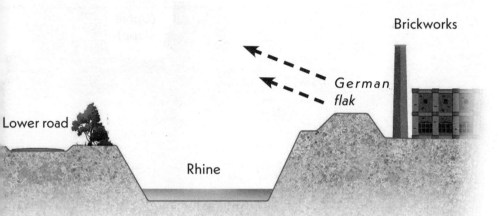

Brickworks

German flak

Lower road

Rhine

Below: Self-propelled guns, panzers, armoured fighting vehicles: with the element of surprise that airborne landings relied on long gone, the German defenders held all the cards on Tuesday morning.

GERMAN ATTACK

SCHOOL (Mackay)

Pt. Lygo

GERMAN ATTACK

SLIT TRENCHES

BRITISH DEFENCE PERIMETER

MORTAR PIT

BRIGADE HQ

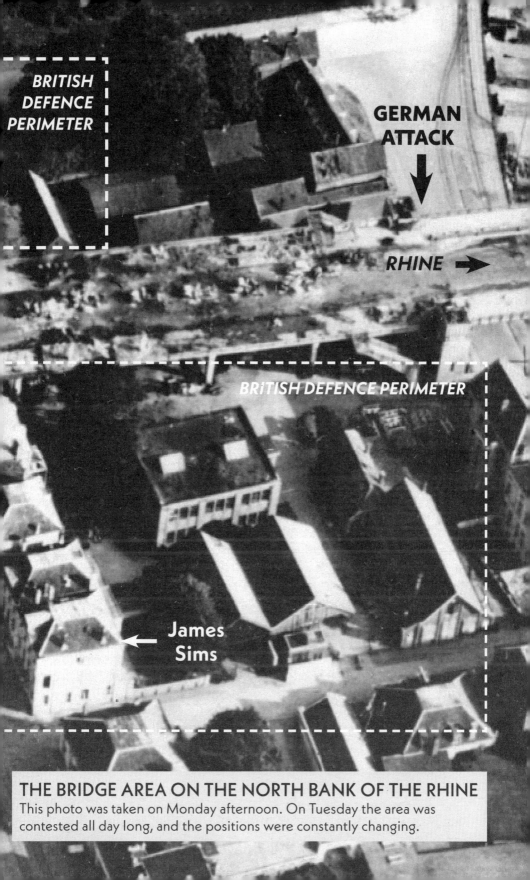

BRITISH
DEFENCE
PERIMETER

GERMAN
ATTACK

RHINE →

BRiTISH DEFENCE PERIMETER

← James
Sims

THE BRIDGE AREA ON THE NORTH BANK OF THE RHINE
This photo was taken on Monday afternoon. On Tuesday the area was
contested all day long, and the positions were constantly changing.

PLATOON BATTLE DRILL FOR CLEARING TWO ROWS OF OCCUPIED HOUSES

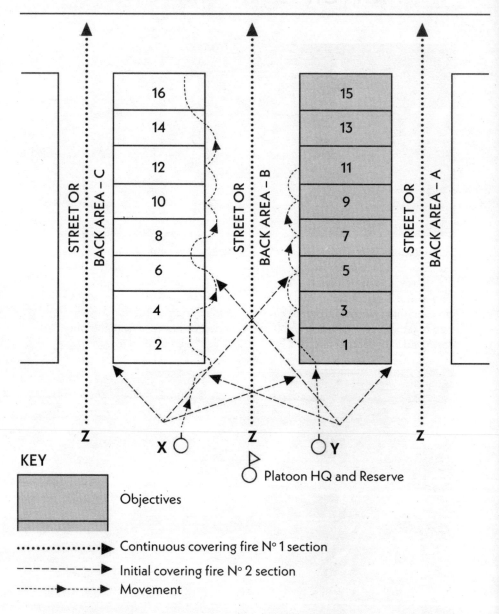

KEY

Objectives

............▶ Continuous covering fire N° 1 section

------▶ Initial covering fire N° 2 section

------▶------▶ Movement

○ Platoon HQ and Reserve

Street fighting was manpower-intensive, and, as the manual said, a three-dimensional space – the enemy might be upstairs. Every room of every house had to be cleared, and while every house offered cover, every open street offered clear lines of fire, every corner a new ambush. This diagram from the instruction manual for clearing one street makes clear the challenges faced by the battalions attacking in the Town.

PRINCIPAL CHARACTERS

Major Robert Cain: in the desperate battle for 'the Monastery' and then at the high ground at Den Brink, Robert Cain of 2nd Battalion South Staffords did everything he could to keep the men together as the battalion was destroyed in the Bottleneck.

Padre Bernard Egan (left): Egan was at the Bridge at Arnhem with Frost and his men. He was injured when the German panzers started to close in on the men at the Bridge on Tuesday evening and ended up in a cellar with the wounded he had been tending to.

Lieutenant-Colonel John Frost: here (centre) on his return from the Bruneval raid, Operation Biting, the only unequivocally successful British airborne operation of the war.

Brigadier John 'Shan' Hackett: (centre) with his boss, Roy Urquhart, on his right and their boss, Monty. Smiles all round. Hackett was cleverer than those around him, and he and they knew it.

Brigadier Philip Hicks: the most experienced man on the ground, 'Pip' Hicks kept his head down and got on with playing the poor hand he had been dealt.

Captain Alexander Lipmann Kessel, RAMC: discovered first-hand German attitudes to the wounded that he found shocking but not exactly surprising.

Brigadier Gerald 'Legs' Lathbury: principal architect of the plan to take the Bridge at Arnhem which had misfired on Sunday and Monday. On Tuesday what was left of his leaderless Brigade would have to pick up the pieces.

Captain Eric Mackay (right) of 1st Parachute Squadron, Royal Engineers, spent Tuesday fighting in and around the school on the eastern side of the ramp that ran north of the Bridge into the Town, ignoring a piece of shrapnel in his foot.

Captain Stuart Mawson, RAMC: Medical Officer with 11th Battalion. Stuart Mawson witnessed the aftermath of his Battalion's disintegration on Tuesday, saying it was like men fleeing a forest fire.

Major Geoffrey Powell: fighting as a company commander in 156 Battalion, Geoffrey Powell witnessed the destruction of 4th Parachute Brigade first-hand.

Captain Lionel Queripel, of 10th Battalion. Queripel's devil-may-care attitude in the battle in the Woods, crossing a road under enemy fire, smoking his pipe, was a source of inspiration for the men fighting on the Amsterdamseweg, even when events ran out of control.

Major General Stansilaw Sosabowski: (left) languishing in England, fog bound, his parachutists unable to go to Arnhem, Sosabowski's Poles were at the back of the airborne queue. How Tuesday ran for the Poles could not have made this clearer. In this picture he is most likely fending off Lieutenant General 'Boy' Browning (right) attempting, yet again, to persuade him to cede control of the 1st Polish Independent Parachute Brigade.

Major-General Roy Urquhart: (right) once he had made it back to Divisional Headquarters at the Hartenstein Hotel, Urquhart could get on with making decisions and taking command. But had the die been cast?

INTRODUCTION

The history of a battle, is not unlike the history of a ball.
Some individuals may recollect all the little events of which
the great result is the battle won or lost, but no individual
can recollect the order in which, or the exact moment at
which, they occurred, which makes all the difference as to
their value or importance.

The Duke of Wellington

SKINNING THE CAT

THE BATTLE OF ARNHEM, Operation Market Garden, has been
present in my imagination for as long as I can remember, a peculiar
and powerful singularity.

I have been drawn to it almost my entire life. Writing about it has
felt both inevitable and impossible. As I have sidled up to history as
a parallel career, the time to grasp this particular nettle has snuck up
on me. So much excellent ink has been spilt, by brilliant writers,
amateur and professional historians alike (I'll leave it to the reader
to decide who is who). It is a battle that is talismanic and indeed
dominant in the British post-war narrative about the final year of
the Second World War in Europe, overshadowing other epic, shattering, bloody victories of the eleven months following D-Day. In
contrast to the ruthless German Army crushing machine that the
British Army had become in 1944, Arnhem offers a last stand, our
last proper defeat of the war, and it casts an irresistible shadow for

anyone who wants to feast on failure, futility, heroism and drama at a time when the war was headed in only one direction.

Arnhem, of course, comes to most people via the movies, in a way that has become impossible to ignore. It is that rare thing, a battle that lives in the popular imagination. The extraordinary *Theirs Is The Glory* set the tone. It is perhaps hard to think of a stranger cinematic artefact: made on the battlefield itself in 1946, the burned-out tanks still present, vivid in black and white, using footage shot during the Battle alongside re-enactment, the players themselves veterans of the Battle. Then, in the 1970s, up against *Star Wars* came *A Bridge Too Far*, Richard Attenborough's paradoxical anti-war movie that made gallant defeat seem so attractive, his camera feasting on the maroon beret glamour his panoply of stars offered him, a glamour that had been tarnished in that decade by more recent bitter events in Northern Ireland. With its gee-whizz can-do Americans, its steely Germans and a heavy helping of tea-drinking Brits, some of whom are awfully unhelpful chaps in the RAF, William Goldman's screenplay set the popular narrative in stone. Chipping away at that narrative seems Sisyphean, but here we are.

The Battle came to me via my father. After his National Service in the mid-1950s, which came at a time of Imperial withdrawal and nuclear expansion, Dad stayed in the Territorial Army as a parachute engineer; he had an appetite for the challenges that being an airborne soldier offered. They played hard, they lived a life of adventure, and the sappers were 'triple hatted': soldiers, engineers, parachutists all at once. It's the parachuting I remember, of course. His squadron practised jumping into the sea off Guernsey, so there were photographs and tales of that when I was a small boy (I suspect now, like so much of this kind of activity, it was an excuse for a jolly), and trips to see him jump from a balloon. I have a vivid, and no doubt embellished, memory of trying to help him with his reserve 'chute' by picking it up by its red handle and being told rather emphatically what a bad idea that was. I'd have been fired across Salisbury Plain by its spring. But Arnhem was part of this picture; officers Dad knew, such as Eric MacKay, had been at Arnhem (as well as others who had fought in Normandy, of course), and one of his NCOs in his TA establishment had fought at the Bridge.

So we went to see *A Bridge Too Far*. I remember the crashes and the bangs, the utterly mind-blowing scenes of the parachute landings, done for real, en masse, but I also remember his niggles with the film: wrong tanks, actors' haircuts, rotten saluting, the mischaracterization of people he knew and events he'd heard about first hand. But I was bitten by the Battle's bug. It became a subject to return to again and again, and something we could and would discuss ad infinitum. We don't do football, see? For my O level I produced a project about the Battle of Arnhem, even visiting the National Archive (or Public Record Office as it was then, presenting a letter from a history teacher as a reference on arrival) where I read the War Diaries. We visited Arnhem on the road from Wolfheze into Oosterbeek where I drank a delicious cold cider – that memory has stuck – and was almost run over by a moped in the cycle lane by the Bridge, a place offering fresh danger forty years after the Battle. Each new book that appeared would get the once-over. Each time I'd find myself willing on the men of 1st Airborne to succeed this once, and each time I'd be disappointed.

When Dad retired, I suggested that he write about Arnhem. This got short shrift: there's nothing new to be said, he said. I found it hard to disagree. And yet, new scholarship emerges, time passes, and fresh perspectives force their way forward, even though the nine days' fighting of the Battle tends to force all accounts of it into the same shape. Once the struggle at the Bridge has ended, the Battle in the Oosterbeek Perimeter becomes a British Alamo, and amidst the endurance, sacrifice and suffering, an echo of repetition and fatalism emerges. So now, in writing finally about Arnhem, how does one avoid these patterns? How can the story be approached afresh?

After all, one of the attractions about the Battle is that it was short and relatively contained. It has this in common with D-Day, the celebration of which often overlooks the ten weeks of savage fighting that followed it, as well as the months of naval and aerial battle that prepared the battle space. The Battle of Arnhem occurred in a contained area too – while the Drop Zones and Landing Zones may be 'too far' from the Bridge, you can cover the distance in an afternoon, and take in most of the key locations along the way. The shape of the place now is essentially as it was then, the relatively new road bridge in the Town notwithstanding. And 1st Airborne's ten thousand or so men is a reasonably finite number of people to keep track of, at least compared to the numbers involved in the colossal actions in Normandy which preceded it and the vast offensives that followed. The Battle's fame has helped it to be well recorded and remembered, and narratives from the men as well as their officers, whose versions of events have tended to dominate the story, are plentiful, abundant even.

So what is your author's approach, and how have I arrived at it? To try to say something new, or perhaps, better put, something else, about the Battle of Arnhem, I am going to focus on one day, Tuesday 19 September 1944, and the Battle that was fought by 1st Airborne Division and 1st Polish Independent Parachute Brigade, as well as the RAF troop transports, who were as much a part of that effort as anyone else. 30 Corps, 101st US Airborne Division and 82nd US Airborne Division, and their efforts to the south to make sure that 2nd Army reached the Rhine at Arnhem, do not feature.

Why? Well, because what I'm hoping to do is place 1st Airborne's experience on the Tuesday in its own context: they had no idea what was happening to the south, all they knew was that the relief they expected by Tuesday had not materialized. They didn't know the ins and outs of what was happening; it was an unknown over which they had no influence. Battalion commanders, Battery commanders and brigadiers see only as far as their battalions, batteries and brigades can see – *if they're lucky*, and luck was something in short supply at Arnhem. So in this book we don't see what lies beyond, because they couldn't see it. Similarly, the Germans and the decisions they were making were opaque to the British. Whatever

decisions General Model made are felt in terms of their consequences rather than explained to the reader, because again, the men
in Arnhem had no knowledge of those decisions, only the immediate consequences of them.

Furthermore, I want to try to avoid some of the fatalism and
hindsight with which the Battle is inevitably freighted. What will
happen next? How are the decisions being made on the day, and the
potential pitfalls of an airborne landing, to be brought back to life
without my solemnly declaring that everyone should have known
better, that the Landing Zones selected were too far from the main
road Bridge in Arnhem, and so on? Men may have known, and even
said so at the time, but there's little doubt they felt the risk was
worth it. Certainly getting there and holding the Bridge would have
felt well within their capabilities.

On that Tuesday, the inheritance of what had gone before in airborne operations played itself out. North Africa, Sicily, Normandy:
these are the key to so much of the Arnhem story. The anatomy of
1st Airborne Division, its muscles, its sinews, its eyes, its ears, its
brains, all were tested to their very limit on Black Tuesday. To investigate this anatomy means we will have to leave Arnhem and look at
their origins and evolution, but I'll try to do that in the context of
how they were understood at the time. These rabbit holes, or digres-
sions, are, I hope, the body of institutional memory, such as it was,
that the men at Arnhem carried with them, which subsequently
informed how the day went.

To try to express this I have decided to create my own convention
for how to discuss the Battle, and divide it into four locations, and
avoid place names and street names. Indeed, in the orders for the
operation, street names were substituted with British street names;
the Arnhem to Ede road was dubbed Ermine Street, for instance.
The fighting happened at **the Bridge**, in **the Town**, where 1st Parachute Brigade did all it could to reach the Bridge, **the Woods**, where
4th Parachute Brigade did what it could to flank the Germans and
get into the Town, and **the Village**, Oosterbeek, where 1st Airborne

Division had set up its headquarters and Divisional Administrative
Area. We will go to England and elsewhere from time to time, but
these four areas will serve as our primary locations. Many of the
men present weren't as familiar with the street names and locations
on maps as later historians have become. Not everyone had a map,
and some of those who did could not read them. Main roads were
'main roads' rather than the Utrechtseweg. This cannot be a hard
and fast rule, but it feels true to the chaos of the day. Furthermore,
although this is an account of one day, it is necessarily incomplete,
the way anyone's picture of the day would have been. This was perhaps a choice between a slender volume or the world's biggest
doorstop volume. I know on your e-reader this is a difference of
nano-microns, but I wanted *Arnhem: Black Tuesday* to be a manageable read.

The day itself I have divided into four easy quarters, Midnight,
Morning, Afternoon and Evening, and while events do not naturally conform to any such tidy schedule, I have tried to keep the
narrative as close to the chronology as possible. One challenge is
that Black Tuesday was a procession of relentless 'Meanwhiles'.
Three o'clock on the afternoon of 19 September 1944 may not have
been the day's climax as such, but everything was happening everywhere, all at once.

To explain where everyone starts on the Tuesday at midnight I
will necessarily have to report what happened on Sunday and
Monday. What happened on Black Tuesday was about so much
more than the two days that preceded it. The shape of the book tries
to reflect this: the storm passes, night falls, and the men brace themselves for whatever is to come. Incredibly, one of the units in this
story has what could be described as a quiet day on 19 September
1944. What happened to them thereafter is another story.

The experiment of looking at a single day does not change the
core element of the story of the Battle of Arnhem. The men of 1st
Airborne Division and their Polish comrades fought with extraordinary tenacity and courage, and while the Battle attracted five

Victoria Crosses – these ultimate awards for gallantry being a reliable barometer for the need of those at the top to wring good news out of bad – putting the day under the microscope has, for me, made the way these men fought and resisted, how they motivated themselves in the face of horrendous losses, even more striking. The men fighting their way into the Town on Tuesday fell into the trap the Germans had set for them after the surprise of the initial landings. What personal resources they had to draw upon are, to this spectator at least, mysterious. That they were able to dust themselves down on Tuesday and continue the fight defies belief. For example, on Tuesday afternoon, Major Robert Cain is described by one of his fellow officers as looking nothing like a future VC winner, yet what he went on to do – beyond the pages of this book – will live forever in the annals of bravery.

The Duke of Wellington's view that the 'history of a battle, is not unlike the history of a ball' feels apposite when it comes to Arnhem. Despite it being essentially a small, contained event, there is much that reveals itself as you start to examine it. Accounts differ, recollections can be at odds, witnesses disagree. Historians are reliant on varying accounts and recollections, seeing the same events from many different angles. Diaries written either in the heat of battle, or at the end of a long and exhausting, intense day, do not agree on timings at all, just as the protagonists in the moment of any given action don't. Some of what has been handed down doesn't quite add up. So, in that sense, Arnhem is Wellington's 'ball'. There was perhaps some irony, then, in the way the men who set off for Arnhem saw it as a 'party' they were loath to miss.

Watching *A Bridge Too Far* with my daughters many years ago, I was struck by how someone who didn't know the story, who didn't know what was going to happen next, might feel as the story played out. Suddenly the old well-worn story was new again, even if the tanks were still wrong. This is my attempt to grab something of that feeling. I thank the reader for their patience and hope they too are left wondering 'what would happen tomorrow?'

KICKING THE DOOR IN

Everyone has a plan until they get punched in the mouth.

Mike Tyson

Operation Market Garden – the overall operation of which the Battle of Arnhem was the British airborne component – evolved, it is generally agreed, from Allied overconfidence. In every post-mortem, in every analysis, this overconfidence has been found wanting by hindsight and of course most damningly by the turn of events themselves.

But in early September 1944, in terms of the big picture, the Allies had a great deal to be confident about and things to look forward to as well – primarily the prospect of an end to the war. It had been clear to everyone by mid-1944 – even those at the very top of the Nazi hierarchy – that Germany was done for. The Allies had pulled off the greatest amphibious landing in military history on D-Day, breached the Atlantic Wall, brought the war back to France in only four years following the total humiliation of Dunkirk. After two months of horrific attritional 'meat-grinder' fighting in Normandy, the British, Canadians, Americans *and* the Poles had worn down the German armies in France to the point of collapse. Allied armies that had been green on D-Day were now battle-hardened and had beaten some of the most feared armies under Hitler's command.

The Battle of the Atlantic had also been won the year before in 1943 – meaning that not long after D-Day, waves of American troops could be shipped directly to Normandy from the United States, rather than dashed across the Channel from England. The strategic bomber offensive which had shattered the Ruhr and immolated Hamburg in July of '43 had reached its tipping point after what became known as the 'Big Week' of 20–25 February 1944, and as well as disrupting German industry had emasculated the German air force; the Luftwaffe had been engaged over Germany and defeated by American fighters. By the time of the Battle of Arnhem, and one of the reasons such an operation was even feasible, the Allies had achieved almost total air supremacy. With their U-boat effort also thwarted by the Allied codebreakers, the Germans had been reduced to fighting in one rather than three dimensions. Allied industrial might was something to which the Germans, with their own factories dispersed and under attack, no longer had any credible response. The folly of challenging three economies each larger than his own was finally and fatally catching up with Hitler. In the East, the Soviet Union had launched a vast offensive, Operation Bagration, in late June 1944, tying up and destroying vast quantities of German men and materiel; in Italy, Rome had fallen the day before Operation Overlord and D-Day had begun. The writing was on the wall.

Moreover, whatever the regime might want to assert, the Germans knew they were losing – Claus von Stauffenberg's attempt to assassinate Hitler in the July plot sprung as much from alarm within the German officer corps at the prospect of defeat as it did from disgust with Nazism. From the Allied perspective it must have felt like it was only a matter of time and that time was of the essence.

The scale of the German defeat in Normandy was seen at the time as decisive, certainly by the Allies. The figures are disputed – in Normandy the Germans had an estimated 450,000 men in the field and around 240,000 were killed or wounded. Escaping the Falaise pocket in August 1944 left 12th SS Panzer Division with only 6 per cent of its armour – reduced from 150 tanks to 10, from 20,000 men to 300. In the retreat across the Seine the Germans left behind 500 tanks. It was the kind of defeat that the Germans had inflicted on France in 1940, total, absolute, though far, far bloodier. Of course, the British hadn't quit after that defeat, but the victory in Normandy had demonstrated overwhelming Allied might in every dimension imaginable – tactically, strategically and operationally. When the German armies retreated in chaos that same month from their disastrous counter-offensive at Mortain, and even though some units were able to escape, it was the end of the German Army in France. General Eisenhower, Supreme Allied Commander, surveyed the damage, comparing it to a scene from Dante: 'It was literally possible to walk for hundreds of yards at a time, stepping on nothing but dead and decaying flesh.' It was only a matter of time. The Nazi regime might be talking about holding on fanatically, but in the end armies could and would break. Allied armies had surrendered for far less, though their governments hadn't capitulated.

Try as one might to look beyond the fact of the disaster at Arnhem, these factors do go some way to understanding why such an ambitious, arguably hare-brained feat of arms might be attempted: it was worth the risk. Decisive and overwhelming might had got the Allies this far and one further demonstration of that might could force the whole house of cards to collapse. Delivering an entire airborne army sixty miles behind enemy lines and seizing the Rhine would qualify as exactly that kind of gesture. The decision, its conception, lay with one man who, even after the operation failed, claimed full responsibility, someone who had never been accused of being hare-brained and who was often criticized for his caution: Bernard Law Montgomery.

Field Marshal Montgomery was one of the genuine star generals the Allies possessed, and by goodness he knew it. At the helm when Eighth Army delivered the first unequivocal British victory of the war at El Alamein in 1942, he had carefully cultivated a narrative of being an instrumental part of the turning of the tide; and in planning the land component of Overlord – which had resulted in an outcome he would later claim he had planned all along – he had been the ascendant Allied general. Perhaps inevitably, by the time of Market Garden he had become almost too difficult for his superiors to handle. Consternation went everywhere Monty went; he was as gifted at rubbing people up the wrong way as he was at command, and tended only to be sensitive to this flaw when things came to a head.

But Monty's style had, one way or another, been a central factor in the defeat of the German armies in Normandy, and despite grinding fighting and heavy casualties his armies remained buoyant and confident, growing in experience and a welcome knowledge that the Germans were beatable. However, the end of the Overlord campaign – which no one had quite planned for – also marked a shift in the balance of Allied power. The American armies now outnumbered the British and Dominion armies, causing Eisenhower to take command of the land campaign, leaving Monty in charge of only the British, DUKEX[1] and Polish armies. It was a demotion for Montgomery, but as a sop for it he was promoted to Field Marshal. Eisenhower, managing a coalition of forces that was now preponderantly American, knew he had, somehow, to contain or entertain Montgomery's ego as well as manage coalition politics with the British. It proved far from straightforward.

British 21st Army Group had advanced huge distances after the breakout at the Falaise Gap, quickly crossing into Belgium – 'The Great Swan' it was called, as armoured units 'swanned' their way through France, going as far and as fast as their tanks could take them. On 1 September, 11th Armoured Division covered sixty miles. Immediate military politics aside, Montgomery was under pressure from the British government about the German rocket attacks that had begun that summer. A mobile V2 site in Rotterdam had been the location of the first launch of a ballistic missile, hitting Chiswick in West London, not far from where I'm writing this. A thrust into Holland by 21st Army Group would prevent these attacks, so Montgomery was keen to deliver on this too. Simply in terms of the land battle there were still many plates to keep spinning.

However, and there is always a however when operating strategically, Allied supply lines were massively overstretched with a front that ran from the North Sea to Switzerland. As the American armies grew, so did the colossal logistic effort to support them.

So it is easy to see the appeal of delivering the enemy a knockout blow. The First World War had ended with Germany's precipitous collapse, which had come after far more modest strategic gains. Eisenhower had opted for a Broad Front strategy and was being lobbied from all sides for priority. At one fractious meeting he had had to remind Monty that he was his boss. Little wonder he chain-smoked four packs a day. But the Arnhem plan had Ike's blessing. General Omar Bradley, Montgomery's nearest equivalent in the US Army, gave the plan the thumbs-up too. One last heave might do it, rather than pausing and consolidating and waiting for the petrol and ammunition to catch up.

Should the Allies breach the last major physical obstacle, the River Rhine, at Arnhem, the Germans might just throw in the towel, and finally the game would be up. Montgomery had looked at many ways to get across the great river, with 1st Allied Airborne Army's deputy commander Lieutenant General Frederick 'Boy' Browning – who had in the wake of D-Day been providing speculative plans for airborne operations, to 'kick the door in' to Germany. One plan was called Operation Comet and it relied on brand-spanking-new airborne forces.

Victory in Normandy seemed to have made the case for airborne warfare on a large scale. Over the summer of 1944, airborne forces had reorganized as 1st Allied Airborne Army, and within this, comprising two American Divisions and one British, was 1st Airborne Corps under Browning himself. While this cutting-edge formation, wildly expensive to train, maintain and deploy, was burning a hole in Allied pockets, it was also looking for a role, as there were no more amphibious landings to support. Its advocates claimed that it offered the possibility of a decisive swift victory. The scene was set for further ambitious operations as the Allies broke out and the Germans tumbled away in retreat in the aftermath of Normandy, with lessons learned and conclusions drawn.

It was in this broad context that the nine days of Arnhem were born from the momentum of victory. They were trying to strike while the iron was hot, to end the war, when it looked like the enemy was done. Montgomery's staff were sufficiently confident that they had drawn up concepts for Operation Gatwick, the next phase following on from Market Garden.

Operation Comet, which preceded Market Garden, was essentially the same concept but with only 1st Airborne Division and the 1. Samodzielna Brygada Spadochronowa (the Polish 1st Independent Parachute Brigade). These units would seize the bridges across all of the water obstacles in Holland up to and including the bridges at Arnhem, thus circumnavigating the defences of the Siegfried Line, offering an encirclement of the German armies in the Netherlands and a buccaneering swing right into Germany itself. The chosen vanguard of 2nd Army, namely 30 Corps, would then break through the German front lines at the Albert Canal, and race up the road through Eindhoven, Nijmegen and on to Arnhem all within forty-eight hours or so. It looked simple on a map, but was actually monstrously complex. When it became clear that Comet would need to be beefed up, Market Garden was conceived. And because Market Garden was a plan hatched in reaction to a changing situation, there was only a week to put it together, some of the planning having been cannibalized from previous operational orders, such as Comet and Operation Linnet and, as we shall see, Operation Transfigure from the previous month. Such was the haste in which the Market Garden gamble was put together – and then given the green light.

D-Day was 17 September, a Sunday. There was one rather major snag: 1st Airborne Division would not be arriving in one lift, but would be spread over three days, with the Poles arriving on D+2. On Sunday the landings had gone well, though the business of getting from the Drop Zones and Landing Zones that day had had mixed results. A portion of the Division, as we shall see, had had to remain at those Drop and Landing Zones to secure them for the lifts to come. Black Tuesday, twenty-four hours in Arnhem, would be a day of decision for 1st Airborne Division, 1. Samodzielna Brygada Spadochronowa and, in the end, the people of the Netherlands. The high-stakes gamble of Market Garden would make it clear that the dice weren't always loaded in the Allies' favour.

The plan broke down as follows: leading the charge for the Bridge was 1st Parachute Brigade: under Brigadier Gerald 'Legs' Lathbury. This Brigade arrived on Sunday in the First Lift. It comprised three battalions, 1st, 2nd and 3rd Battalions of the Parachute Regiment. The plan called for them to proceed from the Drop Zones west of the Village through the Town in order to seize the Arnhem road and railway bridges, and hold them. Lathbury's plan was for the three battalions each to take its own route into the Town, essentially to race one another. With 1st Parachute Brigade were its supporting troops, sappers, signalmen, logistics troops, gunners and so on. Ahead of 1st Brigade the Division's Recce Squadron, in Jeeps equipped with machine guns, were to race on as fast as possible and get to the Bridge first.

At the same time as part of this First Lift, 1st Airlanding Brigade commanded by Brigadier 'Pip' Hicks arrived. This Brigade was made up of three airlanding battalions, 1st Border Regiment, 2nd South Staffordshire Regiment and 7th King's Own Scottish Borderers (KOSB). The majority of these men arrived on Sunday by glider, the remainder on Monday with the Second Lift. Their role in the Arnhem plan was to hold the Drop Zones and Landing Zones required for the Second Lift coming on Monday.

This Second Lift – due on Monday morning – comprised the parts of the Airlanding Brigade that hadn't been able to arrive on Sunday and 4th Parachute Brigade commanded by Brigadier John 'Shan' Hackett. 4th Brigade arrived on Monday in the Second Lift at 1500 hrs, delayed by weather in England. This Brigade comprised three battalions: 156 (an Indian Army Battalion whose convention demanded that the 'th' suffix wasn't part of its name), 10th and 11th Battalions of the Parachute Regiment. Once the Second Lift had arrived, the bulk of 1st Airborne Division would be in the Arnhem area. This Brigade was to make its way round hooking into the Town by a northern route.

    1. Samodzielna Brygada Spadochronowa: Major General Stanislaw

Sosabowski. Waiting in the wings in England, due to set off for Arnhem on Tuesday morning.

The tangle of events and narrative on 19 September 1944 at Arnhem is dictated by the fact that everything was happening everywhere and all at once. The old adages about plans and the possibility of their survival upon contact with the enemy all apply: outlining what the officers in command at Arnhem were trying to achieve, combined with the bitter fruits of their decisions, demands describing a tragic mismatch. Sod's Law stalked 1st Airborne Division in the streets, fields and woodlands of Arnhem that day.

The shape of Black Tuesday is very much dictated by the British Army's adherence to its habits of 'standing to' half an hour before dawn, and making use of first light; certainly those parts of 1st Airborne Division trying to fight on the offensive put this into practice – the attacks in the Town and the Woods were in full flow from 0700 hrs to around 1030 hrs. By 1500 hrs in both locations the outcome of these offensives was clear, and it fell to the officers remaining to make sense of the situation.

The defensive battles being fought at the Bridge and to the west of the Village had their pace dictated by the Germans. The effort the Germans put into these encounters made it clear where they felt their priorities lay – clearing the Bridge and making sure that the approaches to the Town were secure mattered more than putting the British under pressure further west.

The task of 1st Airborne Division (with 1st Polish Independent Parachute Brigade Group under command) was to capture the bridges at Arnhem and to establish a bridgehead round them, so that formations of 30 Corps and Second Army could pass through without delay on their advance northwards.

1st Airborne Division after-battle report

MIDNIGHT

1

THE BRIDGE: THE BESIEGED

... the Airborne Division is not, and was never designed as, a 'suicide force' ... [it] will never be called upon to undertake an operation where the ordinary hazards of modern war, which have been faced by all troops, are considered to be abnormal.

Lieutenant General Frederick 'Boy' Browning

0000 HRS AT THE BRIDGE. The briefest of moments to draw breath.

The officers and men of 1st Parachute Brigade who had successfully made it to the Bridge took stock of a hard day's fighting. As made evident by the uniforms of the dead and from what the men they'd captured told them, the SS had tried to push across the Bridge from the south in the morning, from well after first light, but had been repulsed in pyrotechnic style.

The paratroopers had blazed away from their positions in the houses that surrounded the Bridge's vast off-ramp, and from the other buildings they had occupied on the Sunday evening. Mortars, anti-tank guns, Brens and rifles had cut the Germans down in their armoured cars, half-tracks and lorries. Whatever tactical objective the Germans had been trying to achieve had been answered implacably. The reputation of 1st Airborne for fighting hard, which they had earned in North Africa, was now being affirmed here on the streets of the Netherlands. The only drawback of the morning's fighting was they had burned through a large amount of ammunition,

ammunition they could only afford as long as they were relieved, either from the west, by the rest of the Division, or by 2nd Army, currently forcing its way sixty miles up from the Albert Canal to the south. Allied advances since the Germans had collapsed at Falaise, 'The Great Swan', had confidently eaten up distances like this in the German wake. Everyone knew the Germans were done. Or at least, that they ought to be.

As well as the men from his own Battalion, 2nd Battalion the Parachute Regiment, Lieutenant Colonel Johnny Frost – to whom, as the highest-ranking officer present at the Bridge, command had devolved – had brought with him an assortment of men from 1st Parachute Brigade: Brigade headquarters, the bulk of C company from 3rd Battalion, sappers, gunners, as well as divisional personnel, Royal Army Service Corps (RASC), Royal Electrical and Mechanical Engineers (REME), glider pilots and men from the Recce Squadron. They had all joined Frost's column as it pushed and probed its way east through the Village, on through the Town and on to the Bridge. Some men had been left behind, cut off, injured or simply lost. Frost's orders were also to seize the railway bridge that lay to the east of the Village – the idea being that a platoon would then cross the river and arrive at the road bridge from the south, capturing it from both ends. However, a firefight broke out between Frost's leading platoon and the sappers sent to check the railway bridge for demolitions, only to be upstaged by the Germans using the explosives they'd set and destroying the railway bridge, its spans heaving and collapsing into the river. Another sign that, as Sunday had progressed, the Germans had got their act together and responded to the threat of the British landings.

Frost's men dug slit trenches in the back gardens of the houses they'd occupied, weapons pits, mortar positions and, on the traffic island just to the west of the ramp by the Bridge, positions for the Battalion's 6-pounder anti-tank guns. Spirits were high, the entrenched soldiers steady in the face of the persistent mortaring and shelling the Germans were ladling on to them.

The road bridge at Arnhem, the cherry on the Market Garden cake, had been destroyed in May 1940 by the Dutch Army as the Germans invaded the Lowlands. Repairs had only been completed the month before the British made their attempt to seize it in September of 1944. Called the Rijnbrug, this vast road bridge had been built in the 1930s at the same time as the similarly imposing bridge at Nijmegen, the Waalbrug – also a tiered arch bridge. Visible from miles away, standing well above the Neder Rhine on concrete footings, its steel arch is 120 metres long. In the four years it took to repair the bridge, the Germans had maintained a pontoon crossing. On British maps this pontoon bridge was marked up in the place of the road bridge. There was also a further pontoon bridge about half a mile west of the Rijnbrug; an aerial photograph from the week before Market Garden went ahead showed this pontoon bridge in action.

Nevertheless, it is striking how short on detail the September 'first issue' 1:25,000 maps are. Where the Bridge should be it says, perhaps ominously, 'Slachthuis': 'slaughterhouse'.

Situated on the eastern side of the Town were raised earthwork embankments along which traffic ran down into Arnhem. The twenty-one buildings that the British occupied on the Sunday around the Bridge were homes, offices, council buildings that looked down over the ramp. For dealing with an assault coming directly over the Bridge, as happened on the Monday morning, the buildings proved ideal. But for whatever else the Germans might have in store, the situation might look quite different.

Somehow, and no one at the Bridge knew how, 1st Parachute Brigade's commanding officer, Brigadier Gerald Lathbury, had been separated from his headquarters and had in effect vanished. Maybe he was dead, perhaps he had been captured. Either way he hadn't materialized on Monday, and nor had the rest of his Brigade. Frost had asked his intelligence officer to find him a German captive who spoke English. A Hauptsturmführer, an SS captain, was found. It was soon and shockingly clear to Frost that II SS Panzer Corps – or

at least what had been left of it after Falaise – was in the neighbour-
hood. As far as received opinion was concerned, 9th and 10th SS
Panzer Divisions had been destroyed in the fighting in the Normandy endgame at Falaise. 2nd Battalion's intelligence summary
from Saturday 16 September, three days before, *had* included 9th
and 10th SS Panzer Divisions in its round-up of formations that had
been identified in the area north of Antwerp, but it did not place
them at Arnhem. However, it said:

> 5. <u>To sum up.</u> There is no direct evidence on which to base an
> estimate of the troops in the immediate Divisional Adminis-
> trative Area. ARNHEM, if the enemy main line of defence is
> on the WAAL, will be his vital centre of Line of Communica-
> tions, and will therefore contain a number of troops out of
> the line. It will be strongly defended if the line is manned,
> but at present may be empty while the available troops are
> digging trenches or conducting their fighting withdrawal
> from the ALBERT CANAL.[1]

The Germans could be expected to put their best men into the fighting to the south of Arnhem, where the 'Kampfgruppe Chill'[2] had
fought so doggedly at the Albert Canal in the preceding week or so.
But the presence of these SS soldiers, who were as motivated as any
German soldiers could be at this stage of the war, was somehow a
surprise for a Battalion commander. In 1st Parachute Brigade's
orders there had been no mention of any specific formations beyond
the vaguest 'Enemy is expected to stand with main def position on
River RHINE'.

The man who had signed off on those orders, Brigade Major
Tony Hibbert, was already at the Bridge with Brigade Headquarters.
But with the clock turning midnight and the Battle already three
days old, it was not the time for any more surprises, particularly
when the Allies' strategic intentions were all too clear to the

Germans. The Allies should have known to expect the Germans to throw everyone and everything at the Bridge.

The rest of Monday had seen a series of counter-attacks as the Germans probed at the British positions. The Germans had been fighting with a grim disregard for their own casualties, knowing that the Bridge was the last crossing over the Rhine before Germany – which would then be popped open to the British and the Americans.

Enumerating exactly how many men Frost had with him at the Bridge is difficult as estimates vary and accounts overlap. He had taken 548 men with him to Arnhem on Sunday and had lost nine men killed[3] that day. On Monday another eleven died, including the Battalion's second-in-command, Major David Wallis, who had been killed overnight by sappers of 9th Field Company RE. He had been to visit A Company to discover their condition at the end of the day, but had failed to satisfactorily answer the sappers' challenge in the dark, and they'd opened up on him with a Bren as a legitimate target. Wallis was an old friend of Frost's. The lieutenant colonel had already seen his battalion chewed up in North Africa; now he was losing friends too. Ironically, earlier Wallis had tried sending a pigeon to report the situation at the Bridge, a source of great hilarity as the bird refused to go. 'But nothing was funny now,'[4] thought Frost. Major Digby Tatham-Warter took over command of the Battalion. On Sunday night the Bridge had caught fire, a German ammunition dump had been attacked and cooked off, and the whole area had been lit by the flames as if by daylight. To be able to see in the dark, Frost had ordered a building be set on fire, several wooden huts according to the Brigade HQ Diary. The attempt to repeat the trick backfired, as Frost put it:

> We need not have bothered as our own caught fire, and then the one next door. We managed to stop our own, but all night long various fires were raging and we could see to shoot at two hundred yards.[5]

In the school building on the eastern side of the ramp, Captain Eric Mackay of 1st Parachute Squadron Royal Engineers had had a hard day's fighting. He had no illusions about what he and his men were facing, after the hand-to-hand fighting the first night. At close quarters on the Sunday evening around the school, the combat had been intense and horrific: at one point Mackay put his pistol in the mouth of a German machine gunner who'd poked his head into the school and blew his head off.

Although the men in the school had repelled the SS attack first thing, the school's position on the eastern side of the ramp meant it could be fired on from the far side of the street. However, it was harder for the Germans to close on the building because it was on the ramp and all approaches to it were uphill. Mackay had with him A Troop as well as what he estimated were about fifty RASC personnel, amounting to a small infantry company. On arrival his men had been told to 'bugger off' by B Troop, who'd got there first, but as the day progressed both A and B Troops and Mackay's composite force occupied the main school building. Gunfire went to-and-fro between the school and the building next door. Mackay ordered two of his sappers, George 'Poacher' Paine and Ron 'Pinky' White, who had the medical training required, to help Corporal Roberts of 3rd Battalion with the wounded in the basement.[6] Mackay had also designated the area under the stairs as the mortuary. His men were as busy fighting fires as they were the Germans:

> The enemy promptly set the house next door on fire in another attempt to burn us out. By 9.30 it was going well. A high wind sprang up and burning fragments were blown on to our wooden roof, which soon began to smoulder. The fire-fighting party moved up to the roof with the A.R.P. appliances supplied by the Dutch Government. The whole area was as bright as day, and they immediately came under harassing

machine-gun and sniper fire. Covering fire was given as much as possible from the floor below. Parties were changed frequently on account of the intense heat and tiring nature of the work.

After three hours' fire-fighting, everyone was exhausted, but the danger was past. We had now been fighting almost continuously for thirty-four hours; no one had had any sleep for forty-three hours and very little food and water. There were two dead and seventeen wounded out of fifty. So ended the second day.[7]

Generally, radio contact within the perimeter at the Bridge had been hard to maintain, so who was where and in which house, and what state they were in, was impossible to keep track of. The Parachute Regiment's war cry of 'Whoa Mahomet!' (which they'd adopted in North Africa and knew the Germans couldn't pronounce) was the only guarantee.

Casualties were increasing. Captain Jimmy Logan was 2nd Battalion's Regimental Medical Officer and was taking care of the wounded in the basement of the building that had been designated as Brigade HQ, in the main block of buildings on the opposite side of the ramp from Mackay's school. Logan's job was made all the more difficult by the fact that the Town's water had been cut off as the German forces regained their composure after the initial shock of the assault on Sunday.

By midnight, Captain Logan faced a third day without sleep, with hundreds of wounded men to attend to. What he couldn't do was evacuate them to the Field Ambulance (FA), which was back in the Town, along with the rest of 1st Parachute Brigade.

And yet, all in all the situation at the Bridge at midnight, while far from ideal, didn't seem hopeless. The enemy had been unable to dislodge them, and if the Brigade were able to get through from the Town, and resupply the men at the Bridge with ammunition, they felt they'd be able to hold on for as long as it took 2nd Army to appear. Frost was worried about ammunition, primarily. Water, or the lack of it, was an inconvenience in the immediate term, and would certainly make fire-fighting more challenging. Food they could do without. But ammunition was the only way they could resist. Without it, his men were done for.

2

THE TOWN: THE EMBATTLED

Like everybody else, I completely failed to appreciate the
strength of the opposition we were up against.

Major Anthony Deane-Drummond

AS NIGHT FELL ON SUNDAY, the race for the Bridge had lost momentum. While 2nd Battalion and Brigade HQ had pushed through and taken up positions there, the other two battalions in 1st Parachute Brigade had run into fierce German opposition; the Brigade's plan had already gone awry. Major John Bune, second-in-command of 1st Battalion, had been killed, along with eleven other men. R Company had suffered a catastrophic 50 per cent in casualties in a fierce battle trying to move along the northern route into Arnhem.

The commanding officer of 3rd Parachute Battalion, Lieutenant Colonel John Fitch, had quite the complication to deal with. He had found himself with two senior stowaways in the forms of Major General Roy Urquhart and his brigadier, Gerald Lathbury, who were keen to find out what was happening and urge their battalions on with their advance. Urquhart's Jeep had been struck by a mortar on the edge of the Landing Zone and his radio destroyed; but rather than staying with Divisional Headquarters he set off to investigate. Instead of pushing forward, Fitch had parked his Battalion Headquarters in a house on the main road into the Town, the Utrechtseweg, just to the east of the Village. This pause had been decisive in allowing the Germans to regroup in their defence of the Town.

3rd Parachute Battalion had headed down this same central road

ahead of 1st Battalion, but had endured a similarly sticky and frustrating advance towards the Bridge. One company, C, or at least
some of it, had made it through to the Bridge, but no others. By
Monday any advance in that direction had ground to a halt. The
streets and houses in the eastern stretch of the Village, the high
ground at Den Brink on the outskirts of the Town, the railway line
coming up from the south over the Rhine to meet the main Amsterdam line, the Lombok estate in the Town itself, all feed into the fatal
Bottleneck by St Elisabeth Hospital. The most significant of these is
the lower road along which Frost's men had successfully made their
way and which comes up from where it skirts the riverbank to meet
the main road from the Village – the Utrechtseweg.

At the Bottleneck, all routes having met, the road then splits
once more, with the river road diving down to the right towards the
embankment, where it runs parallel with the water and open to the far
bank, on which stood a brickworks on the reclaimed polder. The other
road – the higher road – carries on straight up the slope towards the
Town, with the hospital on the left, followed by houses with allot-
ments behind them. Behind these are the railway sidings. The
embankment falls steeply back down on the right-hand side towards
the river road.

Heading up the higher road eventually delivers you to the
Museum (or Monastery as it became known), around the bend at
the crest of the hill and then down on into the Town and the railway
station, with houses again on both sides of the road. Fifty metres to
the east of the Bottleneck is the road that runs straight north up to
the railway line, the Zwarteweg with its terrace of two-storey brick
houses on its west side and the hospital on the east, which is where,
on Monday night, 1st Airborne Division's commanding officer,
Major General Roy Urquhart, found himself trapped in the loft of
Number 14.

To get into Arnhem, to get to the Bridge, the battalions had to get
through the Bottleneck in the Town, an area commanded by German
fire and with little or no room for flanking manoeuvres. Sunday and

Monday had proved how difficult it was. On Sunday, 3rd Battalion lost nine men killed, a further eighteen on Monday. Among them were Major Peter Waddy, commander of B Company, killed by a mortar blast, not a mark on his body, alongside his company sergeant major, Reg Allen; there were scores more injured, captured or lost.

By the end of Monday the two battalions from 1st Parachute Brigade were spread out in the houses along the main road to the west of the Bottleneck. The Germans were firing on them from all sides. In the ebb and flow of the battle in the streets to the north of the main road it was clear that they held the railway line, and that, knowing their way around Arnhem, they could turn up anywhere and surprise the British. Losses in the parachute battalions were mounting, and it was clear that the men who were still able to continue were tiring.

German anti-aircraft guns from across the river held up progress in the afternoon but were partly suppressed with mortars and artillery support. Nonetheless, the British troops couldn't get any further east than the Bottleneck. By the end of Monday when 1st Battalion regrouped in the Town, R Company was down to forty men.

Lieutenant Eric Davies of No. 10 Platoon, T Company, 1st Battalion, took part in the typically confused and confusing action and described the people caught up in it:

> The house was still occupied by some screaming Dutch people – what a row! A young girl ran from one house doorway to another and was shot through the upper leg. My medics attended to her, but we had to hold the mother off; she went berserk. Food and drink were offered to us by civilians as the battle raged! I had eight or nine men left with me. I decided to try to advance further as the factory was now cleared. The civilians disappeared, sensibly going to their cellars.[1]

In the fighting that followed, Davies was injured, a bullet passing through both his legs and another through his pack into his neck:

'Old soldiers say that you never see the one that hits you. I did – it was a tracer.'

On Monday another twenty-three men from 1st Battalion were killed. The three rifle companies were being chewed through, and with officers leading from the front and being killed and injured, the challenges of fighting in a built-up area and the leadership required were put under real strain. By the time midnight approached, both battalions – out of contact with each other, short of men, the wounded left along the way, the dead littering the streets and houses of the Town – were determined to push on and get through to Johnny Frost and his boys come what may. But there were reinforcements coming. 2nd Battalion the South Staffords, and 11th Battalion the Parachute Regiment, were on their way to the Town – maybe they would be the difference in forcing a way through the Bottleneck.

3

THE VILLAGE: A QUIET NIGHT?

0900 – No information as to movements of G.O.C.

1st Airborne Division War Diary

LOCATED BETWEEN THE DROP ZONES and Landing Zones of the First and Second Lifts and the Town, with the Woods to the north, Oosterbeek was a hive of activity, with fighting on its fringes and approaches. While Divisional Headquarters had settled into the Hartenstein Hotel, which showed signs of not being too recently abandoned by German officers, the Village began to take on the role of backstage for the Division and what was happening around it. Other HQs gravitated to being within a few hundred yards of the Divisional HQ. The men of the Royal Artillery had positioned their guns on the Landing Zones, while down in the south of the Village by the church the RASC had set up a supply dump. In Regimental Aid Posts and Field Hospitals, medics were tending to the wounded.

21st Independent Parachute Company, the Division's pathfinders, whose work was now done in setting up guidance beacons for the First and Second Lifts, had been slotted into the defences in the north of the Village. This hand-picked company, which included some German Jews among their number, had thus far suffered only one casualty, Corporal Jones. They made their way to new positions for 2300 hrs, commandeering a horse for assistance. It was a quiet night for the Independent Company. They still had to provide navigational aids for the Poles due to arrive on Tuesday, as well as for the scheduled supply drop. But the night was otherwise uneventful.

Also serving as a temporary Divisional reserve were the hundreds of glider pilots who had brought 1st Airborne to Arnhem. The Glider Pilot Regiment had two Wings at Arnhem, Nos. 1 and 2, and these Wings consisted of Squadrons. The men had been trained by both the RAF and the Army, the idea being that they were soldiers first, pilots second. Louis Hagen, a German Jew, in D Squadron No. 1 Wing, had his doubts about how well trained they had been as soldiers but with his fellow glider pilots was waiting patiently for something to do. Come midnight on Monday the column of pilots he had joined that had been heading into Arnhem was dug in along the railway line to the north of the Village.

7th Battalion King's Own Scottish Borderers had spent Sunday and Monday guarding the Landing Zones, and had moved northwest up to Ginkelse Heide (Ginkel Heath) to defend it for the arrival of the Second Lift. The KOSB had been fighting the Germans along the treeline on Monday morning. It had been a bloody day for them, with seventeen men killed (in contrast to none on Sunday). The Germans had attacked their positions with anti-aircraft guns on Sunday night, and at first light it became clear that the Germans were holding the wood in the top corner of the Drop Zone that 4th Brigade were due to land on at 1000 hrs. Because the treelines offered the enemy such great cover, the fighting went on all morning, so it was just as well that the Second Lift had been delayed. By the time the sky filled with parachutes at 1500 hrs, the KOSB at least knew of the enemy presence and were able to engage it, rather than the lift being the point at which the enemy first made contact. When 4th Parachute Brigade arrived there was machine-gun fire on the DZ, some of the heather was aflame, but the KOSB had done their job and suppressed the Germans sufficiently that the landing went off well enough. Freed of this task, the KOSB deployed to the east to join the advance into the Woods. They made slow progress as the roads were congested with the men of 4th Brigade, but as night fell the KOSB were no longer in contact with the enemy and were moving in anticipation of tomorrow.

1st Battalion the Border Regiment was regrouping after two days of guarding the Landing Zones – they fell back into a more defensive posture to the west of the Village. Of all the fighting elements of the Division they had had the quietest time, relatively, with only two men killed on Sunday and then ten on Monday. In the morning, heavy mortaring had destroyed some of the Battalion's Jeeps, and the afternoon, after the Second Lift had come in, had seen men injured on the Landing Zones, strafed by unexpected Luftwaffe fighters. The Border Regiment Diary took stock:

> At 1900 hrs Battalion moved off LZ 'Z' to Phase II position. Many gliders by this time were in flames. All gliders had now arrived, including those missing from first day, with the exception of the CO.[1]

The Border Regiment's arrival by glider as a complete formation on Sunday had gone well except for one major fly in the ointment. Their commanding officer, Lieutenant Colonel Thomas Haddon – a professional soldier and Border Regiment man from the pre-war Army, whose career had seen a stint as Assistant Secretary to the Joint Intelligence Committee after getting out at Dunkirk[2] – hadn't made it to Arnhem. He'd gone to Sicily with the Borders in the abortive glider landings the year before Arnhem, but this time his glider's tow rope had broken just moments after taking off in England, so he was unable to join his men on the Sunday. The following day, as part of the Second Lift, the Dakota tugging his glider was struck by flak, the pilot killed, and Haddon was set down with his staff seventy-five miles away and behind enemy lines. The Battalion was getting on with what it needed to do. By midnight on Monday its commanding officer was still missing; his fate was unknown.

Similarly, the core issue on Monday night, the subject of all the gossip on the ground, was the whereabouts of Major General Urquhart. He had left Divisional Headquarters on Sunday evening and had not been seen since by his men. With the advance into the

Town having failed to make any proper progress, and the Second Lift having arrived, a decision, or set of decisions, about how to proceed with the Battle needed to be made. There was trouble brewing in Urquhart's absence: uncertainty about the fate of the men at the Bridge, whether the battle in the Town could be brought to a successful conclusion, and what new line of advance could be opened in the Woods.

THE WOODS: WAITING FOR TOMORROW

Hostile bombing during night with flares, intermittent and
annoying, no damage.

4th Parachute Brigade War Diary

THE LANDING OF 4TH Parachute Brigade, though contested, had
gone without major incident and the Brigade was preparing to make
its move north of the railway line into the Woods. All three battalions had embarked but had made differing progress: 156 Battalion
were fighting around Wolfheze; 10th Battalion were to 'hold hard'
ready for deployment in the morning; and 11th Battalion had been
sent off to the Town. The War Diary states:

> Task for 19 Sep – Advance between including Road ARNHEM –
> EDE including Railway to secure high ground KOEPEL 712793
> with firm left flank on road.

But before Brigadier Hackett's men could start on this task he had to
fathom what the plan was in his Divisional commander's absence.
Where was the major general anyhow?

5

THE TOWN: THE GENERAL

Destiny is a good thing to accept when it's going your way.
When it isn't, don't call it destiny; call it injustice, treachery,
or simple bad luck.

Joseph Heller, Good as Gold *(1979)*

ROY URQUHART DIDN'T GET MUCH sleep that night, with the grenades in his smock pocket pressing into his chest.

In the loft of the house opposite St Elisabeth Hospital, Urquhart had plenty of time for reflection. He had done what he'd done before, what he'd always done – when commanding 231 (Malta) Brigade in 1943, he had gone forward to find out what was going on. On Sunday he had landed by glider. Urquhart was too big, heavy and old to parachute, at six feet and forty-three years old, and he'd been warned off it by 'Boy' Browning when he'd first taken command of 1st Airborne Division. The landings had gone perfectly, he'd landed on time at 1300 hrs and set up his TAC HQ (Tactical Headquarters) in a wood on the edge of the Landing Zone. He was determined to make sure he knew what was going on. The strange, immediate jump-start to action during an airborne landing offered as much potential confusion to the people landing as it did to the enemy. As soon as they were on the ground, the fluid and essentially chaotic character of airborne operations kicked in.

The previous two years of airborne landings had made this all too clear. On D-Day on 6 June 1944, 6th Airborne Division's First Lift of the night, at around midnight – consisting of glider *coup de main* parties, parachute battalions and their glider-delivered heavy weapons – had essentially been disastrous. Weather had played its part – the bad weather that had famously delayed the embarkation of the vast flotilla hadn't completely passed Normandy by – and aircraft found it hard to locate the intended Drop Zones. Parachutists had been scattered all over the eastern end of Normandy, while battalion commanders (if they even found their battalions) were unable to muster the kind of troop concentrations they had rehearsed with in preparation for Overlord.

At the Merville Battery, Lieutenant Colonel Terence Otway, who later wrote the official history of British Airborne forces, found himself with just 150 men at his rendezvous, rather than the 600 or so he had hoped for. The German guns at the Battery needed to be silenced – they overlooked Sword Beach – so Otway put in his attack anyway. By the end of the assault through the wire, there were only seventy-five or so men still standing. It later transpired that the Battery's guns were not the heavy artillery expected – 100mm guns rather than 150mm – but at least 9th Battalion of the Parachute Regiment had prevailed.

Nor were the top brass in Normandy immune to the effects of the calamitous drop on D-Day. The commanding officer of 3rd Parachute Brigade, Brigadier James 'Speedy' Hill, while marching in a column, looking to join up with the rest of his Brigade, had been mistaken for Germans by Allied aircraft, and strafed and bombed. Jumping into a ditch, the man beneath Hill had been killed and a chunk of Hill's backside had been torn off. He got himself patched up, and despite the doctor saying Hill looked 'bad for morale', he availed himself of a bicycle. Eventually Hill found his way to his headquarters, where he could assess what the state of play was for his Brigade. Before leaving for Normandy, Hill had told his men:

> Gentlemen, in spite of your excellent orders and training, DO NOT BE DAUNTED IF CHAOS REIGNS. It undoubtedly will.[1]

Chaos had undoubtedly reigned the year before in Sicily, the summer of 1943, where 1st Airborne Division's experiences had been even worse. The glider landings had been an almost complete catastrophe – the long journey across the Mediterranean over a nervy Allied fleet at dead of night, glider pilots flying gliders they were unfamiliar with, had delivered on its potential flaws. The parachute landings at the Primosole Bridge on the night of 13–14 July 1943, Operation Fustian, had been calamitous. To everyone's astonishment, German Fallschirmjäger (paratroopers) had landed by parachute simultaneously, resulting in an extra dollop of chaos and confusion for the Allied soldiers being dropped all over Sicily (some men spent the time they should have been fighting hiding on Mount Etna, others, cut off and lost, ate nothing but apples for a fortnight).

And the previous year in North Africa everything that could have gone wrong did go wrong: operations there began with James Hill choosing his Drop Zone from the door of his aircraft, setting the tone for a campaign that seemed as unending as it was frivolous, and profligate in its waste of men who were elite soldiers, expensively trained. The battalions in 1st Parachute Brigade were whittled down in tough fighting in Tunisia, but without any proof of the airborne concept given that the landings they had embarked on had come to nothing. Right from the beginning, airborne landings had been fraught with the possibility of chaos. By the time Arnhem came around, everyone wanted things to run more smoothly than they had done before. No one was keen on dropping (or being dropped) at night. And night landings were only necessary if airborne troops were being dropped in support of men landing on beaches at first light; this was not a requirement of Market Garden. Not having to land at night was something that everyone welcomed wholeheartedly.

But the landings on D-Day of Market Garden had gone perfectly; chaos had not reigned. Quite the opposite. If the mood in 1st Airborne had been one of desperation to get into action and ready to take any risks that might possibly come their way, then their arrival in Holland that Sunday might have felt a bit of an anticlimax. Some gliders had turned over on landing in the soft Dutch soil, their noses getting stuck and pitching them over. Of the men of 1st Parachute Brigade jumping on Sunday, only one man's chute had failed to deploy. There were twisted ankles and dislocated shoulders, the odd kitbag had gone awry, but the general impression had been of a successful exercise. The Germans who'd been in the immediate vicinity of the Drop Zone had put up little resistance, and in general had surrendered. Some of them had even been caught with their girlfriends – it was a Sunday afternoon after all.

Above all, the air plan had worked. It had delivered. Triumphantly. It had given 1st Airborne Division the opportunity to assemble and move on to its objectives in a way that James Hill with half his arse missing in Normandy would have envied. Major General Roy Urquhart knew perfectly well that his fellow airborne officers regarded him as a 'landlubber', and there was concern that he wanted to fight conventionally, form his battalions and brigades up and attack in the standard infantry style, that he just didn't get the way things were done in the airborne fraternity. However, the way the landings had gone – entirely as planned, allowing him to do just that and to form up his men in a deliberate and ordered manner – must have seemed to justify the decision to land so far from the Bridge, with the Village and then the Town in between. Even with problems with the radio net – problems everyone had expected – Urquhart had gone forward, to look at the in between.

Going forward was completely in character for Roy Urquhart. It was perhaps one of the qualities that his patron Montgomery so admired. Montgomery had first come across Urquhart in October 1940, when he'd joined the divisional headquarters of 3rd Division as a staff officer. This was the unit Monty had commanded with great flair in France. Promoted to commander of 5 Corps, in charge of defending southern England, Monty had done what he could to ensure that his old Division became part of his new command, and had kept an eye on the men who had joined 3rd Division after

Dunkirk. Two months later, Urquhart had been promoted to lieutenant colonel and chief of staff in 3rd Division – the kind of
appointment that Monty would have had go across his desk and
that he would have approved.

Montgomery made a point of getting to know his officers, and as
a former staff officer, having learned all about how the British Army
worked under the bonnet during the Great War, he wanted to be
sure that he had the right people in the right positions, determined
as he was to ensure people did things his way and that the people he
regarded as useless were out of the picture. In March 1941, Urquhart
was given command of a battalion in 4th Division. To his chagrin,
however, it was an English battalion, 2nd Battalion the Duke of
Cornwall's Light Infantry. Urquhart may have spoken like an upper-
crust Englishman, but he was in reality a Scot, serving initially in the
Highland Light Infantry. But this was a Montgomery appointment.
As Monty put it:

> I kept command appointments in my own hand, right down
> to and including the battalion or regimental level. Merit,
> leadership, and ability to do the job, were the sole criteria; I
> made it my business to know all commanders, and to insist
> on a high standard. Good senior commanders once chosen
> must be trusted and 'backed' to the limit.[2]

He also went on to say:

> Every officer has his 'ceiling' in rank, beyond which he should
> not be allowed to rise – particularly in wartime. An officer
> may do well when serving under a first-class superior. But
> how will he shape when he finds himself the boss?[3]

Perhaps in the loft at Zwarteweg 14, Urquhart was considering how
he was so far 'shaping' as the boss. Looking at the ceiling in the loft,
perhaps he felt he might have exceeded his own.

Before he'd commanded the Malta Brigade, Urquhart had been chief of staff of the Highland Division, where again he existed firmly in Montgomery's orbit within Eighth Army. He wasn't involved in the actual planning for El Alamein – Operation Lightfoot – but had been present at Corps- and Army-level conferences. Urquhart's Divisional commander, Major General Douglas Wimberley, had impressed him with his command style, running the Highland Division like a battalion, knowing everyone and everything. This, of course, may have been something beyond Urquhart's reach when he came to command 1st Airborne Division, with the Division dispersed around its airbases and not training together. He'd done what he could during the summer of 1944 to get to know his officers but it had been labour-intensive, clocking up hundreds of hours in his personal plane.

Fighting with the Highland Division in the desert had offered Urquhart an insight into the problems engendered by keeping everything moving and staying in touch with what was happening. Wimberley often split his headquarters into three parts, which meant that it was hard for Urquhart to keep track of where his boss actually was, especially when radio communications were at their most haphazard. Urquhart's conclusion was that it was best to keep going forward and eventually you'd find who or what you were looking for. The Highland Division's headquarters could be stretched across hundreds of miles; he had tried to apply this same principle in Arnhem in microcosm – and now here he was stuck in the loft of Zwarteweg 14.

With the Malta Brigade in 1943 this had worked well. As a brigadier in Sicily the same year he had fought with dash. On 19 July he had led his Brigade in a night attack across the River Dittaino, his lead Battalion the Devons driving north towards the town of Agira – Urquhart with them and urging forward motion. With the Canadians alongside, they pushed on to Regalbuto. Sicily involved hard fighting, where the terrain of ridges, hilltop towns and scrubland without any cover favoured the defender. Urquhart was always in the thick of the action, taking a tactical HQ – a Jeep, a radio, and his driver and batman Hopkins – everywhere with him, as well (in the Montgomery style) as having liaison officers who were to be his eyes and ears where he couldn't be.

The Malta Brigade had been apportioned independent brigade group status, so was intended to operate more flexibly than brigades attached to a divisional headquarters – which suited Urquhart's freewheeling style. It was the part of his career he enjoyed the most. As long as radio contact worked, and as long as his main HQ was efficiently run, with hierarchies and roles clearly delineated, he could run his independent Brigade group with vigour. For three weeks' solid fighting on Sicily, this worked really well for him. When the fighting had ended there, 231 Brigade were immediately ear-marked for making the crossing to the mainland.

But it was in Italy, at the River Amato, going forward in a Jeep to check on his vanguard, the Devons, that Urquhart was ambushed. A German armoured car fired on the Jeep, killing the wireless oper-ator, seriously injuring the brigade's intelligence officer, Captain Jennings, and wounding Urquhart in the chest, arms and legs. Perched on the bonnet was the Devons' battalion commander, who miraculously was unhurt. It marked the end of Urquhart's time commanding the Malta Brigade. Once he had recovered, he was invited to Montgomery's headquarters, presumably to give Monty the chance to check him out and make sure he knew how Monty liked things done. Urquhart spent a few days there, under the mutual microscope, watching how the generalissimo did things. The Bri-gade's history, published in 1946, written by one of its intelligence officers, Major R. T. Gilchrist, could not have offered more thor-oughgoing praise about its former CO:

> Most Commanders, having prepared an attack, would be
> content to sit back and watch it run to fruition – but not so
> Brigadier Urquhart. He could not resist throwing himself at
> the enemy and then dragging the rest of the Brigade after

him. He drew on the bank of fortune in a most brazen manner. He was just as liable to be killed or wounded as he stood in the open alongside a tank, on the first day of the fighting whilst a tank battle was in progress, as he was in Italy on the last day of the fighting. The impetus given to the attack by having a commander so far forward was dynamic and cannot be estimated. Nor is it possible to estimate the addition he gave to the morale of the troops when he constantly appeared among them standing erect as if on a drill parade – while they were crouching in their slit trenches. The effect was startling.[4]

Yet here he was, startled himself, at being trapped in the loft of a house in Arnhem opposite St Elisabeth Hospital.

Urquhart's experience in command, his attitude and his connections, make him an understandable appointment for 1st Airborne Division, particularly from Montgomery's point of view. Lieutenant General Frederick 'Boy' Browning, whose networking skills were second to none, clearly felt that Urquhart's face would fit. The Malta Brigade, operating independently, was as much like an airborne Division as anything else the British Army had. And Urquhart had done well with it. He was certainly more experienced than his predecessor but one, Major General George Hopkinson. Another big character in this corner of the Army with no shortage of big characters, Hopkinson had been an energetic and almost monomaniacal advocate of glider warfare. He had been killed on 9 September the previous year, going forward to see how 10th Parachute Battalion was doing at a roadblock near Castellaneta in southern Italy. He'd been hit by gunfire while sticking his head above a wall, literally having a look at what was going on; he had the distinction of being the only British airborne general to be killed during the war. This was perhaps in character for a man like Hopkinson, who wangled his way on to Bomber Command raids as a passenger.

Hopkinson's death had led to a struggle for succession within 1st Airborne's highest echelons: when Brigadier Ernest 'Eric' Down took over, he must have thought the job was his. A tough Parachute Regiment officer who'd been there since before it was known by that name, he should have been the perfect fit. But there were problems, and some intriguing followed:

> The other two brigadiers, Hackett and Lathbury, were not entirely happy about the appointment of Down, who, whilst thoroughly competent, had a reputation as one of the most abrasive officers in the Army.

Whatever their beef with Down was, the two parachute brigadiers got their way, although the upshot was an outsider came in above them. In January of 1944, Urquhart got the job. Down attended one Airborne conference at which he was told he'd been sacked and was being dispatched to the Far East. Over lunch with Urquhart, a disgruntled Down offered advice, and no doubt given his reputation, some home truths about the officers Urquhart was about to inherit and the state of play within the Division.

Nevertheless, Urquhart wasn't the first choice: another landlubber, Bernard 'Swifty' Howlett from 36th Infantry Brigade, a professional cricketer and highly experienced infantry officer, was in the frame for the job, but he had been killed in fighting at the Battle of the Sangro River on 29 November 1943, the day after he'd been told of his promotion.

With Urquhart's stated aversion to private armies, perhaps Montgomery regarded him as the officer to bring 1st Airborne Division to heel, or at least into the fold. But his presence at the front that Sunday when he had joined 3rd Parachute Battalion alongside Brigadier Lathbury must surely have offered its commanding officer, Lieutenant Colonel Fitch, an unhappy reminder of what happened the last time the Divisional commander had come forward; if anything was going to cramp your style as a battalion commander it was your GOC (General Officer Commanding) hanging around your Battalion Headquarters.

On Sunday night, at the end of the first day in Arnhem, when time must have been of the utmost essence, Urquhart had got himself some sleep – 'I dozed fitfully on a settee' – thinking that things were under control. He had spent these critical hours asleep in the belief that he was in good hands: 1st Parachute Brigade's commanding officer Gerald Lathbury had the airborne experience that the major general was so conscious he himself lacked. The plan for getting 1st Brigade from the Drop Zones to the Bridge was Lathbury's, the three routes taken, Lion, Leopard and Tiger, his concept, remnants of Operation Comet, the previous version of the plan to seize the Arnhem bridges. That Lathbury had opted to send all three of his battalions into the Town pell-mell and not hold one back in reserve, as conventional wisdom would have suggested, was something Urquhart had deferred to, just as Lathbury had deferred to the major general's enthusiasm to hare off into the yonder together. Experienced officers knew what luck, good or bad, could do for them. And bad luck was following Roy Urquhart around, right into the loft at Zwarteweg 14.

The loft was tiny, with barely enough room for the three men – along with Urquhart were his intelligence officer, Captain Willie Taylor, and an officer from 3rd Battalion, Captain Jimmy Cleminson. Cleminson had been part of the drama of the fighting in the Town. Earlier on Monday he had seen his best friend, Major Peter Waddy, killed as he attempted to hurl a sticky bomb at a self-propelled gun from the window of a house beside the Bottleneck. The fighting in the Town had devolved into small, bitty and often individual actions as the British, divided and holed up in different houses, fought from where they were, atomized. Now, as the day ended, Cleminson found himself caught in the major general's personal pickle. Cleminson had a moustache that as the hours passed began to bug Urquhart. Cleminson himself described it as being of rather 'heroic proportions', but he can hardly have been worrying about his moustache. What a mess of things Urquhart had made, haring about away from his headquarters, plainly lost, was self-evident to Cleminson, not that it was for him to say.

On Monday afternoon, B Company of 3rd Battalion had found themselves hemmed in both at the Bottleneck and on the embankment. They had fallen back – and it was in the fighting that followed that Major Waddy was killed. Cleminson had spotted Urquhart and Brigadier Lathbury, as well as Captain Taylor, trying to run east, forward towards where the Germans had taken control of the streets. They had left Fitch and his HQ to their own devices earlier and were now tangling themselves up in the confused fighting around the Bottleneck. Urquhart called to Lathbury: 'Come on, Gerald, we must go and have a look!' Considering he had been cut off from his Divisional Headquarters for the best part of twenty-four hours and that Lathbury similarly had been cut off from his Brigade HQ – currently ahead of him at the Bridge – why they weren't repairing west towards the Village and away from the increasingly confused and haphazard fighting in the Town is a question worth asking. Certainly Lathbury had been enjoying himself, throwing sticky bombs and smoke grenades, and almost shooting Urquhart when his Sten gun went off negligently. Cleminson later said, 'Subsequently all General Roy would say was that he wanted to see for himself. Well he certainly did!'[5]

At the time, after Urquhart had exclaimed, 'Come on, Gerald, we must go and have a look!', Cleminson replied, 'For goodness' sake don't – you will only run into a lot of Germans,' but Urquhart bowled on forward, with Lathbury throwing smoke and Taylor running behind. Cleminson's men, who had been fighting since they had landed on Sunday, sensibly hung back, knowing perfectly well that Cleminson was right, and that the Germans could be around any corner. Which of course they were. Lathbury was immediately struck by a bullet in the back and went down, paralysed. They dragged him across the street into the gardens at the back of the houses, and then into one of the houses. A German soldier appeared

at the door: Cleminson and Urquhart shot him dead. Urquhart may
well have been the highest-ranking British officer to kill a German
soldier in the Second World War. He certainly thought so. The
couple in the house took Lathbury down to the cellar[6] while Cleminson, Taylor and Urquhart ran out of the house, through gardens
separated by a warren of shoulder-height fences, and into Zwarteweg
14, a red-brick terraced house opposite the hospital, and took refuge
in the loft. Like so many of the men of 1st Airborne Division in the
houses around them, they were now cut off, in streets where the
Germans were patrolling aggressively, and where chaos reigned.

In the meantime, a German self-propelled gun had parked outside the house. Urquhart considered out loud how they might
escape and favoured making a break for it. Taylor and Cleminson
were not so sure. Cleminson went down the ladder to have a look
and the major general was outvoted. Urquhart would have more
time to ponder what to do overnight. Being a Monty man, he knew
even as they:

> . . . took it in turns to keep watch and although I kept remind-
> ing myself that a commander in battle must never neglect his
> sleep, my mind was too active for sound rest. How far had
> 30 Corps advanced? Had the Americans succeeded at Grave
> and Nijmegen? Perhaps by now the 2nd Battalion had been
> given some help . . . It was very restricting in the little house
> and my frustration was increasing.[7]

They also made a mess needing to relieve themselves in the confines
of the loft, something they found mortifying.[8] The hours crawled by
as the Battle crackled and thudded on through the night. The fate of
the Division and its efforts to get through the Bottleneck to the
Bridge were out of Urquhart's hands. They would wait for dawn.
Urquhart had missed the moment when his reinforcements from
4th Parachute Brigade via the Second Lift arrived, and crucially the
moment of decision as to what to do with these reinforcements. He

knew the battle in the Town had gone awry, but nothing beyond that. He was absent from his headquarters, unable to influence the Battle and now completely cut off.

Whether Hopkinson, Down, Howlett or even Gerald Lathbury, who'd thought the job was his, would have done anything any differently may have run through the major general's head between fitful bursts of slumber. Back at Divisional HQ the decisions that would set the course of the rest of the Battle were being made, and there was nothing straightforward about any of that either. Urquhart's rush to the front had been described since as 'running around like a great wet hen' – so was 1st Airborne now a headless chicken?

THE VILLAGE: DIVISIONAL HEADQUARTERS – THE BRIGADIERS

'Come down quickly. The two Brigadiers are having a flaming row!'

Lieutenant-Colonel Henry Preston,
Assistant Adjutant and Quartermaster-General[1]

If there is disturbance in the camp, the general's authority is weak.

Sun Tzu, The Art of War

BRIGADIER 'SHAN' HACKETT HAD LANDED on Ginkelse Heide a full nine miles to the west of Arnhem at around 1415 hrs to the sound of German machine-gun and mortar fire and the smell of heather burning. There was a sense that the enemy was all around, and there was fighting on the edge of the Drop Zone as the men of 7th Battalion King's Own Scottish Borderers tried to clear part of the DZ. The Second Lift was late. Hackett retrieved his precious walking stick, which he had lost on landing; in the confusion he took some startled surrendering Germans prisoner. Jumping had been difficult – in the sunlight he found it hard to distinguish between the red and green jump lights at the plane's door; besides, characteristically, he had decided to wait to jump until he was satisfied that he was at the right end of the Drop Zone.

The official 4th Parachute Brigade Diary is a skeleton of the document it should have become, thanks to the way events played out, and what there is in its place, or rather as an addition, is Hackett's own diary of the Battle. It is a blend of the personal and the professional. He says that on arriving at the DZ, he 'had some difficulty collecting myself and then numbers of Brigade HQ whom scattered and rather confused'. But within an hour or so of landing, the Brigade was ready to move off, even though the reality of the landing demanded the immediate need to extemporize. For instance, 156 Battalion had had to find new rendezvous points due to the presence of the enemy, which made it clear that things were far from straightforward. By 1515 hrs at least the radio net was up, though the sappers and the field ambulance with 4th Brigade were not yet in contact. But by 1530 hrs the Brigade was a 'going concern', though, by Hackett's reckoning, at about 80 per cent strength. The friction that accompanied airborne landings had come into play; the desire to land in Holland and move on into battle as a coherent unit was, on D+1, not as simple as it had been on Sunday when the enemy had been taken unawares. It was Brigadier Hackett's first operation as an airborne soldier, his Brigade's first landing en masse, and if the immediate discombobulation of landing was one thing, then the information he was about to receive was of a completely different order.

Around the same time, news arrived from Divisional HQ of a change in plan: 11th Battalion would be going into the Town. These orders came from the acting Divisional Commander, Brigadier Hicks, who had taken charge in the absence of Major General Urquhart, though there was both more and perhaps less to it than that. Less to it in that he was, after all, in Urquhart and Lathbury's absence, the only brigadier still in contact with Divisional HQ. Hicks was also the most senior officer who knew the bigger picture, in so far as there was one, with the problematic radio communications. More to it in that Hicks was the man in line for the job. Urquhart's disappearance, which had set in motion a swirl of rumour, had caused a further unforeseen consequence – the question of succession.

Deciding the pecking order of who should take Urquhart's place was not straightforward. Relations between the naturally emollient Urquhart and his brigadiers had been far from ideal, particularly when it came to Hackett. As a former tank soldier, Hackett didn't have Urquhart's full confidence; commanding armour and infantry were very different things. Urquhart had at one point referred to Hackett as a 'broken down cavalryman', something Urquhart recalled in his memoirs years later, along with a petty argument about a walking stick. That he included this suggests some needle between the two men.

Whatever Eric Down must have said over lunch about the three brigadiers under Urquhart's command, Urquhart had decided that Hackett was the last man of the three who should take his place in the order of succession. It ran as follows: Lathbury first, then Hicks, then Hackett. But the chances that the Divisional Commander and his immediate deputy would be absent from Divisional HQ was extremely unlikely to the point of impossible. Except for the fact that Urquhart was in the habit of going forward, and that airborne operations had, up until this point, been characterized by officers disappearing, and men ending up in the wrong place.

However, it was the last-minute ad hoc manner in which Urquhart made clear his preferences that was far from ideal. On Sunday morning, just before they boarded the glider for Holland, he had informed his chief of staff, Lieutenant Colonel Charles Mackenzie, of his preferred line of succession in the event that he was killed or went missing. What he didn't do was tell the brigadiers themselves: after all, Urquhart had it all mentally filed under 'in the unlikely event of'. Urquhart trusted Mackenzie utterly, describing him as:

> . . . a small neat Scot with a small and neat moustache, and a
> large and neat mind. Unhurried, precise, and patient with a
> pleasantly dry sense of humour . . . The perfect staff officer.[2]

Urquhart, having spent a good deal of time in the war as a staff officer, a role he found constricting and tedious, hating the business of interpreting other people's intentions, valued Mackenzie's judgement and trusted him with making sure things ran smoothly. And now that one form of the 'unlikely event' had come to pass, Urquhart's disappearance, it was for Mackenzie to relay the major general's decision on who should succeed him: 'Pip' Hicks was now the next in line. Besides, on Sunday night and Monday morning Hicks was on his own: he was the last brigadier standing.

The oldest man in 1st Airborne Division, turning forty-nine on 25 September, 'Pip' Hicks was by far the most experienced brigadier in the Division, and his record in the Great War was unimpeachable. In 1918 he had been awarded a Military Cross:

> For conspicuous gallantry and devotion to duty during a daylight raid. He commanded his party in a most skilful manner, and was largely responsible for its success. About 50 of the enemy were killed, several of whom were shot by him with his revolver, and two prisoners taken. His conduct was splendid.[3]

By the time Roy Urquhart was commanding 1st Airborne, Hicks's age was beginning to play against him. Being an officer from the Royal Warwickshire Regiment, Montgomery's old regiment, he was known to the generalissimo, who had suggested to Urquhart, himself a relatively sprightly forty-three, that Hicks was perhaps a bit long in the tooth for the airborne pace of things. But the previous year Hicks had done well in Sicily – like so many of his men, his glider had landed in the sea, and he'd swum ashore, rallied his men, fought on, earning a bar to his DSO. Hicks knew what he was doing. Urquhart regarded him as 'the professional infantryman, tall, amiably reserved and practical'.[4] Experience was something Urquhart valued in the private-army world of airborne soldiering, even as there were still jibes that he was new to the airborne way of doing things, that he was a landlubber.

Indeed, that lack of experience was something other officers in 1st Airborne had already identified as a shortcoming in their new boss. Lieutenant Colonel John Frost had weighed Urquhart in these scales too when his new GOC was appointed. Frost put it like this:

> He had had no previous airborne experience, though considerable battle experience, which few of the senior airborne officers could claim. The snag of bringing in a complete newcomer was that however good they might be, they were inclined to think that airborne was just another way of going into battle, whereas in fact the physical, mental and indeed spiritual problems were, when the battle might have to be fought without support from the normal army resources, very different.[5]

Frost also felt that he hadn't seen enough of Urquhart during the summer. That his boss had gone down with malaria during the spring had perhaps passed him by. But Frost's assessment was at odds with what Brigadier Mark Henniker, former Divisional Commander Royal Engineers (CRE), thought:

> He was a good practical soldier, with both feet on the ground, and not too much airy-fairy nonsense about him. We in the Airborne business had built up a kind of mumbo-jumbo, based partly on theory and partly on bitter experience, and it seemed to me that Roy Urquhart was just the man to distinguish the sense from the nonsense in our philosophy.[6]

Henniker, who had come to like Urquhart, was posted away from 1st Airborne before Market Garden, and so didn't get to see him under pressure, in the clinch.

So, command of the Division had fallen to Hicks, the most experienced senior officer it possessed. Despite this experience the defensive tasks his airlanding – glider-borne – Brigade had been given suggested that these soldiers were at the back of the queue behind the parachutists when it came to the business of taking the bridges at Arnhem. For Operation Comet, the aborted operation that had preceded Market Garden, the plan had been to seize bridges all the way to Arnhem using gliders, rather than paratroopers. Opinions varied about the wisdom of this approach. The man in charge favoured the idea, the men who were going to have to do it, less so. Staff Sergeant Jim Wallwork, who had flown in Sicily and then landed the leading Horsa glider at Pegasus Bridge on the night of D-Day, was briefed to land in Nijmegen, at night, and with his co-pilot had planned to surrender to the Germans immediately on landing. When Colonel George Chatterton, his commanding officer, had suggested that his pilots could land as a *coup de main* he was called a murderer – the flak expected at Arnhem made it simply too dangerous. There would be no *coup de main* at Arnhem.

This seemed to fly in the face of 6th Airborne's experience in Normandy, when famously gliders had seized the Caen Canal and Orne River bridges; but this staggering piece of flying aside, 6th Airlanding Brigade had last been deployed in bulk on the evening of D-Day in what was called Operation Manna. The massed gliders of the Brigade arrived to reinforce the parachutists whose drops had been dispersed and had teetered on disaster. As usual, the airlanding soldiers, unless they were used for small-scale *coup de main* operations, got the unglamorous jobs, even though these glider elements had gone rather more according to plan than their parachuting colleagues. The reality was that everything was still a gigantic experiment.

Nevertheless, this distribution of tasks spoke to an unspoken division within British airborne forces between the dashing new para boys and the rather more staid traditional regimental light infantry battalions who had been re-tasked for gliders. The fact that the battalions had more men and were more heavily armed didn't cut through the Parachute Regiment's glamorous force field. No dash for the bridge for 1st Airlanding Brigade with its Border Regiment men, the men of the South Staffords and the King's Own

Scottish Borderers. Their role in the Market Garden plan, guarding the Drop and Landing Zones necessitated by a Second Lift, smacked of mere housekeeping. The fact that flying in by glider was incredibly dangerous didn't seem to make the airlanding role any sexier. Airlanding battalions had less of the 'private army' or 'family business' about them.

Urquhart's absence on the Sunday had been regarded by his chief of staff as understandable and in character, and 'not a cause for concern',[7] but by 0900 hrs on Monday morning – before the Second Lift was due to arrive – it was decided by Mackenzie that now was the time for Hicks to take command of the Division; Hicks was also persuaded, because things were quiet enough around the Drop and Landing Zones he was defending, to send one of his battalions, the South Staffords, or rather half the Battalion (more being due with the Second Lift), into the Town. It was Mackenzie's job to tell Hackett – a man he described as 'touchy' and 'volatile':[8] Urquhart shared his assessment, and also, in the manner of the times, called him 'short'.

Hackett was undeniably something of a thruster. Fiercely intelligent, speaking ten languages, he was Oxford-educated and moreover a keen historian – when at Sandhurst he had written a paper on Saladin and desert warfare. He was from Western Australia but educated in Geelong, Victoria; his father was an Irishman who had emigrated to Australia, became a politician and newspaperman, had John late in life, and died shortly afterwards. Hackett had taken part in counter-insurgency in the Arab revolt in the 1930s but gone on to become a tank man. Badly burned during Operation Crusader in late 1941, he became a staff officer – and crucially and characteristically for a man with ambition he had then gravitated towards GHQ's formation of Special Forces, the Long Range Desert Group, and so on. This made him perfectly placed, once he had recovered from his wounds, to be the man to form 4th Parachute Brigade. He had raised the Brigade himself, took great pride in it, and guarded it jealously.

But it is here that the fragmented nature of 1st Airborne Division came into play, as well as, perhaps, an expression of the hierarchy of the airlanding versus the parachute elements. For better or worse, 4th Parachute Brigade was very much Hackett's private army. Many of his officers were fiercely loyal to him, though not without the caveats that officers of 11th Battalion might have expressed, as we will see later. So, as he was bound to see it, taking a battalion off him was going to be hard news to break. When Mackenzie did so to a protesting Hackett he finished by saying, 'Well, there it is, you will only upset the works if you try to do anything about it.'

Accounts differ about the row on the evening of the Monday, and attempts have since been made to downplay just how heated the argument was, but undoubtedly Hicks had been in Arnhem for twenty-four hours longer than Hackett, was familiar with the situation – or as familiar as he could be in a rapidly changing and confused Battle – and had responded to what was happening as best he could given what he knew: Frost at the Bridge, the stalemate in the Town, the major general missing. In these circumstances, reinforcing the drive into the Town seemed logical, even if the South Staffords were under-strength. None of this tempered Hackett's fury. He wanted an objective beyond simply moving north of the railway line into the Town. That there was no one in charge of the drive to the Bridge also bothered him. And it got worse when Mackenzie revealed Hicks was temporarily taking Urquhart's place. A livid Hackett claimed seniority. In a sense he was correct: he had been made a brigadier three months sooner than Hicks, despite being fourteen years younger and not a veteran of the Great War.

Regardless of his frustration, the decision to send 11th Battalion into the Town had been made long before Hackett had landed. Crucially as to how the rest of 4th Parachute Brigade's day would now play out, Hackett's reaction to this unanticipated set of circumstances was to carry on with trying to advance his Brigade to its Phase II positions.

While it might be plain that things were not unfolding as the plan demanded they did, or as he wanted, Hackett – who described the situation as 'most untidy' – was going to proceed with Plan A regardless. The final straw had come at 2300 hrs when Major James Linton from 2nd Airlanding Battery arrived 'from Div HQ and brought further instructions. I then went to Div HQ, saw Brigadier Hicks.' The source of his fury, Hackett said later, came from his battalion being taken from him and the lack of orders for whatever he was to do next: 'I asked a number of bread-and-butter questions about report lines, fire support and so forth, but no one had thought of these.' He raised the question of his seniority. 'In the end I wrote out some orders to myself and signed them!'[9] At a moment when flexibility and cool heads were required, the incensed and headstrong Hackett was both trying to stick to the original plan and, if he didn't get his way, take command of the Division from someone who had been appointed by his boss, had been there longer than him, and who was more experienced.

Nevertheless, it was with the missing major general, Roy Urquhart, that the buck stopped regarding the argument about where the buck now stopped. He had only mentioned this contingent hierarchy at the last minute, while embarking for Holland, as a kind of afterthought, and only to his chief of staff, Charles Mackenzie. If there was one decision Urquhart made which truly reflected his lack of airborne experience – and how, from the outset, chaos would reign – it is this; if he was going to act in character and go forward, then he should have communicated firmer provision for the possible consequences.

In the Village, despite the noise of battle from the Town a couple of miles to the east, and the sound of sporadic contact with the enemy in the Woods and along the railway line to the north as 4th Brigade took up its positions for the next day, there was relative calm. Divisional troops were going about their business, Jeeps driving from the Landing Zones with stores to the RASC dump near the Hartenstein Hotel, the Pathfinders of 21st Independent Parachute Company moving up ready to mark out the Drop and Landing

Zones for Tuesday's lifts. A September evening in Oosterbeek, the mild weather, the leaves on the tree-lined streets turning to autumn colours, can be a pleasant walk or drive. Not that evening. At the Hartenstein Hotel, Hicks had his maps out, his radio net running, trying to find out what was happening in the Town; when Hackett finally arrived he was, like so many men who went to Arnhem, reminded of an exercise. The two brigadiers – who like so many airborne officers seemed not to have a particular affection for each other – went off into a corner. Hackett expressed his annoyance that a battalion had been taken off him on arrival, though he conceded it was the right one.

On this meeting, the midnight row at Divisional HQ, Hackett's account is tight-lipped, simply noting he returned to his HQ at about 0130 hrs on Tuesday morning. Gossip swirled around this meeting. Accounts say that things were settled amicably, but why would they need to be? As it was, Hackett's entreaties had changed nothing, and Tuesday would proceed as ordered: he would carry on north of the railway line and seize the high ground in the Woods. And, from Hackett's point of view, he would do so as he saw fit.

The vacuum of command had been filled by a strange tension at the top. There was, understandably, a raw desire on the part of the remaining actors to make decisions, and to take control of a battle that was already proceeding nothing like what anyone had expected. An argument about who should be making those decisions had resulted in no real change to the agreed plans, no fresh thinking. How would this shape the day to come? Would men be determined to exert their influence over events, to force the situation to their will, and indeed be able to do so? And what had 1st Airborne brought with it in terms of support? How had the British Army been winning in North-West Europe anyway? Firepower.

7

THE VILLAGE AND THE WOODS: THE GUNS. 1ST LIGHT AIRLANDING REGIMENT, RA

God fights on the side with the best artillery.

Napoleon Bonaparte

BY THE TIME OF ARNHEM, the British Army had come to rely on superb gunnery to take control of and impose its will on the battle-field: and why would it not? German doctrine called for responding to any attack with an immediate counter-attack – British gunners would take this opportunity and rain shells on to German soldiers and vehicles as they formed up for the counter-attack. It exemplified the British philosophy of using 'steel not flesh' to defeat the enemy: technology and machines would do the killing; men would not be put at risk if it could be avoided.

German tactical inflexibility in Normandy had contributed a great deal to delivering the Allied victory there, and the Royal Artillery Corps at the peak of its size had more men and women in it than the Royal Navy. While this included vast resources devoted to anti-aircraft defence in the United Kingdom, artillery in North-West Europe truly was Queen of the Battlefield. The gunners tore through ammunition and gun barrels in the high summer of 1944, and the Germans paid the price. With spotter planes, Forward Observation Officers, complex integrated radio communications, battery fire that could be delivered on a Corps level, every gun at the Commander Royal Artillery's disposal – from 25-pounders, through mediums and up to heavies – could be turned to fire on a target. In the early stages of the Normandy battle this was further bolstered by naval gunnery. Allied artillery was decisive in the European campaign, and integral to the British way of war, used to shatter the enemy in preparation for an offensive or in counter-battery fire once an offensive was underway. Gunnery often made the difference.

This was reflected in the make-up of the army fighting in North-West Europe that 1st Airborne was slated to fight alongside: 18 per cent of the men in 21st Army Group were gunners, 15 per cent infantry. Shells were to be expended to save men's lives. As Montgomery's intelligence supremo Bill Williams put it: 'waste all the ammunition you like, not lives'. Gigantic fire-plans ensued. For example, in Operation Epsom, which ran from 26 to 30 June 1944, over 700 guns were brought to bear. The following month, for Operation Charnwood on 7–9 July, 656 guns were available, as well as naval gunnery. Immediately following Charnwood came Operation Jupiter on 10–11 July, another Corps-sized offensive to seize the high ground at Hill 112 to the west of Caen, for which VIII Corps had a wealth of artillery at its disposal. Each of the three Divisions in the attack used their artillery to support the brigades going forward, augmented by 3rd, 8th and 5th Army Group Royal Artillery from the neighbouring 30 Corps. Five hundred and twelve guns – mediums and heavies – as well as the 15-, 16- and 6-inch guns of HMS *Roberts*, *Rodney* and *Belfast*, which were further bolstered by Typhoons offering ground attack on German positions. In one shoot on 20 July the combined guns available to the Canadians delivered 59 tons of shells in three minutes, what was called a 'murder target'.

As part of the Battle of Caen this was the kind of heavy metal that could be expected to be expended on a two-day battle. The British fought in three dimensions, with air power at their disposal, but the sheer power and ubiquity of artillery meant that even in poor weather indirect fire could be brought to the enemy with tremendous fury. Infantry could operate within this umbrella of fire with quite the degree of confidence. There was German gunnery in reply, but it was nothing like as formidable as what the British had brought to France, and the fear of counter-battery fire from the British went a long way towards cramping the German guns' style; German gunners did what they could to avoid setting off the Allied guns.

The arsenal of destruction available to a Commander Royal Artillery ranged from 7.2-inch heavy guns firing a 200-pound projectile with a range of 19,667 yards (eleven miles), its maximum rate of fire three rounds per minute, through the medium guns at 4.5- and 5.5-inch, their ranges varying depending on the weight of shell fired, to the ubiquitous 25-pounder. (The vagaries of gun classification mean that some are categorized by the equipment's barrel diameter and others by the ostensible weight of the projectile. In artillery parlance the gun is the equipment, the ammunition itself is the weapon, but I may be looser with the terms as we proceed.) A sure rule with gunnery was that accuracy declined with range, and that prolonged firing degraded the equipment further. Weather, wind and air pressure also had an effect. But numbers counted; rate and weight of fire mattered.

A British infantry division could call upon three 25-pounder field regiments, with twenty-four guns per regiment, as its basic artillery resource – in essence it was the division's fourth brigade. It could also, with proper fire-planning and in the event that the guns were available, call upon guns from the corps it was a part of, and even from the army to which its corps answered. This firepower relied on good maps, radio and cable communications, surveying and plentiful supplies of ammunition. That the lines in Normandy were relatively static, for example, meant that gunners had access to excellent mapping, and well-established communications nets; cooperation between the different arms within an army, division or corps was something that became well practised. Most attacks in Normandy would be preceded by artillery barrages of varying intensity – sometimes to bring about surprise the guns would not be called on to soften up the enemy – followed by counter-battery fire and shoots responding to enemy action and requests from the men at the sharp end. Plentiful artillery, what, to the Germans, must have seemed endless supplies of ammunition and heavy guns capable of keeping the stoutest of heads down, were part and parcel of how the British fought. Using gunnery this way was what had enabled the British to win in Normandy.

Things, however, were markedly different for the artillery component in 1st Airborne, constrained as they were like everyone else in the airborne world by what they could bring to the battlefield. The Commander Royal Artillery had to provide the Division with anti-tank defence – each brigade adopting a slightly different approach to its anti-tank component – as well as indirect fire. The anti-tank guns at their disposal were standard British weapons, the 6-pounder Quick Firing anti-tank gun, and its much, much bigger brother the 17-pounder. The 6-pounder had been in action with the British Army since mid-1942 and was, at the kind of close ranges being fought at Arnhem, effective against all German armour, even the daunting Tiger and Tiger 2 tanks. Weighing 1.14 tons it could be readily man-handled by its six-man detachment (strictly speaking, guns don't have 'crews'), and during the Battle of Arnhem men could run and push a gun into position and then scoot away again. With tanks coming around corners or over the brows of inclines, a 6-pounder could be a fairly mobile ambush weapon, and so it proved in Arnhem.

The 6-pounder fired a variety of ammunition, each refinement designed to enhance its ability to kill German armour without the need for a bigger, more powerful gun: for instance, a 'discarding sabot' round, which when fired would fall apart, dropping its outer casing while its central hard tungsten core carried on to the target at greater speed than normal armour-piercing shot. Disabling a tank or discouraging its crew could be enough, though ideally the round went into the tank and ricocheted around, tearing the crew apart or setting fire to the ammunition, batteries and fuel. The Mark 3 carriage had been adapted to fit more easily inside a Horsa glider, its shield had been modified, but with a Jeep it was pretty much the ideal gun for 1st Airborne; a Jeep and gun could be delivered by

Horsa and extricated within half an hour or so, provided the Horsa hadn't landed inconveniently upside down or wrapped itself around a tree.

The 17-pounder, a huge, heavy 3-ton monster of a gun that dwarfed the 6-pounder, had been developed in anticipation of German armour getting heavier and tougher. The 17-pounder gave 1st Airborne the ability to deal with heavy German armour a mile away, though the prospect of such an encounter in a built-up area was perhaps unlikely. The presence of 17-pounders speaks to the anticipation that German armour was to be expected on the ground at Arnhem; 6th Airborne had taken Tetrarch light recce tanks in their Hamilcars – getting them off the Landing Zones had proved difficult in the summer, with suspensions getting tangled in parachute canopy lines. And the titchy Tetrarch's 2-pounder 40mm gun packed none of the punch of the 17-pounder, which had a muzzle velocity of 3,950 feet per second when firing its discarding sabot round, a similar speed to the 6-pounder but a much heavier projectile with at least twice the effective range. It was too heavy to be towed by a Jeep, let alone manhandled by its detachment, so took more time and effort to bring into battle. Towed by a gun tractor, the 17-pounder required the similarly monstrous Hamilcar heavy glider to transport it to Arnhem. The pilots were trained to let the glider's tyres down to try to make unloading more straightforward, but it was a more unwieldy aircraft to operate in every way. Nevertheless, in terms of anti-tank artillery the airborne men were well equipped, comparable with other infantry formations.

In contrast, indirect fire, guns firing from a distance, the firepower that the British Army had made the centre of its way of war and winning, was a very different matter. The decision to go to Arnhem had been based on the whirlwind of victory brought about by the application of the crushing firepower that the Allies had at their disposal. But 1st Allied Airborne Army lacked exactly this kind of battle-winning firepower, determined by the limitations of the airlift. And in turn those limitations made what 1st Airborne Division was able to do, on the offensive and in defending, quite unlike what a line division in the rest of North-West Europe could achieve.

In short, 1st Airborne Division's CRA, Colonel Robert Loder-Symonds, had none of the tools at his disposal that his equivalent in, say, 43rd Wessex Division had. No heavies, no mediums, no 25-pounders. Instead, he had the American 75mm Pack Howitzer M1, which had been designed as a light gun for taking into difficult or challenging terrain. It fired a 14-pound shell, with a maximum range of 9,600 yards (about five and a half miles) and a rate of fire of up to six rounds a minute (which required aiming, loading, firing, clearing the gun every ten seconds). If it was estimated that a 25-pounder round needed to land three feet from a foxhole to injure or kill anyone in it, then the M1 really was the baby of the battlefield in gunnery terms. It had been designed to be broken down for portability, particularly for mountain warfare, to be portable by mules, and had been adopted by the British Airborne gunners because the 25-pounder was simply too big to fit into a Horsa.

With three batteries each consisting of two troops with four guns apiece, the Regiment would fly a gun into battle with two trailers of ammunition, 137 rounds per gun, 125 of which were high explosive, six armour piercing and six smoke. If the guns were to fire their high explosive (HE) at a rate of six rounds per minute, that amounted to twenty minutes or so of indirect fire; and while it was unlikely that the Regiment's guns would be called upon to deliver that kind of fire, it is clear that what 1st Airborne didn't have was sufficient indirect firepower to destroy the Germans if they were able to coax them into a counter-attack, let alone produce the kind of barrage they might need to suppress or disrupt the enemy in the first place. In Arnhem, the firepower playing field had been levelled.

The post-Overlord report put together by 6th Airborne after Normandy dealt directly with the limitations that its divisional artillery offered, and it didn't mince its words. Indeed the directness of the language is striking. On the subject of 'ARTY' (the report reflects the army's addiction to abbreviation and in quoting this report I have expanded on the abbreviations) it states baldly:

> (a) The artillery fire power of the Division is quite inadequate and must be augmented by having additional regiments placed under command. The Royal Artillery staff of an airborne division is insufficient to cope with this additional artillery and should be increased. In its present form it is not even sufficient to cope with the airborne division artillery alone if any casualties are incurred on landing.[1]

The problem plainly stated: 6th Airborne, which had been put together for Operation Overlord, had found its capacity for gunnery wanting. Nevertheless:

> (b) The airlanding Light Regiment of 75mm is a most necessary part of the Division and should be taken as a regiment [e.g. in its entirety] in the early lifts. The guns of this regiment enable brigades to have immediate support of a close nature such as is difficult to obtain from the heavier natures of artillery found in the support division or Army Group Royal Artillery . . .

The light artillery that was integrated with 6th Airborne was 'most necessary', yet 'quite inadequate'. Operation Overlord had been months in the planning, preparation had been in the manner of a 'too big to fail' operation. The battles in Normandy that had followed it (and 6th Airborne's time holding the British left flank) had had the full abundance of Allied resources poured into them. Market Garden was, like Charnwood, Epsom and Jupiter, a Corps-sized operation, indeed it was more than that with the involvement of 1st Allied Airborne Army. But 1st Airborne had been delivered sixty miles away from the 'heavier natures of artillery' that had been an integral part of the Normandy battle system. The report also expressed concerns about anti-tank provision, stating:

> . . . 17 pr anti-tank guns are invaluable . . . The two anti-tank batteries of 16 guns each were found barely sufficient. A third battery is required. The absence of extra front and side shield [the modifications made to the 6-pounder to make it air portable] leads to unnecessary casualties.

The anti-tank battle had been a close-run thing on D-Day, and 6th Airborne had benefited from armoured support, tanks that had come up from landing on Sword beach, from the afternoon of D-Day itself.

But it was the question of communications, of signals, by now utterly essential to the smooth running of British gunnery, that had the report's keenest attention. In fact, more than half of it concerned communications, radio and line. The headline was that the radio gear wasn't up to the job:

> (c) It is open to question whether the types of wireless sets provided for RA communications are in fact the most suitable. The 68R set provided for parachute Forward Observation Officer has a very limited range in enclosed country. A more important factor, however, is the lack of range of the No. 22 set which is the basis of the airborne support net. By the very nature of the airborne operation, the distance between guns and forward brigades must be extreme, and substitution of all No. 22 sets by No. 19 High Frequency is necessary: this particularly applies to the control set at HQ RA (together with the sets at the gun positions).

The lack of range of both radio and artillery at the disposal of 1st Airborne's gunners, and its lack of punch, could only come into play when the Division's plan called for it to be so spread out, at least during the initial stages of the operation. Once – if – all had gone according to plan and the Division was safely inside the Town, around the Bridge, relieved by 2nd Army, covered by its guns, the radio and gunnery issues maybe would be less pressing.

Gunnery in 1st Airborne was organized around who needed to be where and how they had arrived in battle in the first place. Anti-tank batteries were attached to each of the three brigades, ensuring that there would be 6-pounders in the van with infantry. These, however, arrived by glider, so there was the issue of rendezvous after landing. The Division was well equipped in terms of anti-tank weapons, and while these guns were answerable to the Commander Royal Artillery, they were in effect devolved to the battalions they fought alongside. Then, arriving by parachute, were men from each of the batteries, the Forward Observation Officers, their signalmen, with their precious cargo of radios and the sets' power supplies. They too were to go forward and provide coordinates for the guns in their batteries to fire on. Speed was of the essence. Yet the delay in finding a Jeep, on which this essential speed relied, offered a potential hold-up of its own. The batteries, having arrived by glider, would set up and wait for targets to be called in.

A relatively new and additional element was 1 Forward (Airborne) Observation Unit (FOU), RA, whose role was to make contact with the guns in 2nd Army and call in this much more serious firepower once the heavies, mediums and 25-pounders were within range. Their commanding officer, Major Denys Reginald Wight-Boycott, was part of the Division's seaborne tail, attached to 30 Corps. Wight-Boycott had raised 1 FOU; even before D-Day, it was clear that airborne formations needed better fire support. For D-Day with 6th Airborne, officers from the Royal Navy had been trained as parachutists to ensure good cooperation with the guns the Navy had to offer, something which had made a critical difference. Forward observation demanded trust and understanding between the men calling in the targets and the men on the guns – gunners talking to gunners.

A call for volunteers in 21st Army group went out and the rather officer-heavy 1 FOU was established. Commanded in Arnhem by Captain Arthur O'Grady, these officers were distributed among the battalions, waiting for the golden moment when they would be able to literally call in the big guns once 2nd Army, having fought its way up from the south, got within range. There was little to do on Sunday, and Monday was much the same. It wasn't a problem with the radio equipment as such; 2nd Army were simply too far away, and the men got caught up in the melee in the Town and around the Village. But the Light Regiment's Forward Observation Officers were in contact with their guns and bringing in fire.

In the Village on Tuesday morning, calls for 'Mike' targets were coming in from the Bridge and Woods. A 'Mike' target was the concentration of fire on a target of all of a regiment's guns. These calls had come through loud and clear and were being responded to with fire from the 75mm howitzers that Loder-Symonds finally had at his disposal. The Light Regiment's arrival in Arnhem had been far from ideal.

From four different airfields, Manston, Blakehill Farm, Down Ampney and Keevil, No. 1 Battery flew towed by a variety of different aircraft, illustrating the complexity of getting the Regiment's guns to Arnhem. Their arrival was fraught and dispersed. On schedule at 1315 hrs, all but two of 1 Battery's gliders made it to the Landing Zone, one landing in England and another, under Staff Sergeant Leeves, winding up four miles away from Arnhem at Renkum (he would make his way towards the sound of gunfire in the best traditions of the Corps of Artillery and turn up later in the afternoon). The men of 1 Battery organized themselves, figured out who was missing, what kit they had at their disposal, and made contact with the units they were to liaise with. Captains Walker and Lee were sent off to join 7th King's Own Scottish Borderers and Border Regiment battalions to offer fire support, and by 1500 hrs the Battery was dug in by the Landing Zone.

Half an hour later 3 Battery arrived, also somewhat short-handed. Three gliders were missing. The men who had made it had seen the gliders go down and were rattled by it. But by 1500 hrs they had rendezvoused and were ready to move off and recce where they might set up their guns. Almost immediately they were engaged by enemy machine-gun fire, which they dealt with promptly, pushing on to join 1 Battery at the Landing Zone. To defend them they were joined by men from the South Staffords, glider pilots (who were now doing their bit as all-round soldiers) and sappers from 9th Field Company RE.

Like for the rest of 1st Airborne, this was a period of orientation and taking stock of their environment: where were the targets likely to be? Where would be the best place to site the guns? What and who else were around them? The Light Regiment's Diary states that at 1700 hrs Lieutenant Moore 'took a Party up to the lunatic asylum to examine some new German 105mm guns which were being stored there. He found one booby trapped & left them as it looked unlikely that they could be used.' Additional firepower might help, indeed might be essential due to all the missing men and materiel, but time was pressing, and fixing booby-trapped guns was not time best spent. A shoot was called in for a target at a hotel in Wolfheze after 1700 hrs as the light began to fail, but for all that and the occasional nearby exchange of machine-gun fire, the mood was that it was all a bit quiet and there was a dearth of targets. The Regimental Diary states, at around 1800 hrs: 'C.O. "kicking" because there were no targets to fire on, he said we might just as well have come on the next day.'

As it was, the CRA, Loder-Symonds, had made it safely to Arnhem, but his Brigade Major was on one of the gliders that had stalled through a 'broke tow rope'. He would come 'on the next day'. But with him were other staff crucial to the running of the Regiment, the REME officer attached and the Signals Officer RA: they would now arrive on the Monday as part of the Second Lift. It wasn't until Monday at 1700 hrs that all of Loder-Symonds's headquarters team were finally reunited, setting themselves up at the Hartenstein Hotel in a 'first class ready-made dug out with pit prop roof and walls'. Again, a 'quiet night' was noted in the diary. While the battle ground on in the Town and raged at the Bridge, as far as the diary in the Village was concerned the mood was tranquil, and communications in working order.

Loder-Symonds's responsibility was for all of the Division's artillery assets. Commanding 1st Light Airlanding Regiment RA itself, 1st Airborne's indirect rather than anti-tank guns, was Lieutenant Colonel William 'Sheriff' Thompson. On Sunday, Thompson, thirty-four, had been confused about which day he was leaving for Arnhem, but he arrived with his TAC HQ as part of the First Lift. Thompson was pleased with the prospect of landing by daylight. Organizing his men and equipment on landing would be much easier than at night, and while the dire predictions of losses from flak had worried him a couple of days ago, being able to land at the corner of the Landing Zone where he wanted to position his guns was ideal. As it was, he felt that 3 Battery would need to move, in order that its guns could cover the Bridge, so they were all dispatched to the Village, ending up by the church on the lower road.

As well as the guns arriving by glider, the parachute components – attached to the parachute battalions – had dropped on Sunday afternoon, landing at 1415 hrs, quickly making it to their rendezvous and pressing on, picking up six prisoners as they went. Led by Captain Charles Harrison, the 3 Battery Parachute Party, E Troop, consisted of signallers, to facilitate communication between the infantry battalions in the rush for the Bridge and the guns, wherever they might be. Harrison's party joined 1st Parachute Brigade HQ and got on the southern route into the Town, making it to the Bridge with 2nd Battalion 'just in time to hear several German Half Tracks, Armoured Cars & horse drawn transport pass over it'. Harrison found on arrival at the Bridge, once Lieutenant Colonel Frost's men had set themselves up around the northern end, that the radio net wasn't working – the man-portable No. 38 radio set had worked well travelling through the Town, but by the time Harrison was in place at the Bridge it had failed. Not only that but Brigade communications had also failed and the Recce Squadron was also drawing a blank.

With Harrison was Bombardier Leo Hall, a signaller who found Harrison frustratingly vague, and felt it was always best not to ask questions or offer opinions. Hall did, however, figure out what the communications problem was at the Bridge – an 'unsuppressed vehicle'. The electrics on a vehicle could cause a low clicking or popping sound; British and German vehicles were suppressed to prevent this. Hall knew his job inside out, was meticulous in keeping his radio sets going and preserving the life of his batteries (known as 'Dags' because they were made in Dagenham), and reckoned it was a Dutch vehicle that was interfering with the British transmissions. The tall houses in the centre of Arnhem were also an issue. If Hall could get his equipment into a higher Observation Point, then maybe he could get through.

Hall set about getting his set to work, even though he later claimed not to understand how or why he'd been able to do it. Getting the radios out of the Jeeps would help:

> I rigged up the 68 Back-Pack set that Morrison had humped the 6 miles-plus from our Dropping Zone. The aerial reached almost to the apex of the pitched timber-lined roof. Switching on, I found Interference still evident, but much less so than that on the 22. I called up Control (the Battery Command Post) on my 22 set asking '. . . report my signals, over'. (You don't say: 'Are you receiving me?'!) Through the 68 Set came the clear reply, 'O.K. over.' So that was it, cracked: transmit on the reasonably powerful 22 with outdoor aerial and receive on the less powerful 68 with indoor aerial. Don't ask me for technical explanations; I know of none, but I can still feel the glow of satisfaction at overcoming a difficulty vital to Artillery support for the Paras . . .[2]

Incredibly, however, Hall didn't tell Major Dennis Munford, who had taken charge of 1st Parachute Brigade's gunnery, that he'd got through: 'I did slip up.'[3] That's one way of putting it. But by Monday the Royal Artillery radio net was working well.

On Monday the remaining components of the Regiment were due to arrive in the Second Lift, delayed as it was by fog at home. Arriving at 1700 hrs short of a glider carrying guns and ammunitions, 2 Battery quickly joined 1 Battery. The recommendation in 6th Airborne's report that all the guns arrive in the First Lift had not been heeded, the Light Regiment had lost out in the scramble for glider provision, and its efforts were diluted as a result.

Loder-Symonds decided that the following day he would have to reorganize and gather his batteries together, with 3 Battery dug into the grounds around the Oude Kerk, the Old Church, on the lower road at the bottom of the Village, E Troop with its four guns to the west, F Troop with its three to the east. It would work well as a site for the guns as it offered a clearer line of fire for targets in the Town and at the Bridge. The trees in the close country in the Woods by the Landing Zone had hampered the ability of 1 and 3 Batteries to send in indirect fire; the meadows and the polder around the church would make things simpler. The night was 'noisy but uneventful', and 11th Battalion passed through the guns' position and turned east on to the lower road on their way into the Town.

By contrast, Tuesday morning was noisy and very eventful. At 0700 hrs 1 Battery's guns on the Landing Zone were strafed by Focke-Wulf Fw 190 fighters, which came swooping in low, making the most of the absence of Allied fighter cover and the shorter trip from the Reich. Being bounced at first light left the men on the ground wondering where the RAF had got to. Then the morning's work began. With Major Munford calling in shoots from the Bridge, the guns of 3 Battery were landing shells on targets almost on top of the British positions, just the kind of accurate, ballsy gunnery that was needed in the circumstances. German mortar fire came back at the guns, but there was a sense of business as usual, the intense and precise business of gunnery, the targets being called in, the men lugging the ammunition from the dump to each gun position, the teamwork of well-rehearsed drills that the Royal Artillery lived and breathed: bearings called, the gun set, the pull of the lanyard, the shell away, the gun cleared and the drill repeated.

With the 75mm Pack Howitzer, the six-man detachment had tightly defined roles, each man his tasks, all in line with making sure that the gun was able to fire at its maximum rate of six rounds per minute. These roles extended well beyond simply laying, loading and firing the gun. Number 1 was in command of the gun, Number 2 was at the breech, Number 3 on the sights, Number 4 loading, and Numbers 5 and 6 were responsible for the ammunition.

Training was all in the Royal Artillery, so these duties broke down further. In the manual, Number 1 had twenty-six instructions to follow, which were further broken down into constituent parts: that the gun's axle was clamped correctly; that the gun itself had been assembled properly. He had an oil index to check, as well as the gun's mechanisms, ensuring that the sights were tested and adjusted, and – while this might seem obvious, except in the rush and hurly-burly of battle – he had to be sure the gun was not loaded when it was limbered up behind its Jeep. The tools issued with the gun were the tools to be used with the gun, *except in case of an emergency.* Number 1 chose the gun platform unless it had already been selected: the gun in effect was his. He had to watch the recoil of the gun; he had to make sure it was laid properly; he would make sure that the detachment were rotated if they got tired, supervising which ammunition was selected, the fuses for the shells and their timing. He was responsible for the rate of fire, and he gave the order to fire.

On firing the gun the men would assume their positions, kneeling around it. Number 1 knelt to the right of the traversing handspike, clear of the gun's spade so that he could see what was going on. Number 2 was beside the breech, his responsibility (along with the muzzle guard and lubrication and firing the gun itself) pulling the lanyard as ordered by Number 1. Number 3 had the most intricate role, operating the telescope, micrometer and clinometer, which measured elevation, translating the bearing and distance of the target into how the gun should be laid. With line and elevation set, he would say simply 'ready'.

Number 4, when the gun was in action, was expected to have the correct round as ordered in hand at all times, ready to load. With an expected rate of fire of one round every ten seconds, there was no margin for error in the drills. Everything was accounted for, everything was choreographed. The only time the gun could be loaded or fired without the direct order from Number 1 was 'when engaging tanks', when time would be of the essence and laying the gun indirectly was the last thing on anyone's mind.

The 75mm Pack Howitzer did come with a solid shot round for the possible eventuality of this kind of calamity; but on Tuesday morning, as the Regiment sent in its indirect fire, this did seem unlikely. There were 6-pounders in place after all and the fighting in the Town was miles away. There was also provision for how to run the guns in the eventuality of casualties, in which case the detachment could be scaled down. When a man was down, the job done by Numbers 5 and 6, keeping the ammunition flowing, would be covered by one man. In the event of two casualties, a further adjustment would be that one man would take on the roles of Numbers 1 and 2, commanding and firing the gun, and so on. Everything to keep the guns going.

Shoots went in on to the Town, backing 1st Battalion, called in by Captain Harrison. They hit the brickworks south of the river where there were German guns, as well as trying to interrupt the German attacks around St Elisabeth Hospital. Captain Peter Chard with 156 Battalion in the Woods was calling in shoots too. The Royal Artillery radio net was alive with orders and information even as headquarters cursed the breakdown of Divisional communications.

But as the morning progressed, what was becoming clear was that things were beginning to go wrong in the Town – that while:

> . . . 3 Battery engaged numerous targets in the Bridge area . . .
> 1 & 3 Para Battalions & 11 Battalion met heavy resistance at SW
> approaches to Arnhem.

There was only so much the gunners could do, under-powered as they were in terms of the effective punch of the weapons they had brought with them, under-provisioned in the amount of ammunition supplied, and short-handed because of the guns and men lost on the journey from England. The infantry trying to reach the Bridge would have to force their way through the Town without the kind of artillery support that had been winning the war for the British up to this point. So how would the infantry fare in getting through to Frost and his men at the Bridge? How was the morning playing out in the Town?

8

THE TOWN: THE COLONELS ON THE RIVER ROAD

Tuesday, 19th.
0100.   11 Battalion arrived.
0230.   Received order to withdraw to bridgehead at
OOSTERBEEK. Above order cancelled proceed to bridge.
Made Plan.

Lieutenant Colonel David Dobie's account

0200 HRS. IT WAS TIME to decide what to do in the Town. Again.

Gathered in the basement of a house in the Bottleneck, the officers were putting together yet another set of orders. Wearied from two days of struggle, they had to figure out how to get to Lieutenant Colonel Frost at the Bridge. Order and counter-order had come from Divisional HQ – on Monday night Brigadier Hicks had been told that John Frost's force at the Bridge had been wiped out, leading to the cancellation of an attack into the Town at 2130 hrs. Then a withdrawal from the Town was mooted. Keeping track of what was going on in Arnhem was a minute-to-minute affair, with precious time trickling away and the flow of reliable information challenging even the most basic decision-making. Absent major general or not.

Outside was the sound of mortars crashing down, the smell of burning vehicles and the sight of the dead strewn across the streets. In the basement a candle in a bottle guttered. This O Group, a conference called to issue orders for the battle in the Town, had fresh impetus. Frost was still at the Bridge! Contact had been made. He would have to be relieved. At this conference were Lieutenant Colonel David Dobie of 1st Battalion, Lieutenant Colonel Derek McCardie from 2nd Battalion the South Staffords and, eventually, as he was late arriving, Lieutenant Colonel George Lea from 11th Battalion. The hold-up in putting in last night's assault meant that Dobie, who had assumed command of the forces pushing into Arnhem, now had many more men at his disposal than he had had last night, even though 1st Battalion was now down to about 140 men after the previous two days' fighting. Dobie had arrived in Arnhem with 548 men. The rest were dead, wounded or missing, swallowed up in the warren of streets around them. Now that their Second Lift elements were present in the Town, he had virtually the whole of the South Staffords and all of 11th Battalion, which had hurried down from Ginkelse Heide overnight. This would give Dobie many more rifles, and so the decision was made to attack at all costs at 0345, before first light.

Unknown to Dobie, McCardie and Lea, 3rd Parachute Battalion – with whom they were not in contact – had had the same idea, to push on at all costs. Lieutenant Colonel John Fitch had had to endure the burden of Major General Urquhart and Brigadier Lathbury tagging along with his headquarters, and his battle had been micromanaged particularly on Sunday when they had called a halt on the way through the Village. As recounted by Major Alan Bush of B Company:

> If we had not had those two with us, Fitch would probably have followed C Company around that route to the north, but he could hardly move without the approval of both the divisional and brigade commanders – a hopeless situation.[1]

Bush had been with Fitch and his senior guests on Monday, when a German patrol came within 20 yards of them:

I remember one had a big fat arse and I thought, 'What a
target!' They were being very casual. Three of our men were
ready to open fire, but I ordered them not to. RSM Lord was
there and he nodded approval; you can't start a battle with
the divisional commander and the brigadier in the same
house.[2]

Losing them the following morning had freed Fitch somewhat, but
even once his men had gone under the railway line on the lower
road, the Battalion's progress through the Town was slow. And attritional. He'd tried to use the railway line as an axis of advance, but
the Germans had put paid to that. By the time he was preparing to
attack on Tuesday morning he had about fifty men left that he could
call on. He'd arrived on Sunday with a total strength of 588 men.
And while not all of them were riflemen, 3rd Battalion had been cut
to the bone. One of his company commanders, Major Peter Waddy,
was dead, another, Major Mervyn Dennison, was badly injured.
Fitch decided that if the Germans didn't attack during the night, and
they tended not to, especially not with their armour – moving
around at night being too dangerous for tanks – then he would try
again before first light.

    Fitch's plan was to gather his men from the houses they were
holed up in, NCOs and officers moving from building to building
silently. Starting at 0230 hrs, he pulled his men together, hoping to
form a large enough body to be able to get down to the riverbank
and then onwards. There was a little machine-gun fire, but Fitch's
men mustered successfully: 'the plan worked'.[3] At least *that* element
of the plan worked: leap-frogging forward, they got to the other end
of the embankment, a full 1,500 yards, as far as the pontoon bridge,
through bitter mortar and gunfire. The river road was exposed to fire
from the far bank, and whatever scrapes the men could dig were
not enough. Even if he had had twice as many men, the problems
of fighting past the Germans would have remained as intractable,
and Fitch's attack faltered. With a dozen casualties, among them

Regimental Sergeant Major John Lord, he ordered a withdrawal to what the men had christened the Pavilion, a large building on the riverbank, and decided to try again in daylight.

As Fitch's men fell back, in went the 1st Battalion attack, along the same axis. This took both battalions by surprise. It was during this retreat that Dobie had the following exchange with Captain Richard Dorrien-Smith:

> Dobie: Good morning!
> Dorrien-Smith: Where the hell do you think you're going?
> Dobie: I'm going up here.
> Dorrien-Smith: I wouldn't do that if I were you. It's full of mortars and machine guns.
> Dobie: How do you know?
> Dorrien-Smith: Because I've bloody well been there.
> Dobie: Well, come and show us.
> Dorrien-Smith: Not bloody likely.

Fitch realized that while he might be high and dry in the Town, he certainly wasn't alone. S Company of 1st Battalion – which now comprised about a platoon's strength, no more than thirty men – was on the right flank, on the river road. Major Ronald Stark, a larger-than-life officer who had served under Frost in North Africa, ran into exactly the same problems that Fitch had encountered, and demonstrated remarkable coolness under fire, until he was captured with what was left of S Company in some German slit trenches. Fitch's men now had to provide covering fire as 1st Battalion went up against the German brick wall. The Germans were dug in at the far end with slit trenches and oil tanks filled with dirt. Armoured cars had also joined the fray at the far end of the lower road, panzers too, but too far off for any anti-tank response. The German fire was of the kind that military citations and reports call 'withering', and 1st Battalion casualties started to come back through where Fitch had dug his men in, in the bushes on the western end of the embankment. Through the smoke and the undergrowth his men were unable to return fire.

At 0730 hrs Fitch tried again to find fresh positions, but the situation was impossible. The Bottleneck, the Germans on the opposite bank, the armoured cars on the river road, all had defeated him. It was time to get out. As the 3rd Battalion Diary has it, it would be every man for himself:

> On his return casualties were being suffered at an ever increasing rate, and the wounded were being rushed back in small groups every minute. The C.O. held a brief conference with his 2 i/c and Intelligence Officer. It was decided that as his force was slowly being decimated without being able to reply, he would withdraw to the Pavilion and form a strong point there. The orders he gave were that every officer and man would make his way back to that point by the best way he could. No question of fieldcraft this; the whole area seemed covered by fire and the only hope of getting out safely was by speed. The withdrawal began immediately. Casualties were heavy.[4]

Alan Bush was with Fitch when he gave the order to withdraw, about 250 yards from the relative safety of the Pavilion. The mortar fire was moving along the embankment 'steadily, foot by foot' towards where Fitch and what was left of his Battalion were dug in. Fitch had his back to the approaching mortars. Bush could:

> . . . see it coming and said we must get out of there. He told me to get the men back; most of them were behind us; the Colonel was as far forward as anybody.[5]

As they made a break for it, Bush told the injured to head up the slope to St Elisabeth Hospital: 'I don't know whether they made it; with any luck they should have done.'

Making a break for it with Fitch was his intelligence officer, Alexis

Vedeniapine, the son of an exiled Russian Imperial Army officer, who had come to the British Army by way of Vladivostok, Shanghai and Cirencester Agricultural College. Now he was running for his life in Holland. He had risen through the ranks as a volunteer from the early days of airborne forces, had a Military Medal from North Africa and was of the old school of airborne forces – utterly fearless. As they ran back towards the Pavilion, a mortar detonated close by, badly wounding Vedeniapine in the back, the foot and the chest, and killing his commanding officer. Unbelievably, Vedeniapine made it back to the Pavilion. Maybe twenty men remained, wounded and unable to fight. Fitch was dead, 3rd Battalion destroyed.

In the meantime, Lieutenant Colonel Dobie's 1st Battalion committed itself to the attack, with similar results. With Dobie's men was Leo Heaps, twenty-one, a Jewish Canadian officer and veteran of D-Day who had wangled his way into joining 1st Airborne after recovering from wounds he had acquired in France. Heaps had served with the Dorsets in Normandy, and was nominally in charge of 1st Battalion's transport, despite failing Parachute Regiment selection. He had demanded an explanation and interview and was granted his wish. He was very taken with the *esprit de corps* in 1st Battalion. Heaps came from a politically active family and had understandable zeal in wanting to fight the Germans. Perhaps not unlike Vedeniapine, he was a typical adventurer attracted to the airborne ideal:

> There was an esprit de corps about, which infected the very
> marrow in your bones, and compelled you almost to be off
> for new adventure.[6]

Jumping into Arnhem was his first attempt at parachuting. Heaps had taken advice from a fellow officer, Lieutenant Eric Davies, a former ballet dancer, on what to do, and chanted 'Feet together, Shoulders round, Elbows in and watch the ground' on his way down. His kitbag went its own way, his stuff spread all over the

Drop Zone. Once landed, Heaps had commandeered a Bren carrier and in the next couple of days he developed a knack of popping up almost central to events, going backwards and forwards in the Town, performing his own reconnaissance and discovering exactly how difficult things were in the Bottleneck. He'd run into Urquhart and Lathbury on Sunday and been given instructions to take back to Divisional HQ. It was Heaps who had told the colonels at the candlelit O Group that the Bridge was still in British hands and the attack had to go in. Now:

> The morning was full of flying chunks of metal and wounded men. Fire came from every conceivable direction.
>
> . . . I lay flattened behind some trees while Martin and the Dutchman crawled under the jeep for protection. We lay like this for half an hour, while the German guns blew up our men on the lower slopes almost at will. I knew that there would be no advance on the bridge today.[7]

Without PIAT (Projector, Infantry, Anti-Tank) rounds or any 6-pounders to answer the German armour, Gammon Bombs were all that was left, but the Germans weren't letting them get that close, and Dobie's Battalion was pulled apart. At 0600 hrs he took stock: his Battalion was running on fumes, R Company had six men left, S Company fifteen, T Company eight, Battalion HQ ten. For all the prisoners they had taken and Germans they had killed, they couldn't go on. Dobie decided that they should break out and take refuge in the houses, but they were quickly surrounded and shelled into submission. The SS broke into the houses. When Dobie, wounded in the eye and arm, was captured, his 1st Battalion no longer existed.

All the while, hiding in a toilet on the ground floor of a house next to the pontoon bridge was signals officer Major Anthony Deane-Drummond, who had come forward to find out what was going on with the Divisional radio net. Deane-Drummond got caught up in the fighting, led a scratch party of men, and had got as close to Frost as anyone had in the Town. But on Monday night the Germans had burst into the house where Deane-Drummond was hiding out, and he and two others locked themselves in the toilet. Deane-Drummond had escaped before, walking from Italy to Switzerland after the failed Operation Colossus of February 1941, the attempt to blow up an Italian aqueduct. The Germans tried the door, but didn't force it. As the drama of the river road played itself out, Deane-Drummond did what so many of the men cut off from the rest of their comrades did. He laid low, and waited, hoping.

The river road was impassable. Facing resistance like this, these battalions, which had been mauled in preceding days, might not be able to make any progress. But the South Staffords and 11th Battalion were relatively fresh. What were the other battalions in the Town going to be able to do? And how had Johnny Frost's early morning been at the Bridge?

The air was fresh, the morning was beginning to sparkle and all the men looked jaunty and confident. A kind of watchful intentness for the first sight or sound that would proclaim the imminent test of their martial prowess now settled over this keen, battle-eager assembly.

Captain Stuart Mawson, RAMC[1]

MORNING

9

THE BRIDGE: TOTTERING ABOVE THE BOILING TIDE

This was Digby's first battle and I remember him asking, 'I would like to know if this is worse or not so bad as the other things you have been in?' I think I replied, 'Difficult to say. In some ways it is worse and in some ways not. At least we have got food and water. It won't be so good when the ammunition runs out.'[1]

Lieutenant Colonel John Frost to Major Digby Tatham-Warter

ACCORDING TO ORTHODOX British military opinion, the Germans did not like to fight at night, but at Arnhem they had chosen to break with tradition. They continued to probe at Frost's positions, and with grim determination. Monday may have proved fruitless for the Germans as they tried to force the British out of the houses around the Bridge, but it didn't dim their determination. While they were clearly going to have to use panzers and infantry to evict Frost's men, they had also set up mortars and artillery on the southern side of the river, from where they could batter the lodgement almost unmolested. Troops were coming at Frost from all directions, and the enemy had the advantage of being able to bring up fresh men and machines seemingly ad infinitum.

They had a variety of targets to concentrate on, and on Monday they had had some success in winkling the airborne men out of three of the houses on the edge of the perimeter, by simply making them too dangerous to occupy. Frost had consolidated his positions because he had no choice. There was a cluster of buildings, one of which on the western side was tall enough to look down on to the road on the Bridge itself, and two on the opposite side. Some of these had become uninhabitable during the fighting on Monday, as had the factory buildings to the eastern side of the redoubt. These latter structures had been overrun by the end of Monday, leaving the bulk of Frost's forces on the western side of the bridge, on the corner that curved with the road coming from the river and round, parallel with the ramp.

Alongside their infantry, 1st Airborne had landed a vast amount of supporting soldiers as part of its contingent. In the two lifts that took place on Sunday and Monday, 5,850 of the 10,241 men delivered by glider and parachute were in the infantry battalions. The rest were engineers, gunners, signallers, service corps, chaplains, medics, mechanics, the Recce Squadron and so on. A single Horsa glider could deliver a platoon of infantry or a Jeep with four men: 'On average each glider sortie mounted for 1st Airborne on 17 September carried just 8 personnel.'[2] While these men did not count as part of 1st Airborne's bayonet strength, they had at least been trained to fight, even if they perhaps had not expected to be in the thick of it quite yet.

In their positions in the school on the eastern side of the ramp, the sappers of 1st Parachute Squadron RE, who had come to Arnhem to ensure the Bridge wasn't primed for sabotage, were being sorely put to the test. At 0030 hrs the Germans attacked the north and the eastern sides of the building. Forty-five minutes of close combat followed, with the Germans throwing grenades into the ground floor, firing rifle grenades, and having got a machine gun in one of the windows, spraying one of the rooms and the hall.

Captain Eric Mackay's men, a composite force of sappers and RASC personnel, were exhausted from the last three hours of firefighting, made doubly hazardous as the Germans had been sniping at his men as they worked on the roof putting out fires, silhouetted by the flames, lit up as if by daylight. The men had been awake for forty-three hours but nevertheless fought off this attack, Mackay deciding that the rooms the Germans had got into needed to be barricaded and abandoned. Gradually he moved his men upstairs, cutting loopholes in the walls as they went. The Germans were close, really close, so taking advantage of a lull, Mackay ordered his men to bind their boots in rags so they could move around the school building silently. There was debris everywhere, the stone floors 'slippery with blood, especially the stairs'.[3]

The Germans were determined to clear the school, and with it the eastern side of the ramp. At 0200 hrs a large mortar or, according to the squadron's diary, an anti-tank 'bazooka' hit the school with a huge explosion, blinding Mackay's batman, and knocking everyone out as it tore off the south-east corner and blew away part of the first floor. Mackay had been taken below to the basement, where he had been sending his wounded, but having come to his senses he went back upstairs. At 0300 hrs he saw to his complete amazement sixty Germans forming up all around the school, right under the windows, ten feet away, preparing to move in, seemingly convinced by the lack of response from the school – with everyone knocked out – that the building was unoccupied, and that they were going to just waltz in.

Mackay gathered all his able-bodied men to the windows and loopholes of the first floor, 'it all seemed too good to be true',[4] armed with every weapon they could get their hands on. According to the squadron's diary, every unwounded man had two grenades each, pins pulled and ready. When Mackay gave the signal, his troops, sappers and supply corps men, leaning out of the windows, dropped grenades on the Germans and gunned them down. Six Bren guns and Stens churned rounds into the enemy, cutting the careless Germans down, the war cry of 'Whoa Mahomet!' resounding above the din. It was a slaughter, the Germans leaving thirty dead behind as they fled, as well as their mortars and machine guns.

Mackay was satisfied that he had seen them off for the night, and finally got his wounds seen to – he had shrapnel in his foot that had

pinned it to his boot, which even he admitted was very painful. That
he had been running the Battle with this impediment is something
he rather throws away in his account, almost as an afterthought. The
medical orderly tried and failed to extract the metal from his foot,
so Mackay literally soldiered on. Leading his men mattered more
than shrapnel in his shoe. This kind of vicious close combat and
Mackay's eagerness to get stuck in doubtless explains why Frost in
his appreciation as a fighting man thought:

> ... that it was almost a waste to use them as sappers when
> they were so good at killing the enemy. Shock troops in the
> full sublime sense of the words.[5]

Among these sappers was Sapper Emery, who despite his own shrapnel wounds accounted for thirteen Germans, and Sapper Carr for a
further eleven in his time at the Bridge.

Mackay was facing the problems of the siege at the Bridge in all
their varieties: dealing with the wounded, making sure the seriously
injured had sufficient morphine even though there was no prospect
of resupply. Coordination with the other elements of 1st Brigade
around the Bridge was also a challenge, perhaps best reflected in the
fact that Brigade HQ Diary erroneously recorded 'everything had
been fairly quiet during the night', even though they were only a
couple of hundred metres away on the other side of the ramp.

The men fighting at the Bridge were not just isolated from the
rest of the Division, from 2nd Army; they were also isolated from
each other. Patrolling to find out what the enemy was doing and
making sure they remained in touch with the rest of Frost's forces,
so that they could coordinate the defence, were going to be essential as they hung on waiting for relief. Mackay's radio was at least
working, and he informed Frost of his situation at the school, the
strength of his force, and how the early morning had gone. But the
chief problem for all of the men fighting at the Bridge was the question of ammunition. As he hobbled around the school in the

aftermath of the close-quarters massacre at 0300 hrs, Mackay redistributed his men's ammunition, taking rounds from the wounded so as to carefully husband a resource that would be crucial as the day progressed.

Around the school, on the ramp leading up to the Bridge and on the roadway on the Bridge itself, were the burned-out German trucks, half-tracks and armoured cars destroyed in the dogged attack by the SS the previous morning. The German dead lay all around, some of them killed as they debussed from the lorries kitted out with improvised armour in the form of oil barrels filled with sand. This had not been a fair fight by any means, as the still-reeling Germans had fed themselves into Frost's enormous ambush. They had pressed their attack with great resolve, and for that inflicted a high price paid by Frost; not in terms of men – only a few were killed in the two or so hours of that fighting – but in terms of ammunition, the one critical consumable thing that the airborne soldiers could ill afford to waste. After sixteen cancelled operations, the paras had made the most of the moment, thinking that 2nd Army would arrive soon, so what did it matter?

When Frost's men had repulsed this SS attack, they had done so in the confident expectation that their relief by the rest of 1st Parachute Brigade was imminent. By Tuesday morning it was plain such relief wasn't coming. 'We, who were by the bridge, our objective, were firmly sealed in unless more ammunition arrived.'[6] Just how much ammunition the men at the Bridge had is essentially unknowable. The RASC 250 Light Composite Company had brought ammunition trailers to the vicinity of the Bridge, tens of thousands of rounds, yet how many actually reached the Bridge is unclear. Monday morning had been a shooting gallery, and the keyed-up airborne soldiers – finally on an operation – had filled their boots firing at the enemy. Capturing German weapons as Mackay had done would help, but only so far. On Tuesday morning Frost ordered an end to sniping to conserve ammunition despite the fact that it gifted the Germans the opportunity to get closer. It also meant that movement between the houses the British were occupying became much more challenging, further isolating the besieged at the Bridge. Additionally, it meant that manning the 6-pounders, out on the roads covering the approaches to the Bridge, became impossible as the day wore on; without sniper cover, it became too dangerous for the artillery detachments to go out to their guns to fend off the German tanks.

Those gunners with Frost had been working hard to keep the radio net going and deliver fire support from 3 Battery. The day before they had fired 'Mike' targets, full Regimental strikes on the enemy. But Bombardier Leo Hall's successful connection with 3 Battery was now being used not just for gunnery but was being relied on by Brigade HQ for basic contact with Divisional HQ. The OP (Observation Post) itself was in the attic of one of the buildings on the corner, from which Major Dennis Munford could see most of the lodgement. The men took turns up there, not surprisingly attracting a great deal of enemy fire, it being an obvious spot to site an OP. Munford himself had been wounded in the face on Sunday by sniper fire aimed at the OP, making the dangers horribly evident. Unlike Brigade HQ, they certainly didn't think they had had a quiet night, with the incessant noise and shock of shelling and explosions all around them. The attic itself had been damaged and some of the men injured by the resulting fragments and splinters. The Royal Artillery Signallers guarded their radio jealously, the precious No. 22 set kept in a corner, protected by sandbags.

The other Royal Artillery component, 1st Airlanding Anti-Tank Battery, under the command of Major Bill Arnold, had had a good day on Monday. With three rounds of armour-piercing they had cut a v-shaped notch in the wall on the side of the Bridge, so that they could fire through it and hit anything venturing up or down the ramp. Arnold was disappointed that he hadn't been able to bring a 17-pounder with him to the Bridge – the extra firepower would have come in handy. The distances at the Bridge, with tanks or self-propelled guns or half-tracks coming around the corner, were well within the 6-pounder's capacity for destruction. However, deploying the 6-pounder on a hard road surface came with its own problems; the gun carriage's spades needed to be properly wedged into the ground to make sure the gun didn't move when it was fired. By way of illustration, one gun on Monday had been set up without its spades in place and had rebounded back 40 yards with the recoil, injuring two of the detachment operating it.

Lines of sight also posed a problem. This was not like being dug into a hedgerow and facing front, with the enemy pressing from all directions. Here the guns needed to be agile and able to respond to what was spotted coming around whichever corner. Guns could be hooked up to Jeeps and driven forward, if and when they were needed, but without garages in which to store them, they were vulnerable to mortar fire – if not direct hits then splinters shredding tyres puncturing radiators. Manning the guns in the open was becoming more hazardous too, as unanswered sniper and machine-gun fire increased and as the Germans tried to prise the British out of the buildings on the eastern side of the redoubt.

With 1st Airlanding Anti-Tank Battery was Captain Arvian Llewellyn-Jones:

> Deeds of great bravery were quietly completed. 6-pounder rounds of ammunition, ready to explode at any time, were quietly taken from the bonnet of a burning jeep, and loaded into an undamaged one. Guns were unhooked from wrecks, and hooked back to runners.[7]

He knew the situation was desperate but had weighed the advantages and disadvantages of each side. The tanks could traverse rubble, come right in to attack buildings, but could not lower their guns sufficiently to attack the anti-tank crews. Given the size of the area around the Bridge and its layout, these encounters were all happening well within a distance of one hundred yards.

The Royal Army Service Corps (RASC) and Royal Army Ordnance

Corps (RAOC) men who had come to organize supplies in the
planned Divisional Administrative Area had now been necessarily
repurposed into fighting men, while still doing what they could to
perform some of their essential backstage duties. Corporal Austen
Johnson had been tasked with collecting ammunition from the
wounded. He passed it on to the Brigadier's bodyguard – who plainly
had not done a great job, with Lathbury missing in the Town somewhere. The RAOC party foiled a German attempt to plant explosives
on the Bridge with their Bren gun, and took cover when the whole
area was mortared at first light. Like many of the men at the Bridge,
they witnessed a British medical orderly being shot and killed by a
sniper as he escorted three German prisoners from under the Bridge.
One of the Germans ran for it and a Bren gunner shot him dead. Private Ted Mordecai, one of the RAOC men, saw the bullets go straight
through his back and ricochet off the pavement. Everything was happening at very close range; it was impossible not to see the worst.

Doing his rounds was Father Bernard Egan, the Roman Catholic
chaplain who had come with 2nd Battalion, parachuting in on
Sunday. He had been one of the first chaplains in airborne forces,
along with a Methodist, the Reverend R. T. Watkins. They had
developed the tools of their pastoral trade in time for North Africa:
an air-portable communion set, with paten – a mass plate – a chal-
ice and two cruets.

On the Sunday evening, Egan had delighted in hurling a chair
out of a window as the men adapted their surroundings for the
forthcoming siege – the thrill, he thought, came from knowing he
would not be arrested. The cellars were filling up with the wounded,
with no prospect of evacuation. Accompanying 1st Parachute Brigade into Arnhem was 16 (Parachute) Field Ambulance, who had
deployed at St Elisabeth Hospital in the Town, as planned. This successful deployment had been the only element of 1st Parachute
Brigade's scheme to take and hold the bulk of Arnhem that had
actually gone according to plan, and now with Frost cut off at the
Bridge his casualties could not get the surgical care it offered. Now

the men were in battle, Egan's role was directly pastoral, assisting the Regimental Medical Officer, a Glaswegian called Captain Jimmy Logan, with the wounded and the dying. Wearing his dog collar and his Red Cross armband, Egan ran between the buildings, moving from cellar to cellar, doing what he could to keep tabs on his flock. On his travels he ran into Frost leaving a toilet. 'Father,' he said, 'the window is broken, there's a hole in the wall and the roof is gone. But it has a chain and it works.'[8]

Egan's work was short on such moments of levity. One man, with a stomach wound, had been given about quarter of an hour to live by Captain Logan. Knowing the lad was a Catholic, he had sent for Egan. Aware he didn't have long, the boy begged the chaplain to give him a rifle so he could go back to the fighting, so as not to let the Battalion down.

There were also Recce Squadron men at the Bridge; they had been given the job of racing ahead to seize it on Sunday, an effort that had been beset by miscommunication and unexpected German resistance. Even though both Urquhart and Frost regarded him as unpunctual, unreliable even, the adventurous Major Freddie Gough, the Recce Squadron's OC (Officer Commanding), was at least among those who had made it to the Bridge. His squadron's Jeeps had been equipped with Vickers K-guns like those used by the men of the SAS in the desert a couple of years before. These guns now offered more firepower, though their rapid rate of fire meant they chewed through ammunition at breakneck speed.

Frost had spotted Gough grinning like a maniac as he fired his K-guns during the Monday morning attack. But now there was little prospect of doing any reconnaissance and while the Recce Squadron was in theory ready to dash across the Bridge and meet the Poles when they arrived later in the day ('suicide' according to Frost), in the meantime Gough took on the role of Frost's number two. Also with Gough was Trooper Charles 'Darkie' Bolton. Bolton had been set up with a Bren gun pointing down the ramp of the Bridge – Gough liked the cut of his jib. Flicking V signs at the enemy:

Bolton was crawling all over the place, sniping 'and every
time he'd hit a German, he'd grin widely and say there goes
another one of those bastards'.[9]

Gough's driver, Trooper Ronald Brooker:

Just before daylight, the sound of heavy gunfire could be
heard from the direction we had arrived on Sunday. Our spirits rose, and felt sure some at least of the division would arrive
shortly. During the early morning we heard the battle cry of
the 1st Battalion, 'Whoa Mohamed', and a cheer went up.[10]

These battle cries were coming from the west, from the men of 1st
Parachute Brigade trying to make their way along the river road. But
cheer in reply as they might, the men at the Bridge were still on their
own.

Over the road from Brigade HQ in what he called the 'White House'
was Private James Sims. He was a member of the mortar platoon,
one of the new intake after the North Africa and Sicily campaigns.
2nd Battalion had been wasted away by the campaign in Tunisia,
and had to be rebuilt after the botched landings in Sicily. After his
time in the Home Guard, Sims had been an artilleryman and had
been seduced into joining the Parachute Regiment by a recruiting
leaflet which offered a life of adventurous soldiering rather than the
tedium of drilling with a 25-pounder. Seventeen in January 1943, he
volunteered immediately. He filled in the necessary forms with a
mate and passed, leaving Larkhill in Wiltshire and reporting in to
the airborne forces depot at Hardwick Hall Camp near Chesterfield
in Derbyshire. Sims liked the atmosphere at Hardwick Hall: everyone was a volunteer and they were there because they wanted to be.
Tall, standing at six feet, Sims knew he was going to have to get into
shape, and the Army Physical Training Corps' Sergeant 'Basher' Bar-
tlett saw to that. Once again, Sims enjoyed the spirit of the outfit.

Everyone mucked in if there was a job to be done, including the
NCOs. 'Instead of curses you received encouragement.'[11]

By the time Sims had volunteered for selection as a paratrooper,
the process had been refined not just in terms of getting the men fit
and strong, with tough route marches as part of the routine – it also
included a newfangled psychological quotient. If you made it
through the fortnight – and those who didn't were returned to their
units – you had to go for an interview with an Army shrink; the
Parachute Regiment was keen to discover the mental make-up of its
men. Sims and his fellow recruits were far from impressed with this,
and via the grapevine had figured out what was expected of them by
the doctor when asked the immortal question, 'Why do you hate
your mother?' The required answer of the private soldier, the grapevine claimed, was a display of aggression:

> . . . you have to put on the show of fury and jump up, knocking
> the chair over backwards and shout 'what the hell are you on
> about'. Better still, you should reach across and make a grab at
> the psychiatrist then you were sure of a rifle company.[12]

On the last day the recruits took part in an exercise storming mock
German positions. With this stage of the recruitment over, and after
a 'glorious booze up', it was time to go to RAF Ringway, the parachute school near Manchester, and learn how to parachute. Sims
was appalled at the standard of RAF drill but fascinated by the business of learning to parachute.

By February 1944, Ringway was a smoothly operating machine, the
techniques for learning to parachute and master the all-important
landing having been refined and perfected. The Royal Air Force was
mass-producing competent parachutists, not just for the Army but for
the Special Operations Executive (SOE) as well, and any client that
needed to master the cutting-edge techniques on offer. Nevertheless,
the dangers of the business of arriving into battle by parachute were
very present. One moment of carelessness could result in injury or

worse still death. While Sims was on his course, an instructor had fallen from an aircraft having not secured himself to the plane. Devices such as The Fan, which allowed a parachutist to simulate the last part of his fall, lowered a man in a harness to the ground at the same speed as a parachute descent. It was, supposedly, the same force as jumping off a 12-foot wall. The men were trained to tuck in their elbows and their chin, squeeze their feet and knees together as they exited the plane, all to avoid snagging the lines of the opening chute. The helmet that parachutists wore by this stage of the war was distinctive. It wasn't the same broad-brimmed helmet worn by the rest of the British Army, which it was feared might snag on rigging lines. Rather it was essentially a copy of the German Fallschirmjäger helmet. Britain's airborne pioneers weren't averse to pinching good ideas.

A trainee's first jumps were from the dreaded balloon, an eerie and frightening experience. Sims and his mates all agreed that jumping from a plane, with the noise and movement, was far preferable. Being winched up in the basket to the balloon was terrifying enough in itself. Pitched around by the wind and bawled at by the instructor, Sims was so scared when it was his time to jump that he just fell out. Old hands said that the night jump in the balloon was less frightening because you couldn't see anything. The experience cured Sims's fears, and he came to take pride in perfecting his parachuting technique, getting out of the aircraft as quickly as possible, handling his equipment. There were moments of singular humour too; one man at a drop at Tatton Park in Cheshire was caught in a thermal and being a small wiry fellow took a few minutes to descend. From then on, Sims recalled, he was weighted down.

Not that he would have needed it, as the men were laden with equipment. By early 1944, techniques had been developed for every rifleman to carry as much equipment as possible. His rifle would be kept in a valise, jammed under his harness or in the kitbag attached by rope to his leg, which he would lower once he had exited the aircraft. This weighed about seventy pounds.[13] The effect of this added weight was that you would come down a little faster, the kitbag landing beneath you, and then the canopy would take a sort of breath and deposit you more lightly beside it.

At least this was how it worked in theory. On the Drop Zone after landing, it was essential to keep your wits about you and watch out for other falling kitbags. A stick of parachutists would also jump with containers being delivered almost simultaneously. The fifth man in a stick was supposed to shout 'Container! Container! Container!' to remind the aircraft crew to release them. Containers going awry was something the men could ill afford, and they too offered another hazard on the Drop Zone. In a container might be a Welbike, a small motorbike developed for airborne soldiers, as well as ammunition, bicycles and fold-up trolleys, crucial for moving stuff around when setting off for the objective. Personal weapons like Sten guns and pistols often enough would go under the outer smock that parachutists wore. Even though they had been victorious, the Germans on Crete had taught everyone in the airborne business the bitter lesson that landing by parachute with nothing more than a pistol and having to grub around on a Drop Zone looking for weapons containers gave your opponent the chance to inflict vast numbers of casualties.

Parachuting wasn't for everyone, and until qualified you could refuse to jump. You'd be returned to your unit, no harm no foul. Qualified parachutists who refused were court-martialled, given fifty-six days' detention and a return to unit with the offence noted. When the Stirling bomber came online for training, having been unable to keep up with the Lancasters and Halifaxes for Bomber Command sorties over Germany, the men didn't like it. Scores refused to jump from it. Sims at six foot and a bit in his boots and helmet had been told to bend over by a crewman on a Stirling because his head was jamming the control rods on the ceiling of the fuselage.

By the end of his course, 60 of the 165 applicants had passed. They had all faced the dangers of parachuting – men breaking their arms exiting aircraft badly, chutes failing to open (known as a Roman Candle) and men plunging to their deaths. Overcoming that fear was a key ingredient in the parachutist's make-up, as much as whether he hated his mum or not. Little wonder then that these men were motivated, and felt bonded to one another. In 2nd Battalion the men wore a mepacrine-stained gold lanyard made of woven rigging line, rather than the same badges as other airborne troops, to symbolize that bond.

On Sunday, in the chaos of landing, Sims had had trouble finding the rest of the mortar platoon, his veteran pal Slapsie and his Jewish Sergeant Koliakoff.[14] They made it to Arnhem Bridge as part of the great snake of soldiers and Sims settled in what he knew as the White House, a three-storey house next door to the buildings adjacent to the Bridge, on the southern part of the lodgement. They set up an Observation Post for the mortars on the top floor. Opposite the house in the middle of the road was a traffic island into which a mortar pit had been dug. As a member of the mortar platoon, Sims had spent Monday dashing out to the mortar pit and back to the house, running errands. Getting around the lodgement involved jumping through windows, crawling on your belly, dodging fire, anticipating snipers. As the day passed, the need for water became more pressing, and he crawled out to a tap on a pipe in a garden. Lying on his back, he turned the tap on and filled two mess tins as bullets pinged around him.

By the time of Market Garden, it is fair to say Lieutenant Colonel Johnny Frost was a legend within the airborne world. The hard-soldiering, hard-drinking[15] Scot had led his men out from sixty miles behind enemy lines in North Africa; had fought with his battalion in the bizarre confusion of Operation Fustian in Sicily, when German Fallschirmjäger had landed on the same Drop Zone; and most importantly, he was unique among the officers in 1st Airborne Division, in that he had been involved in the only unambiguously successful British airborne operation of the war so far, Operation Biting, on the night of 27 February 1942. Its success had showed what could be done with small-scale airborne raiding. Frost's men had parachuted at night on to the Normandy coast at Bruneval and stolen the Würzburg radar which had been giving off radio signals irresistible to curious British boffins. The raid was a triumph and Frost was feted by the Prime Minister on his safe return. It was just what Churchill had ordered – here was Combined Operations keeping the Hun on his toes and even better, stealing his technology.

When the war began, Frost had been in Syria with the Scottish Rifles, the Cameronians, returning to England in early 1941, where he found the pace of life too slow, shooting grouse in Suffolk to pass the time while on invasion defence duty. His commanding officer wasn't keen on him leaving for what was called at the time the Special Air Service, but Frost was determined to go, for they were looking for captains to be company commanders. As it was, he was appointed adjutant of 2nd Battalion. He felt the interview had gone badly, because his response to a question about discipline had caused one of the officers conducting the interview to raise an eyebrow. But it merely confirmed that Frost was the kind of man they were looking for. As adjutant he was intimately involved in selection and recruitment. James Sims in the mortar platoon had joined the Parachute Regiment in early 1944, when the system was properly established; Frost was there when they were making it up as they went along.

Not that he didn't believe in discipline. He regarded it as self-evident that the German Army's successes came from their strict adherence to discipline; the way that British successes in the desert against the Italians fell away the moment the Germans arrived in North Africa was proof enough of the difference between the British and German armies.

When the recruits started to arrive at Hardwick Hall, they were of variable quality. The requirement was men who were A1 fit, men of good character, and volunteers. However:

> It was inevitable that some Commanding Officers should seize the opportunity of unloading some unwanted material

on to us, but I was amazed to see with what gusto some of
them played the game . . . among those who came nearly half
had no documents, a large number could be labelled lame,
halt or Wind.[16]

Frost had to sort them, returning those he knew he couldn't get into
shape to their regiments, and opting to take a chance on some of
them too. One of the companies quickly evolved into a completely
Scottish body, formed of men only from Scottish regiments, whom
Frost – naturally perhaps – regarded as in better shape than those
from the rest of the United Kingdom.

Later in the war, the Indian Army, which had been raising its own
airborne units made up of men who had volunteered as parachutists, subjected these men to a survey about their attitudes, and why
they had come to airborne forces. Major Harry Pozner, MC, of the
Royal Army Medical Corps, published a study of the psychology of
those troops. He summed up the notion of the ideal man that had
evolved during the selection and training process:

A man in his middle twenties, he averaged about 68 inches in
height and 160 pounds in weight.[17] Wiry and agile his body
was capable of sustaining hard knocks and extreme priva-
tions. Well orientated and with an intelligence above that of
the ordinary soldier he could swiftly assimilate the evidence
of his senses and act instantly and effectively, exploiting to
the full the slightest advantage in the local military situation.
Warily aggressive, his mind could clearly admit the probabil-
ity of mutilation or death and then resolutely put that aside,
knowing in the discharge of his mission with pin-point
accuracy the utmost fulfilment.[18]

In 1942 such an ideal soldier was hard to come by. In his report,
Major Pozner noted that while the response to the call for volunteers was initially 'surprisingly high', the men taking up the challenge

were 'regimental misfits, neurotics with temperamental instability, and mildly warped and deviated mentalities together with the inevitable sensation and glamour-hunters and escapists'. As the war progressed and the need to populate new battalions with airborne soldiers became more pressing, and entire battalions were switched to a parachuting role, the problem of men who were passive in their attitude to their soldiering and were simply going along with the conversion became identified as a problem. A willingness to parachute in itself was not necessarily a good barometer of training. The men needed to have something more about them. 'Fortunately, it was realized from the start that the mere apparent desire to jump did not automatically make a good paratrooper.'

Selection boards were established to refine the process. In the Middle East, where 4th Parachute Brigade had been raised, the fail rate was about 50 per cent. While expressing reservations about the survey results, given the vagueness of some of the men's replies, Pozner still found the numbers interesting. A total of 1,012 men were interviewed, of whom 51.6 per cent wanted to become paratroopers because they liked the idea, felt they were temperamentally suited, thought parachute units were the best, or were 'good sports'. Some 14.3 per cent in one cohort and 27.5 per cent in the second cohort (and one can understand Pozner's concerns about the data) were 'desirous of change', because they disliked being ordinary infantry, were 'browned off', or wanted to see action. Remaining with friends or units also counted for similar numbers. In the first cohort 4.8 per cent wanted the extra money, the jump pay.

Pozner also outlined the problems of training parachutists. The standard required at NCO level to make sure men became competent parachutists was extremely high and specialized. They were also at the mercy of the RAF, in terms of availability of aircraft and the issues that accompanied this – weather, suitable planes, scheduling for training and so on. And as the men were loaded up with increasingly specialized equipment for parachuting into operations, so accidents increased. Jumping with a mortar baseplate in your kitbag, for example, meant you really had to make sure you went out of the door neatly and cleanly.

Pozner outlined four types of parachutists. The naturals, who loved parachuting for itself, as if it were a sport, constituted about 5 per cent of recruits. The second group, at around 15 per cent, were men who once they'd overcome their initial misgivings, came to enjoy jumping and take pride in their prowess at it. Some 70 per cent, he found, were not particular fans of jumping but regarded it as a necessary evil, who experienced anxiety every time they jumped, but an anxiety that didn't affect them as soldiers. The remainder, roughly 10 per cent, were men who found each jump harder and harder, and whose nerves were being burned up by parachuting, creating a mental state not unlike combat fatigue.

Refusing to jump was dissected in Pozner's report, as well as a tendency for men to build up complex rituals and superstitions about jumping. The process of jumping and the anxieties that accompanied it were as follows, according to Pozner:

> In the aeroplane before the order 'Prepare for Action' there are the same mild depressions and introspections. At 'Action Stations' after the static lines are hooked up there is the characteristic conscious effort of will followed by a focal concentration of all the faculties on the impending jump. Immediately preceding the order 'Go' there is in most cases a complete surrender to an attitude of fatalism which has been summed-up in phrases such as, 'Whatever happens, I'm going', 'At any rate it will be quick', 'It's now or never'.

Certainly this is how your author felt the time he jumped from a C47 at 900 feet in 2004. Parachuting didn't necessarily mean you'd make a good soldier, but it helped, concluded Pozner. Frost, who was no fan of the process himself, thought the training and discipline that went with conditioning his men helped enormously, but he also knew what they were like. Adventurous and bored, as often

as not. After months of recruitment, and seeing his men go to RAF
Ringway and return qualified as parachutists, Frost was ordered to
bite the bullet and learn how to parachute himself. However, he
didn't have time to do the whole course, so rather than going from
Ringway straight to Tatton Park, where there was a balloon to practise in, he went up in a plane:

> We smiled at each other the learner parachutist's smile, which
> has no joy or humour in it. One merely uncovers one's teeth
> for a second or two then hides them again quickly lest they
> should start chattering.[19]

His first jump went well, so with his boss, Lieutenant Colonel Fla-
vell, he decided to jump again right away. One wrenched knee later,
and a day trying to walk it off, he was in hospital having the fluid
drained from it, in a ward full of the officers of many nations who
had also hurt themselves parachuting. The next week a group of
officers from the Airlanding Brigade who had crashed in their glider
came to the ward. This was a dangerous business. And it was public
knowledge:

> The chauffeur of an aunt with whom I was staying, on hear-
> ing I had become a parachutist exclaimed disgustedly, 'Why
> that's the surest way of becoming a prisoner there's ever been.'

Frost took command of 2nd Battalion on his way to North Africa at
the end of 1942. They had been sent there to seize airfields: it was in
Frost's view a 'useless adventure' based on sloppy intelligence, which
had squandered the Battalion, killed his second-in-command, and
wasted the hard work turning the army's volunteers, rejects and
adventurers into a competent fighting unit:

> The fact of the matter was that the British Army had no idea
> of how or when the new airborne capability should be used

and our own Brigade set-up was woefully inadequate to
ensure that really dreadful errors should not occur.[20]

However, perhaps unbelievably, 1st Army had called off the offensive that Frost's men were supposed to tie up with; indeed a measure
of the debacle is that this was the only message that his signallers
had received from 1st Army. Bruneval had succeeded because it had
been small-scale, the parameters of the operation limited, the objectives realistic. Raiding the French coast – easy for the RAF to find,
and somewhere the Royal Navy could make the rendezvous – worked
because it was backed with good intelligence. And more importantly didn't leave anyone miles behind enemy lines. But as airborne
operations got bigger, acquired more and more moving parts, and
the stakes became considerably higher, so the risks multiplied.
Market Garden was to be the biggest and consequently the riskiest
of the lot.

Come Tuesday, the men at the Bridge knew that the Germans, despite their every attack having been seen off the day before, were
about to apply more pressure. The roar of engines, the sound of
panzers, half-tracks, whatever they were, limbering up, was unnerv-
ing. Crouching in a slit trench as the Germans mortared and shelled
the houses by the Bridge – and in his mind they were 88mm guns,
because every gun was an 88 – James Sims started to muse on what
being 'bomb-happy' meant when a mortar bomb landed at his feet
and did not go off. Already the men at the Bridge were hanging on
by the slenderest of margins. Infantry they could deal with, especially men as slapdash as the soldiers who had lined themselves up
for the slaughter outside the school at 0300 hrs. But armour was a
different matter. It was now first light and a long, long day lay ahead.

10

THE TOWN: THE DOCTOR

War is the only proper school of the surgeon.

Hippocrates

STUART MAWSON SMOKED HIS FIRST cigarette of the morning and pondered the poor night's sleep he'd had. He had parachuted in the day before with the rest of 4th Parachute Brigade, in the delayed Second Lift, and had then been part of the stop-start advance towards whatever was to happen next. It was around 05 30 hrs and 11th Parachute Battalion was waiting in reserve to go forward and help with the push into the Town. He knew little beyond that – he was a doctor, and military matters weren't his purview. Medicine, a crucial part of 1st Airborne Division's set-up, was his primary concern.

The medicine that 1st Airborne Division brought with it to Arnhem for Market Garden was state of the art. Provision had been made for three field surgeries, where it would be possible to not just carry out the standard business of patching people up or performing rudimentary amputations, but rather deliver a full range of surgical treatments, even when sixty miles behind enemy lines. Equipment had been devised to be parachuted in: surgeons' tables, ventilators, plasma, everything imaginable. Airborne operations were expected to be casualty intensive – every glider after all carried a pair of stretchers and some blankets, given their reputation for landing heavily or even upside down. Jeeps, for evacuating casualties, were essential and utterly precious. Every man carried a field dressing, but care of the morphia styrettes was for the officers. If and when a casualty was treated, a ticket stating who he was, what was wrong with him and when he'd been given his morphia (to avoid a deadly additional dose), was attached to him.

Each of the three brigades in 1st Airborne had its own field ambulance, and having between them experience of North Africa, Sicily and Italy, they had paid careful attention to 6th Airborne's experiences in Normandy, where the key factor had been how quickly the front had stabilized. Within a couple of days, the front-line hospitals were in contact with the rear of Allied lines and the next stop before men were evacuated for further medical attention or convalescence. For an airborne division, the aim was to be able to deliver that same degree of medical care when it was behind enemy lines. Medicine and modernity, it has often been argued, live in eternal lockstep and nowhere more so than in 1st Airborne Division, this most modern of military establishments.

The First World War had seen advances of all kinds in medical treatment, as well as setbacks. Before penicillin and antibiotics, as a result of its great success in the Boer Wars antiseptic had been seen as the way to ensure that men did not die of infection caused by dirt entering the wound, whether it be pieces of uniform, mud, wood or whatever foreign object found its way into the injured man's body. Unfortunately, faced with the damp and filth of the Western Front, this had been an optimistic assessment. Antiseptic treatment had been nigh-on ineffective, and the medical establishment had to think again. The Army was frank in the ambition it had when it came to medicine: it was the job of the doctors to get men fit enough to fight again, and failing that, to get them strong enough to be of use as a worker. Needless to say, doctors, nurses and stretcher-bearers (many of them in 6th Airborne Division being conscientious objectors, unarmed men who had done their airborne training alongside their fighting colleagues) most likely viewed things differently through a lens of medical mercy, but they could at least share the core aim of ensuring that men might be of further use primarily to the Army and then to wider society. The Army's attitude to combat fatigue was that once you were demobilized your mental recovery was none of its business, whereas if you might be someone for whom the Army could still find something useful to do – preferably fight – then they'd take care of you.

There had of course been two major changes between the First and Second World Wars in terms of men and medicine. The relationship between the citizen and the state had been radically altered: the men being conscripted, unlike their predecessors in the Great War, had the vote. Britain's armies were now citizen armies, in the fully fledged sense, and generals, defence ministers and prime ministers were making plans for voters' lives and limbs; avoiding the perception that men's lives were going to be thrown away as cannon fodder, as they had been in the Great War, became central to how the Second World War was to be fought. The course of the war further altered this relationship. With the fall of France in the summer of 1940 there was no doubt that this was a war for national survival, and persuading people to fight to defend Britain was straightforward. In the East, however, the issue was more complicated. The staggering defeats in Singapore, Burma, Malaya and Hong Kong to the Japanese in 1941–2 meant that men were being asked to fight a war of Imperial reconquest rather than of defence. Motivating citizen soldiers, their attitude to how the state valued them, was important in a way it had never been before.

Therefore, the Army may well have possessed its pragmatic attitude to the medical care of its men, but it could hardly say so out loud. Care of its citizen soldiers had to be seen to be done. On Black Tuesday each of the nine infantry battalions had a Regimental Medical Officer, a man who knew the soldiers well and who had trained alongside them, a non-combatant but properly integrated and crucially the first port of call for the wounded. The same standards of physical fitness and endurance would also apply in order that he could keep up with the infantry. Further to this, orderlies were integrated into the battalions to offer instant medical assistance on the battlefield. With these orderlies the medical officer was to liaise with

the Brigade-level field ambulances, sending men 'back' to their surgeries. Crucially, he knew the men and their officers and the culture
of the battalions.

But the quality of care that the medical officer and Army could
offer had been radically changed by the second major development
since the Great War: the successful manufacture of penicillin and
antibiotics. Alexander Fleming's discovery of penicillin in September
1928 had happened in good enough time for it to be put to use, by
the Allies at least. As well as sulphonamide for dusting injuries, penicillin took centre stage in British and American combat medicine
and was directly responsible for a huge increase in successful out-
comes. As Fleming himself put it, not altogether modestly, perhaps:

> The results achieved [from using penicillin] led to a saving of
> manpower and reduction in wound-complications and
> recovery in hospitals, in supplies of drugs and equipment, in
> surgeons and nurse time which it is impossible either to com-
> pute or to appreciate.[1]

Due to penicillin's discovery and its emergence as a critical way of
saving men from infection and blood poisoning, and with the
arrival of war, it became clear that the British medical establishment
would have to decide what to do with its discovery. Two sentiments
ran in parallel: that no medical breakthrough this important could
be kept from the rest of mankind; and that it would be far better for
everyone if the Germans did not get their hands on it.

In America, two weeks after Pearl Harbor, in late December 1941,
Roosevelt set up an Office of Censorship to ensure that no one got
hold of the information needed to make penicillin – while at the
same time the US Army resolved the principle that enemy combat-
ants should receive the same treatment as Allied men, and if that
meant treating them with penicillin then so be it. During 1941 the
British became concerned that an attempt to get hold of a culture
of Alexander Fleming's penicillin mould might come from a

biochemical company in Switzerland, and so Fleming was encouraged to make sure this didn't happen. The Germans never managed to get hold of Fleming's culture.

Indeed, given their reputation for being adept at scientific and technical innovation, Germany's failure to invest in medical technology is striking. In 1942 there were just two people in Germany working on developing penicillin, with a third joining them on loan from the Wehrmacht. Compare that with the brainpower and Reichsmarks being spent on rocket and cruise-missile technology!

Tellingly, for such an important medical project, the Hoechst Dye Works in Frankfurt was the centre of German research efforts into the new medicine. Before the war German medics had concluded that sulphonamide did enough of an anti-bacterial job cleaning wounds and that penicillin simply wasn't worth investing in. In 1942 penicillin in the United States and Britain was being mass produced in ways that speak volumes about very differing attitudes to mass production. Whereas the British produced cultures in countless tiny glass bottles, the Americans had developed vast vats using a deep fermentation process to churn the stuff out. All this time the Allies were keeping tabs on German medical progress and knew how far they were running ahead. It was only in 1943 that attitudes changed and German production was finally turned around; but even then its field medicine could only boast a penicillin wound-dusting agent by the time of D-Day in June 1944. Penicillin itself wasn't brought into their field medicine until the month after the Battle of Arnhem – too little, too late.

As well as realizing the efficacy of penicillin too late to save perhaps hundreds of thousands of lives and limbs, German attitudes to medicine were also shot through with Nazi ideology, and consequently distorted. Given the T4 'euthanasia' programme, which had been murdering disabled children and adults deemed a burden by the Nazi state, it is hardly surprising that the attitude among the Germans' battlefield medics stood in stark contrast to the British Army's core aim of bringing men back to the front line or production line as soon and as best as possible. After the Battle of Arnhem, while being held as a prisoner of war by the Germans and asked to meet and debrief his opposite numbers, Captain Alexander Lipmann Kessel, RAMC, a South African who had worked as a surgeon in St Elisabeth Hospital, discovered to his horror the state of German field medicine. He had already formed a pretty low opinion of their handiwork when he had had to deal with men who had come into the hospital having previously been treated by the Germans.

Lipman Kessel's opposite numbers from 9th SS Panzer Division breezily told him that men with stomach and head injuries weren't worth saving, and that euthanasia by morphia was the best option for them. Given that British field medicine had succeeded in delivering a 60 per cent survival rate for abdominal wounds[2] – by far the hardest wounds to treat, with the possibility of huge blood loss, multiple points of injury, faecal matter getting into the wounds and so on – it shocked Lipmann Kessel to learn that German surgeons didn't consider those wounds worth the effort. Head injuries too. The men, they said, were going to be of no use anyway. 'Any other approach is sentimentality, not surgery.'[3] Lipmann Kessel was revolted but unsurprised at this attitude; he was also somewhat perplexed that they hadn't spotted that he was a Jew. Unless they had, and picking his brains was more important. He also realized that their methods for dealing with shock and blood loss were hopelessly out of date. Whether constrained by the shortages that characterized the German war effort, or an asleep-at-the-wheel attitude to medical innovation, or morbid fatalistic pragmatism, these doctors, who didn't think their men worth saving, were from the SS: a clear sign to Lipmann Kessel that Nazism's death wish extended even to what it regarded as the cream of its soldiery.

Of course, there were people in Germany who could get their hands on penicillin and benefit from it – or rather one person: Hitler. The Führer's personal doctor, Theodor Morell – who himself claimed to have invented penicillin and was allowed by Hitler to take credit – had treated Hitler with penicillin eye drops after the July 1944 bomb plot. It's not clear whether Morell used American drugs, but penicillin was good enough for the Führer – just not for the ordinary *Landser* fighting for the Fatherland.

Like the rest of the Division, the medical effort was planned to arrive piecemeal. On the Sunday afternoon after landing, two parts of 1st Parachute Brigade's plan had come off. Elements of 2nd Parachute Battalion had reached the Bridge along the lower road, while 16 (Parachute) Field Ambulance, the field surgery attached to 1st Parachute Brigade, had made its way to St Elisabeth Hospital, at the top of the embankment at the entrance to the Town, right next to the Bottleneck. The long-term plan was that the other two field ambulances, the 133 with 4th Parachute Brigade and the 181 with the Airlanding Brigade, would set up in the Municipal Hospital and pool resources later. Once the Town was occupied, St Elisabeth Hospital would be in the centre of the Divisional Administrative Area and it came with staff and supplies – though there was a question of what to do with the patients already there. For the opening stage of the operation, the field ambulances would answer to their respective brigades, deploying wherever was expedient; then if all went well, they would run the dressing stations on rotation and begin the evacuation of casualties by road and air. Like so much else airborne, hard planning, complexity and contingency sat alongside one another.

From the beginning of the development of airborne forces it had been clear that medicine would be central to this new and experimental form of warfare. With the novelty of transporting soldiers by glider to the battlefield, one of the immediate questions was finding a way to alleviate airsickness. Drugs were tried but in the end it was decided that landing and being in action were a sufficient psychological distraction to cure the men instantly – doubtless the relief of having landed safely and in one piece also helped.

The airborne field ambulance that emerged was modelled by Lieutenant General 'Boy' Browning on cavalry field ambulances[4] at the recommendation of his Assistant Director of Medical Services, Colonel Arthur 'Austin' Eagger. When injured, men would be taken to a

Dressing Station, a Regimental Aid Post (RAP), and then on to the Main Dressing Station (MDS) if they needed surgery – 10 per cent of casualties did. Surgeons were expected to perform 1.8 operations per hour, and do twelve hours on, twelve off. Technically, a field ambulance should be able to deal with 330 surgical cases a day – more than half a Battalion's worth. The overall mortality rate, if a soldier was successfully delivered to a field ambulance, was estimated at 1 per cent.

By 1944, the RAMC side of airborne forces was state of the art for the Allies. In Normandy, 6th Airborne Division's surgeons had performed 397 surgeries, including seventy-two amputations and one appendectomy. Containers for bringing in blood and plasma had been devised, as well as an airborne ventilator, collapsible surgeons' tables and specialized packs for airborne medicine called 'Don' and 'Sugar' that contained immediate kit for treating the wounded: cigarettes – the essential Second World War ration – anaesthetics, drugs, dressings, and inevitably, tea, milk and sugar. But like so much in the airborne set-up, there was an unsettled contradiction: patients with abdominal wounds could not be moved for up to ten to fourteen days, therefore provision to treat men for this long was a requirement of any airborne operation. Yet any initial lift could only really manage to deliver forty-eight hours' worth of medicines. Herein lay the tension between the immediate tactical limitations of airborne landings and the necessities they threw up. Not unlike the question of needing to take particular care of ammunition expenditure, medicines would be in short supply if things didn't go according to plan. Airborne resupply, a central part of the air plan, was critical to medical planning. Even more critical was being relieved, in that it would remove any constraints enforced by contingency.

Each field ambulance differed slightly in its war strength in terms of numbers, and 16 (Parachute) Field Ambulance, which had successfully set up at St Elisabeth Hospital, had ten officers and 125 other ranks. The parachute battalions, as mentioned above, each had a medical officer like Captain Stuart Mawson, RAMC, and eighteen other ranks comprising the medical section. The Parachute Brigade HQs also had a couple of officers apiece and six other ranks. The airlanding battalions each had a medical officer but fewer orderlies, as did supporting units. As well as the men landing by parachute, there were more men and equipment in the seaborne tail, and a Medical Stores Depot, planned to be delivered by plane to Deelen airfield at the successful breakout from Arnhem. In the meantime, though – however long that meantime might be – aerial resupply would keep the field ambulances stocked with surgical equipment and materials.

A field ambulance was commanded by a lieutenant colonel with the equivalent authority to a battalion commander. As well as nursing orderlies, anaesthetists, clerks and so on, it was complemented with a sapper for carpentry duties – the expectation being there would be a need to improvise when setting up in the field – along with mechanics and RASC personnel for the critical task of resupply. There were thirty-four 'vehicle drivers', outnumbering any of the other trades, and at least thirteen stretcher-bearers (British soldiers would call out for 'stretcher-bearers' rather than for a 'medic').

As for every other unit in 1st Airborne Division, Jeeps were essential to the airborne medical effort and had to be delivered by glider. The Parachute Battalion medical officers and their orderlies might arrive by parachute, but the equipment they relied on came by glider. A frenzy of unloading and rendezvousing followed landing, accompanied by the immediate and necessary question of keeping supplies flowing. As it was, 2nd Army were expected within a couple of days, well within the planned window of existing supply and immediate air resupply, so when Tuesday dawned, things were looking in good order for the field ambulances. As long as St Elisabeth Hospital remained accessible, the soldiers in the Town could be treated. But with the Battle sliding out of 1st Airborne's control, that vital resource too was soon in the balance.

At around 0800 hrs on Monday the Germans had taken the hospital as the Battle ebbed and flowed around it. A bitter negotiation with the Germans ensued. The field ambulance commanding officer was taken away by the enemy, though they allowed the second-in-command, Major Cedric Longland, with two surgical teams – including a pair of surgeons and a pair of anaesthetists with fourteen other ranks – to carry on working, while the SS nominally controlled the hospital. During the day the hospital changed hands several times. In the evening German officers returned and demanded the complete removal of the British from the hospital. The Germans claimed grenades had been thrown from the hospital windows; given the closeness of the combat and the aggression shown by both sides, this was not an unlikely proposition.

Captain Lipmann Kessel was one of the surgeons who carried on working – although his surgery drew enemy spectators. He used what German he had to demand that he be allowed to operate in peace, shouting at the Germans to leave, and, on one occasion, to make his point, performing a particularly gruesome amputation to force them to clear the room. He described the confusion:

> Other German soldiers were wandering round the hospital, poking their guns into cupboards and under patients' blankets, but I was kept too busy in the theatre to think much about them and, when I came out at midday for some food, I found two of our own soldiers drinking coffee and joking with the Dutch nurses. Was the Division again in control?[5]

Despite the roar and chaos of battle, the men lay still in their beds ('unless delirious') – disturbed occasionally by stray rounds or grenades flying in through windows and walls, and on one occasion:

> . . . when a bunch of SS men wandered through the building and amused themselves by firing machine-gun bursts over the helpless bodies in the corridors, killing one patient and wounding two others.[6]

Lipmann Kessel spotted something else in the confusion too:

From the windows we got glimpses of what seemed private
skirmishes between small groups from the two sides and
once, between cases, I happened to spot none other than the
Division's CO, General Urquhart, with a couple of aides
edging his way past some houses.[7]

It was into the deadly maelstrom in the Town, at the Bottleneck,
around St Elisabeth Hospital, that Stuart Mawson's 11th Parachute
Battalion was now, on Tuesday morning, being fed.

Men who were wounded and unable to get to an aid post, who had
fallen through the cracks, received what care they could wherever it
was available. On Tuesday morning, a few streets away from the
hospital, Captain Peter Stainforth RE was being tended to by Dutch
nurses in the cellar of an old people's home called Hoogstede. He
didn't know how he had got there. A veteran of North Africa and
Sicily, Stainforth had been wounded before in North Africa, but on
that occasion he had found his way to a Regimental Aid Post – 1st
Parachute Brigade in March 1943 were in the line being used as
normal infantry so they had a stable medical set-up. Now, in September 1944, Stainforth had been part of the team of sappers from
1st Parachute Squadron RE who had been given the job of making
sure the railway bridge across the Rhine was not mined for further
destruction. It had been blown up by the Germans when C Company from Frost's 2nd Battalion had got there on the Sunday
afternoon. By the time he arrived – having torn his trousers on some
barbed wire – Stainforth and his men spent several hours looking
for explosives on the bridge but drew a blank. He and his men were
'dog tired' and in the darkness they had found some sheds to sleep
in, in turns, the men keeping watch. They managed to grab three
hours' rest. They were on their own, out of touch with the rest of the
Squadron and the Brigade, not entirely sure of where they were,
who was around them, and what was going on – not unlike their
major general in his loft.

As they set off on the Monday morning they found other men in a similar situation:

> . . . four more paratroopers came out of a house and joined us. They were a corporal and two privates of the 2nd Battalion who had become separated from the others in a clash the night before and a medical orderly who had remained behind with the wounded. We all went on together.[8]

Making their way underneath the railway bridge into the outskirts of the Town, and avoiding being ambushed by German fighting patrols coming down the railway line, they leapfrogged their way forward to St Elisabeth Hospital, which at this point on Monday morning – likely around 0700 hrs – was back in British hands.

Realizing that the Bridge was being held, and, owing to the fact that the Germans had now interposed a force between 2nd Battalion and themselves, going forward and trying to get through to rejoin the Battalion would be futile. Stainforth decided to double back to the high ground half a mile west of the hospital at Den Brink, dodging an armoured car and a party of Germans searching the gardens in the Lombok estate.

It was on reaching Den Brink that Stainforth was wounded. Den Brink, with its wooded grounds sloping down towards the main road, was already criss-crossed with German slit trenches. When he and his party were fired on, thinking it was just a sniper and spotting one German running, Stainforth tried to drop the man with a long burst from his Sten gun. But suddenly the place was a warren of Germans running in every direction, as surprised as he was. Thinking 'Why haven't I been killed yet?',[9] Stainforth and his party sprinted back towards the houses in the estate, but just before he got into cover he was hit in his side by a bullet. He looked around him; one of the sappers with him was leaning against a tree, dying. Stainforth then made it into cover, while the rest of the paras made themselves scarce. Fortunately, the Germans did not pursue them or investigate, and a medical orderly was able to come over to treat his wound, despite Stainforth having tried to shoo him away, remarking it had 'gone right through', and had made 'a nice clean hole, too'.

The orderly plugged the holes with field dressings. These rectangular packs, khaki coloured, came with instructions written on them so that anyone could use them; to an orderly well trained with this kit, it would have been second nature. Typically, the instructions would read:

TO OPEN: Outer Cover: Break thread holding flap. Inner Waterproof Cover: tear apart at the uncemented corner where indicated by the arrow.

CONTENTS: Two Dressings in Waterproof Covers, each consisting of a gauze pad stitched to a bandage and a safety pin.

DIRECTIONS FOR USE. Take the folded ends of the bandage in each hand, and keeping the bandage taut, apply the gauze pad to the wound and fix the bandage.

One dressing to be used for each wound.

In the case of head wounds when respirators have to be worn care should be taken to adjust the pad so that it does not interfere with the fit of the facepiece.

DO NOT HANDLE THE GAUZE OR WOUND.[10]

The orderly gave Stainforth ten sulphanilamide tablets to swallow and injected him with morphine from his own supply of styrettes; as an officer he was carrying the morphia himself. The orderly would have drawn up a ticket, but with the morphine taking effect, Stainforth felt relaxed and a little sleepy. They lay the rest of the night in a ditch under some ivy, fighting all around them. Stainforth spent some time on a stretcher, and then when it became clear that he wouldn't be able to get back to Oosterbeek for treatment, or forwards to St Elisabeth Hospital, he found himself at Hoogstede, the stretcher-bearers alerted to its presence by a Red Cross flag flying from its roof.

On arrival the Dutch nurses had stood over Stainforth discussing what to do about him, one asking him in perfect English where he was hurt. They took him out of his uniform and his underwear and put him in bright yellow pyjamas. He felt close to death at this time, sleeping in one of the sisters' beds, numb with pain and exhaustion. Dawn came as a relief on Tuesday: he was still alive. The day itself was 'uneventful'. In the cellar there were about twenty-five people, the inmates of the old people's home and three British wounded and a pair of SS men: 'I wondered whether I had anything to do with them being there: both were suffering from a generous pepper-ing of 9mm about the legs.'[11] There was no way of telling how the Battle was going – until one of the nurses said that the Jeep and bike had black crosses painted on them. Helpless in the basement, unable to get to a Regimental Aid Post let alone a field ambulance, Peter Stainforth had to bear his wounds without the medicine the Division had brought with it.

Away from the mayhem of the Town, in the Village, it was decided by the Assistant Director of Medical Services for the Division, Col-onel Graeme Warrack, that the other two field ambulances, as well as stragglers from the 16th who had got separated from the rest of their unit, should pool the bulk of their resources in the Schoonoord Hotel, the large guest house and dining spot on the crossroads on the western side of the Village, where the main conurbation petered out into parkland and holiday homes. The Schoonoord sat three hundred metres or so from the Hartenstein Hotel, where Divisional HQ anxiously awaited news of Major General Urqu-hart. The Village had been a holiday destination before the war, with walks in the woods and bed and breakfast for well-to-do Dutch people. The crossroads sat on the route that ran east through the Village towards the Town and was intersected by the road that ran down to the river from Oosterbeek railway station in the north and then left on to the most southerly route towards the Bridge, the lower road. The roads were already strewn with rubbish as men had moved down them on their way to battle – soldiers discarding fag packets, sweet wrappers, as well as the respirators they'd had to bring but knew they wouldn't need. The Schoonoord was an ideal spot for a hospital in the Divisional Administrative Area – the closest thing the Division had to a rear on the Tuesday, well furnished with communications. The to-and-fro of Jeeps bearing casualties announced where it was. It was ideal. For now.

Meanwhile Stuart Mawson, at the 11th Battalion Aid Post in the Town, knew that 16 (Parachute) Field Ambulance had successfully set itself up in St Elisabeth Hospital. He'd been cold in the night and didn't feel at his best after a rough landing on Ginkelse Heide the day before. At 0530 hrs his orderlies, Adams and Dwyer, had woken him with a mug of tea and had filled him in on the 'gen'. They'd been on the move all day previously and, exhausted, Mawson had managed to sleep through the opening assaults of the morning on the lower road by what was left of 1st Parachute Brigade. He had been far enough back that the noise hadn't disturbed him. Only the odd rifle shot rang out.

Although 4th Parachute Brigade had landed on a contested Drop Zone, Mawson was mainly concerned with the fact he'd been concussed, losing one of his front teeth when he bashed his mouth on the bottle of medicinal brandy in his haversack; characteristically, his mind had been on the medical rather than the military aspects of his arrival in Holland.

He didn't think of himself as a military man: he'd been a hospital doctor before the war, and was most comfortable slotting into a role and getting on with caring for the injured. On his way from the Drop Zone to the Village, he had treated Major Richard ('Dickie') Lonsdale, 11th Battalion's second-in-command, who had been hit on his hand by flak on his way into the Drop Zone, but who, despite the seriousness of his injury, refused to see a surgeon. There had been a sense of urgency all round.

11th Parachute Battalion, commanded by Lieutenant Colonel George Lea, had been removed from 4th Parachute Brigade – to the fury of 4th Brigade's OC Brigadier Hackett – and sent into the Town to aid the push to relieve the Bridge. Mawson didn't know about the row at Divisional HQ between Hackett and Hicks that had accompanied this decision. Nevertheless, the change of plan, the new move, was pretty much the only thing that Mawson did know about from his perspective; when he awoke the 'gen' was that they were waiting for Lea to return with his Battalion's orders. Mawson ate his breakfast and surveyed the scene, the Battalion waiting in dead ground along the street that sat nearest the river and east of the railway bridge before it would move on up into the Town – if he felt anything it was perhaps complacency:

> I had not seen a casualty since leaving the rendezvous and was lulled by this non-event into a feeling of immunity, I felt the worst was over. Maybe a battle was about to develop, but I just could not anticipate it as something that might result in men dying or flesh being torn from bodies, certainly not from mine.[12]

Only the day before, the men had been referring to the operation as an 'exercise' even as they moved forward towards the sound of fighting. Mawson felt he was like the 'rear wagon of a large goods train', waiting for it to move forward. His contact with Battalion HQ – without a radio – relied on sending a runner forward, hoping that the runner would make it back. Otherwise Mawson would have to rely on what he could glean from around him.

Mortar rounds started to land with a crack around them, so Mawson, Dwyer and Adams decided to look for better cover – as veterans of North Africa and Sicily, Mawson was happy to defer to their judgement. They chose a concrete drive between two houses, set up their Red Cross flag, and immediately the first of the casualties started to come in. A man shot in the leg, patched up with a field dressing. Mawson gave him a shot of morphia – the man was 'almost apologetic' at having been hit by a machine gun as he had run across a road. Nonetheless, it meant that the stretcher-bearers were getting to casualties and transporting them back to the medical officer.

Time passed and more and more men started to drift back from the front – such as there was a front. Walking wounded brought with them the news that the Battalion did not seem to be making any progress. Men from other units would pass by too, heading towards the sound of battle in the Town; even though the Battalion's own Jeeps with its ammunition and supplies were still parked along the road, waiting.

Suddenly, by his reckoning at about 0930 hrs (though plainly, when cross-referenced with other accounts, much earlier, sometime after 0700 hrs), Mawson received a surprise visit. Major General Urquhart appeared in his Jeep with his driver, pulling up and quizzing Mawson intently, trying to find out anything he could. Urquhart had been able to escape from the house when the German armoured fighting vehicle parked under his loft window had fired up its engine and departed as a party of men from the South Staffords came skirmishing into Zwarteweg. Making their break for it, Urquhart and the others ran around the corner to find another party of officers and men from the South Staffords, as well as assorted others. Among them was Lieutenant Ben Lockett, from A Troop of 1st Airlanding Anti-Tank Battery, part of 1st Parachute Brigade's anti-tank component. He hadn't clocked who Urquhart was at first, he'd never seen his GOC before, but quickly realized from the way one of his colleagues was behaving who this unknown officer was:

> He seemed somewhat bemused and completely out of touch with reality. When I understood that he had been holed-up, the thing began to make a bit more sense . . .[13]

Getting back to Divisional Headquarters – wherever that might be – was Urquhart's priority, even though as it turned out he was only a hundred yards or so from where Colonels George Lea and Derek McCardie were, as they were still figuring out what to do. Since his escape from the loft opposite St Elisabeth Hospital, Urquhart had done everything he could to find out what was going on. Quizzing Mawson was doubtless part of this.

Urquhart's sudden appearance serves to emphasize how little individuals might know on the ground – telling Mawson 'in case you don't know, although I expect you do, there's a CCP [Casualty Clearing Point] recently set up a quarter of a mile back'. He was right: Mawson didn't know. Mawson thanked Urquhart, who responded with a smile and a thumbs-up and drove off. In his inexperience Mawson thought that seeing the major general must mean things were under control, an illusion which was to be shattered immediately by an intensification of fire and the appearance of more casualties.

As the morning drew on and the day warmed up, casualties began to trickle back and Mawson decided he should move to somewhere that wasn't quite so vulnerable to mortar fire. The house on whose drive he had set up his Regimental Aid Post had a garage, and after a brief discussion with Dwyer and Adams, he decided to ask the owners' permission to make use of their home. The family let Mawson into the house and offered him the chance to clean himself up in their downstairs loo. As he did so he decided that he couldn't bear to bring his men and their bloody work into the pristine suburban house, and asked if the garage would instead be suitable. After exchanging pleasantries with the family about the imminent Allied victory – as well as suggesting that they should stay in the cellar, at least while there was fighting going on – they offered to clear the garage and let him set up shop. A collapsible canoe and a pram went into the garden. Mawson and his team started to process the wounded, who 'lay on their stretchers quietly and patiently, saying nothing but intently watching every movement of the RAMC men'. A sniper fired the odd shot in their direction, as the movement of men and Jeeps attracted enemy attention. Mawson, however, turned his mind to treatment of the wounded. Later, in his memoir, he outlined what he was trying to achieve:

Above: A glider pilot's view: the tug lurking above the glider, the Dutch coast below. The skill required to fly these wooden aircraft and the intensity of the training made the pilots a precious asset, even though the gilders themselves (**below**) were essentially disposable, and a perilous way to come to battle.

'Sheriff' Thompson features in one of the many iconic pictures from Arnhem on the Sunday; he is on the left clutching two kit bags. The wreckage of a Horsa in the background, and the men puzzling over what to do about it, indicates the danger inherent in this means of transport, even when arriving on LZs that were deemed ideal. On Tuesday afternoon Thompson saved 1st Airborne Division from a rout.

A supply basket comes in to land, not far from the main ammunition dump and Divisional Headquarters, the Hartenstein Hotel. Jeeps and their trailers were essential for getting men and supplies around; the Jeep here has men in the trailer. Jeeps parked in the open here were extremely vulnerable to mortar fire.

Supplies falling into the trees. Much needed stuff falling out of reach was a deadly temptation for some men desperate for ammunition and food. But with Supply Zone S behind the German blocking line, most of the supplies fell into the hands of the enemy.

Some containers and panniers did reach the men in the Village, though nothing like the amounts the Division needed to keep itself going. The plan for air resupply, which was in its infancy, required that the land battle go as expected. By 1500hrs on Black Tuesday this was very much not the case.

Private Morris of Acton, London. Sten gun at the ready and Major General Urquhart's airborne pennant over his shoulder. Morris is using the airborne variant of the Sten, the MKIV, with its wooden stock.

A mortar crew from the 1st Battalion the Border Regiment engages the enemy at very close range, the tube almost vertical. They are Privates Norman 'Jock' Knight (obscured), Ron 'Ginger' Tierney (facing camera) and Corporal Jim McDowell.

Men of the Light Regiment with the 75mm M1 howitzer. While the gun detachments were excellently trained, their fire accurate and prompt, their comms generally excellent in Arnhem, the gun itself was simply not up to the task. They could not deliver the kind of firepower the Allies had built their way of war around.

'Gallipoli II', one of the 1st Battalion the Border Regiment's 6-pounders, which were named after Great War battles. In withdrawing from the brickworks at Renkum on Monday, B Company left behind two of their precious anti-tank guns, 'Ypres' and 'Somme', leaving them short of cover on Black Tuesday. It was perhaps their good fortune they had a relatively quiet day.

Men of R Company of 1st Battalion, which took 50 per cent casualties in the fighting around Wolfheze on Sunday night, before it even got into the Town. Second from the left, holding the cigarette, is Corporal Alfred Reynolds, 24, who was later killed in the push towards the Bridge.

Men of the 2nd Battalion the South Staffords on their way into the Town. The Staffs came in the First and Second Lifts, and were fed piecemeal into the Town. A long column like this could be easily held up, the men dispersing or getting cut off.

A complication for 1st Airborne Division, short of food and water, as well as shelter, was taking care of German prisoners of war. The Division had brought sixty-nine Military Policemen with it, who, as well as directing traffic, had to deal with the POWs. These were kept in the tennis courts near the Hartenstein Hotel. The youngster on the left looks quite happy that for him the war is over.

This photo was marked up as 'the master race at work' by the photographer Sergeant Dennis Smith. They're preparing firewood; hanging from the tree are mess tins. The man guarding them is wearing the Medical Research Council body armour that some men wore at Arnhem, with three plates: chest, crotch and lower back.

A PIAT crew of C Troop, 1st Airlanding Reconnaissance Squadron, covering a road near Wolfheze, on Monday. The British man-portable anti-tank weapon the PIAT was most effective at other-side-of-the-road distances. The container on the left, propped up on the tree, holds spare PIAT bombs; it was made of cardboard. PIATs were the second line of anti-tank defence after the 6-pounder, and ahead of the Gammon bomb, which you had to be close enough to throw at a tank.

Dug in with a Bren gun. Behind the men is a wire garden fence. These fences were useful in channelling the enemy into fields of fire when in defence, 21st Independent Parachute Company chose a house on a hillside with these fences on Tuesday morning to drive the enemy on to their guns.

My concern, having taken the immediate measures required
for the saving of life and limb, arrest of haemorrhage, com-
bating of shock, relief of pain and the prevention of further
damage through movement or infection, was now to see
them safely off my hands to where the really skilled treatment was available; that mending and repair work which
determines the outcome, not only from the point of view of
life but also from that of appearance and later usefulness.[14]

Just as Mawson got down to the business of triage, John Lawson
from the 133rd (Parachute) Field Ambulance, a fellow RAMC captain, appeared. They knew each other from exercises and Mawson
was reassured to see a familiar face. They exchanged pleasantries
and news. Lawson was on his way to try to make contact with the
field ambulance in St Elisabeth Hospital. He had also set up a Casualty Clearing Post in a barn about half a mile back; he was
wondering whether it would be possible to take the men who
needed surgery forward for treatment. Refusing the offer of a cup of
tea but accepting a cigarette, Lawson bade farewell but left his Jeep
behind to help with further evacuation and made his way forward,
towards the sound of the fighting.

At St Elisabeth Hospital the Battle raged on. On reaching the Divisional Administrative Area, Major General Urquhart had reported
what he knew of what was happening in the Town, and then told
Colonel Graeme Warrack, Assistant Director of Medical Services at
Divisional HQ,[15] that the hospital sat right in the middle of the
most contested part of the Town. With radio communication intermittent at best, it was decided to contact the hospital using the
existing Dutch phone network. An Army Dental Corps officer and
dentist, who had been working as an anaesthetist, Captain D. Ridler,
took the call in a phone box at the hospital front door, the conversation interrupted by explosions and machine-gun fire. Some
reports suggested the Germans had set up a mortar behind the

hospital and were lobbing bombs directly over it, making effective counter-mortar fire more difficult.

With the noise of machine-gun fire, mortars and a self-propelled gun at the end of the street in the background, Ridler reported back to Colonel Warrack the state of play in the hospital. There were one hundred casualties, he said, with about twenty staff to treat them. Ridler is reported as having signed off that 'the detachment was in good shape and comparatively speaking, all was well'[16] to the crash of a huge explosion. It was with this phlegmatic attitude that the surgical team and orderlies of 16 (Parachute) Field Ambulance would have to carry on until relief (if any) came.

Mawson marvelled once more at Sergeant Adams's ability to make a cup of tea regardless of the situation. They pondered what was happening back at home in England. Well, that depended on what time it was. It was coming up to 1100 hrs. 11th Parachute Battalion was about to fight its last battle.

11

THE TOWN: THE BATTALION

In front of a large hospital (Queen Elisabeth's) on a hill overlooking the river in ARNHEM. We met the S. STAFFS, who were apparently putting in an attack over the crest of the hill. 'A' Coy, on non-receipt of orders, pushed on through the other unit. (I think all our Walkie-Talkies were by now defective or non-existent.) The C.O. established his HQ in front of the hospital, and 'B' Coy dug in around the front at eastern side of the building. About 1000 hrs 'B' Coy was withdrawn to the West of the Hospital and took up positions covering several of the main roads. We were machine-gunned, but no tanks or infantry appeared. There was a lot of gun-fire behind the Hospital, but the situation was not at all clear.

11th Parachute Battalion War Diary for Tuesday morning

11TH PARACHUTE BATTALION HAD FOUGHT in just one battle before, on Kos. This obscure battle on one of the Greek Dodecanese islands began for the men of 11th Battalion on the night of 14 September 1943, when A Company had flown out of Cyprus and jumped at 0115 hrs, their job being to seize the airfield with the assistance of the Special Boat Service, who had been inserted twenty-four hours previously. The SBS fired a Very flare from the Drop Zone and everything went perfectly. A Company then made their way in stolen transport, buses and trucks to the airfield at Antimachia and the Italians duly surrendered. Several days of acting as a flying column followed. The Germans counter-attacked by bombing the airfield, and the British, who had not allocated enough fighter cover for Kos, could not defend the island.

Fortunately for A Company they were withdrawn on 24 September, returning to Cyprus. The Germans continued to build pressure from the air, reducing the RAF and South African Air Force squadrons' ability to defend the island. The ratchet suitably tightened, with the Germans dominant in the air, the following week they invaded Kos, on 3 October, landing men by boat and parachute in Operation Polar Bear. They were outnumbered by what was left of the Durham Light Infantry and the RAF Regiment troops (as well as aircraftsmen and crew), but they retained the initiative and more importantly air dominance. Try as the British might, and unable to coordinate with their new co-belligerents, the 3,500 Italians on the island, they couldn't stop the Germans from capturing the airfield, in a kind of mini rerun of the Battle of Crete of May 1941 (though nothing like as costly for the Germans). Insertion by parachute worked on Kos for the Germans – if not for the British. Like Crete, a British evacuation followed and then a massacre, the Germans murdering 103 Italian officers as a reprisal. A Company had had a lucky escape.

The operation on Kos was in 11th Battalion's backyard. Raised in the Middle East, from scratch, it was the creation of General Headquarters Middle East. Expert opinion, attracted to the modernity and as yet untested possibilities of airborne troops, felt that using paratroopers in the desert to capture enemy prisoners would have sped things along at, for instance, the Battle of El Alamein. Lieutenant Colonel John Hackett was given the job of raising the new 4th Parachute Brigade. Its nucleus was the Indian 156 Battalion (its name changed from 151 Battalion in an effort to confuse the Germans – and later readers perhaps),[1] which had moved to Kabrit in Egypt from India in November 1942. 11th Parachute Battalion was the Brigade's third – junior – Battalion, and something of an orphan: for all his zeal in getting things started, Brigadier Hackett found it a challenge to get it up to war strength.

The battalion had been formed on 4 March 1943, in response to a simple problem. The British were beginning to run out of men. Although it amounted to nothing like the manpower crisis that would affect things come autumn of the following year, casualties in the Middle East meant that existing units were having a hard enough time replenishing their ranks without the need to man brand-new units. For all that it offered a life of adventure as well as the extra two shillings jump pay – and regular infantry battalions did not like losing their more motivated men to the airborne fraternity anyway – 4th Parachute Brigade simply couldn't get the staff, and because 11th Battalion came third after 156 Battalion and 10th Battalion, it was particularly difficult for them to attract new recruits. Nevertheless, the men did come from somewhere eventually; the 1st Special Air Service Regiment was being run down, and a core of men from there were successfully persuaded to join 11th Battalion. Deals were done too: some units would offer a bunch of men rather than lose key experienced personnel, after which those men would be assessed and put through jump school.

Training in Egypt by the Suez Canal and then Palestine, based in a camp at Ramat David near Haifa – jumps by the Sea of Galilee, a demonstration jump in Gaza and so on – followed. But 11th Battalion remained the third, junior, battalion, lowest in the pecking order – and the other two battalions were sent to Tunisia in April of 1943. After Kos, the men returned to Ramat David as part of another brilliant Allied deception in which they were there to represent the '4th Airborne Division', yet another fictitious formation.

But the gravitational pull of Operation Overlord began to exert itself, even on units as far from home as 11th Battalion, and it returned by ship to Great Britain, arriving in Liverpool on 4 January 1944. More training ensued, with a focus on parachuting and integrating the Battalion into 4th Parachute Brigade. In the meantime the other battalions had been sent to fight in Italy, landing by boat in Taranto as part of Operation Slapstick. The first half of 1944 was a time of 'hurry up and wait'. Just as 4th Brigade was untested as a whole, so 11th Battalion compounded this problem in being untested as well and without anything to prepare for, beyond training.

This period quickly became a problem for 11th Battalion. Since their inception, airborne units had suffered from the tension that existed between men who were well motivated to get at the enemy and wanted more action than a conventional unit could offer, and the prosaic business of hurrying up and waiting, doing nothing much more than training and standing by. 1st Airborne Division's new role was to be part of Strategic Headquarters Allied Expeditionary Force's (SHAEF) 'strategic reserve'. This meant waiting for something to come up – anathema to men of adventure, and a major problem for troops who had been trained consciously to be extra-aggressive and self-sufficient. Airborne soldiers, as we have seen, underwent a process of psychological assessment, were instructed in close-up fighting techniques, and of course were put through the process of parachute training – probably as reliable a means as any of testing a man's mettle. The men of 11th Battalion, though untried, were as well trained and keyed up as any in the British Army: they had done training drops at company and battalion level, as well as having acted as the opposition in a training exercise for 6th Airborne's D-Day rehearsals, Exercise Mush, in April 1944. This was the one and only Divisional-scale exercise 1st Airborne undertook.

With all this waiting around, problems of discipline began to emerge. Tensions manifested themselves in different ways. Men going absent without leave. Drinking, fighting. The various halts and cancellations, accompanied by the confinements to camp that came with an anticlimax over and over again, had begun to eat into morale. In 11th Battalion in June a dispute about drawing pay erupted. Men in arrears left camp without their passes in a mass walkout. Lieutenant Colonel Micky Thomas, who had founded and raised the Battalion under extremely trying circumstances, at the back of the queue and left out of 4th Parachute Brigade's main set-up for so long, was fired by Brigadier Hackett, who said he was 'too much of a gentleman' for the job, a sour reward for his efforts. His men at least knew how to act together and for each other's interests – and Thomas was hardly responsible for the situation regarding pay. His fellow officers considered returning to their units too; Thomas talked them out of it. By the time of the Battle of Arnhem, Thomas had been killed on Mont Pinçon in Normandy while fighting with 5th Battalion the Wiltshires.

So on Black Tuesday the late Micky Thomas's successor, Lieutenant Colonel George Lea – who had been Hackett's Brigade Major and thus a trusted appointment – was facing an unenviable task. He had been ordered to separate from 4th Parachute Brigade and make himself available to 1st Parachute Brigade in the Town. This order, of course, hadn't come from Brigadier Hackett but from Brigadier Hicks, who had chosen the 11th because their rendezvous after landing had placed them closer to the Town than 156 and 10th Battalions. The men had come up the lower road in good order, and Lea made himself known to Lieutenant Colonel Dobie of 1st Battalion, arriving late at the O Group in the cellar. Initially it was agreed that the 11th would serve as the Brigade's reserve, but it became clear quite quickly that 1st and 3rd Battalions were so depleted as a result of Monday's fighting that the 11th would have to become involved right away. Lea himself was very active in going forward and assessing the situation, going through the Bottleneck into the Town and making sure that A Company were working with the South Staffords in pushing forward past St Elisabeth Hospital. While Stuart Mawson set up his Regimental Aid Post at the Battalion's rear half a mile or so back with C Company in reserve, Jeeps and men waiting on the roadside, A and B Companies were engaging with the enemy, who were surrounding them on three sides.

Immediately the problems associated with fighting in a built-up area came into play. Previous exercises had been in countryside, at most involving small villages, but Arnhem was as urbanized an environment as any British soldiers had fought in. In Ortona, Italy, the year before, Canadian troops had had to fight house by house, floor by floor, to winkle the Germans out, 'mouse-holing', blowing holes in walls and working their way through buildings. But they had armoured support, tanks working to deliver close and heavy fire. This was of course dangerous for the tanks, every street corner offered a possible ambush by anti-tank gun or man-portable anti-tank weapon, but if the tanks and infantry cooperation paid off properly, as it had at Ortona, then the Germans could be winkled out. In a grim reflection of Arnhem, the German soldiers in Ortona had been paratroopers.

Fighting in a built-up area (acronymically known as FIBUA) is incredibly challenging, particularly without universal radio communications, something well beyond the reach of the British Army in the Second World War. Coordinating men who are taking cover, establishing bases, regrouping, tending to the wounded, figuring out what to do in different slit trenches in the countryside is one thing; doing it when they are in buildings is quite another (*see diagram on p. xxxii*). 11th Battalion's War Diary makes it clear that the company-level walkie-talkies were not working, as was usual, but in this urban environment it was a further embuggerance that compounded the problems faced by Lieutenant Colonel Lea. Cohesion was instantly at stake.

The British Army manual 'Fighting in Built-Up Areas' – Military Training Pamphlet No. 55, published in 1943 – laid out the contradictions and problems, while at the same time asserting that although built-up areas favoured the defender, it was just like fighting anywhere else. Five points into the manual it states this:

> 5. The ground. No other battlefield includes ground both so open and so close. In every street are coverless stretches affording ideal fields of fire. In every street are numerous protected firing positions, hiding places, and sources of ambush. It follows that fighting will nearly always be at close quarters, casualties high, and the nerve strain for both sides heavy.[2]

And if there was one thing that lightly equipped parachute troops could do – as was playing out at the Bridge – it was defend themselves. Attacking in a built-up area, an area that favoured defence, was a challenge of a different order, as Montgomery and his staff had found trying to clear Caen in the summer of 1944. In the end they had resorted to getting Bomber Command to come in and flatten the place – though of course that in itself radically changes the environment.

When a built-up area is the scene of a prolonged period of fighting, however, many of its characteristics will be modified. When a whole sector of a town is reduced to rubble, the piles of debris render the area analogous to close country providing much cover; they will also restrict movement, except on foot.[3] Lieutenant Colonel Lea was not yet facing such a 'modified' environment, and he was making sure he was well forward with A Company ensuring his grip, but because movement across streets, hampered by mortars, machine guns and artillery from the other side of the river, was impossible, he found it hard to keep tabs on the whole of the Battalion: the manual calls this 'conspicuous movement', 'restricted manoeuvre', 'difficulty of locating fire'. Not helping matters was the fact that jumbled up in the action that morning were men from other battalions who had been involved in the assault the day before, stragglers, wounded, men who had simply found themselves left behind either by an advance or a withdrawal. Further down the manual still, but in bold at least, was the problem of **'civilians'**.

The manual's summary reads like a prediction of how Black Tuesday might run:

> Fighting in built-up areas reduces the advantages enjoyed in open warfare by the side that is superior in mobile equipment and vehicles; it involves chiefly infantry action, in the form of small, numerous, and independent battles; and its dominant feature is an abundance of cover interspersed with short, open fields of fire. Such fighting, therefore, favours the

defence, except possibly at night. In addition, it requires
increased manpower for a given area. Above all, because of
the enclosed nature of the fighting, success depends on the
determination, cunning, and trained observation of the individual. Heavy shelling and air bombing at the right place and
time may be more decisive in built-up areas than in the field.[4]

Battalions like the 11th may have possessed 'determination, cunning, and trained observation of the individual', but what they
lacked was access to heavy shelling and air bombing, and above all
manpower.

Parachute Regiment battalions were small, operating on a different structure to regular British Army battalions, in that they were
triangular. A conventional infantry battalion had deeper manpower
pockets, with four rifle companies to a Parachute battalion's three.
In North Africa, when 1st Parachute Brigade had been put into the
line because 1st Army had been short of infantry, the paratroopers
had quickly established a reputation for fearlessness and aggression.
However, their triangular company structure meant they burned
through men much faster than the larger, regular battalions. A
normal battalion might operate with three companies forward and
one in reserve – a Parachute battalion did not have that luxury.

Furthermore, line battalions would operate an LOB system – Left
Out of Battle – to ensure that there were spare men held back in the
event of disaster. Regrettably, Lea's LOB men were still in England.
So A and B Companies went forward, while C was left in reserve,
deployed in a part of the Town they had not been designated to
attack. 11th Battalion went into Arnhem on the Monday with 571
men, comprising Battalion Headquarters, Headquarters Company,
the Signals Platoon, Support Company, an Assault Platoon, Mortar
Platoon, Medium Machine Gun Platoon, and then its three rifle
companies, A, B and C, each with three platoons.

The company broke down as follows: Company Headquarters
with two officers and thirteen other ranks, a clerk, a quartermaster,

a storeman, etc. There were two batmen, one of whom doubled as a driver – there was also a company pool of PIATs. At company level there were four nursing orderlies who would liaise with the Regimental Medical Officer, in this case Stuart Mawson. The sharp end, the infantry platoons, boasted – at full strength – their subaltern and thirty-three other ranks. The platoon commander would have a headquarters, with a batman who doubled as a signaller, a sergeant as second-in-command, and a headquarters orderly/runner. The platoon HQ held a Bren gun just in case. The platoons numbered ten men each and were split into rifle and gun groups, the latter running two Bren guns.[5]

In total, then, a company commander had at his disposal some 90 riflemen, whereas a battalion commander had 270 or so, depending on absences and illness, and men injuring themselves on landing. Like all other Parachute Regiment battalions, 11th Battalion's blade was not as sharp as it might have been. The glider-borne airlanding battalions in 1st Airlanding Brigade each had four rifle companies. But they were being held back to defend the Landing Zones and kept away from the battle in the Town, where numbers might make a difference – a drawback of arriving in more than one Lift – with the exception of the 2nd South Staffords, who were now joining the battle in the Town.

Above all, what street fighting really required was automatic weapons, and density of firepower, to keep the enemy's head down. Airborne soldiers were encouraged to shoot well in their training, to practise good musketry and make every shot count. The demands of street fighting ran counter to this. Rifles, the manual stated, were perfectly useful in street fighting for sniping, but it did concede that automatic carbines were the ideal weapon for the environment. For the paras, this meant Sten guns, the 9mm sub-machine gun, a weapon designed to be a simple, cheap, yet robust answer to the German MP40 – known as the *Schmeisser*. But as Lieutenant Colonel Johnny Frost had found at the Bridge, the key problem was that whatever the weapon, ammunition was being consumed at a prodigious rate, and, as German armour began to assert itself, Sten guns were of little help.

What these airborne battalions were being asked to do, largely because the previous two days had not panned out as hoped, was simply becoming beyond them. All the training in aggression and stamina – and the men of the 11th were now beginning to feel the strain of very little sleep and the enervation of combat – would count for nothing in an increasingly uneven struggle. The defender has no need to hold the initiative, but simply to anticipate the attacker's approach. With the Bottleneck by the hospital, even the most inexperienced Germans could hold up 1st Airborne. Whoever they were, Panzer SS or the widely expected 'ear and stomach' soldiers – pressed men who were otherwise medically unfit to fight – soldiers, the challenges the Germans faced were nothing compared to what George Lea and the other lieutenant colonels were facing on the Tuesday morning, if they wanted to advance.

As the Germans ranged their mortars and Lieutenant Colonel Lea rushed between A and B Companies, the remnants of 1st Parachute Brigade and the South Staffords were feeding themselves into the Bottleneck. On the river road Lieutenant Colonel Fitch's attack had been crushed, David Dobie's men were being torn apart, and the South Staffords were fighting along the higher road towards the Monastery. In the flames, smoke and noise of battle, who was who, and who was where, men in their airborne smocks indistinguishable from their fellows, four different lieutenant colonels trying to assert themselves, no one was properly in charge. The fire from the German side was murderous. Ammunition or the lack of it – in particular PIAT ammunition – became critically important as the Germans sent self-propelled guns into the fray.

To the north of the main road, the Lombok estate offered the Germans the perfect defender's advantage for fighting in a built-up area. At the top, the northern end, of the estate was the railway, cut into the high ground that rose from the river's meander. This railway line served the Germans' needs perfectly – it cut right through the centre of the battlefield and exacerbated the Bottleneck. The estate was built on a grid with wide streets running down from the railway line. If you wanted to move from west to east, laterally, you had to run the gap between each line of houses. Controlling the railway line meant that the Germans were able to bring men directly to the station and then on to the line at the top of the estate slope. For the defenders, new technology had come into play, a variation of the MG42 weapon set in a tripod that could be used to fire indirectly, using it to close down streets. As the War Diary says, 'we were machine gunned . . . a lot of gun-fire'. And with the Germans firing mortars as well, there was no way to respond effectively with counter-mortar fire in such an enclosed space: getting into the open to do so was fraught with danger.

Fighting panzers was no more straightforward. The 6-pounders would have to be concealed, and then, when a tank was spotted, rushed into action. The men manning the guns, manhandling them into position, waiting for the tanks to come on to them, additionally had to brave mortar and machine-gun fire, not to mention the flak guns over on the other side of the river.

Gunner Len Clarke, with E Troop of 2nd (Oban) Airlanding Anti-Tank Battery, was lurking with his 6-pounder in a front garden, his line of fire facing the hospital. His gun engaged an approaching tank, but only once his troop commander, Lieutenant Bob Glover, had pulled rank and insisted on aiming the gun himself. Three rounds from the 6-pounder hit the tank and it stopped. Clarke and Glover then made themselves scarce. Another gun, commanded by Captain P. A. Taylor alongside 11th Battalion, was also stalking tanks, but the Germans had armour in abundance. Taking it on required great nerve and not a little luck.

As Lieutenant Colonel Lea tried to coordinate his attacks with those of 1st Parachute Brigade, word came from Divisional Headquarters of a change of plan. With 11th Battalion in its half-in, half-out role as the reserve in the Town, Major General Urquhart changed his mind. Or rather changed the decisions that had been made in his absence. Even though he could barely make out the order due to the bad reception on his radio, George Lea was ordered to withdraw from the push for the Bridge and turn his Battalion's efforts towards meeting up with 4th Parachute Brigade, which was due to be advancing down the northern side of the railway line, as outlined in the original Market Garden plan. Lieutenant Colonel Lea was to take and hold the high ground at Den Brink beside the prison and west of the Lombok estate. The fact that it must have been clear by now that the Germans controlled the railway line seems not to have been factored into Urquhart's decision. In ordering 11th Battalion away from a battle in the balance towards one that was not playing out as expected is hard to explain. After more than a day away from his headquarters, time he described as 'idiocy', Urquhart wanted to try to get a grip on events, to make decisions. He had an eye to taking control of the simultaneous battle to which Brigadier Hackett had committed 4th Parachute Brigade in the Woods. So, at around 0930 hrs, Lea was ordered to redirect his efforts to the high ground at Den Brink.

Lieutenant Colonel Lea may have been unhappy with his new orders, but now he still had to regroup by falling back from the South Staffords, leaving them isolated further along the higher road. If they were counter-attacked by the Germans they would have no reserve, in the form of 11th Battalion, as originally planned. George Lea climbed into a Jeep to make his way to B Company and spread the news. Once again, his radios and walkie-talkies weren't working, and with his second-in-command, Major 'Dickie' Lonsdale, in Oosterbeek and injured, Lea would have to do all this personally. While the manual may have suggested that a built-up area offered him the chance to have a personal influence on things, it also placed him in the broad areas with no cover. Critically, his men were going to have to leave their dug-in positions and therefore be exposed. Finding men from 1st Parachute Battalion and discovering a 17-pounder anti-tank gun concealed just behind the Bottleneck, he added them to his increasingly improvised force to reorganize his men and carry out his new orders.

But what effect would pulling back have on 2nd Battalion the South Staffordshire Regiment, whose left flank A Company was protecting? Would the men at The Monastery be able to hold on?

12

THE TOWN: THE MONASTERY

Others from the direction of the riverbank fired directly into the hollow, which now became an absolute death trap.

2nd Battalion South Staffords War Diary

LIEUTENANT COLONEL McCARDIE had had to adapt. 2nd Battalion the South Staffordshire Regiment had not arrived in its entirety on the Sunday. The allocation of a large portion of the initial airlift to Lieutenant General 'Boy' Browning's headquarters had put paid to that. Browning and his staff had landed to the south near Nijmegen. Browning, who had cooked up the Market Garden plan for Montgomery, wanted to be there at the moment of victory, and so had taken up thirty-eight gliders to get his Tactical Headquarters to Holland. Half of the South Staffords had to stay at home. As 1st Airlanding Brigade's reserve, the South Staffords were lower in the pecking order. The Brigade's task was to hold the Drop and Landing Zones needed for the lifts that would follow D-Day on the Sunday, so the South Staffords would have to wait until D+1 to be present in full strength.

Still, while not ideal this was better than what had happened the previous year in the landings on Sicily, when McCardie's glider had been forced to ditch after being cast off early by his tug pilot. He'd swum ashore; some of the men who couldn't face the two-mile swim had remained on the glider. When he finally made it to dry land, he walked inland, barefoot, hooking up with some Commandos and realizing that the Battalion hadn't made it to its rendezvous.

He noted in his account that the timings were approximate because his wrist watch had been 'put out of action by sea water'. In short, the landings had been a complete calamity.

Of the 1,730 men who had set off for Sicily in the summer of 1943 by glider, 326 had drowned. The South Staffords' role of honour grimly reflected this – scores of men from the South Staffords who'd flown there had 'no known grave'. Operation Ladbroke, the airborne component of Operation Husky, the invasion of Sicily, had underlined how important it was for glider crews and tug pilots to work well together. That the British the next year had stuck with a gliderborne delivery of soldiers after the disaster of 1943 was a testament perhaps to the power of optimism over experience. A Landing Zone that allowed for gliders to descend and land in an orderly manner – in daylight – reassured both officers and men. On the Sunday the War Diary reported:

> Battalion 1st lift consisting of BHQ, B & D Coys, one pl Vickers and HC Pl Mortars, landed at RIJERS CAMP (662815). One Pl B Coy did not arrive, and B Coy HQ glider cast off over England. Battalion took up defensive position round L.Zs.

By comparison, Sunday itself had been stress-free: the Germans had been taken by surprise. On Monday they weren't surprised any more. And the weather had changed. The Second Lift wouldn't be on time:

> 18th September 1944
> Place: Brize Norton
>
> Owing to 'Met' report take off put off until 1015 hrs. Rain at Manston, low light cloud Brize Norton. Take off on time, 1 A Coy glider broke tow rope while circling airfield made good landing, hitched up and took off again. All our gliders at LZ OK. Newspapers full of airborne landing on Holland. Photographs.

The *Daily Herald* headline read 'AIRBORNE ARMY CAPTURES DUTCH TOWNS NEAR REICH BORDER: Thousands of Paratroops Landed Before AA Guns Opened Fire'. The *Daily Mail*, with its banner 'For King and Empire', ran with 'AIRBORNE INVADERS OPEN BATTLE OF THE RHINE', quoting Monty's 'Onward into the Reich'. The *Daily Express* offered Monty saying of the Germans that it was 'Doubtful How Long They Can Fight'. The mood around Market Garden, the feeling that it was the right time to do something this audacious, extended well beyond 1st Airborne Division. Whatever surprise the enemy had experienced on Sunday had truly dissipated a day later, particularly when you could read about the Allied intentions for Market Garden in the papers: the kind of over-confidence that was a hallmark of the whole adventure. But the Second Lift, if nothing else, demonstrated that while the Allies might have deep pockets, there were still limits to what they could do – they couldn't land everyone at once:

Place: Holland

Battalion moved off at 0930 hrs through WOLFHEZEN into ARNHEM with the object of relieving 1st Para Battalion at Arnhem Rd Bridge. Held up for a few hours north of OOST-ERBEEK (708702) but got through and entered town at about 1900 hrs, where contact was made with remnants of 1st and 3rd Para Battalions (726776), under heavy fire from German defences on high ground north of ARNHEM. During the afternoon the second lift consisting of Rear BHQ, A Coy, and C Coy, one pl Vickers, Jeep Pl, Mortars, and two ATk pls, landed. B Coy HQ glider also landed with this lift. Second lift moved down into Arnhem during the night and A Coy reached the Battalion about midnight. Remainder of second lift held up; got through at first light.

The Battalion, comparatively intact, was now in the Town, ready to add its weight to the attempt to relieve Lieutenant Colonel Frost at the Bridge. And unlike its parachuting equivalents, the glider-borne 2nd South Staffords had heft in terms of numbers.

Landing men by glider offered the British Army all sorts of advantages that parachuting couldn't. Men dropped from an aircraft would always have the issue of needing to land safely, get rid of their parachute, manhandle their kit, find one another and muster at a rendezvous point. A glider-landing saved you all that bother. A glider that landed in the right place essentially delivered a platoon of soldiers together, as one. As long as it landed the right way up. A glider landing in the right place delivered a tactical effect with a possible strategic outcome, if the tug pilot didn't let the glider go early and into the sea. A glider landing in the right place allowed the army to save time and money by only needing to train two pilots rather than thirty parachutists. As long as the pilots weren't incapacitated by ground fire and the glider wasn't rendered pilotless. Or if the glider broke up because it wasn't loaded properly. Or flew into a mountainside. Or was shot down by over-eager and poorly briefed Allied naval anti-aircraft fire. And of course, and most importantly, as long as you had the weather you needed to be able to proceed in the first place.[1] Nevertheless, gliders still offered airborne planners the closest thing they could get to a concentration of force.

Moreover, what they offered the airlanding elements of British airborne divisions was more men and more stuff. Airlanding battalions had four companies of riflemen, each with four platoons. The idea was that a company could be delivered in five Horsa gliders. 2nd South Staffords could transport 767 men, around 200 more soldiers than the equivalent battalions in 1st Parachute Brigade. They were arranged differently too, in terms of their anti-tank capability – they had integrated anti-tank platoons in a battalion support company. Parachute battalions had batteries attached because a Parachute battalion's heavy equipment and supplies had to be brought to the battlefield by glider; 6- and 17-pounder anti-tank guns were too large to be dropped by parachute. Given they required the similarly monstrous Hamilcar glider to deliver them to the battlefield, 17-pounders and their ammunition and gun tractors arguably represented a serious opportunity cost in terms of space (one 17-pounder detachment fired all of two rounds in the course of the entire Battle). That said, the Airlanding Brigade's battalions like 2nd South Staffords packed a punch; or at least they would have done if they were able to assemble and advance all at once. Which, thanks to the air plan, they weren't.

So Derek McCardie would have to adapt. After the O Group with David Dobie from 1st Battalion and George Lea from the 11th, the attack had got underway. The War Diary states:

> At 0445 the Battalion moved off for the Road Bridge through the main street of the town. They were followed by the 11th Para Battalion; remnants of 1st and 3rd under Lt-Col Dobie, at the same time, started along the river bank.

This push into the Town was to have more heft than the previous effort by the remnants of Fitch's 3rd Battalion earlier in the morning, though by this stage the battlefield was congested, men from 1st Battalion making their way as best they could from the scrub and the end of the river road. The South Staffords were to take the high road, above the embankment, which offered them houses to work their way through rather than the improvised slit trenches and minimal cover of the river road and the scrub.

The South Staffords delayed, waiting for their remaining companies to arrive, but then McCardie decided to press on. Following him was 11th Battalion – McCardie's understanding was that he would be backed by Lieutenant Colonel Lea's men. Once they were underway they made good progress, chasing away the self-propelled gun that had sat outside Major General Urquhart's loft, liberating St Elisabeth Hospital, and moving on through the slice of buildings between the higher road and the railway to the north. At the top of the embankment and south of the bend in the higher road was the building that the South Staffords referred to as The

Monastery. It is a simple example of the confusion around the battle in the Town that this was a museum, not a monastery, and referred to as such by the other units in the fight for the Town (if they referred to it at all).

The Monastery sits back from the road slightly down the slope of the embankment. Along the higher road it has a black iron fence, with trees and gardens around it. Its dome marks it out as a different space from the many tall houses on the northern side of the higher road opposite, with its white columns suggesting municipal grandness. The South Staffords dug in around The Monastery, but their opportunity to get across the road or in and out of the position was curtailed by the black iron fence. The higher road, with its tramlines and overhead cables, then ran downhill into the Town a few hundred metres from the railway station, but beyond The Monastery on the southern side of the road there was no cover. Down the road, where the first houses of the other side of the street stood, was as far as anyone had got in the push into the Town on the Monday. In this road stood German self-propelled guns and half-tracks, nose to tail.

Getting to The Monastery had been costly. Immediately after crossing the start line at about 0500 hrs, D Company encountered a party of the enemy around the hospital, and though they saw them off, their strength was reduced some 60 per cent. German 20mm anti-aircraft cannon were firing from across the river. This was the enemy's anti-aircraft ordnance so feared by the air planners when deciding on where to deliver the Division now repurposed in a ground role. It was firing on pre-sited locations, street corners and the few places that seemed to offer cover, while MG42s fired on fixed lines. The Germans weren't short of ammunition so could simply keep firing at random into where they guessed the British would be trying to advance. In the early morning light, the church spire in the Town was silhouetted by the flames from the houses already burning there and around the Bridge as German tracer rounds tore up the streets.

Keeping the men going forward was critical. D Company's commander, Major J. E. Phillip, was wounded, hit in the stomach. His second-in-command was Captain E. M. 'Oscar' Wyss, who before the war had worked in his parents' restaurant in Burslem in Staffordshire. Like McCardie, Wyss had been in Sicily, delivered off target in his Horsa, been taken prisoner and held in an actual prison. He had made himself busy and useful during the South Staffords' advance into the Town, dealing with snipers and keeping the men going, doing the essential stuff that fighting in a built-up area required of infantry company officers.

But as the fighting intensified, Wyss took it upon himself to spur D Company on, walking among the men, yelling at them to move forward. It still wasn't light. Private R. C. S. Edwards, 21 Platoon, D Company, describes the action:

> We now came to a wide, exposed, riverside stretch of road in front of the St Elisabeth's Hospital and all hell seemed to let loose on us. We were out in the open and must have been like targets in a shooting gallery. All 'Jerry' had to do was line his guns and mortars along the gap, a quarter mile wide, and fire. He could not miss. Yet still Captain Wyss ran up and down, totally ignoring all the stuff and metal flying about him, his voice growing ever hoarser, 'On, On, On, D Company On, On', where men flagged, faltered or hesitated, he was there. You could not crawl on your stomach and watch him standing upright. You had to follow his lead. I laid what smoke bombs I had with me along the gap, where I thought they would do most good, then put my head down and ran like a harrier for the far side. I stumbled over the dead and dying, slithered in pools of blood, until I reached the partial shelter afforded by the houses and buildings. Here I found most of those that had got across the gap were sheltering in a dell by the side of the Museum.[2]

Given the confines of the battlefield, the smoke would have announced the intentions of the South Staffords as much as it concealed their position.

The men had to follow his lead: Wyss got himself and his men to The Monastery despite everything. His actions were mentioned in dispatches:

> After leading the forward troops through a very heavy and prolonged concentration of artillery fire, Captain Wyss advanced straight up the main road which was swept with fire from at least six machine guns. There was no cover available and no alternative route. Had Captain Wyss hesitated, the whole attack would have faltered. After an advance of some five hundred yards, two German tanks appeared and began to shoot up the column from behind a house. Captain Wyss at once seized a P.I.A.T. and, firing from the middle of the road without cover of any kind, scored a hit on the first tank and caused both of them to withdraw.[3]

Described as 'a character and well-liked and respected by all', and unable to pronounce his Rs ('wallying his twoops'), once Wyss and his men reached The Monastery he continued urging them on and taking on the responsibility (and immense personal risk) of using the PIAT to keep the German armour at bay. But his luck eventually ran out. Sergeant Norman Howes, from A Company:

> . . . heard Lt Col McCardie shout out, 'OSCAR, CAN YOU DO ANYTHING ABOUT THAT BLOODY TANK' . . . I heard Oscar shout out 'WIGHT-HO! SIR'. I then heard a terrible burst of Spandau – just like ripping linen. I heard Oscar call out 'Oh-Oh-Oh' and then silence. I could not see his body but I would guess it was about 10 metres away. The Padre Captain Buchanan was to my left and he said to me 'Cannot

we go and help him?' I replied 'Sir, He's dead'. My bravery was
not as great as his Christianity.[4]

It was around 0600 hrs when D Company had properly dug in
around The Monastery – it had taken two hours to get there from
the start of the attack some 400 metres back. 11th Battalion were, as
we have seen, caught up in this action, holding the South Staffords'
left flank on the other side of the road. B Company was coming up
but was considerably short of men.

As it grew lighter, the Germans were able to bring more targeted
fire to bear, particularly on the dell to the west of The Monastery. A
stand-off developed. The Germans couldn't get their infantry past
The Monastery, but similarly the men of the South Staffords knew
that appearing at a window would earn them a shelling. With them
was Lieutenant David Russell of 2nd Parachute Battalion, commanding 7 Platoon, who had been separated from their own
battalion on the Sunday, and then again from the men of 3rd Battalion whom they'd joined up with the day before:

> We were ordered to occupy the upstairs rooms and observe,
> but as no-one seemed interested in our reports, we carried on
> our own battle with any enemy movement we saw. We passed
> a target to the South Staffs Mortar Officer, who was in action
> close to the Museum, and at a minimum range, after a couple
> of sighting rounds, he engaged a M.G. post with great
> success – certainly it never came into action.[5]

Unable to bring 6-pounders up the slope on the higher road, the
South Staffords held on without serious anti-tank coverage. Also
with dawn had arrived the German armour. A combination of Bren
gunfire and PIAT bombs had encouraged the German tanks or self-
propelled guns to back off – the gunfire would force the vehicle's
commander to stay inside with the hatch down, and then, if the
man operating the PIAT could get close enough and get a bead on

the panzer, a blow from a PIAT bomb could be enough to get them to withdraw.

The Battalion War Diary from around this time reads:

> The Battalion continued to fight off the enemy and at about 0900 hrs tanks appeared. These were held off for about two hours by PIATs, but at approx 1100 hrs when all PIAT ammunition was exhausted, the tanks overran the position, inflicting heavy casualties and splitting the Battalion into pockets.

In the grounds of The Monastery there were men from A, B and D Companies, dug into the gardens beneath the lip of the road. Men from A Company had fought their way into the houses on the other side of the road, ideally to offer the chance of a further advance in towards the Town, and to attack the German blocking positions. Among them from B Company was Major Robert Cain.

Cain was a day late. His glider had been part of the First Lift on Sunday, but the tow rope had broken and anticlimactically he had landed in a field fifteen miles south-west of Canterbury; his pilot, Sergeant McGeary, complained that the same thing had happened to him on D-Day. Cain had rushed back to RAF Manston to try to find another glider but without initial success. Undeterred, he and his men cannibalized the seats from damaged and defunct gliders and fitted them to one they found without seats. At thirty-five, Cain was one of the older officers in the South Staffords.

Trying again with the Second Lift, he had finally caught up with his battalion. On his way into the Town, Cain had several encounters that sum up the surreal chaos of the battle coming to Arnhem: children smashing a framed photo of Hitler to pieces; a Dutchman in his nightshirt who offered him a wounded soldier's rifle and pack, mouthing the word 'Germans' while putting his fingers to his head, pistol-like; a German self-propelled gun with men patrolling, whom Cain attacked with a Bren gun, firing from the hip, killing the Germans.

Cain had realized that the PIAT was going to be central to his men's survival, especially if the advance to The Monastery was to be the high-water mark of the South Staffords this Tuesday morning. Together with Major Jock Buchanan of the South Staffords' Support Company, Cain ran the gauntlet to get PIAT ammunition forward to The Monastery and supply Lieutenant Dupenois with more rounds.

The PIAT itself was an effective enough close-range anti-tank weapon, if a somewhat peculiar piece of equipment. A spigot mortar, it fired a charge with a fine point, the idea being that the energy of the blast would be focused through the fine point and punch a hole through the skin of an armoured vehicle, or at least detach some metal inside it, which in turn would bounce around the inside of the tank causing damage to the crew. Now, and with hindsight, the PIAT might seem unconventional. It wasn't a recoil-less rocket system like the American bazookas or the German *Panzerschrecks*, but rather it fired its projectile by means of a charge triggered by a powerful spring. It says a little about the British Army in September 1944 that it was entirely conventional, the Army's premium one-man portable anti-tank weapon which had replaced the obsolete Boys anti-tank rifle.

Cocking the PIAT was far from easy: a man would have to put his feet on the shoulder plate and pull the cocking handle against the spring. This was even harder done when lying down, but the PIAT operator needed to make sure he was concealed from the armour-supporting infantry, as its practical range was under 50 yards. On firing, the PIAT bomb would be lobbed by its charge at the target; siting required offsetting the trajectory of the bomb, combined with some good luck and a little judgement. Men well trained or well practised on the PIAT, like many in the Town and the Village, could take on most, if not all, German armour providing they could get close enough. One huge advantage of the PIAT was the fact that it didn't give off the great whoosh and bang of its American and German equivalents and thus didn't reveal its operator's position so readily. Without a pyrotechnic flash, it also had the advantage of not setting fire to the curtains of the bedroom you might be hiding in. Men had been sceptical about this heavy, cumbersome piece of kit, but in close quarters it quickly proved its worth. It worked well as a short-range mortar too. In the fighting at The Monastery, mortars were being engaged with the enemy at such short range that their second-stage fuses were being disabled and the mortars fired from almost vertical tubes.

Major Cain wanted to try to break the deadlock. He knew there were British 6-pounders further down the hill. If he could deal with the German infantry accompanying the armour then he would, he figured, be able to coax that armour on to the guns. This the War Diary characterized as a:

> . . . period of waiting while the 11th Battalion prepared their attack, and all the time German opposition was definitely on the increase. In fact from about 0800 hrs the Battalion passed definitely on to the defensive. At that time a force, estimated at about one coy of German infantry, attacked D Coy on the right from the SE.

German infantry could be repulsed, 'easily' the War Diary even said, but their armour was much more of a problem.

Cain had decided to redeploy some men to the other side of the road and hold the houses there. This, he thought, would at least offer a second field of fire to the South Staffords and relieve the pressure on The Monastery. His men moved on to the first floors and prepared to defend the buildings. Immediately he realized this would not work, as it gave the Germans the chance to systematically shell the buildings his men had occupied. Rather than risking any infantry, they would simply smash and burn the South Staffords out. Nevertheless, with 11th Battalion on their left shoulder, there remained a chance of a flanking action that could hook round the Germans and relieve the situation on the higher road. Lieutenant Colonel McCardie started to hedge his bets and ordered his transport back to the Village and the Divisional HQ area.

What Divisional HQ knew about how the South Staffords were getting on, however, was sketchy, as the Divisional Signals War Diary makes clear: radio communications were still proving problematic, though there wasn't much Division could do in the immediate circumstances:

> At 0905 hrs the No 58 p set with 2 South Staffs was heard on the Div Comd net but it was so weak that comm could not be established. At 0947 hrs this was reestablished.

The Hartenstein's Divisional signals network was in contact with all but Lieutenant Colonel Frost at the Bridge, the Phantom and Recce radio net were working, and Public Relations were directly in touch with the War Office. Not that this made any difference in the Town.

The South Staffords War Diary for this part of the morning is confused, its accounts overlapping and, in some cases, contradicting each other. But that is hardly surprising. Times were approximate, men from different units were all jumbled together as we have seen, and all the while on the South Staffs' right flank, fighting on the lower road, were the men from what was left of 1st Parachute Brigade. They were being hammered from across the river, and, as on the higher road, increasingly by tanks and self-propelled guns. Fending off the tanks was the best they could hope for. What the South Staffs and the rest of the men fighting their way into the Town were not doing and could not do – because of the urgency to reach the Bridge and move forward – was lure the German armour on to the anti-tank guns that lay further back, to the west of the Bottleneck.

In 2nd Army in Normandy, anti-tank screens to deal with a German counter-attack were the norm, with German armour being tempted on to the guns. But now, with their 6-pounders so far back and unable to help, the South Staffords, caught in the confines of the Town, had to fight in narrow streets rather than open spaces which would have given them the ability to turn the enemy's flank. In turn, 1st Airborne's men were unable to bring their state-of-the-art anti-tank firepower to bear. Little wonder that the HQRA (Headquarters Royal Artillery) War Diary report wrote in a tone that seems to suggest exasperation:

> To give the details of the loss of each gun would be impossible, but four basic reasons are suggested.
>
> (1) The misuse of the 17 Pounders by using them as mobile Anti-Tank guns in the forward areas.
>
> (2) The failure of the infantry to realise that the tank must come to the gun and NOT the gun to the tank.
>
> (3) If the Infantry require a gun forward they must stay to see it out again.
>
> (4) The absence of any PIAT or similar projector for the flank or rear defence or for hunting local hulled down tanks.[6]

With Major Cain was Lieutenant Dupenois of B Company, who 'particularly distinguished himself by his bold use of this weapon' – but, as Cain observed, while fire from the PIAT might have hit the German armour, he was sure none of the tanks was actually knocked out. The PIAT worked as a deterrent, not a killer blow. So the tanks kept coming.

Further west, at around 1000 hrs, the 6-pounder under the command of Captain P. A. Taylor was able to have an effect. When the men of 11th Battalion were surprised by 'a number of tanks . . . considerable confusion ensued'. He was able to knock one tank out, and then stalk and hit another – but there had been nothing systematic about this defence. It was nothing more than a reflex action and only underlined what trouble the men in the Town were in.

By around 1100 hrs, six hours after they had commenced their attack on the Town, the PIAT ammunition had run out. The houses opposite The Monastery were on fire from German shelling. While the men in them tried to carry on firing on the enemy, without PIAT ammunition and with the tanks standing off out of range, the situation was sliding out of Lieutenant Colonel McCardie's control.

At a hastily called O Group, Cain observed that McCardie was worn out, done. Little wonder – the South Staffords were being pulled apart. The Monastery was being reduced to rubble, the building was in flames, the dell behind it wide open both to mortar fire and artillery from across the river: a 'deathtrap'. The flanking attack of 11th Battalion was, as far as McCardie knew, still pending, but the South Staffords' position had become untenable.

What remained of The Monastery was filling up with casualties. The Regimental Medical Officer, 'Basher' Brownscombe, had set up shop there with the help of the chaplain, a Church of Ireland man named Alan Buchanan. The chaplain saw the way the wind was blowing and had made the decision to evacuate The Monastery when the Germans – 'a large party of Boche' – having infiltrated the houses on the other side of the street, suddenly rushed the South Staffords. They were overwhelmed. A Company in the houses opposite – cut off from what was happening across the road – didn't receive the order to leave, or at least that's what the War Diary suggests. Major Cain ran for his life with a small party. Dashing through the flames back towards the Bottleneck, he eventually found some reassuringly deep trenches across the road from St Elisabeth Hospital, the South Staffords' 'square one', dug, he thought, for air-raid protection:

> Battalion HQ disappeared completely and it is believed, although still unconfirmed, that they were run down by a tank while in the act of withdrawing. The C.O. [McCardie] and 2IC have both been reported as wounded and prisoners of war.[7]

The South Staffords had fought their way into the Town and been dashed on the rocks of an implacable German defence before them. The men on the lower road had been similarly shattered, though without the relatively beguiling luxury of houses from which to fight. Having failed to relieve the South Staffords, 11th Battalion had been ordered to try to marry up with the rest of 4th Parachute Brigade, which was currently in the Woods. Perhaps there was another route into the Town, and the German flank could be turned. Perhaps Brigadier Hackett's men were going to save the day. And Major General Urquhart was clearly back in charge if fresh orders were coming in from Division. Captain Mawson at his aid post had met Urquhart when the major general had stopped to speak to him, heading west in his Jeep earlier in the morning. The command vacuum was over, so what decisions could, and did, 1st Airborne's returning commanding officer make?

13

THE VILLAGE: DIVISIONAL HQ AND ELSEWHERE

As it turned out, it would have been better if I had stayed a little longer to assess the local situation thereabouts and to co-ordinate these thrusts personally; for in the desperate and confused hours before us it became only too painfully clear that what was needed above all else was some co-ordination among the units fighting their way into Arnhem. If I had known this, I would have taken control on the spot.

Roy Urquhart, Arnhem

MAJOR GENERAL URQUHART'S RETURN TO Divisional HQ brought one drama to an end at least; Brigadier 'Pip' Hicks could return to 1st Airlanding Brigade's HQ and get on with handling his Brigade's tasks, albeit minus the 7th King's Own Scottish Borderers, who were still under Brigadier Hackett's command. Urquhart's chief of staff, Charles Mackenzie, quickly briefed his boss about Frost's force at the Bridge, the battalions now forcing their way into the Bottleneck, and the plan for Hackett to make for the high ground north of the railway line in the Woods.

Urquhart's batman, Hancock, appeared with tea and shaving kit and generally tidied him up. In the centre of the Divisional Administrative Area there remained an odd feeling of detachment, calm even, an acknowledgement that the fighting or the fighting to come was beyond the confines of the gentle streets and parkland of western Oosterbeek, a marked contrast to the bloody, knife-edge struggles at the Bridge and in the Town. The difference could hardly have been more pronounced, despite the odd mortar crashing in. The Germans were not bothering with the fringes of Oosterbeek at this time on Tuesday morning.

Urquhart's first decision – on a morning of decisions – was to ensure someone was in charge in the Town. He knew Brigadier Gerald Lathbury was *hors de combat* – he'd seen it for himself – but he'd rushed back to his headquarters without taking time to find the senior officers in the Town. Moreover, neither Hicks nor Hackett, for all their midnight drama, had thought to appoint someone to take control of the battle in the Town. Urquhart chose Hicks's number two, Colonel Hilaro Barlow, second-in-command of 1st Airlanding Brigade, for the task. In the event of Market Garden being a success, Barlow's appointed role was town commandant of Arnhem. Aged thirty-seven and from an army family, Barlow was every inch a professional soldier, had raised one of the parachute battalions, the 7th, from scratch, and had been running 1st Airlanding Brigade's battle while Hicks had been in charge of the Division.

At around 0800 hrs Barlow and his batman set off in a Jeep with a radio set, on their way to take control of the four battalions in the Town. At last, some semblance of order would be brought to things in the bid to reach John Frost.

Barlow never made it. Divisional HQ never heard from him again, and as is clear from the progress of the battle in the Town above, he did not feature in the fate of the battalions fighting there. As Barlow and his batman, Lance Corporal Raymond Singer, made their way into the Town, they ran into men from the South Staffords and Barlow stopped to ask a captain what was going on when suddenly mortaring began. As they ran to a house for cover a mortar crashed down on them, obliterating Barlow and killing Singer. As the chaos erupted in the Town, and the battalions continued to lose their cohesion, Barlow's death became a story of mysterious disappearance: 'he was never seen again'.

Bad luck continued to dog Roy Urquhart. He might be safely

back in his headquarters making decisions, but his ability to exert influence over the battle for the Town was snuffed out, and he didn't know it. The situation was changing quickly, and taking command of it was becoming harder and harder. Perhaps that critical moment would never come again.

Aware that Hackett might still be fuming after the row in the early hours, the next decision Urquhart took was to make sure things were on track in the Woods. He sent Charles Mackenzie and with him Colonel Loder-Symonds, Commander Royal Artillery, to 4th Parachute Brigade's HQ. He wanted to know how Hackett was getting on, and to ensure he knew what support he could expect in terms of gunnery. Urquhart's envoys relayed the message that, should Hackett have the time, the GOC would like to see him in person. Times for this differ quite dramatically: the Divisional Diary says it was at 0845 hrs, Hackett's diary 1000 hrs. On any other day travelling in a Jeep, Hackett's HQ, on the far side of the railway line, was a ten-minute drive at most. But with mortars clanging in, Me 109s suddenly above them, or the odd sniper taking shots, it was a longer and less straightforward journey. Even though the exact extent of the difficulties that 1st Airborne faced were becoming clear to Urquhart, he made no changes to Hackett's plans that morning. Changing course in the Woods was not going to be an option.

Making use of the apparent calm at Divisional HQ was George Pare, padre to the No. 1 Glider Pilot Wing. Pare had flown out in the First Lift on Sunday alongside Lieutenant Colonel Murray, his CO; Murray had piloted Major General Urquhart's Horsa glider and Pare was excited at the prospect of going into action before the war was almost over. Pare had found the landing, in glittering sunlight, unimaginable by comparison with what he'd experienced a year before in Sicily. Like so many of the men landing on Sunday, his march into the Village had given him the chance to sample Dutch hospitality, trying some ersatz coffee, and to talk to the locals who reassured him how much they hated the Germans. As soon as the shooting began, the civilians understandably dispersed. But the mood was still hugely confident; the consensus that Sunday afternoon was that the war was as good as over.

Padre Pare had helped with the wounded in the aftermath of the landings, noting that the Germans were scrupulously respectful of the Red Cross. Moving men out of burning gliders, he realized several times that he was leaving himself exposed to German machine-gun fire, which lifted when he moved men into the open and away from the gliders. He had had to rebuke one man who was unable to leave the body of his dead comrade, to get the man off the Landing Zone. There were fifteen chaplains as part of 1st Airborne's complement, who arrived as and when the units they accompanied did. When chaplains were first attached to airborne units they realized pretty quickly that they would have to undergo parachute training and endure the same hardships as the men to whom they were offering succour. In North Africa and Sicily the padres had become an integral part of the field ambulance, extending their role to the care of the wounded, the dying and the dead. Pare's duties, therefore, included the burial of the dead, even the enemy.

Generalmajor Friedrich Kussin had been the Stadtkommandant of Arnhem until Sunday afternoon, when he had run into the men of 3rd Battalion, the platoon commanded by Jimmy Cleminson, whose moustache Major General Urquhart would find so irksome in the loft on Monday night. Kussin had driven straight into Cleminson's men as they moved on from their Drop Zone: not that they knew who he was – to the men he was a German general and almost instantly a dead one at that. Perhaps capturing him might have been more sensible. But what could better symbolize the enemy being caught out by the epic Allied landings than one of the enemy's top brass being gunned down?

Cleminson had had to stop his men from continuing to fire at Kussin's car, as ammunition was more precious than their enthusiasm. Kussin's body, hanging half out of his Citroën, his scalp torn open on the tarmac, his cigarette burned down to his dead fingers, was seen by hundreds of British soldiers as they made their way east towards battle. With him were his driver and batman, Gefreiter Josef Willeke, and Unteroffizier Max Köster. To the troops rushing by, they were merely dead Germans. Kussin had been trying to find out what was going on and left his headquarters to get the gen on what the German response was. If anyone illustrated the perils of rushing around an airborne battlefield, it was the late Generalmajor. That something similar hadn't happened to Roy Urquhart was perhaps miraculous. The following day, Monday, Sergeant Dennis Smith of the Army Film and Photograph Unit had used a few seconds of his precious footage to film the dead Generalmajor as men streamed past him. It is one of the most striking images from the Battle, even if the black-and-white means we can't see his red tabs the way the men who killed him did. But come Tuesday, his body needed to be buried.

Having finally bedded down at about 0300 hrs on Tuesday morning, a couple of hours later Padre Pare rose, had something to eat and made his way to the Hartenstein Hotel. He caught up with Lieutenant Colonel Murray and the rest of the staff from the Wing, who had taken one of the rooms in the hotel as their headquarters and home. Pare had lost his backpack, but there was food enough prepared by Murray's batman. There was much talk of course that Urquhart was missing. In one respect the rumours were right, on the other hand they were wrong, also suggesting that the Assistant Director of Medical Services – the Division's chief medical officer Colonel Warrack – had been taken prisoner. On the battlefield rumours were not reliable, but for all that while 'the news was not so good . . . everybody was confident'.[1]

The padre wasn't the only man with faith that morning. While he went looking for the senior chaplain, Pare came down the steps of the Hartenstein Hotel at the very moment Urquhart reappeared – Pare was stunned to see him. As Urquhart explained where he had been and his adventures in escaping, Pare noted that the moment offered a 'great resurgence in confidence'.[2] Whatever might be happening elsewhere – and who truly knew what that was at the

Hartenstein at that point – Roy Urquhart's reappearance gave the men in the Divisional Administrative Area the boost they felt they needed. This diversion aside, Pare then met up with the senior chaplain, 'Bill' Harlow. They ate some stew and then Harlow gave Pare his tasks for the morning: burying the dead, and among them Generalmajor Kussin.

Pare took a Jeep, his batman and driver, and a couple of young German prisoners of war he had been loaned. The POWs sat on the bonnet of the Jeep as he drove back to the crossroads on the main road at Wolfheze. The POWs had been promised food for their labours and Pare gave them chocolate and cigarettes; he didn't feel any particular animosity towards the Germans. A single grave was dug on the roadside for all three men: Kussin, Willeke and Köster. The body of a Dutch woman was also lying nearby, but Pare decided to leave her there. As they were burying the Generalmajor and his two colleagues, German planes flew over and buzzed the Divisional Administrative Area, so Pare made the small party take cover under the trees lining the road. In this idle moment, he struck up conversation with the German POWs, whom he reckoned were seventeen or eighteen years old. He asked them what they thought of the war. Their answers are fascinating:

> 'Don't you think war is foolish?' I asked.
> 'No.'
> 'Why not?'
> 'Germany must live.'
> 'She is living.'
> 'Yes, but we must have space to live.'
> 'You have space enough.'
> 'But you have an Empire. We must fight.'
> Several questions and answers gave me similar replies.[3]

Given that Pare knew that the war was almost over, and the feeling within the Division that it was time to get into action before it was too late, this exchange points straight at why the Germans, especially ones this young, might still be fighting, and also why they might believe that the war was not yet over.

With crosses made from wood gathered from the house by the crossroads, and having tidied up the grave of a soldier from Chester buried by the men guarding the crossroads, Pare and his charges headed back towards the Hartenstein Hotel. They picked up two more corpses, loaded them on stretchers on to the Jeep, and then took them back to Divisional HQ, where the two German POWs buried them before rejoining the other POWs being kept in the tennis courts next to the Hartenstein.

Among the hundreds of glider pilots who had landed on Sunday and Monday was Sergeant Louis Hagen. He was a German Jew, his father a banker who had had the money and connections to enable Louis to escape Germany. Louis Hagen had a freewheeling spirit. He had spent the early period of the war during which he was an illegal alien likely to be interned working in theatres, sleeping in their scene docks. He drove a car – even though he wasn't allowed so much as a bicycle – and in the end, when up before the beak to argue for his liberty, called on his Liberal Party connections to vouch for him. Although he described himself as a light-hearted young man at the time of Market Garden, Hagen had the measure of the enemy. In 1934, when he was eighteen, he had sent a postcard to his sister bawdily lampooning the Blackshirts. Unfortunately, she left the card lying around where it was discovered by a maid. Louis was arrested at work at BMW and imprisoned in Torgau castle, which had been repurposed as a concentration camp. He spent six weeks there, witnessing and experiencing degrading torture. This personal brush with Nazi tyranny sent the family into action – it was time to leave Germany before it was too late.

While Louis managed to dodge any consequences for ignoring the regulations surrounding his being an illegal alien, the law did eventually catch up with him in England, and the authorities then wanted to try him for desertion. Life as a German Jew in Britain during the war was a sliding floor. He joined the Pioneer Corps, where aliens were trusted with digging ditches but not much else. As the war progressed, things became less restrictive and he volunteered for a series of different trades within the Army. But it was the Glider Pilot Regiment that had captured his imagination:

> One of the very last regiments that was prepared to accept 'enemy aliens' was the Army Air Corps' Glider Pilot Regiment, which was officially formed on 24 February 1942. Of course I immediately volunteered for this: to become a pilot was the ultimate goal, not only for me, but also for thousands of other soldiers of all ranks.
>
> I have never been to an interview in such a state of excitement. I felt that if I was accepted I would be the luckiest man alive. I still remember how I disliked being treated as a third-class citizen in Germany and a foreigner in Britain. Becoming a British pilot would be a miraculous change.[4]

Even though he found a great deal of the work that went with it rather challenging, Hagen took immense pride in his training. He also bucked against the baggage that came with the way the Glider Pilot Regiment had been set up – the men were trained as pilots by the RAF but treated as Guardsmen by the Regiment's NCOs. Hagen did not appreciate the latter – he had an aversion to Army bullshit. It almost cost him his job; thankfully, his potential as a pilot in the end overrode his aptitude for ironing creases.

On Sunday he and his lead pilot had flown in three men from 156 Battalion and a Jeep. After a struggle with getting the tail off and the runners down for the Jeep to get away, Hagen and 'Mac' made their way to the rendezvous on the edge of the Landing Zone. Around the Wolfheze level crossing they saw a confusion of Jeeps and guns and men organizing themselves and leaving the LZ areas. In the melee, Hagen spotted another pilot who had ripped him off for a fiver when going on leave. They had a brief argument about it and then fell about laughing at the thought of conducting such petty business while on an operation. The surreal turns kept coming: as he passed the lunatic asylum, whose patients had been turfed out to make way for British casualties, in the crowds of soldiers flirting with Dutch girls Hagen was then mistaken by some Dutch nurses for Prince Bernhard of the Netherlands. He gave away sweets and cigarettes, made his excuses and left. The glider pilots formed up in a column and marched on towards Arnhem cursing their heavy backpacks. After turning round and coming back half the way they'd come, though no one explained why, at 0200 hrs on Tuesday they'd bedded down for the night.

In effect the Glider Pilot Wings were part of Urquhart's Divisional reserve. They had been trained, in theory at least, to be all-round soldiers with Guards Brigade-style discipline. But they were a long way from being infantry specialists like the men of the parachute or airlanding brigades. With their skill as pilots, they were a precious asset. American glider pilots, by contrast, were not trained as soldiers and would return to a rendezvous and sit things out. During the Normandy landings, 6th Airborne's glider pilots had been evacuated within a couple of days of D-Day. At Arnhem this was planned to be the case too, if and when 2nd Army arrived. For now, though, the glider pilots were a rather useful chunk of potential manpower at the Division's disposal.

One of the men who'd been recycled from Normandy was Captain Iain Muir. He'd taken to his role as an all-round soldier, being a former gunner, and had been mentioned in despatches for manning a 6-pounder in the fighting around Ranville. Muir took command of the group of thirty glider pilots that Louis Hagen was a part of, when they were then placed under the command of A Company of 156 Battalion. After standing-to before first light, they went back to a wood near the original rendezvous.

As they waited, they were strafed by German fighters. Just moments before, the glider pilots had been arguing what kind of aircraft they were – only to be settled when the planes opened fire on them. No one was hurt but this was not meant to be happening. Then the order came for the glider pilots to clear the nearby wood of the enemy. The battle for the Woods was about to begin. Having proved himself as a pilot, Hagen would now have to find out what kind of soldier he truly was.

Coalescing around the Divisional Administrative Area were the service troops of 1st Airborne Division. Within the glider detail of the two lifts, there were 863 items listed as 'other vehicles'. The Jeep was central to the way the Division would function. They were used for everything, from the Recce Squadron's attempt on Sunday to dash to the Bridge, stymied as it was by indecision, poor communication and enemy ambush, to moving men, guns, supplies, the wounded – Jeeps were ubiquitous and essential. The Jeeps used by British airborne forces had been literally cut down in size by Nuffield Mechanizations and Aero Limited to reduce weight and width, to make sure they would fit into a Horsa glider. They were further adapted, and the techniques to load them and artillery pieces and other loads into gliders refined, at the Airborne Forces Development Centre at Amesbury Abbey. This incorporated an experimental REME workshop. And the REME were in Arnhem to keep the Jeeps going.

Like the other arms of 1st Airborne, the REME's craftsmen and mechanics were distributed among the fighting units where they would be needed, as well as having a central Divisional workshop, the Advance Workshop Detachment. The REME itself was a new Regiment, founded in 1942 and designed to maintain other existing Corps: the Ordnance Corps, the Sappers, Signals, Service and the Royal Artillery. However, because the REME was new, its men were not allowed to take on the work of pre-existing established unit mechanics. Seventy-five men from the REME went to Arnhem, twenty-seven of them with the fighting units in what were designated Light Aid Detachments. Many had already served in Sicily and some had worked with Popski's Private Army in North Africa (named after its founder and CO, Lieutenant-Colonel Vladimir 'Popski' Peniakoff). They too were keen to get into action.

The men in Arnhem were the tip of the REME effort. There was a seaborne REME component too, though that hadn't been part of the original plan. Under the command of Lieutenant Colonel Richard T. L. Shorrock, who had been part of 'Boy' Browning's core 'Dungeon Party', a group of officers whose job it was to brainstorm airborne warfare ideas, this party had not got to Holland as planned. An engineer and haulage man in the brick trade, managing production in Marston outside Bedford, Shorrock had the experience ideally suited to running a large mechanical and logistic concern. Slated to fly into Brussels with a fully independent workshop, he had been thwarted; his men had had to unload their gliders and travel to Holland by sea. On 19 September he was caught up in a 2nd Army traffic jam.

Joe Roberts[5] did get to Arnhem, however. Roberts was the REME clerk. Four Horsa gliders bearing mechanics were despatched to Arnhem, with motorcycles, hand trailers and folding bikes. Landing on Sunday in REME glider No. 4, Roberts had travelled with a welder, Corporal Bonthron, Craftsman Fielding, a 'tele mech', and Artificer Quartermaster Sergeant Turner with a Jeep and welding trailer. Getting from the Landing Zone and finding other REME personnel had proved tricky for Roberts and his folding bike. Spotting another REME man at Wolfheze, Roberts hitched a lift in a Jeep, passing Generalmajor Kussin's body at the crossroads. When the Jeep stopped in a queue of traffic he saw his unit cycling past him. He unfolded his bike and chased after them. Roberts's job was to do the workshop's paperwork, though as things got hotter he didn't get much done. But there was nevertheless work aplenty, keeping guns in good order, repairing Jeeps and maintaining radios. Sergeant John Morrison, who was an Armament Artificer, Telemechanics, wrote:

> On the wireless side, we had to do a good deal of improvisation. One thing of which we were called on to do pretty

frequently was the repair of battery leads. Perhaps the most unusual job we did was to improvise a choke for a No. 76 set by scraping down a piece of wire until we got the resistance right.

The armourers were even busier. Their Quartermasters went out with a jeep round the units in their various positions collecting damaged equipment and taking out the repaired stuff. This repair work was very important, for there were no replacements and there was a lot of damage done to the small arms and automatics by the kind of fighting that was going on.[6]

For the REME men in the Divisional Administrative Area, the same sense of calm reigned. For the Craftsmen in the fighting elements, things were very different, as they were caught up in events, having to fight as infantry. And there were three very different battles being fought – at the Bridge, in the Town and in the Woods.

Hanging over Urquhart, beyond the questions of what to do in the Town and the Woods, was the matter of 1st Airborne's timetable. Whatever freedom of action he may have had in deciding which officers to send where and how to employ his battalions on Tuesday morning, he was restricted in what he could do by the air plan. The Third Lift was expected that morning – the Polish parachutists, their gliders and heavy equipment, as well as a further supply drop.

Yesterday's lift had been held up by the weather in England. Had 4th Parachute Brigade arrived on time (the appearance of German fighters over the Drop and Landing Zones notwithstanding), Brigadier Hackett's men might have tipped the balance on Monday. As it was, they wouldn't be going into action until first light on Tuesday. Time hadn't been squandered so much as lost. For all his misfortune that came from going forward, for all the enemy's intervention on Sunday which had held up his 1st Parachute Brigade, the weather had a vote, a casting vote it could be said. And in delaying the Second Lift, the weather had picked its side.

Urquhart and his staff were keenly aware that this was far from ideal. The scale of the air side of Market Garden is hard to overstate. The RAF had committed two Groups, 38 and 46, offering a total of sixteen squadrons, of Dakotas and Stirlings and the odd Albemarle. These aircraft and their crews were needed elsewhere, as the Allied lines grew longer in the Great Swan out of Normandy. Aircraft had been needed to augment the remaining Mulberry Harbours' ability to keep up with the need for fuel, food and ammunition.[7] Time diverted from that primary task was viewed extremely jealously by everyone outside the airborne world. But changing an air plan with so many moving parts – squadrons to contact, re-brief, re-route, altering the timetable – would be next to impossible. Cooperation and contact between 1st Airborne and the air elements would need to work perfectly for Urquhart to be able to make any changes to Tuesday's timetable. What he wanted to do was redirect the Poles from their planned Drop Zone on the south of the river to the Drop Zone near the Village, and make sure that the supply drop would not go to the planned Drop Zone 'S', which he knew his men did not hold. He was worried the Poles might be in for a 'sticky reception'.

Given that 1st Airborne's ability to act rested on cooperation with its air component, there was a surprising lack of belt and braces in its approach to making sure it was something that would run smoothly. Urquhart recollected ordering a change to Tuesday's air plan: 'these messages however did not get through,' he recalled. At 0947 hrs the Divisional Signals Diary reported that 'Phantom' – a pair of officers from the GHQ Liaison Regiment – was in contact with 30 Corps, as well as the Public Relations radio with the War Office. So the means to speak to London as well as 2nd Army were in place. Urquhart therefore had his messages sent.

With the issue of air cooperation hanging over him, and hoping for answers from England to his requests for changes, Urquhart found a further irksome problem around air power exerting itself that morning. German fighter aircraft were in the skies over Arnhem. The mere presence of the Luftwaffe over the Arnhem battlefield was a shock after a summer during which it had been conspicuous by its absence. The Allies had dominance of the skies. Certainly, the men of 1st Airborne waiting in England to go into action, reading the papers about what was happening in Normandy during the summer, would have got the impression that the Allies had air cover on tap. Close air support, the hallmark of Operation Overlord that summer: where was it now?

The system in place in Normandy, 2nd Tactical Air Force's 'cab rank', in which squadrons of Typhoons and Thunderbolts would attack targets they were called to and then look for further targets of opportunity, was dependent on two things: proximity to the front and good radio communications. Montgomery had a keen understanding of how decisive tactical air power could be. It was something he had sought to get right in the desert and he had developed a close working relationship with Air Marshal Sir Arthur Coningham ('Maori' or 'Mary' by nickname). Their personal relationship had undergone the usual Monty ups and downs, and once Operation Overlord was in full flow it had deteriorated almost completely. But they had at least developed a winning formula and reputation for plastering the Germans with aerial firepower that complemented the available artillery.

A central priority of the Normandy landings had been establishing airfields within the lodgement. Building airstrips had begun the day after D-Day. As a result, aircraft were available within minutes when called upon, or in the skies above, often for sorties lasting no longer than an hour, without the need to fly across the Channel before being at the disposal of the land forces. How 2nd Tactical Air Force had played its role in the Normandy campaign was central to the logistic, tactical and strategic picture of Operation Overlord. The aircraft were prioritized and integrated. However, this process had taken the entire campaign to refine and perfect, and the weather would of course once again cast its vote. Also at Montgomery's disposal were aircraft from Bomber Command – redirected from

strategic bombing over Bomber Harris's near-dead body. As we have
seen, when faced with the problem of capturing a city, Caen, in the
east of Normandy, Bomber Command had been called upon to
completely destroy the city rather than waste soldiers' lives on street
fighting.

But the changing nature of the campaign also changed what tactical air power could accomplish. While fighter bombers dominated
the skies and broke the Lüttich counter-offensive between 7 and 11
August, and queued over the German land army during the battle
for the Falaise Gap that followed, this dominance was merely a
function of the way the battle had played out. German resistance
had slowed down the development of the front, giving the Allies
time to build up their airfields between Caen and Bayeux. The
muscle memory and expertise that had been built up over the two
and a half months of fighting in Normandy, as well as the plain tactical advantage of having aircraft immediately on hand, were
dissipated by the break out and the Great Swan that followed.
Having adapted to the Overlord battle, 2nd Tactical Air Force would
have to adapt again. Pressure on resources, transport and equipment came into play. Provision was made to have three forward
operational airfields keeping up with Monty's advance. One option
was to use captured German airfields, but these had been smashed
up by the RAF and USAAF during the campaign and then liberally
mined and booby-trapped by the retreating Luftwaffe. In addition,
sappers were hard pressed with bridging tasks to keep the tanks
moving. Transport was hard to coordinate and always, always in
short supply. Ensuring telephone communications for the forward
airfields was similarly challenging.

In short, by September, 2nd Tactical Air Force was operating under
radically different circumstances to the Normandy campaign in
which it had dominated the skies. However, the existing communications net with 2nd Army remained; the muscle memory of
calling in fighter bombers was still in place in 2nd Army, and with

21st Army Group's systems. But 1st Airborne Division was not a part of either: Urquhart's men were not practised and seasoned close-air-support clients. The impression the men of 1st Airborne may have got of Allied air power over the summer, as they waited across the Channel to go into battle, and the expectations they brought with them to Arnhem, were not aligned with the reality of the situation.

So, with Typhoon squadrons from 83 Group based around Brussels and Antwerp, there were fighter bombers available to 2nd Army. But the commitments demanded of them by Market Garden were very different from what had been asked of them in Normandy. With 30 Corps, US 82nd and 101st Airborne in the 'corridor' to Arnhem, not forgetting the two other Corps in 21st Army Group, there were a lot of bases to cover.

Crucially – after all, this was central to the strategy Market Garden had embraced – Arnhem itself was one hundred miles north-east from where 83 Group's planes were stationed. Time over target was reduced: precious fuel spent getting there compromised how long the Typhoons had to loiter. Furthermore, picking out and striking targets in built-up areas was that much more difficult than in open countryside, especially if pilots wanted to be confident of not killing British soldiers. D-Day had seen a litany of such bloody accidents; more recently the tragedy of the USAAF bombing ahead of the bomb-line at the start of Operation Cobra, killing 111 men and injuring 490 on the ground, even when 8th US Air Force had known where these men were. For an airborne operation in terrain unfamiliar to pilots and soldiers alike, the possibility of such tragic mistakes was a near certainty. And of course there was the weather to consider. It was September, nearing the Equinox. While fighters were available for flak suppression on Sunday, the weather delayed them on Monday, and a bomb-line around the supply flights would be in effect on Tuesday, to avoid striking men on the ground. Yet events as they were playing out on the ground meant that at best the bomb-line was out of date.

Air support for Market Garden was going to do what it was capable of doing, rather than what some people, perhaps unfamiliar with its capabilities and their complexities, might imagine it could. And, remarkably, Sir Arthur Coningham, whose frustration with transport aircraft being held back for the series of airborne operations had been widely broadcast, was only consulted regarding Market Garden on Saturday 16 September, three days before Roy Urquhart needed to call on a change to the air plan. Whether they worked or not, radios were not what was shaping the air battle. The sheer gigantic complexity of running a tactical air force on the move was challenge enough.

But Padre Pare's observation that confidence was high on Tuesday morning is perhaps reflected in the decisions that were made at Divisional Headquarters, and perhaps the state of play between the personalities in 1st Airborne. Despite landing late, 4th Parachute Brigade were going to try to execute the plan that had been cooked up the week before. Hackett's desire to do something decisive with his Brigade – or rather what he had been left with – had been the key factor in launching the battle for the Woods, and Urquhart didn't see reason in the hour or so after he had reappeared to disagree. Perhaps he didn't fancy another row with the fiery Hackett, whose enthusiasm to get into the Germans could not be faulted. The Woods were where 1st Airborne could open a fresh angle of attack. They were going to stick, essentially, to Plan A. And meanwhile, elsewhere, Plan A seemed to be working.

14

THE VILLAGE: ALARUMS AND EXCURSIONS IN THE WEST

At 1900 hrs Battalion moved off LZ 'Z' to Phase II position.
Many gliders by this time were in flames. All gliders had
now arrived, including those missing from first day, with the
exception of the CO.

1st Battalion Border Regiment Diary

ALTHOUGH THEIR COMMANDING OFFICER, Lieutenant Colonel
Haddon, hadn't made it to Holland, 1st Battalion the Border Regiment had had a time less dramatic than the men in the Town, and
had fought its battles tidily. They had been ordered to defend the
Drop Zones and Landing Zones for the Second Lift, so by the end of
Monday their task was complete. As the westernmost units of 1st Airborne, the Battalion's four companies had been guarding the vast
open spaces that comprised LZ-X and LZ-Z: A Company at the top
in the wooded area that backed on to the railway line; C Company
back at Wolfheze by the asylum; and D Company at the bottom of
the Landing Zones. A Company had lost seven men when they had
run out to greet fighter planes they had mistaken for Allied aircraft,
but it was B Company who had had by far the toughest day.

B Company were situated in the hamlet of Renkum, three miles
west of Oosterbeek on the Utrechtseweg, the road that ran up away
from the river and into the centre of the Village. On the Sunday they
had taken up a well-established position in the brickworks that

overlooked the river and the road. Being thorough, they had quickly laid a line for communications with Battalion HQ.

Rushing reinforcements into Arnhem, the Germans had sent men along this road. At first light it became clear that they had occupied a house opposite B Company's stronghold. A morning of firefights followed, during which two German prisoners captured the day before were killed. Even though the Germans had B Company surrounded, carelessness seemed to characterize the German approach, as officers strolled around with maps, unaware of where B Company's machine guns might be sighted. When Lieutenant Joe Harvey alerted Battalion HQ to their predicament, they were ordered to 'fight your way out!'

By 1400 hrs it was obvious that they were outnumbered and outgunned. The Germans had got their act together and were now pressing hard, sniping machine-gun posts and then setting a stable on fire as a marker for directing mortars. A hastily devised plan for withdrawal by B Company was hatched. If the Germans could be convinced the brickworks remained occupied, there was dead ground to the rear that would allow B Company to slip away and head east. As 11 Platoon created the illusion that the company was still in place, the rest made their way out, with fixed bayonets as a precaution, just as it appeared a major attack was going in on the brickworks. They only recovered one of their Jeeps, and spiked two of their anti-tank guns – named after battles of the Great War: 'Ypres' and 'Somme'. The men also left behind their small packs and brought ammunition instead, the old airborne dilemma of bullets versus food. Thinking that 2nd Army would arrive soon, what did it matter? The company had handled itself extremely well, and while men had been lost, guns notwithstanding, it had escaped mostly intact. On getting back in contact with the rest of the Battalion, Joe Harvey wrote:

> We were greeted as conquering heroes. After all, we had knocked off quite a lot of the enemy; we had been surrounded by a far superior force; and we had fought our way

out. It hardly seemed necessary at the time to tell people that
we had sneaked out through the back entrance.[1]

However, Monday's action at the brickworks made it plain that the
Germans were taking the landings at Arnhem seriously, and that a
company isolated, away from the mutual covering fire of the rest of
its Battalion, could end up in deep trouble very quickly. Being
defeated piecemeal by the Germans was not something B Company
could countenance. D Company, being closest to the fighting at the
brickworks and the western entry point for German reinforcements,
also fought off probing attacks. One of their anti-tank guns, 'Gallipoli', engaged a German tank at about one hundred yards. After
'Gallipoli' fired one round, the panzer withdrew.

The men on the guns were struggling with the new armour-
piercing sabot round with which they had been equipped and
which comprised 75 per cent of the ammunition brought to Arnhem.
This made the 6-pounder a much more effective anti-tank weapon –
if one had trained with it. The discarding sabot, the tungsten dart's
casing that flew out of the gun and fell away when the round
was fired, was confusing the gunners who mistook it for the fall of
shot – the flight of the round on to the target – so they didn't like it
one bit. 'The gun-layers had reached a high degree of efficacy with
the old ammunition and to send us to war with this new ammunition we all believed was an error of judgement.'[2] The Commander
Royal Artillery, Colonel Robert Loder-Symonds, concurred in his
report:

> Sabot proved very difficult to observe, though whenever used
> invariably silenced the opposition. It was never possible to
> check up the amount of damage done by any one round.
>
> I am of the opinion that if we had studied more closely
> the type of country we were to fight in, with ammunition per-
> formance in mind, a greater proportion of APCBC (as against
> SABOT) would have been taken.[3]

This suggests that the new round was something the men hadn't been trained with adequately. As ever, having the snazziest and best kit only gave you an advantage if it was matched with the right training.

At the end of Monday, the four Border companies had moved to their Phase II positions, leaving the Landing Zones behind them, gliders still burning in the gloom, and tightened up back towards the Village. After all of its exertions at the brickworks, B Company made its way through the crossroads at Wolfheze, where General-major Kussin's body lay half out of his shot-up Citroën. Moving around in the early morning dark to take up their positions, their day had ended quietly, but ten men had been killed.

Unlike the parachute battalions, which were fresh creations, 1st Battalion the Border Regiment was an old army fighting Battalion that in 1936 had helped to suppress the Arab Revolt in Palestine. The men had subsequently fought as part of the British Expeditionary Force sent to France in 1939, and had retreated from Tournai, jinking around Lille, on their way back to Dunkirk and escape. The campaign in France had been costly, 250 men killed, wounded or taken prisoner. Rebuilding followed in 1940 and 1941, and with it a new role. The Battalion joined 31st Independent Infantry Brigade, with 1st Battalion Royal Ulster Rifles, 2nd Battalion Ox and Bucks, and 2nd Battalion South Staffordshire Regiment. They were despatched to Wales for training in the Black Mountains. Indian muleteers joined the Battalion to handle the mules carrying the mortar ammunition.

In September 1941, 31st Brigade was re-badged again as 1st Air-landing Brigade, and Brigadier George Hopkinson selected to command it. 1st Borderers said goodbye to the mules and hello to the emerging glider technology. The Horsa glider, which would be their means of transport to Arnhem, had not yet been unveiled, and the Hotspur was the glider of choice. Having moved to Salisbury Plain, trials began. In December a Hotspur crashed, killing six on board. Mercifully the Hotspur only carried a maximum of eight troops. The men of 1st Borderers were well engaged with their new role, men volunteering to be pilots and to take flight in the new aircraft regardless of how obviously dangerous they were. But, like the parachute battalions, they were stalled by the RAF's reluctance to spare aircraft as tugs and the still undefined role for airborne forces. Hopkinson was evangelical in his belief that gliders were the way forward, and demonstrations were laid on for Winston Churchill to show what progress had been made with this new weapon.

Horsa gliders finally started to appear in 1942 and these offered planners the possibility of landing entire platoons. But it was to take many months of rehearsals, exercises and theorizing before they were used operationally, in Operation Freshman, the attempt in November 1942 to destroy the Vemork Norsk Hydro heavy-water plant in Telemark, Norway. It was a complete failure: the pair of Horsas crashed and the sappers on board were either killed then or murdered afterwards by the Germans. A Halifax tug was also lost, which neatly illustrated the issues the Air Ministry had about loaning precious bombers. The Special Operations Executive (SOE) informed London of the fate of the men who had been murdered.

As 1943 dawned, the North Africa campaign loomed on the horizon, 1st Parachute Brigade having already been dispatched there in November. Commanding the Division such as it was, the evangelical Hopkinson was not going to miss a chance to prove his contention that delivering men by gliders would work better than inserting them by parachute. And thus was the disaster in Sicily set in motion. Of 1st Airlanding Brigade and the Glider Pilot Regiment, 600 men were killed. 1st Battalion the Border Regiment set off for Sicily with 796 men and returned to North Africa with 15 officers and 214 other ranks. The almost terminally depleted Airlanding Brigade was kept back from the landings in Italy. If Sicily was supposed to make the case for inserting men by glider, then the case definitely hadn't been made; but the powers that be stuck with the idea, the lessons of the landings were taken on, training for pilots of both the gliders and their tugs improved, and plans refined.

Replacement troops were drafted in and the Battalion was gradually rebuilt to include Canadian officers from the CANLOAN
scheme, which by 1944 was in full flow, even though it had delivered
fewer volunteers than hoped; the reasoning was that the Canadian
Army had a surplus of officers and could spare them. Six hundred
and seventy-three men were eventually recruited, short of the fifteen
hundred hoped for. The War Office was picky about whom it took,
demanding volunteers who were fit, already qualified and trained.
French Canadians were viewed as a potential liability: 'some officers
who were quite understandable in ordinary conversation became
unintelligible over a No. 18 radio set in the heat of battle'.[4] These
men started arriving in April and managed to fit in well with their
units. Four served with the Border Regiment in Arnhem.

Tuesday had started quietly. The Borderers were dug in. By mid-
morning there were reports that the enemy had crossed the Rhine,
using a ferry at Doorwerth a couple of miles west. Had B Company
not left Renkum on Monday afternoon, they would have had to
deal with these Germans in their rear as well as those out front.
Under a mortar bombardment, pressure and casualties started to
mount, though realistically nothing like what those battalions
trying to advance towards the Bridge were suffering. In defensive
positions, the Borderers could hold fast, keep their lines tidy, with
the companies working in combination to keep the Germans at bay.
Unfortunately 17 Platoon in C Company had lost a hand trolley in
the morning's mortaring, and with it their ammunition supply, but
otherwise things were ticking over relatively calmly. The Germans
were after all putting their main effort into protecting the approaches
to the Bridge. And anyway, a supply run was due at 1500 hrs. There
would be more ammo: the plan said so.

These new positions were in the woods and parkland to the east
of Oosterbeek, amidst a terrain of rolling hillocks, quite different to
the dense forestry to the north of the Village where 4th Parachute
Brigade were fighting.

The southern approaches might be secure on the western side of the Village, but it was around A Company's position, near the railway line, that concern was growing that the Germans might prise their way through. Self-propelled guns were reported by men of 156 Battalion on the Borderers' doorstep. Losing the Wolfheze level crossing to the Germans would effectively amputate 4th Brigade from the rest of the Division. Added to this were jitters caused by civilian sources in the morning, filtered through the remaining member of the 'Jedburgh' team who had accompanied Urquhart's headquarters to liaise with the local population and the Dutch Resistance. The three-man 'Jedburgh' team – team 'Claude', consisting of two Americans and a Dutchman, Jacob Groenewoud – had parachuted in on Sunday. Groenewoud and Lieutenant Harvey Todd had got to the Bridge with Johnny Frost's column, while Technical Sergeant Carl Scott had stayed behind with Divisional HQ. There were alarming reports of one hundred enemy tanks on their way from Apeldoorn. The Division may have had a quiet morning in the Village, but it was the possibility of the afternoon going awry in the west – the way it had in the east with the battle in the Town going so wrong for the battalions fighting there and the increasingly worrying situation in the Woods to the north – that had Urquhart spooked. It was with these altogether alarming concerns in mind that the major general took himself off to see Brigadier Hackett.

15

THE WOODS: THE BRIGADE

High ground is the king of the battlefield. If you have it, you can control the battle space far more effectively than if you don't. There's always a lot of talk about 'high ground' in military chat, but what does it mean? It can be the high ground of the Miteirya Ridge at Alamein, although that rise, imperceptible when one is walking up it, is only about 40 feet above sea level. You only know you're there when you can suddenly see a mile ahead. Or it can mean the bluffs above Omaha Beach, perhaps 200 feet high. Or a knoll, or a mountain such as Monte Cassino. It's all relative, but in battle, both sides want to control it.

James Holland, conversation with the author, February 2024

IT WAS THE HIGH GROUND that would dominate in the battle for the Woods. High is relative when talking of Holland, of course, but Arnhem itself and the area 1st Airborne was fighting over was not the flat fen of popular imagination. Equally, there's a sorry lack of windmills around Arnhem. The high ground that slopes up away from the railway completely dominates this stretch of the country-side to the north of the Village. Taking control of such ground is a military reflex action, born of plain necessity.

But to act on this reflex and to seize this high ground, the approach the British would have to make was across a patchwork of open fields, farmhouses and woods that ran up to the Amsterdamsweg, the major road leading into Arnhem; this was where 4th Parachute Brigade's two remaining battalions, the 156 and the 10th, were to fight. 10th Battalion would be swinging around to the left, 156 pushing past 7th Battalion King's Own Scottish Borderers (KOSB), who had gone forward to hold the Landing Zone ready for Tuesday's Third Lift, the Poles. The KOSB had been forced back to the area around the farmhouse compound at Johanna Hoeve, having fought a brisk firefight while making for the feature to the east known as Koppel the night before. This encounter offered an early suggestion of how an attack beyond Johanna Hoeve and on towards Arnhem on the axis of the Amsterdamseweg might go. The expectation had to be that the Germans held the high ground.

The treelines along the slope offered the defending Germans another advantage: the benefit of cover, concealment. The only option for the British was to advance in the open, uphill. In plain sight. Not only that but the Germans, lurking in the trees in their field-grey this Tuesday morning, possessed far greater firepower than the light infantry coming at them. Although the British artillery net was working, Forward Observation Officers were in place with the battalions and shoots could be ordered on to the German positions, such as they could be seen; nevertheless, the light guns lacked the weight of fire and the ammunition to suppress the enemy effectively, let alone destroy them. The idea of an infantry Brigade taking on this kind of task in Normandy, virtually spontaneously, without a fire plan that had already flattened the Woods and battered every likely German hiding place and strongpoint, keeping the enemy's head down until the last possible moment, would have been unthinkable. And certainly not without armoured support, which was the way the Germans had been ground to dust in Normandy. Yet these attacks still went in.

This piece of territory offered the Germans a further advantage as the defender. With his back to the railway line, the attacker cannot get his guns and vehicles into effective positions without going to the railway crossings at either end of the approach. Furthermore, there were only two ways in and out of the area north of the railway line: back west towards the level crossing at Wolfheze; or forwards to the bridge at Oosterbeek station. Between these two access points, the railway line sat proud on an embankment and then ran down into a cutting to the east, which men could scramble up and down on foot, but which was not suitable for the support weapons, ammunition, medics and all the essentials the Brigade needed to maintain the attack.

There was a very real risk that this equipment and the men with it would be trapped on the wrong side of the railway line, blocked at either end, unable to escape. So whatever 4th Brigade was going to do, it had to be decisive. 1st Brigade had already come unstuck trying to move into Arnhem against a better-armed enemy, Germans who, while they didn't necessarily outnumber the British, had the advantage of not needing to do much more than blunt their attack, stymie their progress, create delay. The Germans knew Arnhem and its environs better than the British, who didn't know it at all. As the military adage goes, time spent on reconnaissance is never time wasted, but the awkward truth of an airborne landing is that there is little time or opportunity to be spent on reconnaissance. You land, you fight where you find yourself. Where the enemy might be is something you find out the hard way.

It is about two and a half miles from the level crossing at Wolfheze eastwards to the bridge at Oosterbeek station, an area tilting south-east towards the Town, and this was the space within which 4th Parachute Brigade and its commanding officer, Brigadier Hackett, would attempt to change the course of the Battle of Arnhem. With his headquarters, his staff, their Jeeps, radios, signallers and runners tucked up in the strip of trees that ran alongside the railway line, roughly equidistant between the two railway crossings, Hackett made his move.

Taking the lead for 4th Parachute Brigade, 156 Battalion was commanded by Lieutenant Colonel Sir Richard de Bacquencourt Des Voeux. Des Voeux was a Grenadier Guard, a smart chap, one of 'Boy' Browning's staff and a member of the 'Dungeon Party', the airborne

brainstorming think tank. Des Voeux had broken his leg parachuting into North Africa, and hobbled about thereafter; even in this
world of super-fit parachutists exceptions could be made.

Des Voeux's Battalion had been given two tasks for the morning,
ultimately to get on to the high ground at Koppel; but in order to do
this, first they would have to seize Lichtenbeek, east of the Johanna
Hoeve farm. With Des Voeux was Captain Peter Chard of the Light
Regiment – his radio net was working, so he had access to all the fire
support that the Division's guns could offer. 10th Battalion was to
flank 156 Battalion, while 7th King's Own Scottish Borderers held the
farmhouse compound and fields around it at Johanna Hoeve; these
fields were the Landing Zone for the Poles scheduled to arrive in the
morning. 7th KOSB were committed to holding the Landing Zone,
and while they were under Hackett's command he left them as they
were, and did not involve them in his attack. Like Brigadier Lathbury
when he ordered all three of his battalions to make for the Bridge,
rather than holding one back and using it to add weight where it
might be needed, Hackett wasn't keeping a Battalion in reserve. He
was going to commit everything he had from first light.

For 156 Battalion everything happened very quickly. At 0330 hrs
(roughly the same time the attacks went in in the Town) they had
established their firm base in the Woods, after a troubled night
fighting around a house in Wolfheze. An hour and a half later they
were ordered to prepare to put in the preliminary attack on Lichtenbeek. Des Voeux had returned from Brigade HQ, where Hackett had
made clear to his officers that Johnny Frost's 2nd Battalion were
hard pressed at the Bridge and that the Brigade needed to get
through to them immediately. Commanding B Company was Major
John Waddy. He pithily outlined the problem he was facing:

> We had absolutely no idea what opposition was ahead of us,
> despite the fact the 1st Battalion had been through the area
> two nights before and met heavy opposition and managed to
> bypass it . . .[1]

Yet 1st Battalion had lost at least half of one of its companies in the process. Waddy's comment puts us right into the position of the fighting man. This is the reality of how the ordinary soldier sees things. Even at the level of company commander, he doesn't know where he is, or where he's going – and it's a million miles from the arguments that hang around Arnhem about Ultra intelligence and what, before Market Garden, may or may not have been known about German strength. Waddy and his comrades would be fighting without artillery or close air support. The PBI, the Poor Bloody Infantry (Airborne), were going to have to make a fist of it, regardless. Nonetheless, Hackett's company commanders trusted their boss's judgement. At 0700 hrs C Company, backed by B Company, made their way forward as their 'first bound towards the objective', and took it without incident.

Major Geoffrey Powell commanding C Company had a dim view of what was in store for 156 Battalion, sizing up the exact problem with what they were embarking upon:

> The scene ahead brought back memories of fanciful training exercises on the plains of Northern India with troops crossing vast expanses of open ground covered by imaginary fire of palpable insufficiency. The ground ahead today was just as open, and the covering fire was just as inadequate. For this type of attack, a regiment of guns would not have been too much . . . The covering fire was a joke. This slope was a death trap. Within the next couple of minutes all of us could well be dead or wounded. This was the problem which always faced airborne troops fighting without heavy weapons. We were bluffing. We would survive only if the Boche ran away. They had to be more frightened than we were.[2]

The other men fighting in the Town had observed that the training they had done, in their case battalion-sized advances in open country on Salisbury Plain, had left them ill-prepared for fighting on the narrow streets of Arnhem. Yet here was 156 Battalion doing exactly what they'd trained for, and Powell knew in his heart that it was up to the enemy to run away rather than engage. This time they didn't engage – 'never was anti-climax more welcome' – and there ahead of them anyway was 7th KOSB dug in and around Johanna Hoeve. For now at least things seemed to be under control.

Set in the centre were 7th KOSB, dug in and around the Johanna Hoeve compound, performing the dual role of being the base from which the Brigade would attack and holding the Landing Zone in these same fields where the Poles were scheduled to land. Among the KOSB was the mechanic Albert Blockwell:

> We got to the house OK there was a big, square yard at the rear of the house, surrounded by hay barns etc. At first we drove the Jeeps and trailers into a big barn until we realised that if this place was hit we would lose the whole lot . . . Rob and I managed to get a brew going crouched down behind an old cart. The brew was half on the boil when Jerry's mortaring came pretty close, but mortars or not I was determined to have that char . . . I was feeling pretty tired for we had no sleep during the night and there was no prospect of any during the day.[3]

Blockwell had arrived the day before, making full use of the sick bag in the Horsa over the North Sea. Today was a different matter, with bullets zipping about, smacking into the farmhouse, and with the ever-increasing mortar fire there was plenty to keep him awake. Men drifted back from the attack ahead of him and the Jeeps were soon needed to evacuate the wounded. The aid post was only 300 yards away and Albert had heard it had been captured by the Germans; 7th KOSB were cheek by jowl with the enemy, meaning any landing that might come in on the Landing Zone could be contested. Sent to collect supplies from out on the LZ, bouncing around in a Jeep, Albert and his mates were strafed by German aircraft. Luckily he was unscathed. The noises of battle surrounded him as 4th Parachute Brigade went over their start lines.

Lieutenant Colonel Des Voeux's men of 156 Battalion made good progress and C Company took the first ridge without any opposition. So far so good. As they got into position they made contact with 7th KOSB at Johanna Hoeve over to their left. Ahead of them to the east was the road that ran from the Amsterdamseweg down to the Village, the Dreijenseweg, slicing from north to south, finishing at the critical railway bridge at the top of the Village. Des Voeux's men would have to get across this road. The ditches that ran alongside it were the only cover on offer. The road also afforded the Germans an axis along which its armour could prowl, as well as fixed lines down which machine guns and cannon could fire. Without the necessary recce, these were problems that were only being revealed in the moment.

Confident that things were going well, Des Voeux made his next move – ordering C Company to take and hold the rest of the ridge, while A and B Companies were to get ready to move on and seize the next two ridges. With A Company went Battalion Headquarters. Commanding A Company was a veteran of Tunisia and Italy, Major John Pott MC, Johnny Frost's brother-in-law (having married Frost's sister Diana in 1941). Pott had fought with the King's Own Royal Regiment in Iraq and the Western Desert, and was a tough and enthusiastic soldier who loved the glamour of parachuting. He was also very religious. Training with 156 Battalion in Palestine had been like holy catnip to him. During exercises near the Sea of Galilee he liked to read his Bible and ponder the scenery and the miracles Jesus had wrought thereabouts. Pott and Des Voeux went together into C Company's position to have a good look at what was in front of them – but the woods were too dense for them to make any judgement: 'nothing useful could be seen'. Essentially this would be a reconnaissance in force. What was the German presence likely to be? There was only one way to find out: fight.

It was at this point that Brigadier Hackett appeared and urged 156 Battalion on, re-emphasizing that they needed to get to the Bridge as quickly as possible. Given the resistance the Germans had shown in this area only two days earlier, and the obvious build-up of armour and flak guns repurposed as anti-personnel weapons in the fighting so far, Hackett must have been seeking to inspire rather than offer a realistic objective. His professed scepticism before Market Garden – and certainly he had been noisily critical of Operation Comet – was something he didn't let interfere with his decision-making, nor his approach to leadership on Black Tuesday. By hook or by crook, 4th Parachute Brigade was going to get to the Bridge.

At 0830 hrs A Company put in their attack, bringing with them a 6-pounder and an improvised platoon of about thirty glider pilots that had been hastily attached to 156 Battalion, including Louis Hagen. A Company's attack lasted about half an hour. On reaching the road, the Dreijenseweg, Pott's men were immediately pinned down. In response Pott tried to get A Company to break out and to flank where he thought the German fire was coming from, but it was all around; German half-tracks equipped with 20mm flak guns were moving about and pouring fire into the very ditches where his men had taken cover – 'death-traps' according to the Regimental Diary. German light machine guns, dug into the Woods, covered the road and their flanks. Hagen's glider pilots were part of this flanking attack, but they were held up from going in by enemy fire. In such conditions, it was impossible for Pott to coordinate his platoons; his company was being slowly strangled, his officers were being hit, and all attempts to stalk and destroy the German half-tracks failed.

The makeshift platoon of glider pilots were ordered into a copse, up on to the high ground, to clear it of the enemy. Rather than dumping their Bergens (backpacks) with their food and equipment, to return to later, they moved up to the hill and the trees fully laden, crawling, spreading out in the foliage. As the sound of firing grew louder, the inexperienced Louis Hagen couldn't tell whose guns were whose. This was after all his first contact with the enemy. The two 'parachute officers' with them, named as Captains Muir and Smith[4] in the 156 Diary, coaxed the men on, yelling at them to stay in shape and keep together.

Louis was the last man out on the left flank. As he was urged forward by the two officers, Hagen psyched himself up to hate the Germans he would soon need to kill. His mind took him back to when he had witnessed another Jewish boy being bullied in school, and his own cowardice in not speaking up as a fellow Jew, then to the concentration camp at Torgau, and also the sight of SA and SS men in their uniforms strutting proudly around his home town of Potsdam:

> I remembered how I used to dream of a most wonderful miracle by which these self-made Gods would be deprived of their uniform and power. When all those who looked up to them would realise that they were the most ignorant and ridiculous bunch of people mankind had ever produced. The realisation that this was the glorious moment in which I could help this dream to come true gave me a feeling of incredible joy and elation. The circle had been completed, justice was being done . . . and all this in my time. I was ready to take on anything and anybody that was German.[5]

If the German teenagers that Padre Pare had encountered on Tuesday morning when he buried Generalmajor Kussin were motivated by the need for Germany to live, Louis Hagen was their polar opposite. It was time for Germany to die. Suitably pumped up, Louis embarked on his part in the miracle.

Reaching the treeline, they discovered a clearing that had been recently cut, with logs piled up in it. The clearing dipped down and then rose again to yet another treeline, 200 yards on, where the German positions were. Hagen could hear vehicles' engines revving and men shouting, shouting that he understood. As they entered the clearing the Germans opened fire. Consumed by his fighting rage, Louis dumped his rucksack so he could move more quickly, and ran on, heedless. One of the parachute officers was crying out in pain. Seeing only one other pilot nearby, Hagen got up and ran towards where the Germans were, hurtling down the dip in the clearing in plain view. With bullets flying all around him, he threw himself to the ground. To compose himself he watched some ants going about their business, oblivious to the noise and danger. Louis couldn't see the Germans, but he could hear them. And he could hear them arguing about him, arguing about whether they should go after him, before concluding he was most likely dead so there was no need, and then whether they needed to bring heavier kit up to bolster their position.

It dawned on Louis that these soldiers, far from being exemplars of the German war machine at its finest, were pretty average opposition:

> The more I listened to them, the more I realised what a badly disciplined and poor crowd they were and how easily we could have got them if we had only made a properly planned attack.[6]

But he was stuck, caught between the squabbling Germans and his own side. He dropped his rifle and ran, running and ducking for cover, tripping over branches and brambles. He realized in the confusion that both sides were firing at him. When he got up to run, he would try to shout out to tell his own side to stop shooting at him, but each time the clatter of gunfire drowned him out. He wished he had a glider ID flag, but only lead pilots were issued with these. Only when he threw away his grenade – which he'd forgotten about in the hullabaloo – and explained who he was, was he allowed back to the British lines. Although he spoke fluent English, his German accent may not have helped. The glider pilots were unfamiliar to the men from 156 Battalion they were now fighting alongside. Still fired up with fighting rage, he told the officer and the men around him that they should attack the Germans, their morale was low! – he could attest to that, he'd heard them talking. A hasty plan to attack was made, and as Louis steeled himself to go at the Germans once more, a huge crash came: a self-propelled gun had opened fire, the second shot knocking out six men on the left flank.

Going forward was now impossible. The lieutenant who'd led them into the clearing to start with was still out there somewhere, injured, and another four men had been hit in the initial attack. Louis persuaded two other men to help him find the lieutenant. They found him soon enough, but he was dead. They decided to leave the body. It was too dangerous. Recovering the dead would only put them all at further risk, and for what?

Meanwhile Major Pott's men, pinned down along the Dreijenseweg, were under increasingly deadly pressure, and his officers were paying the price as they attempted to get a grip on the situation and counter-attack. Lieutenant Stanley Watling of 4 Platoon was killed trying to get his men over the road. Captain Terry Rodgers was killed mopping up. Lieutenant Delacour of 5 Platoon was also dead. Unable to evacuate the wounded, the injured were treated as best they could be in situ.

There were desperate efforts to attack the German armour. Without a PIAT, Sergeant George Sheldrake stalked a half-track, going into a building hoping to lob a 2-inch mortar bomb into the vehicle, but he 'shortly returned bleeding and without the mortar'. The enemy started to close in on A Company, throwing stick grenades into the ditches.

But Pott was not done. Rallying what was left of his men, and quite rightly reasoning there was no point remaining where they were, he ordered them up to the high ground beyond the road that was their objective, the feature known as Koppel. Before they set off for the top of the ridge, and in the face of increasing enemy fire, the evangelical Pott stood up and addressed the wounded, Sheldrake among them. As the rounds flew about him, Pott told his men that the Lord was with them, even in this bleakest of moments, and while he may have led his men to disaster, the Lord would take care of them:

I am sorry that I have only led the Company to death and
pain; but remember there is another Commander Who is
'The Way, the Truth and the Life', and I am committing you
into his hands as I leave you now. Lord Jesus watch over him,
please.[7]

Caught off balance, or confident that they had blunted the British
attack and that they could still finish Major Pott's diminished band,
the Germans didn't interfere with his dash up to where he had
decided he would dig in. But Pott's men had been spotted; 250 yards
away was a German officer with binoculars watching them. They
shot him, but the Germans came on regardless, a platoon's worth,
before the Brits had had time to dig in. Holding their fire until the
enemy were 20 yards away, A Company fixed bayonets and charged
down off the high ground. Taking a German MG34 machine gun in
the process, they waited for the enemy's next move. Although by
now most of his men were dead or wounded, and with only six men
left from A Company, Pott steeled himself and the survivors for
another charge. He himself was shot through his left leg and his
right hand. The end had surely come.

A Company may have reached and held its objective for an hour,
but it had been destroyed in the process. By 1430 hrs the high point
of 156 Battalion's assault east towards Arnhem was over. How had
the other companies fared?

News had not made it back to Battalion HQ that A Company
had experienced such a bloody start to their advance, so B Company
moved off as planned half an hour later at 0900 hrs, immediately
running into the same level of resistance. Major John Waddy, the B
Company commander, who had brought a German MP40 *Schmeisser*
sub-machine gun with him from England rather than a Sten gun,
set off with his men east into the Woods, having been told that there
were only a few snipers around. Consequently, he expected the
advance of 300–400 yards to the high ground to go without much
of a hitch. He'd been horribly misinformed. The Germans reacted

furiously, initially with light machine-gun fire, and then he found a
bitter warning sign of what was to come:

> I came to a clearing of felled timber, and by a pile of logs
> there was the Platoon HQ of A Company, all dead.[8]

With the sounds of A Company's battle ringing out ahead, John
Waddy and his men were carrying on along a ride in the Woods
when suddenly an anti-aircraft cannon began slamming high explosive into his lead platoon, cutting the men down, shattering trees
and sending deadly splinters flying, as well as the red-hot steel from
the rounds themselves. The flak gun was only about 150 yards away,
a twin-barrelled automatic mounted on a half-track. Waddy and his
men crept forward, determined to knock it out. Fifteen yards from
the half-track, like Louis Hagen, he was close enough to hear the
crew shouting over the noise of the cannon, as well as the revving
engines of what Waddy sensed were plenty more vehicles. He was
getting ready to attack when a sniper in the trees above the half-
track shot the man next to him through the head, and then Waddy
himself in the stomach. Falling, he fired his pistol at the sniper:

> I collapsed and lay doggo, until I heard a crashing through
> the bushes and a large Rhodesian private, Ben Diedricks (we
> had about 20 Rhodesians serving in our battalion since our
> stay in the Middle East), picked me up in his arms and carried
> me back some 200 yards to Company HQ. At the battalion
> RAP our doctor, John Buck, must have thought that I had had
> it for all he did was to chuck me his silver whisky flask![9]

At 0930 hrs the support company and Battalion HQ had put in their
own counter-attack, but to little effect. B Company had not made it
over the road, and had fast been reduced to a rump; the fight for the
high ground had already consumed two-thirds of 156 Battalion
within an hour of crossing their start line. An hour later Brigadier

Hackett was still under the misapprehension that the situation was 'much tidier'. When word reached him of the mauling taken by 156 Battalion, he observed: 'Battalion had now for the moment shot its bolt. Bosche [*sic*] apparently very sensitive to any threat to that high ground.'[10] But making this discovery had cost him dear. The military imperatives around high ground mattered as much to the Boche as they did to anyone.

C Company of 156 Battalion, who had made the first move that morning and then been held in reserve by Des Voeux, had been spared the disaster at the Dreijenseweg and would have to wait for now. It was quite clear that the rest of 156 Battalion's move east had faltered, perhaps fatally. Regardless, it was 10th Battalion's turn to make their push on the Amsterdamseweg, aiming to reach the crossroads between the main road and the Dreijenseweg. They were now the northernmost component of 1st Airborne Division, and still had some distance to go overnight, starting at 0300 hrs to move up to their start line. The essential plan was that 10th Battalion would move down along the south side of the Amsterdamseweg, but go no further north and serve as the firm left flank for 156 Battalion to ensure that the Brigade's advance itself could not be flanked or encircled.

10th Battalion moved forward and made their way across Landing Zone S and through the positions of 7th King's Own Scottish Borderers, avoiding making the mistake some of 156 Battalion had made and identifying the KOSB correctly as British soldiers. In the gloom it was hard to tell who was who, but there was no exchange of fire this time.

The two key features on the main road were the Pumping Station, a tall brick building with a fenced-off compound, and the crossroads. At the crossroads was an inn, a travellers' rest which offered the occupying Germans a view all the way down the Amsterdamseweg. Anyone coming along the road or attempting to cross it would be spotted. In order to control the road, 10th Battalion would have to take both the Pumping Station and the crossroads.

But immediately the Germans made it known that they were in the vicinity, making contact the very moment when Lieutenant Colonel Smyth, leading from the front, turned his Jeep on to the road from a track in the Woods. A half-track with a flak gun opened up, destroying the Jeep but leaving Smyth unscathed. Several of the men had put their packs on the Jeep, so they lost their kit along with food and cigarettes. One man, who'd been volunteered to take a look up the road, had his head blown off. Two more men were blown to pieces by a flak gun as they tried to get across the road. Pinned down, options were few, so the Battalion fell back from the edge of the road and continued east towards the crossroads, out of view. All of this before 0730 hrs: it was becoming clear that the Woods were going to be stoutly defended.

Lieutenant Colonel Kenneth 'Kidney' Smyth, who'd raised 10th Battalion himself, decided that what he needed to do was get across the main road and flank the crossroads. (Smyth had been at the sharp end in Italy, and it was his forward position at Castellaneta that Lieutenant General Hopkinson had been visiting when he was killed the previous year.) Smyth's Monday had also been far from ideal, when he discovered at the rendezvous on the Drop Zone on Ginkelse Heide that he was about one hundred men short.

By the following morning Smyth was looking for solutions. He asked Brigade HQ for permission to flank: permission was granted. If he moved his men further west he would be able to cross the road in the reverse slope, where his men couldn't be seen from the inn at the crossroads or the Pumping Station. A Company was furthest back so they were sent to find the dead ground where the road could be safely crossed. In charge of A Company, about one hundred men strong now, was Captain Lionel Queripel, who had taken over after the company commander, Major Anson, had been shot down on his way to Arnhem. Using a smokescreen to cover the road, they ran across and fanned out to the north.

Queripel asked for volunteers to go forward and recce the next feature ahead of them. There was another road a few hundred yards

further north that ran parallel to the main road, and no one knew
for sure where the enemy was, nor how wide a flanking manoeuvre
A Company could pull. A patrol was put together, Sergeant Tex Banwell and three volunteers. They crept into the trees, up to the next
track ahead, turning right towards where the Pumping Station was.
They came to a tall fence, and to their shock they found behind it
panzers, their engines ticking over. On seeing the patrol, one tank
crew sprang to life. Banwell and his three colleagues turned tail,
back along the side of the track, almost running straight into a
German patrol coming the other way. The four men hit the deck, lay
flat, as the tank fired shells into the trees to flush them out. Using
the bushes as cover, Banwell got the men back to Queripel, but the
news was stark. With panzers behind the Pumping Station, there
could be no flanking action around it. Queripel now had no choice
but to move along in parallel with B Company on the south side of
the road.

B and D Company had meanwhile reached the inn at the crossroads at about 0900 hrs, eliciting murderous fire from self-propelled
guns and flak cannons. B Company tried to exploit the open space
on the side of the road, but the men were cut down, quickly ruling
this option out. Private George Taylor recalled:

> We were held up by some Germans who were in some build-
> ings. I had several Spandaus and we kept exchanging fire with
> them. The barrel got so hot that we had to urinate on it to
> cool it down before we could change it; the hot urine spurted
> back on to me. We were in shallow scrapes at the edge of a
> wood about 50 to 75 yards from the Germans and eventually
> decided that we had to move out. It was just then that 'Nick'
> Walter the number one on the Bren was killed – just the one
> hit in the temple. I did not even know he was hit at first. I had
> to take the Bren from him and leave him, he was still on the
> firing position. That was the first time I'd ever seen anyone
> dead. It all affected me very deeply. He was my best friend.[11]

B Company pulled back some 200 yards, using the slope as it fell away from the crossroads to make it harder for the Germans to direct their fire on to them. But they were hardly out of the frying pan. Behind them were Battalion HQ and the support company, and medics were coming up to deal with the incessant stream of wounded. To make matters worse, the Germans began shelling and mortaring them as they went. Heads down, there was no further prospect of going forward; they would now defend the Brigade's left flank from the south side of the road. Meanwhile A Company, without the option of outflanking the Pumping Station, were now directly embroiled in it. Things were fast running out of control for Lieutenant Colonel Smyth, if indeed he had ever had any prospect of controlling the situation. German armoured fighting vehicles were moving freely on the road, and it seemed there was little that could be done about them.

In the midst of this carnage and the unrelenting pressure from the Germans, Lionel Queripel crossed the main road several times, on one occasion rescuing Sergeant Francis Fitzpatrick, who had been:

> . . . hit by a burst of fire from a Spandau machine gun in the neck back and shoulder. Queripel picked me up as dead from a ditch and carried me across the main road to the RAP [Regimental Aid Post].[12]

Queripel's trips across the road – smoking his pipe, the very picture of cool under pressure – were to make sure he remained in constant contact with Smyth: what then was their next move? Smyth decided that they should lie in wait and not attack until they saw the whites of the Germans' eyes: allow the tanks to come right upon them at a range at which their Hawkins mines and Gammon Bombs might be effective. The problem was stark. Without armoured support, artillery or a proper anti-tank screen, they were stripped bare – what could parachute infantry possibly do against armour? As they waited, a stalemate developed, with vehicles' engines roaring on the other side of the road and the Germans standing off, avoiding the trap Smyth had set for them.

Suddenly the Pumping Station blew up, its roof heaving up and collapsing on to the building. 'The landlord won't like that,' said Smyth.

Two of Smyth's companies were now trapped on the south side of the road. Another attempt to flank the road was made by D Company, but again the Germans had all the open space covered; their tanks were sitting well back and firing half a dozen shells, taking a pause and firing half a dozen more. Mortar fire too was pouring in. As were the wounded to the Regimental Aid Post. This was not as disjointed an action as 156 Battalion's, but it was just as deadly. It was becoming clear that 10th Battalion would have to extract itself from its predicament. The Battalion's mortars were doing what they could to reply to the German mortaring and shelling, but in the extremely close environment of the Woods it was impossible to deploy mortars at such short range and against estimated enemy mortar positions – firing on the panzers was more practicable, but had no real impact. Smyth's six mortars nevertheless fired until they ran out of ammunition, and a whole mortar crew was killed when it took a direct hit from enemy counter-mortar fire. Even if the Light Regiment were able to offer any fire support, and there is a debate about whether they could, it would not have amounted to much. The 75mm gun didn't offer anything like the knock-out power or even the nuisance effect that Smyth's men needed to keep the Germans distracted. The panzers sat back and pounded the 200-yard lodgement.

In its quest to find a way through, 10th Battalion was being eaten alive.

And then, crisis.

It is against text-book teaching to break off an engagement
and withdraw from the battlefield in broad daylight.

Lieutenant Colonel Robert Payton Reid
7th Kings Own Scottish Borderers[1]

AFTERNOON

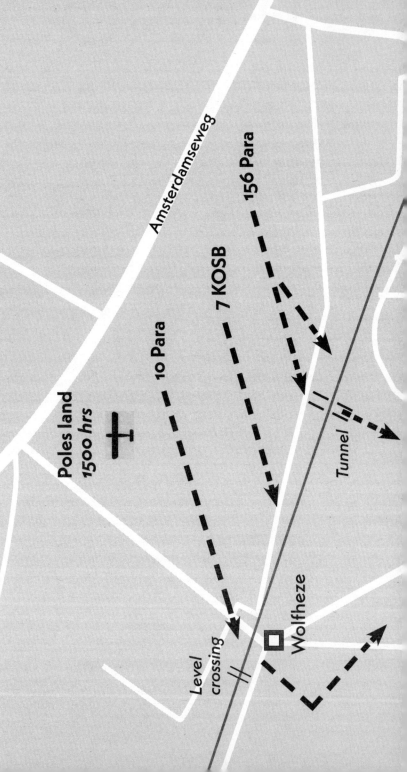

THE WOODS: AFTERNOON (The Retreat)

VELUWE

Amsterdamseweg

156 Para

7 KOSB

10 Para

Poles land
1500 hrs

Tunnel

Level
crossing

Wolfheze

16

THE TOWN: ON THE BRINK

Peter Cook: I want you to lay down your life, Perkins. We
need a futile gesture at this stage. It will raise the whole tone
of the war. Get up in a crate, Perkins, pop over to Bremen,
take a shufti, don't come back. Goodbye, Perkins. God, I
wish I was going too.
Jonathan Miller: Goodbye, sir – or is it – *au revoir?*
Peter Cook: No, Perkins.

Beyond the Fringe, 'Aftermyth of War', 1961

BY 1100 HRS IN THE TOWN the fighting for The Monastery had
ended, but incredibly, the South Staffords had yet more to do.

The high ground at Den Brink back towards the Village had been
earmarked by Division for capture. It seems that after a morning of
such heavy fighting what the battalions in the Town were still capable of was something that hadn't been grasped back at Divisional
Headquarters. Things were moving very fast, and for every move
that 1st Airborne made, the Germans were inflicting deadly punish-
ment. High ground figures large in military thinking, as we have
seen, and for all the obvious and right reasons, but the losses the
South Staffords had taken, and the difficulties of getting away from
the enemy, who was far better armed and hot on their heels, make
such a change of plan seem wildly optimistic at best. In small groups
the men made their way west, trying to make the best of what little
cover there was. They moved in behind 11th Parachute Battalion,
who were waiting on their new orders in the streets around the

Bottleneck – the calm before the storm that Captain Stuart Mawson was to experience in the dressing station in his garage.

Only about one hundred men from the South Staffords came back from The Monastery. As the senior officer there, Major Cain took charge. C Company's commander, Major Philip Wright, had gone forward to try to find Lieutenant Colonel McCardie. Wright was killed in the attempt. In his absence Captain Dickens took over. At the Bottleneck there were 6-pounders, which offered some protection from marauding tanks. The houses were burning and the dead and the wounded of both sides were everywhere. And just as they were getting organized, the men from 1st and 3rd Battalions fell back through C Company, their move to break through to the Bridge also spent. The South Staffs had to take stock.

Among the missing was Lieutenant Jack Reynolds. With No. 1 Mortar Platoon, Reynolds understood the potential for dislocation and confusion in an airborne landing; his experiences in Sicily had left him with few illusions about how things might go. Reynolds was unimpressed with the briefing he'd received, that they hadn't been told about the 'road below us which ran alongside the river, which was rather important as that's where the German tanks went'.[1] He'd flown from Manston in Kent on Sunday; the men had been issued with a rum ration before they took off: 'the army don't indulge in that sort of generosity very often'. Once he'd got off the Landing Zone, Reynolds found that the operation was delivering exactly the kind of chaos he'd anticipated. Although he was a mortar platoon officer (and trained signaller), Reynolds had been sent forward on a bike by Brigadier Hicks: 'You're my eyes,' said Hicks, seeming to assume Reynolds was a recce man. Puzzled by this request when he had a mortar platoon to look after, Reynolds still did as he was told, ditching the bike when he was fired upon. He rejoined his mortar platoon in time to move off with the rest of the South Staffords. A fraught advance up into the Town followed and he arrived at 'I think it was a Monastery of some sort'. On arrival he saw Captain Ernest Wyss's dead body. Reynolds's platoon were dug into the hollow. The disorientation of street fighting was one thing, but finding one's way around the streets was another:

> We had no maps, we had no idea where we were, other than [the way to] the bridge was to follow the line of the river . . . you had no idea where anybody was . . . I'd no news at all of anything and no instructions no orders . . . fragmented wasn't the word for it, it was ridiculous . . . nobody knew where anybody was, I mean it was complete chaos, all fighting your own little battles.[2]

Despite not knowing where he was or what was going on, Reynolds had gone forward, frustrated that there was nowhere to set up his mortars. With him was a signaller, with his No. 18 radio set. He told the signaller to drop the radio, which didn't work and instantly made him a target. He knew that German tanks were working their way along the lower road, and he was concerned that they would before long get around behind The Monastery. Reynolds lost all sense of time, and having gone forward he found himself on his own. Working his way back, grabbing rifles and firing at the enemy, doing what he could to keep the fight going, he came upon some men from Battalion headquarters who had hunkered down in a slit trench, hoping for the best.

Reynolds was finally captured when a panzer had parked next to his slit trench. Without food, water or ammunition there was nowhere to go. Even though he noted that being captured meant you had to do exactly as you were told, Jack Reynolds was to go down in Arnhem legend as the man who flicked a V sign at a German film cameraman. 'They didn't know what that meant. The Germans thought I was giving them the Victory sign from Churchill.'[3] They were marched off as a group, and the photographs of Reynolds and the men he'd been captured with show filthy, exhausted, pensive men, smoking cigarettes. They look relieved that their ordeal was over, but they do not look defeated. The uncertainty of being taken prisoner hangs over them instead.

Lieutenant Ben Lockett, the gunnery officer who had encountered the 'bemused' Major General Urquhart earlier that morning, had been wounded in a duel between a 6-pounder and a panzer. Like so many of the men in the Town, he also was taken prisoner. He said of his experience:

> The psychological effect of this was appalling. I suppose I had anticipated every conceivable eventuality except becoming a POW.[4]

It was as he made his way back to C Company that Major Cain encountered Lieutenant Colonel Lea of 11th Battalion, whose men were also getting ready to form up and make their move on the high ground at Den Brink, anticipating the arrival of the rest of 4th Parachute Brigade down the Amsterdamseweg. Taking Den Brink would afford 11th Battalion control of the approach down this main road into Arnhem. That 4th Brigade was being torn to pieces and had made no progress was not yet known to the men in the Town, or indeed at Divisional HQ. Cain gathered together the men he had into two composite platoons, which was all the South Staffords could now offer in terms of a cohesive – and commandable – group of men.

They went forward and took up position on the corner of the imposing prison building, which sits between the Lombok estate and the rising slope at Den Brink. There Cain was sucker-punched. His men got on to the hillside easily enough – near where Peter Stainforth had been wounded on Monday – without casualties, when suddenly, ten minutes later, the mortaring began. The ground was hard and full of roots, and the men found it impossible to dig in. Mortars were exploding in trees, splinters cutting the men to pieces where they lay. Lieutenant Badger, commanding what was left of C Company, was killed. Panzers followed the mortaring, initially firing on the jail, as if convinced the British were inside. Lieutenant Philip Turner, a Canadian officer with C Company, reported:

> There was little we could do but put our heads down and trust to luck, but the Germans, as usual, were reluctant to follow up the mortaring with an infantry attack. Instead, they sent two Tiger tanks into the woods after us, which came crashing through the trees, firing as they came.[5]

The South Staffords could get nothing right in the vice of the German defence. Den Brink was another objective they might have been able to reach but that they could not hold.

This new wave of mortaring also caught 11th Battalion in the open as its men formed up to try to carry out their new orders to link up with 4th Brigade's drive for the Amsterdamseweg. Further back in the Battalion's positions, Stuart Mawson at his aid post noticed the sudden change. He had been listening to the sound of fire from further into the Town, watching the men come back in their dribs and drabs, the walking wounded making their own way to find him, and Jeeps bringing back those who could not help themselves.

Then suddenly everything changed: 'There was a whistle and a very loud crash like the sound of cars in collision followed rapidly by others in the near vicinity. I stood momentarily, mug of tea in hand, stunned by the unexpectedness of it, then headed tea and all for the ground.'[6] Mawson's inexperience asserted itself. He asked Sergeant Dwyer whose mortars were firing at them and Dwyer went forward to have a look. When Jeeps started emerging from the smoke and men came running after them out of the chaos, Mawson realized he would have to shut up shop quickly. He started loading the wounded up on to the Jeeps he had at the aid post. He suddenly found himself feeling lost, alone, isolated, and out of his depth. He was a doctor after all, not a military man: what was happening? Immediately it became clear that his Battalion was retreating. One man driving a Jeep told him that they had been ordered back, out of range. Houses were on fire, tiles crashing off roofs, trees shattering. The peaceful leafy suburb he had found that morning as an ideal location for his aid post was now at the epicentre of a whirlwind of death and injury:

> There was a trickle of men emerging singly or in small groups from the Holocaust like animals escaping from a forest fire, dodging and weaving through the gardens dropping and rising with the whistles and crashes of the mortars.

He may have been no soldier, but Mawson could see what was going wrong. In the face of a concerted counter-attack by mortars, men cut off from their officers were making their own decisions, and there were the tell-tale signs that panic might be beginning to set in. One corporal he spoke to from the Battalion headquarters company enraged Mawson by not calling him 'Sir' and smoking a cigarette while they spoke. With no officers around, the corporal had taken matters into his own hands. The house he was hiding in had become unsafe, and the Jeeps were withdrawing. What else was he going to do but retreat?

Mawson collared a sergeant, who described the situation. The Germans had Spandaus everywhere, the streets weren't safe, the Battalion had been broken up by mortar fire. The sergeant's decision had been to 'just run like hell and hope for the best'. Mawson was the only officer left in the area, and he wasn't a soldier or tactician; nevertheless he ordered the sergeant tell his men to take up defensive positions where they were. Ten minutes later the mortaring started up again, the Germans having resighted their mortars directly on to Mawson's location. Within moments, the bombs whistled in right on top of him, each one seemingly closer, each one threatening oblivion:

> Death was very near and all around . . . a sudden very close near miss did it. My chains snapped and I found myself

leaping to my feet waving my arms about and shouting wildly 'Come on Sergeant. Come on. The barn. The CCP. We must find the barn. All follow me.'

And with these words I ran blindly away down the road not once casting my eyes behind me.[7]

The battle in the Town that had begun at 0300 hrs was over. The retreat was underway, the enemy rampant. The men at the Bridge were on their own.

17

THE BRIDGE: NO RELIEF

Now death stalked the streets.

Private James Sims

WITH NO SIGN OF RELIEF from the Town to the west, and nothing beyond rumours of 2nd Army in the south, rumours which Bombardier Leo Hall didn't believe for one minute, the middle of the day saw a new intensity to the German efforts to take back the Bridge. The longer that Lieutenant Colonel Frost held the Bridge, the harder it might be for the Germans to prevent the Allies getting through at Nijmegen twelve miles to the south.

The attacks continued relentlessly. The Germans had begun to infiltrate to the east of the Bridge and with no pressure on their flanks they had complete freedom to organize as they wished. With Frost's ban on sniping, the enemy were able to get even closer. Kettling Frost like this was much smarter and subtler than the SS's bludgeoning death ride from the south of the Bridge on Monday, which had resulted in slaughter. With control of the railway station, the Germans could bring in fresh men and equipment from the Reich; the classic Clausewitzian strategic dynamic of whose supply lines were shortest was now tilted firmly in Germany's favour.

Closing on the office building directly to the east of the Bridge, known as 'ɪo' in the 2nd Parachute Battalion Diary, three tanks – or self-propelled guns – approached. The distinction was perhaps academic at best as they clanked along the roads to the positions held by Lieutenant Andrew McDermont's 3 Platoon. The tanks were able to move right up to McDermont's position and shell him and his men from extremely close range, smashing up the buildings, starting fires, causing casualties, trying to force them out. This was a canny place to bring armour in, concealed as it was from the 6-pounders around the other side of the lodgement. Now 3 Platoon was in trouble, and the eastern side of the Bridge, and the buildings the British held, were in peril. Again.

Three days into Market Garden, the presence of German armour could no longer be regarded as a surprise. On the Sunday, the armoured cars and flak guns that the airborne soldiers advancing through the Village, the Town and on to the Bridge had encountered pretty much tallied with expectations. The armoured cars had been difficult enough to deal with, appearing around corners and firing on the 'snake' of the 2nd Battalion men. As for who they were fighting, on the Sunday one of Frost's scouts had returned from an unexpected encounter with a German sentry at the Bridge. When asked who the German soldier was, he had replied, 'Oh, he says he's Panzer SS, sir' – more than a clue that there might be tanks about.

Armour of course is mobile and can be delivered to where it's needed. The headlong rush of Market Garden's preparation was as unlike the months and months of preparation that had gone into Operation Overlord as it could possibly be. There was no equivalent of the systematic strategic and tactical effort to suffocate the German ability to draft in reinforcements. Thanks to Allied air power in Normandy, German formations were unable to move during the day; reinforcements arrived late or got dramatically written down, literally decimated. Allied strategy aimed to destroy the enemy's assets even before he got them to the battlefield. Paradoxically, the fact that the Germans were no longer subject to the limitations brought about by this kind of relentless air attack was the result of previous Allied success. It had taken the Allies months to throttle the Normandy battlefield. Now things were moving too fast. The speed of the Allied advance that Market Garden was hoping to exploit, the rush of the Great Swan from Normandy to the Belgian border, had cancelled out the war-winning advantage that had made it possible – and here in Arnhem as a result there were panzers.

These armoured fighting vehicles, described and later identified as Panzer IIIs, may have been out of date in September 1944, certainly in the terms by which tanks often get measured – their potential against other tanks, their speed, their armament, their armour and so on. However, against paratroopers without armoured support of their own, running low on ammunition, with 6-pounder anti-tank guns limited on how they could be deployed, the panzers were still a very potent threat. If what the Germans needed to do was drive men out of the buildings around the Bridge, a Panzer III medium tank was more than adequate to the task.

The Panzer III had first appeared on the battlefield in 1940. State of the art on its debut, it had worked well for the Germans in the desert and on the steppes in 1941 and 1942, but by 1944, as any Tank Top Trumps person will tell you, it was utterly outclassed. Allied tanks – even British tanks, which had been plagued with being under-gunned in terms of anti-tank ordnance – had caught up with German tank design and were being built in vast quantities by 1944. Sherman tanks and chassis were being turned out in their tens of thousands, T-34s and other Soviet types too. Tank-busting guns had been fitted to tanks as well as to so-called 'tank destroyers'. The Germans, through expediency and the kind of practice that years of defeat in defence had given them, had become adept at operating tanks, self-propelled guns and a variety of armour in different combinations within units. Because they had to, they operated these mish-mash formations with great tactical flexibility, different panzers taking on different roles.

The Panzer III had none of the glamour of its larger feline cousins, but had been used in every role the chassis could deliver, and was arguably the most successful panzer that German industry produced. Operation Barbarossa's lightning-fast and astonishingly deep drives into the Soviet Union in 1941 had been achieved with Panzer IIIs. The Panzer III had done particularly well for the

Panzerarmee against the British 2-pounder 'pop gun' that had been designed to fight the Germans in the close country of North-West Europe rather than the wide-open spaces of the North African theatre. This mismatch had helped to deliver the Germans easy wins in the desert until the 6-pounder made its debut on the battlefield, along with effective tactical air power.

The Panzer III had also been successfully adapted as a self-propelled gun, the *Stug*, the *Sturmgeschütz* ('assault gun'). This design went back to 1936. The Germans, doing their serious tank thinking long before anyone else, had anticipated the limitations of turret-mounting a gun on the Panzer III, and found that the best way to fit a larger gun with a bigger breech was to remove the turret and fit the gun into the hull. Initially, this adaptation was supposed to work in an infantry-support rather than anti-tank role, but come 1941, it was found the larger 75mm anti-tank weapon would fit into the Panzer III chassis. Crucially, not having a turret made the vehicles simpler and cheaper to build. The whole vehicle would be moved to align the gun on the target, then aim, not unlike a field gun on its gun carriage. This kind of make-do-and-mend approach to tank types served the Germans remarkably well and suited their fundamental inability to mass-produce in the Soviet or American style. Panzer IIIs were vulnerable to hand-held anti-tank weapons such as the PIAT, or for the more desperate or intrepid, the Gammon Bomb, the plastic-explosive grenade. Naturally, both of these British options demanded that the men get close enough to engage the panzers. A panzer driving up to a building might indeed get close enough to be in range of any hand-held anti-tank weapons inside the building, but if the German infantry could put down enough covering fire, or the tank could pump enough rounds into the building the men were sheltering in, then those options might not apply.

So it didn't matter whether these were Tiger tanks or Mk IIIs, or, in some cases over in the Village, repurposed French tanks that had been captured in 1940, they were still utterly effective in street fighting against lightly armed opponents. These tanks had got right in close to the building east of the Bridge, out of the reach of the 6-pounders, and were shelling Lieutenant McDermont and his men out of their position. Obsolescence in this case was relative. When all a tank had to do was trundle across a street, over the rubble and debris of battle, its tracks grinding on the tarmac, the five-man crew with their hatches closed to protect themselves from small-arms fire, who cared what its top speed was? The shells these tanks were firing were destructive enough. The tank was the Top Trump. The tank wasn't obsolete: you were.

McDermont was under the command of Captain Tony Frank, who had taken over A Company after Digby Tatham-Warter had been given command of 2nd Battalion while Frost was still in over-all charge of the forces assembled at the Bridge. Frank ordered McDermont and 3 Platoon out of the house while he took a PIAT and a handful of PIAT bombs with him to see off the tanks. Frank was a veteran of Sicily. He had taken a break from his Classics degree at Cambridge to join the Army. A keen sportsman, originally in the Lancashire Fusiliers, he had volunteered for airborne forces. In Sicily he had been in the thick of things during the Primosole Bridge adventure, despite his stick having landed all over the shop and the rest of the Battalion being widely dispersed. Now, having emerged from the house with the PIAT, Frank hit one of the tanks, disabling it, while the other two withdrew. Accounts differ, but in his citation for the US Silver Star, two more tanks appeared, and he engaged those panzers also with the PIAT, seeing them off too: 'in all three tanks were hit and all withdrew'.[1] The PIAT at close range was able to at least force a decision out of the Germans, though of course time and firepower were on their side. Frank had engaged them at a distance of 40 yards.

Nevertheless, no good deed goes unpunished, and Tatham-Warter came over from Battalion HQ to bollock Frank for letting McDermont and his men withdraw from the house. 3 Platoon – fifteen to twenty men in Frank's account – were now under the Bridge, safe from mortar fire and shelling at least, resting up. Frank rejoined the men to order them to retake the house, and make sure that the men east of the Bridge in the school could remain in touch with those on the west side. As Frank described it:

> . . . they set off from underneath the bridge, all very tired, just shrugging their shoulders and going back, but in no defeatist mood or anything like that. They went back and pushed the Germans out; there was probably about the same number of Huns. McDermont was shot as he went along the hall – in the lower stomach, I think; he was conscious, but there was a lot of blood. I jabbed him with morphine, and he was taken away.[2]

The Battalion Diary noted McDermont was 'badly wounded (doubtful he will ever recover)' and he joined the wounded in the cellars. A further German infantry counter-attack came over the ramp on the other side of the house and 3 Platoon and Tony Frank saw them off. That the Germans were successfully infiltrating and getting this close was a mark of the pressure the Bridge was under after midday. The men were holding on, and at great cost to the Germans, but as British officers were killed or wounded, and positions were threatened, the need to be relieved was being felt more and more keenly. After all, today was the day when relief was supposed to arrive, was it not?

However, there was news, and good news, though somewhat qualified: all morning at 1st Parachute Brigade HQ there had been oblique radio chatter, Canadian voices coming through over the air. Given the relative absence of Canadians in 1st Airborne, CANLOAN officers aside – unlike 6th Airborne, which boasted a Battalion of Canadian paratroopers – this suggested that 2nd Army were nearby.

At 1000 hrs, in a one-sided conversation – 'We were unable to receive them loud and clear but they appeared to be able to hear us'[3] – 30 Corps had been successfully informed that elements of 1st Parachute Brigade had the Bridge secured. Inevitably, 30 Corps were asked when they could be expected. The reply was, of course, uncertain, offered no guarantees, but they were on their way, saying they were some twenty miles south and were about to put in an attack to take Nijmegen Bridge. None of this quite added up.

None of this could have been reassuring. The implication was clear: a river assault at Nijmegen, nothing at all straightforward, meant that something had gone wrong to the south. The Bridge at Nijmegen had not yet been captured; tanks would not simply roll on north to Arnhem. Relief could and would not come today of all days. Time was ticking by. German resistance so far had made it clear that they were far from finished, and with the objective of Market Garden so plain now, three days into the operation, the fact that 30 Corps 'hoped to be with us soon' offered only the slenderest of hope. They'd just have to hold on. Even as the panzers lined up to shell the houses and mortars rained down, morale seemed remarkably robust. When the internal radio net was working at the Bridge, Lieutenant Colonel Frost could have been spared too much personal leadership as he moved from position to position to check on his men's progress; nevertheless this kind of leadership is exactly what he provided.

At the school on the eastern side of the ramp, the sappers were under renewed pressure. From his viewpoint down to the river out of the south side of the school, Eric Mackay was keenly aware of the pressure that McDermont was under in 'Io'. Mackay knew that the building had been lost with the arrival of the tanks along the waterfront and was worried that if they peeled off and made their way up the road to his east, he could be cut off from the rest of the lodgement. Mackay radioed Frost to warn him that he could not keep going on his side of the Bridge if Monday's attacks were repeated. Frost ordered him to hold on at all costs. 'Second Army was still five miles away and we could hear the heavy guns firing steadily,' Mackay would later write.[4] Not only that: 'The B.B.C. said everything was going according to plan and that relief was imminent.' What else could they say?

Around noon, due north of the school, the Germans attempted to set up a mortar, suggesting that they had not quite entirely figured out the extent of the British positions or the determination with which they were being defended. Mackay and his men let them set up the mortar, then killed the crew and destroyed the mortar. From 1230 hrs to about 1500 hrs the fighting became even fiercer: with pressure from the south, the house that McDermont was in had fallen, and there were renewed attacks from the east. A mortar with a delayed-action bomb crashed through the roof 'and burst in my command post, killing one and wounding another. At that moment I was looking out of the east face, for something suspicious was happening in the houses opposite.'[5] The buildings across the road to the east had been infiltrated by Germans in greater strength than the day before. With close-up mortaring and machine-gun fire from these houses, the pressure became more and more intense. But first there was the immediate threat of enemy armour.

Mackay described the panzers' arrival laconically – one of his men cried out:

> 'We're all right; there's a couple of Churchills outside.' I hurried over to find myself looking down at a couple of German Mark III tanks. I held a short course in tank recognition immediately.[6]

As the tanks pushed up from the waterfront, Mackay's men engaged the infantry accompanying them, killing several Germans and driving them off. At which point, the Mk IIIs turned their attention to the schoolhouse and started shelling the building's southern room: 'We could do nothing about this, so moved out of the room till it finished.'[7] As Tony Frank drove the tanks off and retook the house to the south, Mackay turned his attention to the houses to his east and set about eliminating those machine-gun positions one by one, 'the same old gag as yesterday'. This involved using a Bren gun firing on 'remote control', probably using a rifle pull-through, and then, when the Germans returned fire on the Bren, responding with everything else he had. One by one the rooms opposite were cleared. Mortars hit the school directly eleven times. Fires raged.

Acts of intense personal bravery became commonplace. Private Robert Lygo was number 1 on the PIAT in the building with McDermont and No. 3 Platoon. The PIAT had a two-man crew, one aiming and firing the spigot mortar, the other keeping the bombs flowing. Before the Panzer IIIs attacked that afternoon, three armoured cars came to recce the eastern defences and started firing at the building. Lygo was handy with the PIAT, and firing four bombs repelled the armoured cars with three direct hits even though their fire 'was directed almost entirely against him'.[8] Then came the panzers. He destroyed one of them even as it fired at him. Lygo's PIAT was the last one left in the eastern defences; in the rubble of the building to the east of Arnhem Bridge, seemingly oblivious to the danger, Robert Lygo held the panzers at bay.

Coolness under fire was the order of the day. The hopelessness of the situation demanded it. Major Tatham-Warter had been projecting visible sangfroid, sporting a bowler hat he had scavenged and carrying an umbrella. Father Egan, doing his rounds of the wounded, found himself trapped by a mortar barrage, unable to cross the street. Digby offered to join him – 'Don't worry I've got an umbrella' – and strolled across the road with him. This was Tatham-Warter's first battle; he was an Oxfordshire and Buckinghamshire ('The Ox and Bucks') Light Infantry man, a canny and charismatic operator, who had used bugle calls to gather his company at the rendezvous on the Drop Zone on Sunday. His sense was that the men needed a recognizable leader, someone visible, and the umbrella served this purpose well. He hadn't brought it with him but had picked it up in a house on his way to the Bridge. Given that his predecessor as second-in-command of 2nd Battalion, Major David Wallis, had been killed by accident failing to answer a challenge, carrying an umbrella seems a less wacky and rather more pragmatic means of identifying oneself. As Tatham-Warter understood it, the sappers had heard 'kamerad' when Wallis said 'second-in-command'.[9] The umbrella would act as insurance against this lethal possibility.

The officers at the Bridge did what they could to exude confidence. Remarkably, Frost made sure he walked briskly between buildings rather than ran.[10] He wore his beret and his battledress rather than his helmet and his smock, trading safety for visibility. Moments of levity still, somehow, occurred. On his travels checking up on the men, Frost had sent two men from B Company, Corporal Chilton and Private Goodwin, to get a message to the school. Mortars crashed around them, so they had taken refuge in a building that turned out to be a smithy – the only problem was the blacksmith seemed to be in the habit of disposing of his shit in the forge's coals. The place stank, they stank. Something to laugh about at the bleakest of times.

Another 'Ox and Bucks' man was Lieutenant Jack Grayburn, who had joined the Parachute Regiment because he was dissatisfied with being a normal infantryman. He had acquired the nickname 'Mad Jack' in the Ox and Bucks. He then found the endless hanging around that came with being an airborne soldier frustrating. At Arnhem he was finally getting what he had joined for. Commanding No. 2 Platoon in A Company, Grayburn had led an attempt to cross the Bridge on Sunday night. He'd been shot through the shoulder. He still carried on, in great pain, moving from place to place, organizing his men in occupying the houses around the Bridge and directing them to dig slit trenches in the embankment. Trenches were dug into the gardens behind the buildings too, though the men had poor fields of fire.

With No. 3 Platoon was Private Roland Janovsky. He had ended up in a house on the other side of the Bridge, on the ground floor with his mate 'Robbo' Robertson. Janovsky had been up in the slit trenches on the embankment. The house had radiators at the windows – mod cons for 1944 – but, as he put it, 'metal radiators . . . were not good protection against ricocheting objects'.[11] He was able, somehow, to find an upside when it came to his building being attacked by tanks – 'luckily' they fired armour-piercing rounds which went straight through the house rather than blowing it up. The cellar filled up with the wounded. He did not know what was done with the dead.

Major Stanley 'Bombs' Panter MC, with S Company, kept his men going with the help of a captured German food truck. He distributed cigars for the men in his two buildings as well as a tot of cherry brandy. He patrolled hard; they weren't letting the Germans simply come to them. Panter's problems were the same as everyone else's: water and ammo, particularly PIAT rounds. S Company Assault Platoon had been putting out anti-tank mines, but 'the position now was becoming rather tricky'.[12] The numbers of wounded were increasing, and while they could be treated then and there, there was no option of evacuating them to somewhere safer where they could be cared for. Frost popped in to congratulate Panter's mortar crew 'after a particularly heavy mortar shoot'.[13] But it was relentless. Panter led from the front, calling corrections to his mortar crew via his batman, stalking a self-propelled gun, shooting Germans, and preventing his men in the confusion from shooting some of the men from 3rd Battalion who had made it to the Bridge on Sunday. The small, embattled redoubt at the Bridge was holding on by every means possible, placing huge demands on the men and their leaders.

Private James Sims in the 'White House' had had his tot of brandy; Sergeant Smith had taken one look at him and made him take a slug from the bottle. Sims's day as the mortar platoon gopher had continued, and he had been told to make himself 'generally useful'. Sims had, however, been left in the mortar pit in the traffic island by the rest of the mortar section at the bottom of one of the slit trenches. He'd had to run across the road; shots were fired, but none connected. The mortars were out of ammunition. Sims had been lucky.

A telephone rang out in the 'White House'. He was told not to answer it, Sergeant Smith saying, 'That's Jerry ringing up, but the lady of the house isn't at home, got it?'[14] The phones became a feature of more humour – a story went around that one paratrooper had called the Arnhem exchange and asked to be put through to Winston Churchill. Sims felt that this robust humour was one of the things keeping them going. Certainly, as the youngest man, he drew comfort from it. For all the laughs, and the soldier playing a banjo on the staircase, it was the death of his best mate Slapsie, cut in half by a cannon shell, that had brought Sims up short. Slapsie had been at Narvik, was a former commando, and had taken Sims under his wing: 'his death cast a cloud over all of us'.[15] It was with the brandy inside him that Sims volunteered to return to the mortar pits in the island to recover a Bren gun. Sergeant Jackman reasoned the best thing to do was to dash out of the front door – the enemy would never expect it. Sims ran to the pits and recovered the Bren gun, though he didn't find a magazine to go with it. He offered 'half-heartedly' to have another look, but the consensus was that he'd used up his luck with the one trip and the enemy would be unlikely to let him get away with it again.

Captain Llewellyn-Jones was worried about being burned out: the enemy were using phosphorous mortar rounds and then shooting men running from the burning buildings. 'The builders' yard in which the anti-tank guns had been assembled was a panchromatic blaze of burning fabric and unmixed paints and solvents.'[16]

In the OP (observation post) Major Dennis Munford – who described Tuesday as a day of constant heavy pounding – was calling in shots from 3 Battery at the church. At the end of the ramp the Germans set up a 105mm howitzer in plain view. This gun attracted everyone's attention and it appears in lots of accounts. Munford reckoned it was only 200 yards away – he wryly noted that visibility was excellent because the church roof had been blown off. The radio set was in the corner, protected with sandbags. Munford called in the howitzer as a 'Mike One' target, asking the guns of all batteries to fire on it.

Bombardier Leo Hall recalled that the radio set wasn't working at the time but that the mortar section dealt with the howitzer.

Munford's recollection is that 3 Battery wouldn't shoot at first – he had after all given the guns what was, within the margin of error, his own position to fire on. He asked Brigade Major Tony Hibbert if he could order the strike in anyway – the OP was in the Brigade HQ building, so this was easily done – and with permission granted he asked for the first round to be smoke so that he could spot the fall of shot properly; indeed the smoke would make it easy for everyone to spot it. The first round went more than 200 yards long, then 3 Battery struck the target. Or the mortars did, or the Bren guns. Either way, in the confusion, the howitzer on its doomed excursion had attracted everyone's attention. If memories differ and accounts collide, this can hardly be surprising. The men had been on the go since very early on Sunday morning, and if events blur and haze together, if attribution of a target destroyed in the noise and raging battle can't quite be pinned down, is that at all surprising? Although these men were young and fit, and some of them had taken Benzedrine, their endless adrenalized state, heightened senses and, put bluntly, the fear they were having to contain might blur recollection.

Johnny Frost grappled with this issue. His officers were tireless – why, he was tireless – but he was familiar with the corrosive effect of fear. Fear might be short-lived, it might be suppressed, but it was ever present. Citations for bravery may say that someone showed no fear, but that was merely because they suppressed it successfully:

> 'Fear will make even cavalry dig, and without tools', so the old saying goes. But fear is rather a dirty word in the best military circles, and is seldom if ever mentioned, yet, as an emotion experienced by everyone to a greater or lesser degree, it is a most potent factor in war.[17]

In so many accounts of Black Tuesday, fear is put aside, left unmentioned. According to the legend, the men are doing well, the boys are cheerful. There was the question of trying to control and contain fear and with it the received wisdom that panic was contagious: keeping up appearances truly mattered. Frost tried to treat the whole situation as if it were ridiculous. And in some sense it was. They had been sent to achieve what was fast becoming plainly impossible: 'well here we are, for better or worse', his adjutant Captain Francis Hoyer-Millar had shouted from the ramp of the Bridge. For better or worse, there they were.

At 1530 hrs a Focke-Wulf Fw 190 came over and attacked the men on the Bridge. It dropped its bomb, which bounced off the ramp and skidded away, missing its target. As the pilot pulled up, trying to dodge the hail of machine-gun fire from the ground, his plane struck the church tower. At the Bridge, no matter what the Germans threw at them, there was still reason to cheer.

'Great joy all round,'[18] said Mackay.

18

THE WOODS: DISENGAGE

At the same time 'B' Company appeared somehow to have
been drawn into the battle, and the fire which we could hear
must be the German response to this attack. It sounded
most unpleasant.

Major Geoffrey Powell[1]

WITH THE SOUNDS OF BATTLE all too clear in the Village as the
fighting on the Dreijenseweg and the Amsterdamseweg reached its
crescendo, and Hackett's battalions were being pulled apart quickly
and ruthlessly by the men and armour in the German blocking line,
it was fast becoming clear that things were not running according to
any sort of plan. Around 1330 hrs Major General Urquhart decided
that he would have to see for himself exactly how 4th Parachute Brigade was getting on with its northern thrust, so he set off by Jeep to
find its commanding officer in his headquarters on the other side of
the railway embankment. Hackett had not taken up his offer of visiting Divisional Headquarters earlier in the morning, and while
Mackenzie and Loder-Symonds had paid him a visit at 1030 hrs to
make sure that Division knew what he was up to, this would be
Urquhart's first sight of Hackett since arriving in Holland. Urquhart's concern was the Division was going to be defeated in detail,
rather than fighting as a whole. The Germans were applying pressure to all of the Division's moving parts, his rifle strength burning
up in its attempts to get into the Town and relieve Frost, an aspir-
ation that seemed more and more unlikely as the minutes ticked by.

Urquhart knew that the bridge at the station in the right-hand corner of the Village was not safe to drive across. Although the Village had been relatively calm overnight, around dawn it was now becoming increasingly insecure. Getting to the top of the road, he turned left and drove west. Similarly dangerous was the level crossing at Wolfheze, which was also subject to shelling and mortaring. Urquhart had already used up more than his fair share of luck for one operation. The smart thing to do would be to ditch the Jeep and take a shortcut over the railway line. He scrambled up the embankment, marched down the track itself, and discovered Hackett's HQ in the trees lining the track. As Urquhart arrived at about 1420 hrs, the headquarters was strafed by Me 109s, but his luck held again and he wasn't hurt. The major general and the brigadier exchanged pleasantries, Hackett saying how delighted he was to see his GOC after the rumours of his disappearance.

Together they reviewed Hackett's situation. The attacks into the treelines and up to the roads were being stiffly resisted. Urquhart looked across the fields with his binoculars and saw men moving about on the other side of the open space that was due to be a Landing Zone when the Poles arrived, whenever that might be. The reality was that it was clear everything had gone to hell, that the northern thrust was failing, that the Germans were quite capable of anticipating whatever 1st Airborne might try to do, that any thrust would be parried. Hackett didn't put it quite like that, saying something along the lines of:

'Unless the enemy alters his plans in such a way as to favour us,' he told me, 'there's not much future for the brigade in its present line of advance.'[2]

Neither of them, however, were quite ready to concede that the northern thrust had failed. There may be no way in through the Bottleneck, but would it be possible to try something else? Perhaps bring the Brigade back south of the railway, regroup, and attempt a different approach? Most importantly, Urquhart wanted to 'tie in' 4th Parachute Brigade with the rest of the Division, though feeding them into the Town when things had gone so badly there was probably not an option likely to succeed. 1st Airborne was not acting in concert: 4th Parachute Brigade and its fiery brigadier had been doing their own thing. Here was the muddle in what had been decided in Urquhart's absence playing out: despite it being obvious that the situation in Arnhem was nothing like what had been anticipated by the planners the week before in England, Hackett was essentially sticking to the original Market Garden plan. This was perhaps a consequence of 1st Airborne being a Division that had been created piecemeal and that had never operated as a whole, its leadership politicized and broiling with backchat. Time was of the essence, for sure, but time had run out two days ago. If Hackett had found the night before to be a most untidy situation, what was it now?

Hackett was also concerned about cutting his losses north of the railway line, and most importantly shoring up his exits. The railway line meant retreat would be a complex affair. Getting his vehicles, guns and wounded out before the Germans counter-attacked – which they were bound to – was going to be essential if the northern thrust was to be abandoned. An alternative of pushing down the main road and meeting up with 11th Battalion, which had been redirected to Den Brink, was also mooted, 'later, if possible'.[3] Hackett and Urquhart couldn't know at this point that Hackett's other Battalion had been caught in the open in the Lombok estate and dismembered. They discussed this possibility and then Urquhart left, wanting to get back to his headquarters and assess the Division as a whole before instructing Hackett what to do. Urquhart bade the brigadier farewell, scrambled back up over the embankment, back to his Jeep and back to the Hartenstein Hotel.

Like Urquhart's, Hackett's predicament was that whatever decisions he might make he was making them too late, or at least with an incomplete picture of what was happening. The decision to send his two leading battalions into the Woods and up against the German blocking line, companies being pulled apart in under an hour, was the decision he would have resisted if preserving his Brigade were the aim. Just as Brigadier Gerald Lathbury had thought that his three battalions could race each other into the Town and to the Bridge unimpeded, so Hackett seems to have thought the Germans would not have anticipated his advance north of the railway line. His battalions, wrecked as they were, would not have the strength to fight their way out; the understatement he had employed when he said that 156 'had shot their bolt' now seemed faintly foolish. The Germans had no real decisions to make. As long as 1st Airborne were contained, things would inevitably progress in their favour.

Hackett had sent all but one of his troops of sappers from 4th Parachute Squadron RE to keep an eye on the level crossing at Wolfheze, and on his western exit from north of the railway line. During the morning, 133 Field Ambulance had moved out of the lunatic asylum and made for the Schoonoord Hotel at the crossroads in the centre of the Village. But no sooner had Urquhart returned to his headquarters than Hackett changed his mind. The level crossing at Wolfheze was under threat, with an attack coming from the northwest, potentially cutting off 4th Brigade. There were also reports that a division's worth of men was approaching. A sergeant from 156 Battalion had reported encountering a German self-propelled gun and an armoured car in the gap between Wolfheze and the Border Regiment's northernmost position. He'd been close enough to hear the Germans in the vehicles talking, so he reported the news first to Brigadier Hicks's HQ at 1st Airlanding Brigade, and it was then passed on to Divisional Headquarters at the Hartenstein Hotel. This stew of potential bad news demonstrated for Urquhart that time was up for adventures north of the railway line. It was instead time to take control and retrench.

What is clear now is just how unclear the picture that Hackett had was: the Divisional Diary makes no mention of the sudden threat of an enemy presence at Wolfheze, and the Border Regiment Diary notes no such major push either, even though they were guarding that western side of the Division. Brigadier Hicks also came to visit Hackett's headquarters and Hackett informed him of the new move of Lieutenant Colonel Smyth's 10th Battalion in light of this anticipated attack. His battalions were in such a parlous state he would need to extract them somehow, regardless of whether this major attack materialized or not: what he knew of the state those battalions were in is also unclear.

At once Hackett ordered Smyth and 10th Battalion to disengage from the fight around the Pumping Station and head for Wolfheze to secure his rear exit. On everyone's mind was the question of a German counter-attack. German defensive doctrine dogmatically emphasized the need to counter-attack, the thinking being that your opponent would spend a great deal of effort in the attack and not have time to reorganize quickly enough back into a defensive posture. This same doctrine had been what the Allied guns had learned to exploit so well in the last couple of years – the Germans could be relied upon to behave in a reflexive manner, and that would offer your artillery a target and an opportunity. In these circumstances 1st Airborne did not possess the means to do this with any true degree of effectiveness, and certainly not on the scale that had broken up so many determined German counter-attacks in Italy and Normandy. Unfortunately, 10th Battalion had not given the Germans much of a bloody nose, and had shown their hand in terms of the meagre firepower they possessed. Nevertheless, they were still more intact than 156 Battalion, and were dug in on the road, and for now, thankfully, not in contact with the enemy. On receiving the order to withdraw, Lieutenant Colonel Smyth seemed unimpressed – the Germans hadn't dislodged him yet: 'it's an order so let's get on with it'.[4] They'd been told to get going in fifteen minutes, unseemly haste for such a difficult and dangerous manoeuvre.

While Smyth might have been out of contact with the enemy, at that moment B Company were still under attack, involving hand-to-hand fighting and more panzers to boot. A Company were still on the far side of the Amsterdamseweg, where Captain Queripel had

been so nonchalantly crossing the road back and forth. A runner was
sent and he was filled in on the withdrawal. He lined his men up and
sent them dashing across the road. The Germans were firing down
the Amsterdamseweg, and they were firing into the Woods. The men
of A Company ran for it, firing back at anything that moved. Total
chaos and confusion reigned. Some men got caught on the far side
of the road, others were cut off from their comrades as unit cohesion
disintegrated. Jeeps carrying the wounded tried to drive west. Queripel, in his maroon beret, again a centre of calm amidst the chaos, a
.45 pistol in each hand, was shepherding his men over the road.

At the crossroads and the travellers' rest, where the Germans had
effectively placed a full stop for anyone trying to go further east into
Arnhem, the confusion played out in an unexpected manner. During
10th Battalion's retreat the Poles' glider lift had arrived (as we shall
see shortly). As B Company pulled back out of the Woods and
towards the Landing Zone, they encountered a force of Germans
whom they mistook for Poles. The Germans didn't speak English –
but nor did they speak Polish. There was a moment's hesitation, and
then a close-quarters firefight when the penny dropped that they
were Germans, not Poles. Sergeant Thomas Bentley wrote:

> Men we thought were Poles were Germans. There was a ter-
> rific skirmish. Sergeant Joe Sunley and Sergeant Harry
> Houghton were with us and they were terrific. We went out
> by pure guts: shouting and screaming. From then on, control
> was nearly impossible. I had to leave the remaining four mor-
> tars. My entire platoon except four men were missing.[5]

The way out of the Woods for 10th Battalion was now into open
country, with the Germans in hot pursuit.

At much the same time Major Pott, commanding officer of A Company from 156 Battalion, lay on the high ground at Koppel, unable to
walk, his leg broken, his wrist shattered. The Germans marched away

the walking wounded and left him there, once they'd made sure he had no weapons on him. He called out, alone, hoping someone might be about. His batman, Private Scott, and three other men appeared from where they had been lying low. They wrapped their boss in jackets taken from the dead to keep him warm, and he ordered them to find their way back to the Battalion. Pott would wait it out.

Major Geoffrey Powell's C Company had been offering fire support to A and B Companies as they had gone into the Woods, and had therefore been spared the hard fighting on the Dreijenseweg. C Company was the most coherent part of 156 Battalion left – at least until the order to withdraw came, which tested the company and Powell sorely. As the surge to the Dreijenseweg had petered out, the Germans had turned their attention to them, with snipers trying to pick off the officers. Powell ordered his officers and NCOs – who all knew each other anyway, and whom the men knew just as well too – to cut off their badges of rank. A sergeant's stripes on his smock sleeves were large enough to be spotted at a distance, and officers' pips and crowns gave away who they were, though of course so did actions like moving from position to position, pointing and ordering the men about. Binoculars and map cases too. With some grumbling, the adjutant had cut off his captain's crowns. The mortaring, which had been so effective all day, intensified.

Powell's forward platoons had been mortared after the crescendo of noise around A Company's attack had died down. They had no idea how the attack had gone, and Powell had no clue where Major Pott had got to, whether he had reached Koppel. The noise had been horrendous, ferocious: laconically, Powell thought 'it sounded most unpleasant'.[6]

One of Powell's men had been killed by one of the first mortar bombs to land by their slit trenches, another was wounded in the backside, and the rest of his men had taken this as a firm message regarding the virtues of digging in properly. The soil was sandy and not too resistant, even with the barely adequate fold-away 1937-issue entrenching tool. The slit trenches went in quickly, the men covering them with logs if they could grab them. While the trees in the Woods presented danger in the form of splinters from exploding mortars, so they also offered some protection. Powell's men had not even been in Arnhem for a day, but they knew how to dig now and were acquiring a good eye for how best to survive. There was no pattern to the mortaring, so every second getting dug in was precious.

Powell became concerned his platoons were too far apart now that the battle on the road had died down, and that they would not be able to withstand a concerted attack by the enemy. The walkie-talkies weren't working either. His platoon furthest forward, 9 Platoon, seemed to be most in danger, as there was the sound of engines revving ahead of them. He sent a runner. The moment the runner had vanished, one of the section commanders from 8 Platoon appeared, ashen-faced. This sergeant had been shot through the elbow; he had news of the situation further forward. The Germans were moving up and down the road in their armour, sweeping 9 Platoon's position with fire, out of range of anything the platoon could throw at them. Another sergeant was dead. Their commanding officer also: 'already nearly half of the sergeants had become casualties'.[7] In the parachute battalions, so as to make sure that the infantry sections possessed experienced leadership, they were commanded by sergeants. The pressure that Powell's men were under now, and the deadly business of being in one of those leadership roles, were making themselves obvious. Hence the need to remove badges of rank. And the need to keep it together.

With the radios not working, machine-gun fire creeping on to their positions, the random mortaring, Powell, like so many officers at Arnhem, knew what the crux of the issue was:

> Wireless batteries, food, water and ammunition: the four requisites for survival. The batteries were finished; we could exist for a time without food and water but ammunition we must have, and this was becoming scarce as well. We must get some more soon or we would be finished.

The mortaring was now quite unpredictable. The Germans would wait for a quarter of an hour, then mortar somewhere with no one in it, then return to dropping bombs on C Company's positions. C Company had no answer, no counter-battery fire. The German armour was similarly aimless, tooling about up and down the Drei-jenseweg, brassing up whatever it fancied; and by the same token there was nothing C Company could do about that either. Powell estimated the Germans were firing twenty rounds for every one his men fired, so the enemy could plainly afford to be profligate. His men were maintaining their fire discipline, only shooting at what they could see, but the weight of German fire was a bald assertion of dominance. C Company were keeping their heads down, while the Germans were doing whatever they liked. An unequal struggle was unfolding north of the railway line. Powell's men were also honing their instincts and not making for cover unless they heard a mortar they could judge as being nearby.

Once the slit trenches were dug and the wounded tended to, the dead were buried, if they could be, in shallow graves. As Powell gathered his thoughts and assessed his company's situation some simple truths revealed themselves: the element of surprise, the 'main supporting weapon of airborne troops', had failed them, and 'the Boche had stopped us reaching the bridge'.[8] Powell had his emotions under control. But the predicament that 4th Brigade was in – its advance defeated, progress impossible and German armour right on top of them, that they were now on the defensive less than a day after arriving – was one that nobody had accounted for. There was much to ponder, even for a lowly company commander.

The Battle had come to find even 156 Battalion's headquarters. Coming up behind A and B Company, the men of the HQ ran into machine-gun fire, and then armour. The Regimental Sergeant Major, Robert Gay, took it on himself to deal with the panzer. However, all he had at his disposal was a Gammon Bomb. The No. 82 grenade had been developed by a Captain R. S. Gammon of the Parachute Regiment. The eponymous weapon was one of those Second World

War anti-tank weapons that would guarantee the user either glory or, more likely, serious injury or death. It detonated on impact. Which meant you had to be close enough to throw it at what you wanted it to impact on. What was unique about the Gammon Bomb was that the amount of charge it delivered was variable. It had a stockinette bag that the user would fill with the appropriate amount of explosives, and then hurl at the tank or machine-gun emplacement or whatever proximate target needed to be dealt with. The Gammon Bomb had replaced the No. 74 sticky bomb, which contained 3.5 pounds of nitroglycerine in a glass sphere, a delicate and temperamental weapon even more dangerous to the user than the Gammon Bomb. Moreover, it wasn't as adaptable as the Gammon Bomb – a Gammon Bomb's fabric pouch could be stuffed with extra explosives. You'd unscrew the cap, pull the fabric fuse, and the weapon would prime itself in flight. But for the men of Battalion HQ to be using Gammon Bombs against armour was a sure sign they were running out of options.

Robert Gay took with him Private Gerald Flamberg, who had already been wounded in the shoulder when he had stalked a tank and thrown a Gammon Bomb from 30 feet to hit it. They got close but the panzer crew spotted Gay and he was shot through the legs. Flamberg pulled him away and bundled him into a Jeep. Incredibly, even in this tension and the heat of combat, a moment of embarrassment could rear its head. Shortly afterwards, collecting ammunition for his company, Powell found Gay sitting in the Jeep and reprimanded him for not pulling his weight. Strangely, Gay didn't respond as Powell thought he might. Instead he told him quietly and in control of his great pain that he'd been shot through the legs. Shame-faced, Powell apologized and returned to his men.

The situation was changing rapidly. 156 Battalion was crumbling, with only C Company in anything like the shape it should be. Then, in the midst of this tumbling round of orders and enemy threats, came the throbbing sounds of approaching aircraft.

19

1500 HRS: SKIES OVER ARNHEM

And now, in this fateful afternoon of Tuesday 19 September, everything began to go awry.

Roy Urquhart, Arnhem

D+2
OBJECT RESUPPLY AND STRENGTHENING AND CAPTURE OF ANOTHER DZ NW OF ARNHEM. 144 A/C ENGAGED, 120 SUCCESSFUL. 10 A/C REPORTED MISSING, SOME MAY HAVE DELIVERED GLIDERS BEFORE BECOMING CASUALTIES. OPERATIONS NO LONGER HAVING ELEMENT OF SURPRISE, PRODUCED CONSIDERABLY STIFFER OPPOSITION FROM ENEMY.

38 Group Intel summary

AT 1500 HRS THAT AFTERNOON, everything that could go wrong for 1st Airborne Division did go wrong. Eight minutes in which everything came undone.

1st Airborne Division had sought to pioneer ideas regarding resupply, working from a blank page and looking at the lessons of the Far East, where supply by air had come to be central to the campaign in Burma. None of these ideas had yet been fully put to the test, but the core principle was that an airborne force would take supplies of ammunition, food, medicine and all the other essentials needed to continue the fight sixty miles behind enemy lines. Like landing a whole division behind enemy lines, this relied entirely on air supremacy, which the Allies had by this stage of the war. Without it, an operation like Market Garden couldn't even be considered. In order for aircraft to drop supplies they would have to fly low and slow over the supply Drop Zones. Flak would have to be suppressed and a German fighter response neutralized. The men of the Royal Army Service Corps (RASC) on the ground in Arnhem, who were ready to collect, collate and dispatch those supplies, had until this point been running what amounted to a quartermaster's supply chain, zipping around in Jeeps delivering goods from their trailers. But the entire way the Division had been designed meant that D+2, Tuesday, was critical particularly in terms of ammunition and medicine. Men of course could fight on without food – up to a point – but not without ammunition.

The supply plan of 1st Airborne wasn't just built around air supply. There were three components. Getting the men and gliders and kit ready at the airfields they would fly from was the initial mammoth task, albeit one they had been through several times with all the abortive operations that summer. There was to be a second resupply by air and then a third wave – a large element of RASC troops who would not be dropped behind enemy lines but who would be arriving in Jeeps and trucks with 2nd Army (or whoever was relieving the Division). By the time Market Garden came around, this third wave had already left the United Kingdom.

The seaborne tail had departed for Europe a whole month before the rest of the Division, under orders for Operation Transfigure. This operation was planned to cut German lines across the Seine as the German army retreated from its shattering defeat in Normandy. 1st Allied Airborne Army was going to deploy Major General Urquhart's men, the Poles and 101st Airborne Division, landing at Rambouillet St Arnoult on 16 and 17 August. Like all the other operations preceding Market Garden, Operation Transfigure had been cancelled, with events moving too fast in France. Despite this, 1st Airborne's seaborne tail had left for France on 12 August, setting off for the Port of London from their bases in Lincolnshire and then disembarking at Juno beach in Normandy. The Ordnance Field Park Seaborne echelon – the road-transported ammunition alone – was quite the convoy:

> . . . [it] included ten binned 3-tonners, four GS 3-tonners, one
> 3-tonner for battery charging and another for battery storage.
> There were also two 15-cwt GS vehicles and a 15-cwt water
> truck, two jeeps each fitted for carrying four stretchers, thir-
> teen 4x4 5-cwt vehicles, ten binned trailers and six GS
> trailers.[1]

The materiel, however, was the tip of the iceberg. 1st Airborne's sea-borne echelon comprised 84 officers, 2,180 other ranks and 1,100 vehicles. Who, on the afternoon of Black Tuesday, were all sat in a gigantic traffic jam: '1000 – Div HQ message stating no move of Coln "A" before 1500 hrs today received. No move of Column "A" before 0500 hrs.'[2]

Unfortunately, Operation Transfigure happened to coincide with a major reorganization of supply within 1st Allied Airborne Army, the penny having dropped that so far inadequate provision had been made for resupplying any possible future airborne operations. This was pretty poor timing for the officers involved, now on the wrong side of the Channel. And, remarkably, it had been realized that there was nothing in place for capturing an airfield and exploit-ing it, another possible use of airborne troops as the advance towards Germany continued. The Germans had taken the lead with airborne forces from the start of the war, and seizing an airfield was central to how they used them; an airfield could be rapidly reinforced. Crete in 1941 in particular had been a success after Maleme airfield had been captured by the Fallschirmjäger. Given that the Allies had taken their cue from the Germans in developing airborne forces, it seems quite the oversight that this was not something properly in place. Since D-Day, exactly what one could do with airborne soldiers was a question now looking for an answer; operations were being put together in a swirl of uncertainty and reorganization. The officers trying to plan for any airborne operation – something they were doing every other week as putative operations came and went – were also having to design and then redesign the systems they were using. The sheer scale of the airborne undertaking cannot be over-stated; likewise the vulnerability of any airborne division to its logistic limitations. Given the congestion on the road to Arnhem from the Albert Canal, all the necessary stuff, this precious stuff, was a long way off from arriving.

When the Transfigure seaborne echelon reached France and the operation was then cancelled, they found themselves without anyone to relieve. On arrival the echelon had to find somewhere to set up, at the same time as making sure they were ready to go at a moment's notice. At least they were across the Channel, and no longer waiting in England, having the piss taken by men from other units for being airborne but nowhere near the battlefront. However, they were now cut off from the rest of 1st Airborne Division, effect-ively out of commission, playing hurry up and wait 400-odd miles away in France, where transport was in short supply, and their precious resources of Jeeps and trucks were being eyed enviously by all comers. Supply was stretched even for conventional Allied forces. The complexity of trying to keep abreast of supply requirements from the other side of the Channel, even when the Division had not been deployed on an operation, generated an altogether understandable response within planning. Overall operational orders might change, the objective might be completely different, but the task of supply remained essentially the same, and so did the solutions. The mate-riel would be packaged up, prepared, sent and dispatched until the operation was complete. The paradox was, however, that in order to be adaptable to the fast-changing front in North-West Europe and the constant churn of cancelled operations, the planning in itself became necessarily inflexible, set in stone. Orders were merely being reis-sued with the code name of the operation changed, but little else.

So, paradoxically, even when the plan changed, the plan wouldn't change. Just as 1st Parachute Brigade had used the same plan to rush for the Bridge as Brigadier Lathbury had prepared for the cancelled Operation Comet, so the supply scales and schedules remained in place: on an administrative order from the RASC to 4th Parachute Brigade's HQ it referred to plans being the same as for Operation Linnet, another of the cancelled operations from earlier in the summer.

The air element was becoming ever more complex. Coordination with the RAF and the prioritization of Transport Command planes was an issue in itself. Every aircraft supplying an airborne division was not available to SHAEF's standard supply operations. Nevertheless, as Market Garden became inevitable, plans to supply the men landed in Arnhem were finally put in place. Despite the hope that 2nd Army would reach Arnhem within two days, provision was made to supply for four days and even with the scheduled drops built into the plan there were measures devised to try to squeeze more into the initial lifts. Additional supplies were allocated to each Horsa glider.

Three of the vast Hamilcar gliders on Monday's Second Lift were packed with tons of supplies. Hamilcar No. 1 contained twenty panniers of ammunition for 1st Airlanding Light Regiment's 75mm pack howitzers, fifteen panniers of 6-pounder anti-tank rounds, sixty rounds of 17-pounder armour-piercing shot, as well as five panniers of 3-inch mortar bombs, serious vital ordnance that the Division would need for defending itself against German armour. No. 2 held sixteen panniers of Royal Engineers assorted stores, ten panniers of the 75mm ammunition, ten panniers of 6-pounder rounds, six panniers of mortar bombs, thirty rounds for the 17-pounders, barbed wire, mines and mine signs, pick heads and shafts, and screw pickets. No. 3 held yet more engineering stores, 6-pounder rounds, mortar bombs and thirty panniers of ordnance stores.[3] It is clear from these manifests that 1st Airborne was expecting to face German panzers. The contents of these three gliders would keep the men of

As the Battle continued, so more and more of 1st Airborne's transport was destroyed, making the business of resupply and relief harder. The Jeep, which so handily fitted into a Horsa glider, was a fragile and precious asset.

Stretcher-bearers move a wounded man in the parkland behind the Hartenstein Hotel. In the background is an ammunition and fuel dump, tyre tracks leading to it. The handrail in the foreground is on the stairs into the Hotel.

Generalmajor Kussin lies dead in the road. He had been ambushed by men of Jimmy Cleminson's platoon as they made their way towards Arnhem. At midnight on the 19th, Cleminson was in the attic with another wayward Major General, Roy Urquhart, cut off from his command as his Division needed someone in charge. Kussin's fate could easily have been Urquhart's. Padre Pare buried Kussin on Tuesday morning.

Corporal Ron Mills of 181 Airlanding Field Ambulance kneels at the Wolfheze graveside of Trooper William McKinlay Edmond from C Troop, 1st Airlanding Recce Squadron. Edmond was killed in the Recce Squadron's attempted rush to the Bridge on the Sunday. Some of the Recce Squadron did get their Jeeps to the Bridge, but like so much on Sunday it had gone nothing like according to plan.

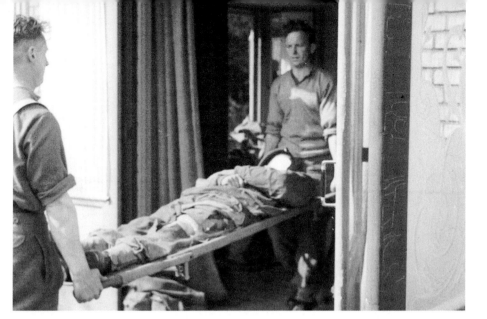

Above: Here at an improvised dressing station in Wolfheze, the wounded are triaged and tended to. The three Field Ambulances had much to do on Black Tuesday: 133 and 181 Field Ambulances had to relocate to the Village, while 16th Field Ambulance remained set up semi-permanently in the St Elisabeth Hospital.

Below: A Dutch woman (the official caption says 'possibly a nun') helps with the wounded. Captain Stuart Mawson, Regimental Medical Officer for 11th Battalion, was assisted on Black Tuesday by an anonymous Dutch girl who at the end of the day went home to her parents.

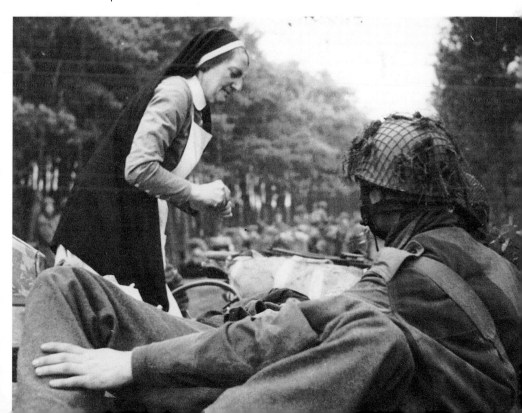

Men leaving the Landing Zones had to contend with the locals' delight at their arrival. The Battle quickly became a deadly business for spectators.

Soldiers from the 21st Independent Parachute Company, as Pathfinders, were the first to land, and were fast to sample the local hospitality. Their role was to make sure the three lifts landed in the right place. By Tuesday afternoon the supply zone was in enemy hands.

The Division's medicine was state of the art, with air-portable surgical equipment specifically designed for the task of treating the wounded. Yet alongside this preparation was the need to extemporize and a reliance on resupply: even the most modern medical provision had its limits.

Gradually the Division acquired prisoners, among them teenagers, fighting because Germany 'needed to live'.

Getting his copy written here is reporter Alan Wood, who was the *Daily Express*'s man on the ground at Arnhem. The following year he lost a leg crossing the Rhine again, parachuting at Wesel. 'We have lost all sense of time' he reported, later in the Battle.

Cleaning weapons, brewing tea, men in slit trenches near the Hartenstein take a moment. Behind them are the tennis courts where German POWs were kept – they too had dug trenches to protect themselves from mortars and artillery.

A soldier at a window in the Hartenstein Hotel, Divisional HQ. On Tuesday morning headquarters was relatively calm, the fighting elsewhere; by the end of the day it was the epicentre of the Battle.

A radio operator watches in his slit trench with a comrade, headphones on, Sten guns ready. The Sten gun lacked stopping power except at very close range.

A Jeep cooks off, another one lost. The .303 SMLE rifle that 1st Airborne had taken with it to Arnhem was an ideal defensive weapon, but not so good on the offensive in built-up areas.

Lieutenant Jack Reynolds shows the German film cameraman just what he thinks of him as he is marched away as a prisoner of war after the struggle for The Monastery.

the RASC and the RAOC busy on the Monday, though the men led by Major Bill Chidgey RAOC were able to claim the stores from only two of the three monster gliders because of enemy mortaring on the Landing Zone. This was fine for the initial supplies, but the supplies to come on D+2 were the key to 1st Airborne's ability to continue the fight.

Waiting for these supplies were the RASC based in the Divisional Administrative Area under Lieutenant Colonel Michael Packe. He had been the driving force behind the reorganization of the previous month, but here Packe was on the ground, making sure things ran smoothly. He was on hand for Divisional HQ, his headquarters in a cellar within spitting distance of the Hartenstein Hotel. In their efforts to keep the Division stocked, the RAOC contingent worked hand in glove with the RASC. The Ordnance Field Park – the ammunition dump – was also handily situated across the main road from the Hartenstein. Using commandeered German and civilian vehicles as planned, in addition to their own four Jeeps, the men of the RASC had spent Monday ferrying ammunition about the Divisional Administrative Area. Packe had nine soldiers. When the Second Lift came in, a convoy of six Jeeps to take ammunition to 1st Parachute Brigade in the Town was quickly assembled, the idea being it would go to the Bridge. By Monday night it was clear that this wasn't an option and the ammunition was decanted into a pair of Bren carriers which caught up with the Brigade ready for its renewed assault on the Town and the Bottleneck on Tuesday morning.

But Tuesday's drops were critical – they were all about replenishing the Division as a whole. In all, 388 tons of supplies were due to be delivered, a 'quartermaster's dream' of resupply. Weapons, 589 of all types, from Sten guns to mortars, including 171 Bren guns – the idea being that these weapons would be collected, taken to the Ordnance Field Park, and then redistributed to any units in need of them – were packed and ready in England. Millions of rounds too: 1,272,200 rounds of Sten ammunition; 1,641,630 rounds of .303 bandolier ammunition, as well as the same amount of the Mark VIII rounds for the Vickers heavy machine gun. These rounds were designed to send the projectile further than the standard .303 projectile and the men were discouraged from using them with rifles and Bren guns; but on the Tuesday, with the way the day was unfolding, every little would have helped. Some 823,756 rounds of .303 tracer too. Also due were 16,000 PIAT bombs. How critical these bombs were to the survival of 1st Airborne Division had been played out with bitter experience in the Town around The Monastery in the morning, and could have made the difference between hanging on until 2nd Army arrived and being overrun. Radios too: 164 sets were on their way, as well as 1,200 stretchers.

As well as the supply drop, the gliders bringing the transport and heavy weapons of 1st Independent Polish Parachute Brigade would be flying from England to land at Landing Zone L. Fog had interfered with these plans already. Ten gliders had made the trip on Monday, the remaining thirty-five would leave on Tuesday. Not only would they be landing on a different day, they were going to be landing on a different side of the Rhine to the parachute element, which was due to land south of the river on Tuesday morning. The air plan had been put together in the expectation that with Arnhem Bridge being held, the Poles would land to the south of it and then link up with their anti-tank weapons and supplies within the Town. This kind of dislocation was something that had not been considered for the British parachute brigades on D-Day, who had landed near enough to their gliders to rendezvous with their anti-tank guns and Jeeps in order to leave for the Bridge in good time. The air plan had been built around the need to deploy the entire Division, as well as the Poles. The assessment of exactly where gliders could land had been a key part of how the plan for Arnhem was put together, and came directly from previous experience. The reasoning was sound, the decision to land them miles from the parachute soldiers they were to support, less so. The churn of planning, coupled with the determination to send as many airborne soldiers as possible on any given operation, regardless of the

complications that might throw up, was now the tail that had begun
to wag the dog.

Squadron Leader Lawrence Wright RAFVR, who worked on the
RAF side of airborne planning at 38 Group, had found the months
after D-Day exasperating:

> Over and above these official planning tasks, we were plagued
> by amateur strategists. When a call from some Airborne officer
> asked for an immediate report on some new landing area, one
> might not know whether the plan had any higher authority, or
> was a mere private enterprise that the caller hoped to sell . . .
> From time to time my khaki counterpart at Moor Park would
> tip me off not to waste time on area A; that the bush telegraph
> advised B or C; we would explore one each and swop overlays;
> all this at a time when A alone was under official consider-
> ation. The week after, I might give him a like tip-off.[4]

There had been moments of farce, maps falling off the back of lorries, 'bloody awful titles' for operations such as Infatuate, an office
filling up with obsolete plans, disagreements about how to spell
Operation Comet: '. . . FOR OPERATION COMMET READ OPER-
ATION COMMET READ FOR OPERATION COMMET READ
OPERATION COMET . . .'[5] Officers were realizing they were trying to
plan a new operation using the same maps from the previous one.

Wright had been central to choosing the glider Landing Zones. It
was his assessment of the ground that had led to Major General
Urquhart choosing the vast Landing Zones west of the Village.
Wright had studied the polder south of the river and knew, from his
assessment of landing gliders in tiny fields in Sicily, that the ground
was impossible for a landing of this scale:

> Extending almost continuously southward from the river
> bank is a vast area that might be thought, from a glance at a
> small-scale map or even from a superficial view on the spot,

to be ideal Airborne terrain, flat and free from walls or hedges.
But all this is reclaimed, low-lying, soft polderland, cut up by
countless ditches and banks into small fields, with very sparse
road or track access.[6]

The tiny fields, soft and intersected by ditches, would make trying to
land hundreds of gliders on D-Day of Market Garden almost impossible. All the effort that had gone into making gliders quick and easy
to unload, and the concentration of force they afforded, would be
squandered on trying to negotiate the ditches and dykes. Closer to
the Bridge the terrain became even worse:

> In a 3-mile radius from the bridge, only one group of fields
> deserved closer study: the 'Malburgsche Polder'. This was
> enclosed on two sides by power transmission lines, and
> ringed all round by a dyke 8 feet high. The flak map showed
> a battery of 6 heavy and 6 light A.A. guns on this perimeter,
> and the tugs would have had to fly on after release over the
> airfield area predicted to be thick with flak. If a tug had to
> jink, and shed its glider, or if the glider was shot down, they
> might just as well never have started. During deplaning and
> unloading (which often took half-an-hour) the whole area
> would have been under observation and fire from good cover
> on the higher north bank. We accepted the Malburgsche
> Polder as a D.Z. for the parachute reinforcements to drop on
> the third day . . . but Chatterton and his staff supported our
> view that it was quite unfit for mass glider landings.[7]

The ground to the west of Arnhem was different, precisely because
it wasn't reclaimed polder land, and therefore not soft and boggy.
The 65 feet it was elevated above sea level made the crucial difference, and its vast fields were not cut up by ditches and dykes. Gliders
and their precious heavy equipment could not be risked south of
the river, and parachutists were better off landing near the gliders

with that equipment: the main landings would therefore have to happen north of the river.

This was a reality that Urquhart had accepted, indeed embraced. In the hurly-burly of putting Market Garden together, Wright had briefed the major general on their options for a successful landing:

> We had thoroughly thrashed out the landing zone problem with his Intelligence officers for about a fortnight [this shows the overlap with the plan for COMET], when I went to Moor Park for a final agreement with them. My arrival threatened to spoil their plan to take an hour off for a well-earned swim, but the General hearing of this, sent them off and summoned me; thus I was honoured with a first-hand exposition of his thoughts about Arnhem. I found him alone in the garden, seemingly painting a landscape, but his easel held the battle picture. He was of course fully aware of the basic dilemma . . . We shall be too thin on the ground, he predicted, and he reopened the question of landing gliders on the polder, making me restate the pros and cons of the terrain. It was not for the Air side, not even for Holly[8] or for Leigh-Mallory, to say whether greater losses would be suffered in landing on bad ground near the objective, in a flak area, than in fighting several miles towards it with a force initially intact. That was for Urquhart to judge, and he chose the latter. We were soon writing our orders accordingly.

What would happen on Tuesday afternoon was cemented in this meeting.

What impact this would have on the Poles and their ability to engage the enemy was left for their commanding officer, General Stanislaw Sosabowski, to figure out. Yet again his men were being treated like an afterthought by 1st Allied Airborne Army, or to put a shine on it, a handy asset should they be needed. The extent of his tribulations, waiting as he was at an English airfield to leave for Arnhem, we shall see shortly.

But events on the Tuesday were far from as expected only the day before. The push through the Woods into the Town had failed. As it was, these gliders of Tuesday's expected Third Lift and the Supply Lift were delayed by bad weather in England. The Polish Brigade HQ's Diary reads:

> 19th September 1944
>> Place: Down Ampney and Tar Rushton
>> 1200 – T.O. of 35 Gliders.
>> Place: Spanhoe & Saltby
>> 1000 & 1500 – Para lift of Bde Gp waits to take off; T.O.
> postponed 24 hrs on order Air Force because of bad weather.

Leaving on Tuesday at midday, those aircraft that weren't held up by the weather set off for Arnhem, oblivious to the fact that their supply Drop Zone and Landing Zone L might be a battlefield. The journey there was far more challenging than it had been on the previous two days. The two Stirling crews from 190 Squadron had a torrid time delivering the Poles. Pilot Officer Jones returned, having delivered his glider successfully, although he had, ominously, encountered 'a certain amount' of flight flak. Flying Officer Bebarfald's Stirling ran into low cloud over the Dutch coast and the glider had run ahead of him, almost snagging the tug with its tow rope, which had then broken. The Horsa went into the sea, its pilots killed, and three men were spotted getting into a dinghy that the Stirling dropped for them.

Flying out of Keevil in Wiltshire, 196 Squadron experienced similar difficulties. In an understatement of some magnitude, their diary calls it 'a bad day for glider towing'. Four gliders out of the nine they were flying to Arnhem cast off prematurely, one ditching into the sea. Two Stirlings had engine trouble.

At Tarrant Rushton in Dorset 298 Squadron were due to deliver ten Horsas and five Hamilcars. The Hamilcars – which were chalked to bring in the men and machines needed to lay a metal airstrip – were cancelled, and take-off for the remaining gliders was delayed until 1210 hrs.

Already at this point the Glider Pilot Regiment had effectively run out of pilots, and if any more were going to be required, they would need to come from the men relieved at Arnhem. Low cloud over the Channel did finally give way to clearer weather over the Netherlands, but on arrival at Arnhem there was 'much more' flak to greet them. The 298 Squadron Diary mentions seeing gliders shot down but none of them from their lift. It was clear that things were hotting up.

The tugs took the gliders across the Channel at low level – 1,000 to 1,500 feet. But once again radio communications became an issue. After the event, Urquhart claimed to have tried to get through to 1st Allied Airborne Army headquarters to inform them that his Landing and Drop Zones were under pressure, but now there was a breakdown beyond his ken and control. This time fighter cover hadn't been provided – for Sunday's lifts there had been vast fighter sweeps that had suppressed flak all the way from the coast to the Rhine. But word hadn't reached 2nd Tactical Airforce that the Third Lift had been delayed. The 160 or so Spitfires and Mustangs that had assembled at the rendezvous to accompany the airstream therefore hung around for a bit and then sacked off their escort duties. The Army wasn't talking to the Air Force – and the Air Force wasn't talking to itself. Whatever the state of communications on the ground in Arnhem and the difficulties with radios they might have been having – difficulties that had been priced in by the soldiers dealing with them, who knew the radio sets were unreliable – this was the kind of breakdown in operational communication that could only compound things for the men both in the air and on the ground.

Ahead of the Poles was the Supply Lift, consisting of 163 aircraft bringing in tons of crucial supplies. Everyone in the Village and the Woods – especially in the Village, where the Battle was happening somewhere else – stopped what they were doing and watched. Men waved, trying to divert the planes from approaching the German-held Supply Drop Zone V, to the east of the Dreijenseweg and behind the German blocking line – no more than a mile out of reach beyond the German guns, but a mile nonetheless.

The fleet of Stirlings and Dakotas came in low and slow. In the aircraft were the dispatching crews, part of the RASC contingent who had trained in getting the panniers and containers into and then out of the aircraft. But neither aircraft had been designed with delivering supplies from low level in mind: the Dakota was unarmed and unarmoured. In the Stirling two dispatchers would work with the pilot and aircrew to get the load dropped as fast as possible; in the Dakota a four-man crew did the same. The Dakota did at least have a rig for delivering supplies, tracks that ran the panniers and containers down through the plane and out of the door. The angle at which the aircraft sat made loading it more demanding than the Stirling. In the Dakota the men had to push the supplies uphill inside the plane. While more on the level, the Stirling didn't have the dispatching mechanism – the materiel had to be thrown out of the bomb deck by hand.

Dispatching was hard physical work, and dangerous. The men had to contend with heavy loads whipping out of the aircraft, flak, flying very low, all of which put the dispatchers at great risk. Some had been trained to use a parachute, some had not. Driver H. C. Simmonds RASC, 253 Airborne Composite Company RASC, stated:

> We had no parachute training at all. When they were issued
> from stores we were told to strap it on, pull the ring, turn our
> head to one side, count ten and hope.[9]

Wearing a parachute when manhandling the panniers was regarded as overcomplicated. One dispatcher in the 253 Company was snagged by a disappearing pannier and whipped out of the plane to his death. From his Dakota, the crew of dispatcher Harry Simmonds could make out the battle on the ground as 10th Battalion withdrew. His aircraft contained plastic explosives and petrol. Tracer struck his aircraft, one round jamming in the rollers of the supply rig and burning itself out. The flak around the Supply Drop Zone V was intense, cutting through the airframes. Men were hit and injured in the planes even as they tried to get the loads on to the arranged Drop Zone.

On the ground everyone, except the German flak gunners of course, stopped to watch the supply drop. From the lawn outside the Hartenstein Hotel, Major General Urquhart felt he had a ringside seat. If the battle in the Woods had been audible from the hotel, an armada of low-flying planes dropping supplies less than a mile and a half away filled the whole sky. And everyone in 1st Airborne Division knew the planes were lining up to drop their supplies, inadvertently, on the enemy. A bitter spectacle ensued, Urquhart wrote:

> Our signals requesting changed dropping points for supplies were not received, so now we were forced to witness the first act of the re-supply tragedy of Arnhem as the RAF crews flew through violent and intense flak in order to drop their loads accurately – on dropping points which we no longer held. On the ground, the troops tried by every means possible to attract the attention of these gallant crews: they waved, they paid out parachute material, they lit beacons. Into the deadly anti-aircraft fire the aircraft came on at a thousand feet maintaining courses without a single exception until their loads were delivered. Only to us on the ground was the agonizing irony of all this known. The Germans were getting most of the stuff.[10]

Harold Bruce of 21st Independent Company saw it too:

> Our expectations were even surpassed when the gliders and planes came in at long last, four hours late. The gliders landed

more or less alright, but the supply planes had a hell of a time. We observed one Dakota making two runs over the DZ with one of his engines on fire. He made sure of dropping all his supplies in the right place, and once his mission was completed he just disintegrated. Six more planes were lost that time.[11]

Louis Hagen was making a cup of tea in the Woods when he saw the planes coming in: 'They were so helpless; I have never seen anything to illustrate the word "helpless" more horribly.'[12] Padre Pare 'watched in agony at the terrible drama'.

Private John Stanleigh from 21st Independent Company felt the same. The day before had been a lark by comparison, and besides 'the ordinary soldier has not got much of a battle plan in his mind'. He thought the planes were Lancasters:

> ... we realised that every supply drop the Germans were simply waiting for our Lancasters to come down as low as possible ... and shot them down ... just like flies, coming down, burning, out of the air. It was terrible I can't describe ... how it felt to see these boys shot down. One of them managed to get out before it hit the ground.[13]

Among the survivors was a man who'd brought Stanleigh to Arnhem on Sunday, whom Stanleigh had entrusted with a letter to his fiancée in case he didn't come back. Along with the few other survivors he was given a rifle and told to get on with it. He still had the letter. He hadn't posted it.

Captain Christopher James RAMC, with 181 Field Ambulance, who had left the Tafelberg Hotel to deal with some wounded down towards the river, noted:

> It was an awful sight, that is the only word that fits the occasion ... The sky was full of planes flying low and so very

slowly, with containers falling out of them, some with and some without parachutes. Those planes seemed painfully slow to us as we watched, they were surrounded with little smoke blotches of exploding flak. Several planes although burning, continued their low, slow steady flight whilst their load was delivered, the pilots knowing they had little chance of survival. They were too low for the occupants to have any chance of a parachute jump. Such an exhibition of courage I never wish to see again, nor do I wish to be so awe-inspired.[14]

There was the ear-shattering sound of flak, shells tearing mercilessly through the sky. One Dakota, its starboard engine burning, came in low and slow, turned to make another run, flames consuming its wing as its crew hurled the panniers from the plane. This was Flight Lieutenant David 'Lummy' Lord's plane, a Dakota Mk III, KG374, from 271 Squadron in 46 Group. The Dakota's aircrew, bar one survivor, Flying Officer King, went down with Lord; six men were lost. Four of the dead were dispatchers from the 63 Airborne Composite Company, RASC. Lord had flown to Arnhem the day before with the Second Lift. At the end of their first run the dispatch crew told Lord there were two canisters yet to be dropped. He turned around and made his second run. Losing height as he went, the men dropped the canisters, and as soon as they were clear Lord yelled, 'Bail out! Bail out! For God's sake bail out!' while still at the controls. Sapper Stanley Holden from 4th Squadron RE stated:

> People were shouting for it to leave, 'Fuck off', as by now its engines was [sic] well alight. It was in a bad way and getting more than its share of ack-ack fire.[15]

The wing exploded, bringing the plane down north of Landing Zone S. Major Geoffrey Powell of C Company simply remarked, 'That bugger got a VC.' This agonizing eight-minute run was recalled by all. The air dispatch crew were all killed: they had delivered to the last.[16] Another plane from 271 Squadron also failed to return, Pilot Officer Wilson's Dakota FZ626. A third plane's engine was hit, but its pilot, Flight Lieutenant Hallom, was able to coax his Dakota home.

The other squadrons in 46 Group suffered similarly; like the crews in 271 Squadron they had found the cloud cover challenging – describing it as '10/10ths'. Two planes were lost – the surviving crew members complained that they had been diverted to a southern route for the trip, which they described as 'not pleasant'. Of the six planes sent by 512 Squadron all but one returned. Flying Officer Campbell had had to set down near Brussels, his plane shot up by flak. Also part of the supply drop, 575 Squadron sent sixteen planes with 256 panniers and sixteen bundles of bedding, losing Dakota KG388 flown by Flight Lieutenant Slack.

Plenty of aircraft needed repairs on their return, reporting burst tyres on landing and other complications. Such losses were in effect felt twice over – for every day that air supply was diverted from meeting the needs of SHAEF's armies in Europe, logistics got more difficult. Every plane lost made that task harder still. These aircraft were a precious strategic asset. The luck of the draw meant that the 437 (RCAF) Squadron were spared the ordeal for 19 September.

Disaster reigned among the aircrews. 38 Group also took a kicking. The 190 Squadron Diary reads as a litany of losses:

> Later 16 Stirlings took off at 13.00 hrs to drop 384 Containers and 64 Panniers in the Arnhem area. Very heavy flak was encountered and many aircraft returned damaged. W/O Pelletier in F/O Pascoe's crew was wounded in the shoulder also one despatcher as well. F/S Coeshott did not return and there was no news of his aircraft. S/L Gilliard failed to return. Whilst over the DZ his aircraft was hit by two shells severing the controls. The order to bale out was given and S/L Bantoft who was Second Pilot – F/O Cullen, Bomb Aimer, F/O Lawton Navigator, the F/E F/S Byrne and 1 Despatcher baled

out. It is thought that the WOP F/O Lane baled out but no confirmation. It is believed that S/L Gilliard did not bale out and that F/O McEwen was also probable lost. F/O Cullen and F/O Lawton landed behind enemy lines and eventually reached Britain. F/S Byrne was seen in Arnhem hospital by F/O Cullen and is believed to be a prisoner of war.[17]

Navigator Reginald Lawton bailed out of Stirling LJ934 successfully, later telling his MI9 escape handlers that there were too many Germans about to move before dark. He bumped into a 1st Airborne patrol who took him to the Light Regiment gun positions by the church. Here Lawton met up again with Squadron Leader Bantoft, the Second Pilot in his Stirling, who was also lucky to survive. Back at RAF Fairford in Gloucestershire no one had any idea the men were still alive – as far as they were concerned, this Stirling and its crew were lost.

In 196 Squadron the Australian pilot Warrant Officer Keith Prowd had been hit by flak just as he lined up alongside another plane – the pilots waved to one another and then his outer starboard engine burst into flames. On board the aircraft was Leonard Hooker from the Fleet Air Arm, an air mechanic from HMS *Daedalus*. Prowd didn't know him, and he wasn't on the crew list. Hooker had hitched a lift. As the Stirling started to go down – Prowd later noting wryly that a four-engined Stirling didn't handle well on one engine – the men prepared to escape. Hooker said he'd be hanging on to one of the crew – his parachute was beyond the main spar, which was on fire. Prowd jumped at what he thought was 550 feet; on landing he looked up to heaven and asked, 'What do YOU want me for?'[18] He found out soon enough. His navigator Mike Powderhill had been cut down by German machine-gun fire, his legs torn open, his crotch visible. Prowd – with permission from the German guarding him – covered him up, heartbroken at his friend's loss of dignity in death. The other crew members had been shot at and wounded as they came down on their chutes. Hooker did not survive.

Stanley Maxted, the Canadian correspondent who had flown to Arnhem with 1st Airborne, recorded the guns as the supply planes came in. The recordings suddenly take the listener into a present moment. His descriptions of what was happening, of the men running out to collect the ammunition and food as it landed around them, cheering and whooping, are somewhat undercut by his saying, 'they're such fighters if they can only get the stuff to fight with',[19] and the crackle and sudden boom of the German flak in the background. Cracking with dismay, his voice is interrupted by loud explosions as he tries to describe the scene, taking care to say he hasn't seen any planes hit. Maxted's voice falters with disbelief, and he leaves the microphone open to convey the sound of gunfire greeting the planes.

At the Bridge, Captain Eric Mackay had missed all this: at roughly the same time he was cheering the Focke-Wulf Fw 190 that had hit the church tower.

Watching on the ground, one Trooper Smith from the Recce Squadron was injured, hit in the eye by a piece of falling flak. Soon enough it became clear that the supplies weren't going to reach the men of 1st Airborne. But there was more hell to come: on the ground it would be a perfect disaster for the Poles.

20

ENGLAND AND THE WOODS: THE POLES

'Hal, what are the Poles doing at this point?'
'They were back in England, scratching their balls.'

The author in conversation with Hal Sosabowski,
September 2020

THE MEN OF I. SAMODZIELNA Brygada Spadochronowa were not volunteers: 'Can you give me any reason why only the brave should die?' asked their commanding officer Major General Stanislaw Sosabowski, perhaps not rhetorically. He liked a whiff of melodrama; those arriving at his training ground were greeted with a sign that read, 'If you are looking for death you have come to the right place.' Their motto was 'Najkrótszą drogą': By the Shortest Way.

These Poles were men who knew exactly who the enemy were and what they were doing. These exiles were of a different quality to the rest of the airborne fraternity. They had developed their own way of doing things and were resolute in their determination to remain independent of the British airborne set-up. Their long-term aim was to fight for Poland itself, and with the Warsaw Uprising ongoing, men in the Brygada, who had expected to be parachuted in to help liberate their city, had been on hunger strike. But they hadn't been sent to Normandy, they weren't fighting with Władysław Anders and his Polish 2nd Corps in Italy, and they had an unfulfilled airborne role. How could they not be destined for Warsaw?

Throughout the summer, Lieutenant General 'Boy' Browning had played cat and mouse with Sosabowski, trying to persuade him to commit to fighting under his command while at the same time offering him independence of command. Vexed by this, Sosabowski did what he could to fend off Browning, whom he found charming – like so many did. Browning's powers of persuasion had after all resulted in the British airborne establishment taking literal flight. But Sosabowski remained adamant he was his own man and his men were his. Browning was also competing with the Special Operations Executive (SOE) for the Poles' attention. SOE was keen on fomenting uprisings in Europe – setting it ablaze – and the Brygada's association with SOE's aims ran contrary to Browning's intentions.

Sosabowski had built the Brygada himself in Scotland at Largo House in Fife, where he and his men had been sent in September 1941. He had selected the officers and men personally for his Parachute Brigade, and at Largo House he developed techniques and equipment for training parachutists independently of the British. His men spent two weeks at the Monkey Grove or Malpi Gaj, an obstacle course in the trees around Largo House. This was doubly demanding as Sosabowski's men had all made the arduous journey from the Soviet Union and many were suffering from malnutrition.

Not only did the British airborne project have to justify their existence and cost to the War Office and the Air Ministry, but the Poles also found they were up against an additional grain of prejudice and mistrust. The men Sosabowski had sent to RAF Ringway near Manchester for parachute training were irked by the rudeness of the instructors there. That said, Sosabowski's manners and old-fashioned charm disarmed plenty of the people he was having to deal with in Scotland. He began preparing his men unofficially for their airborne role. The Malpi Gaj was a series of planks and jumps, balance beams and walls up in the trees at Largo House. Sosabowski was concerned with getting his men fit and agile and fearless. With a grant he had a tower constructed that simulated a parachute fall. The man would climb to the top, put on his harness and jump; the instructor could pause the fall and offer landing tips to the dangling recruit. These innovations made their way to Ringway and Hardwick Hall in Derbyshire soon enough. Sosabowski himself trained as a parachutist at Ringway – he was determined not to ask anything of his men that he wasn't prepared to do himself. His attitude was not unlike Johnny Frost's. He was frightened of parachuting. Of course he was:

> And so it was for most of us. All parachutists are afraid and, in my opinion, those who claim otherwise are either liars or very unimaginative.[1]

Sosabowski also drew up articles of faith for his men. They had to 'be strong, courageous, highly disciplined and well trained. Conscious of his part in modern war, he will not hesitate to sacrifice his life if it is necessary . . . he must keep smiling in the face of death.'

Since establishing the Brigade, Sosabowski had clung fiercely to its independence despite the best efforts of others to disrupt him. He had been sent by other Polish units a tranche of NCOs who had committed a variety of offences; men who had been dumped on him. Sosabowski's instinct was to offer the men amnesty – perhaps they had been badly managed – and give them a chance to prove themselves. Sosabowski felt confident he could deal with and train these men regardless of their past. What he really needed were guarantees that his command would remain his own. In 1942 an agreement was hammered out that the 1. Samodzielna Brygada Spadochronowa would remain under Polish command and, crucially, be used only in Poland. In November that year colours were made for the Brygada and duly consecrated in Warsaw, though it was not possible to smuggle them out for another two years. With the whole Brygada parading together for the first time on 15 June 1944, the colours were presented by the Polish President Władysław Raczkiewicz. (The Brigade had also been presented with home-made colours by the 'kind ladies' of Fife the previous year, and while they were of sentimental value, these Polish colours were the real deal.) Raczkiewicz and his cabinet had made it to France after the invasion of Poland in 1939, and then on to Britain after France collapsed the following year. Although he had entered into the Sikorski-Mayski agreement with the Soviets on 30 July 1941 in the wake of Operation Barbarossa the previous month, an agreement that had freed tens of thousands of Poles to fight the Nazis, the very existence of Raczkiewicz and his colleagues' government in exile by the latter part of 1944 was a source of great friction between the Soviets and the British government. Stalin had no intention of dealing with anyone other than his own Poles.

By the summer of 1944 the Allies were keen to get everyone that they possibly could into action. In July 1. Dywizja Pancerna – 1st Polish Armoured Division – was deployed in Normandy under the command of II Canadian Corps. Commanded by Major General Stanislaw Maczek, they joined battle on 8 August as part of Operation Totalize, fighting an epic battle at Mont Ormel in Normandy. Sosabowski had been under constant pressure the year before to give up on fighting only in Poland. In May of 1943 'Boy' Browning had informed him that he was asking General Alan Brooke to go back on his agreement with the Polish government in exile. Parachute troops of any country were an expensive resource. According to his account, Sosabowski pushed back – where would he get replacements for the moment if and when his men had to go to Poland? Browning told him not to worry – he would make up the numbers with British airborne soldiers. Besides, he would love to work alongside Sosabowski and his Brygada.

While he found Browning charming, Sosabowski saw this conversation as purest machination from one of the great wartime empire builders. Browning was trying to get him into his orbit, even demanding that the Brygada relocate to Salisbury Plain. Tempting as that might be – they would have better access to aircraft for training and so on – it was clearly a land grab. The Brygada was the

Polish government in exile's only remaining reserve. General Anders' men of II Polish Corps were already fighting now in Italy.

The pressure continued. Even Monty paid them a visit. In March 1944 Sosabowski sought to clarify – again – what his role was. The Polish government drew up compromise conditions – one major operation, withdrawal after 15 per cent casualties, not to be used in the early stages of the invasion, and planes for operations in Poland to be discussed. But it remained a fact that 2,000 airborne soldiers being dropped in to help the Polish Home Army, which according to SOE's estimates in 1944 was some 750,000 strong, might not be the best use of the Brygada. Nevertheless, the tussle continued, with Churchill rating the Brygada's symbolism if nothing else – it might lack numbers but it had political value far out of proportion to its actual strength. On D-Day, after a further exchange of letters between Sosabowski, the Polish chief of staff and Montgomery, Monty refused to be held to any conditions – he wanted these fine fighting troops at his disposal. Hanging over all of this horse-trading there was also the unspoken fear that the fighting might never reach Poland and that the Brygada might never be deployed, and thus that its men and its training were doomed to be a wasted asset.

Gradually, Sosabowski – and the Polish government – were worn down. Sosabowski had tried everything, even stating that his men were not sufficiently trained for operations in Normandy, which given his pride in his men must have taken some doing. On D-Day the Polish government handed over the Brygada 'lock stock and barrel, with no conditions at all'[2] to the Allies, with a hope that it might be used in Poland at some point in the future. Things then changed rapidly – Sosabowski was told to be ready to mobilize for the start of July. However, on 22 June Charles Mackenzie – Urquhart's chief of staff – alerted Sosabowski that he would need to be ready for an operation on 6 July. This was not the understanding Sosabowski had been working to. He wasn't ready. His men weren't ready. But now that Operation Overlord was underway, Maczek's

men would soon be committed to battle. With the airborne forces
desperately in need of something to do other than being put into the
line as regular infantry, and requiring some sort of justification for
their expensive existence, it was getting harder and harder for Sosabowski to retain his independence. A meeting was arranged for 25 June.

Sosabowski reported to Browning at Moor Park near Rickmans-
worth in Hertfordshire. Eric Down – the man Urquhart had replaced
at 1st Airborne Division at the start of the year – was also there. The
meeting was frosty – and extraordinary. Browning, who had not
been to see the Brygada for more than a year, breezily asserted that
the Poles were better trained than 1st Parachute Brigade had been
when they were sent into action in Tunisia. A new deadline, 1 August,
was agreed on to have the Brygada ready to take part in an airborne
operation, and talk of liberating Poland was quietly sidelined. Eric
Down joined Sosabowski in Scotland, and helped him get the Brigade into shape. They were finally allocated Dakotas for parachute
training. At the same time, the revolving door of planned and then
cancelled airborne operations that plagued 1st Airborne Division
and caused it such morale problems was still turning. But Sosabowski had acceded to Browning, so whether he felt the Brygada was
ready or not, it was now Browning's call.

And then came the Warsaw Uprising:

> On July 25th General Bor, Commander-in-Chief of the Home
> Army, sent the following telegram to General Sosnkowski
> [the Poles' Commander-in-Chief in the UK]: We are ready to
> start fighting for Warsaw. The arrival of the Parachute Brigade
> will be of important military and political value. Please
> arrange for the airfields in Warsaw to be bombed. I shall
> report when we start.
>
> So about six weeks after we had been switched to British
> command, the call we had all been living for came. We did
> not answer it. It was not surprising that the whole Brigade felt
> very strongly over the political actions which prevented us

carrying out our pledge. The whole world knows what happened in Warsaw: how Polish patriots rose against the Germans as the Russian troops approached the city and how the Russians deliberately stopped, leaving the Germans to wipe out the Home Army. Can you imagine our bitterness and our inner defeat?[3]

So, in addition to the on-off start-stop of cancelled operations, it was with the tragedy of the Warsaw Uprising hanging over them that the Brygada went to Arnhem. On 10 August the Brygada was placed under the command of 1st Airborne Division, affording Urquhart a fourth brigade, albeit one under-strength. The Brygada had been scheduled to take part in Operation Transfigure, which had been so close to happening that the seaborne tail was still in Europe. At the planning conference for that operation, Sosabowski first met Urquhart, whom he liked. He also thanked God it never went ahead. Other operations followed:

Someone, somewhere, with a vivid imagination, optimism and little knowledge, was producing parachute battle orders with the same frequency and ease as a conjuror producing rabbits from a top hat.[4]

Sosabowski, however, still voiced his concerns. He asked for his orders in writing. He didn't like the choice of Drop Zones, he didn't like that his men were being flown in separate lifts and that the lifts were on different sides of the Rhine. He didn't like much either that his artillery would be coming in the seaborne tail. And he certainly didn't like that the Brygada would be arriving on D+2, when things were scheduled to be over anyway with the arrival of 2nd Army. Brigadier Hackett, Sosabowski recalled, told him that a British general would never have got away with voicing his opinions in such a forthright style. Sosabowski's semi-detached attitude was giving him licence to speak out of turn and wind people up in equal measure.

At a planning conference on 9 September he made his feelings clear to both Urquhart and Browning, the latter now bored with dealing with Sosabowski. Browning was as keen as any in 1st Allied Airborne Army for Market Garden to go ahead; he wanted to get himself a victory. He would fly his headquarters by glider to Nijmegen, taking up quite a slice of the lift himself, some thirty-two Horsas and five Waco gliders. The Horsas would have had enough lift to deliver a Battalion of airlanding infantry. When Sosabowski challenged Browning, 'he replied rather lightly: "The Red Devils and the Polish Paratroopers can do anything."'[5]

Still, based on past experience, there remained a feeling that Market Garden would be cancelled. The twist for the Poles was that while it went ahead, their contribution was postponed. At least, the parachute component. On Monday the papers were full of how successfully Sunday's landings had gone. On Tuesday morning the weather had changed; it was foggy. The parachute element of the Brygada, the infantry and others without heavier equipment were scheduled to fly with the 314th and 315th Troop Carrier Groups of the USAAF based at RAF Spanhoe, north of Corby in Northamptonshire. They drew their chutes, checked their equipment, said their goodbyes, drank coffee from the YMCA: they hurried up and waited. The lift was on hold. The weather was no good. It was not until 1500 hrs that Tuesday's parachute lift was cancelled for certain. But the fog had cleared where the gliders were flying from and that element of the Third Lift had gone ahead. On the Landing Zone at Johanna Hoeve the Poles were about to land.

Coming in through a hail of fire, as 10th and 156 Battalions were retreating from their abortive attack in the Woods, the gliders containing the Poles' anti-tank weapons, a near-full complement of 6-pounders, came in to land. The same German flak weapons which had been used to such deadly effect against the parachute infantry now turned skywards – it was also a misfortune of timing that the

Germans did not have to choose whom to shoot at. The battalions were both retreating and not engaging the enemy. With the Poles were eight other gliders, carrying loads which had been unsuccessful on the previous days. The usual problems of towing gliders had had their effect even before they got to Arnhem. The weather may have been good enough to leave Keevil in Wiltshire and Tarrant Rushton in Dorset, but poor visibility had made the crossing fraught. Gliders had cast off early, and despite having been redirected to the southern route to avoid flak, the enemy still did what it could to interfere. By the time the thirty gliders that had made it to Landing Zone L were casting off their tow ropes, they had the Germans' undivided attention.

With German flak guns trained directly on the plywood aircraft, it was carnage. One glider spun out of control, somersaulting as it hit the ground. Pilots were killed instantly as they crash-landed. Heavy landings were the order of the moment, gliders coming in too fast, their loads rendered unrecoverable, their crews subsequently hospitalized. The Polish war correspondent Marek Swiecicki, who had arrived at Arnhem with the First Lift on Sunday, was there. Only that morning he had interviewed Polish POWs in German uniforms in the tennis courts behind the Hartenstein Hotel. The Poles were from Silesia in western 'German' Poland. One was forty-two and said he had been threatened with his family being sent to Oświęcim. Another had been working as forced labour and was conscripted into the Wehrmacht. There were Cossacks, Ukrainians, Russians, and other Soviet subject peoples, who were not as enthused about the likelihood of the war ending as the Poles, fearing whatever fate the Soviet Union had in store for men who had worn German uniform.

In the afternoon, Marek Swiecicki watched the Horsas come in:

> One of the gliders broke up in the air like a child's toy, and a jeep, an anti-tank gun and people flew out of it. We had never expected things to be so bad, so very bad.[6]

He could see the gliders being torn open by German machine-gun fire, the men desperately trying to unload under fire from the enemy. Swiecicki went to find some of the Poles who had escaped the Landing Zone. Among them was Second Lieutenant Wróblewski of No. 1 Anti-Tank Platoon, his legs and ribs broken:

> Beside him lay a corporal with two bullets in his chest. But there were only a few wounded or whole. The majority, the great majority, had remained on the landing ground, or were taken prisoner.[7]

Of the ninety-three Polish soldiers who had left England, nine were killed or mortally wounded. As the remainder fled the Landing Zone, confusion erupted between the retreating paratroopers and the chasing Germans, the dreaded language barrier of having the Poles fight alongside the British delivering its worst. The Poles fired on the British, the British fired on the Poles, the British didn't fire on some Germans, mistaking them for Poles. It was chaos.

Sergeant Sid Dadd of C Squadron No. 1 Wing found himself caught up in the fighting around the railway line and the retreating 4th Brigade:

> The paratroopers were driven out of the woods in front of us by flame-throwing tanks and we retreated back over the level crossing at Wolfheze. Staff Sergeant White was shot in the lung. Later we had the gun positioned in a drive through woods next to the crossroads and knocked out a tank. Finally we could not move the gun as the tyres were shot to pieces.[8]

Only three of the Poles' 6-pounders were recovered. The Third Lift had been nothing but a disaster. It had reaped the bitter rewards of the drawbacks in its planning, flaws compounded by the weather in England, how the battle had gone on the ground in Arnhem, and a fatal over-appreciation of what parachute infantry could achieve: the Red Devils and the Polish paratroopers couldn't 'do anything'.

The survivors joined the surge of retreating men of 4th Parachute Brigade as they disengaged from the enemy. The rest of the 1. Samodzielna Brygada Spadochronowa waited at RAF Spanhoe for the weather to be better the next day, oblivious to what had befallen their comrades. On the Third Lift was Sosabowski's personal Jeep, its owner still in England. It was unloaded and then captured, allowing the Germans to broadcast that Sosabowski had been killed. For that he had no comeback. The Germans were having everything their way. By 1600 hrs could anything possibly go right for Roy Urquhart and his men?

21

THE WOODS TO THE VILLAGE: CRUMBS OF COMFORT?

'It's not the despair, Laura. I can stand the despair. It's the hope!'

John Cleese, Clockwise *by Michael Frayn*

LOUIS HAGEN MAY HAVE BEEN trained as a glider pilot first and a soldier second, and at that, a soldier allergic to the Brigade of Guards discipline he'd been subjected to in his training, but he knew a retreat when he saw one. The Poles had landed, his first combat had ended, and now in a large crowd he too started for Wolfheze. He had abandoned his tea as he watched the Poles coming in, and the order came to move away: 'it was a long stream of troops, moving back slowly'. The men were heading for the railway line, which they would follow back to Wolfheze. Brigadier Hackett's unenviable plan was that they would then turn the corner left and down into the Village. This was a longer route than if they had gone east and south towards the Oosterbeek railway station level crossing, but he felt that given the German presence on the Drei-jenseweg and the likely resistance there it would be safer to pull his remaining chestnuts out of the fire towards Wolfheze. German machine-gun fire streamed across the field, not aimed at anyone or anything in particular but sufficiently full of intent to keep them moving.

Major Geoffrey Powell and his men of C Company, 156 Battalion, had watched in disbelief as the Poles had come in to land, a delicious second helping of targets for the German flak guns and machine guns in the Woods. When the Poles then mistakenly fired on them, Powell's men had shown great restraint: these Poles after all, a gun crew, had missed. Some choice words were exchanged, and then the Poles joined one of Powell's platoons as an extra section, digging in along with everyone else. Like so many of the men in Arnhem that day who'd come in specialized roles, they now found themselves fighting as infantry. Once everyone had calmed down and one of the Poles – whose name as far as Powell was concerned was 'Peter' – had taken charge of his compatriots, the Poles had a good laugh about what had happened. Powell remained unamused. There wasn't much to laugh about. He knew what trouble they were in.

Lieutenant Colonel Des Voeux now paid Powell a visit and briefed him on a rather less organized withdrawal with timings and bounds than had first been considered. They were to withdraw right away. Being intact, C Company was to do what it could to cover the retreat, as well as withdraw to Wolfheze when the time came. Des Voeux then ordered Lieutenant Kenyon-Bell with No. 9 Platoon to 'stay until the last'.

7th King's Own Scottish Borderers were also turning tail. With the Poles' lift completed and the battle for the high ground over, there was little or no point in the Scots waiting at Johanna Hoeve to guard the Landing Zone. Nevertheless, there was dismay that they had been ordered to withdraw. When the order came they had just repulsed a German infantry attack, and were feeling confident; in Urquhart's memoir he quoted an unnamed officer saying, 'You just can't get up and rush away from the enemy in daylight like that, you just can't bloody well do it!'[1] Among the men rushing away was the mechanic Albert Blockwell. He had spent the day dug in around Johanna Hoeve, been out into the Landing Zone to collect whatever supplies he could in his Jeep, watched men stream back from the attack into the Woods, and equally had looked on with despair at the Poles arriving in their gliders:

> I watched another glider hover slowly over the field, I could see tracer bullets pouring into it . . . I couldn't watch it hit the ground – perhaps it was full of lads, I don't know, it was horrible to see. It's one thing seeing lads going down fighting, it's another to see them go down without a chance.[2]

Dug in with a Jeep and five mates and a Vickers gun, Blockwell didn't need to be told twice when the order came to get out. They made for the railway embankment, joining a gaggle of vehicles and a growing crowd of men on the track heading south.

Major Geoffrey Powell knew he had to walk, but also knew that he couldn't, and absolutely shouldn't, no matter how urgent the situation, break into a run. But the crowd of men some 500-strong moving across the open field of the Landing Zone were not in any kind of order. With the road, the high ground and the treelines behind them, where only a few hours earlier they had advanced with such purpose, and the Poles' gliders still burning on the Landing Zone, this was C Company's moment of supreme vulnerability.

If the German self-propelled guns and flak panzers emerged from the treeline now, the men of 4th Parachute Brigade were there for the taking. Powell's company was split up, there were glider pilots, gunners and sappers, and the newly landed Poles too, surging, all moving away from the threat any which way they could. Powell felt the urge to try to control the throng, to get the men into order, men who only a matter of hours ago had moved up to their start lines like a model display. But what could he do? How could he lead at this moment when the men seemed leaderless? If he ran to get to the head of the column, they'd all run too. Panic was contagious. Even if he wasn't panicking himself.

Brigadier Hackett's recollection in later life was that the withdrawal was orderly and controlled. The account he wrote not long after Market Garden, however, differs:

> Great energy and even violence was needed [by] the officers
> of Brigade HQ to prevent some confusion.[3]

Major Michael Page from the Headquarters Company of 156 Battalion resorted to threatening to shoot any man who ran past him.

Mortar bombs dropped in around them. Jeeps weaved through the crowd. The depleted 7th King's Own Scottish Borderers were joining now, extricating themselves from guarding the Landing Zone. A Company of the KOSB had got cut off trying to head for the railway line, and instead headed east and were caught in the open, surrounded. They surrendered wholesale – in effect disappearing. The KOSB Diary states: 'What occurred on A Coy front is shrouded in mystery since no representative of that Coy appeared at the RV . . . Of A Coy there was no sign.'

Back in the Woods the Germans were following hard on the retreat; and at Wolfheze they were making themselves known too, firing on the men who had got back there. Hackett's wafer-thin plan to extract his Brigade began to fray. There was one consolation, though. A tunnel had been discovered under the railway about 500 metres west of the Wolfheze level crossing, a brick and concrete drainage culvert.

Major Aeneas Perkins of 4th Squadron RE had recced the embankment and found both the culvert and a livestock track up the embankment. Incredibly, miraculously, a Jeep could fit inside and through it. Suddenly there was a chance to get the Brigade's transport away from the trap north of the railway line and down towards the rest of the Division. Perkins split the squadron, placing a troop at either end of the tunnel, and sent men on to Wolfheze to cover the level crossing. His presence of mind offered 4th Parachute Brigade's transport a small crumb of comfort. Even so some men were trying to drive up and over the embankment, doing what they could to bounce and heave the 17-pounders over the railway tracks, with mixed results. In the words of sapper Alan Gauntlet:

> It took eight men to bounce a jeep with trailer over each track. We managed four, but then one became completely stuck, unable to move. With sniper fire and mortar shells all around we started losing men, so we made a run for it.[4]

Hackett himself became involved in organizing to get the transport through: ammunition, anti-tank guns, Jeeps, all the essentials he needed for his Brigade to survive. The sappers had come up trumps with their discovery. The tunnel, a scene of revving engines, men pushing and shoving Jeeps into position – the heavier they were weighted down on their shocks the better the fit, wheels spinning on the sandy soil – was the Brigade's sole piece of good fortune on Black Tuesday. Everything else had gone wrong.

Above them, the fighting around the Wolfheze level crossing intensified. 10th Battalion had been in better shape than 156 Battalion after the morning attacks, and their role in Hackett's manoeuvre, once they had disengaged from the enemy and moved to Wolfheze, was to get over the railway line and put a defensive screen around the crossing. Men from 10th Battalion were also converging on the railway line, while a rearguard led by Captain Queripel formed about 400 metres from the tunnel between the railway line and the Amsterdamseweg, fighting their way back towards Wolfheze.

As they went, they had bumped into enemy parties and strong-points. One such was a captured 6-pounder protected by machine guns. Captain Queripel, brandishing his trusty pair of pistols, had overpowered and killed the crew on the gun, recapturing it. He then found himself cut off with a small group of men; accounts differ as to where, but he took their remaining grenades and ordered them back. Sergeant Joe Sunley was one of the group. He recalled that

they had made it around the level crossing to the south of the railway line. Where Queripel was last seen might be in doubt, but his
bravery was not:

> Captain Queripel said 'Sunley get these men out of here.' I
> told them to do so and Queripel said, 'That means you too
> Sunley.' I answered, 'Sir if you stay so do I.' I was told 'that was
> an order' and reluctantly I went. Queripel had taken my 36
> grenades before I left and I never saw him again.[5]

By this point Lionel Queripel was wounded in the face and the
arms. Sergeant Thomas Bentley recalled seeing the top of his head
sticking out of a hole as he flung a German potato-masher grenade
back at the enemy. He was never seen again. Queripel was twenty-
four and it was his first battle.[6] He had just completed a company
commanders' course.

Powell meanwhile had consulted with Lieutenant Colonel Des
Voeux about the next course of action. It was decided to order the
remainder of C Company and forty men from B Company up over
the railway embankment, the tunnel being congested with traffic.
Unfortunately, the men were silhouetted as they reached the top.
German rounds and mortar bombs smacked into them as they
scrambled up it. Powell waited and watched with Des Voeux, called
to 9 Platoon, who had now caught up with him, and once the rump
of B Company had gone over the top of the embankment he called
out to the rest of his men to follow:

> I started up the bank . . . Hauling myself up the steep cinder-
> blackened slope, clutching at bushes to check slipping feet, I
> noticed that the enemy fire had quickened. This was a little
> like clambering across the firing butts on the range in the
> middle of a machine-gun practice . . . Then a burst of Span-
> dau fire ricocheted off the Railway Line, the bullets whistling
> over my head. On the heath below, a couple of mortar bombs

exploded. This was not a place to linger. The sustained noise from behind suggested that the German armour was on our tails. Heaving myself up, I jumped for the slope, boots ploughing into the loose soil and cinders as if I were running down the side of a mountain.[7]

At the bottom of the slope were more trees, into which the men who had gone before him had disappeared. There was no sign of the men behind him. Powell toyed with going back to find out what had happened to them, but the ongoing sounds of battle convinced him this might not be the best course of action. And besides, he needed to keep the men he was with in shape rather than go off and risk getting killed looking for others. The only options on offer were tough ones. And it was then, in the peace of a glade, away from the sounds of battle and danger, that Powell and the men with him discovered the cargo containers.

The 1500 hrs supply drop had left containers scattered across the Divisional area, as well as the Supply Zone 'S', which lay behind the German blocking line. Once the lift had passed, the men of the RASC and RAOC got on with collecting whatever panniers and containers they could, their Jeeps utterly essential to this work. Their morning had delivered on their training as mobile quartermasters: distributing ammunition and keeping the Divisional area ticking over, running rounds recovered from the Hamilcars landed on Monday to the Light Regiment batteries, and making use of petrol pumps in the Village to augment the fuel needed to keep the Jeeps running. Major Bill Chidgey of the RAOC enjoyed himself, particularly not having to do the paperwork:

> I personally enjoyed issuing stores, mostly vehicle and wireless items, without paperwork and without the hassle of normal bureaucratic processes.[8]

But the afternoon saw the need for a dramatic switch in tactics. Men who had flown to Arnhem with the prospect of carrying on with the non-combat roles they were trained for were now going to have to fight. Glider pilots like Louis Hagen were expecting that they might have to pick up their rifles and dig in, but the RASC and RAOC men were not so prepared.

As ever it was ammunition they needed, ammunition and medicine – fast. Even knowing that 2nd Army were at Nijmegen by now and going to be a day late, for 1st Airborne to last the course and deal with whatever the enemy had in store, bullets and bandages were essential.

Scheduled to be dropped that afternoon were 388 tons of stores. Twenty tons, a mere 5.4 per cent, were collected by the men standing by for it, although a considerable amount was collected where it fell and put to immediate use – one estimate is another one hundred tons got into British hands.[9] Men who had found themselves in possession of a rifle and sub-machine gun ammunition were unlikely to hand the materiel in so that the RAOC could redistribute it. The diary for 1st (Airborne) Divisional Ordnance Field Park for Black Tuesday sums it up:

Re supply arrived at 15.00 hours of which very little received.

They obviously needed food too. In their small packs – many of which had been dumped, lost or abandoned in the day's hectic fighting – the men carried a twenty-four-hour ration pack. The pack was designed to provide a soldier with 4,000 calories, and fit into the aluminium mess tin each man carried. They were under strict orders not to eat this food before they embarked, and officers had to maintain strict food discipline. Cigarettes, being a morale booster and an appetite suppressant, were issued too, in a twenty-fag tin. Clearly marked up on the ration pack in block capitals, to avoid culinary mishaps, there were biscuits, a meat block, an oatmeal block, chocolate, boiled sweets, instant tea, chewing gum, salt and sugar. And they'd thought of everything – also four pieces of toilet paper. There was also the 'compo' composite ration pack, designed to feed fourteen men for one day, or multiples and divisions thereof. The compo pack had a variety of foodstuffs to fend off boredom through repetition, but the men were not meant to eat it for more than six weeks on the trot. This came with eighty-four sheets of toilet paper.

But it was the supplies that made it on to or right beside Supply Zone 'S' that had caused the most anguish. Tantalizingly close, SZ S was the other side of the Dreijenseweg, the very road that 156 Battalion had wrecked itself trying to take. With the sounds of battle around, the exact outcome in the Woods and the strength of the Germans on the road were still unknown in the Village. Commander RASC Lieutenant Colonel Michael Packe ordered his men out to collect what they could. Panniers and containers with their canopies and shroud lines were tangled in treetops or on fencing. Captain Desmond 'Paddy' Kavanagh took Packe at his word, and wanted to do more. Kavanagh took three Jeeps to recce the supply zone, and sent another to the Bridge to deliver ammunition. These aspirations suggest how slowly news of how things had gone in the Town and in the Woods had travelled. The Jeep heading through the Town to the Bridge got as far as St Elisabeth Hospital. The driver, R. G. Pearce, noted:

> Here we were stopped by an officer who asked what we were doing. On hearing he told us we should go back, we wouldn't get 300 yards.[10]

Kavanagh decided he needed to recce the other side of the Dreijenseweg too. His men got ready to go.

Kavanagh put his foot down, and they raced ahead, past bloody scenes of battle. All around them, the dead. The Germans were in full control of the road beyond the bridge over the railway cutting.

Despite laying down covering fire with a Bren across the railway bridge, the first Jeep was hit as soon as it crossed. A pile-up of the Jeeps following ensued. Kavanagh, having landed his men it, was determined to make amends. But in the heat of the Battle he made a peculiar mistake – perhaps a result of being a soldier second, or just poor luck. He swapped his Sten gun for the Bren gun of his driver, Burnham Clarke. What they didn't do was swap ammunition. Clarke stated:

> He exchanged his Sten for my Bren and said: 'When I stand up you all run back over the bridge.' This he did, standing in the road and obviously diverting attention to himself.[11]

Kavanagh told his men to run for it. Clarke fired his Sten back at the houses by the road where the German fire was coming from, though he couldn't reload, having only Bren gun ammunition on him. Under cover of Clarke's fire those few men still standing got away, but Kavanagh was never seen again. On being captured, it became very clear to the RASC men what they had driven into: self-propelled guns, armour and plentiful Germans. They never stood a chance; the supplies out of reach and too dangerous to recover. Clarke said of Kavanagh:

> Captain Kavanagh's gallantry was a lasting memorial and an inspiration to all who knew him. In my opinion this officer deserved a decoration. Kavanagh was one of the best.[12]

Meanwhile the rest of 250 Light Company were in the corridor that stretched interminably from Eindhoven into Holland. They had only finally got moving towards Arnhem on Tuesday afternoon. In the rain in the traffic jam was 'Paddy' Kavanagh's best friend, Captain Richard Adams. He had been with the seaborne tail when it had left for the continent prematurely in August, in anticipation of the cancelled Operation Transfigure. Adams had watched the Second

Lift go over on Monday and his assumption was that 2nd Army was 'making whoopee'[13] with 1st Airborne Division.

Collecting supplies had failed. Word went out that the fourteen-man compo pack would have to be divided up into a third of a portion per man per day. The British 1st Airborne Division was running on fumes.

In the clearing just beyond where Major Powell had come over the railway embankment, the cry went up. His men had found containers. It was quiet for now, the sounds of battle muffled by the barrier of the embankment and the trees around them. A moment away from the bedlam of the retreat. Powell felt an urgent need to speak to someone about what was happening, but most of all he knew he couldn't let his men know what he thought of the ongoing debacle. Keeping up appearances was an essential part of command – he admired the way that Hackett appeared to be completely imperturbable and in control of himself, a completely reassuring presence. Getting things off his chest would have to wait. Instead, though, here was an opportunity to replenish supplies. Powell had been in Arnhem for more than twenty-four hours now, and in his distraction commanding C Company he had forgotten how hungry he was. He had enough tobacco to keep his pipe going, but these containers were a small crumb of comfort. Things were finally looking up.

His men prised the containers open: in them, ammunition for 6-pounder anti-tank guns. No use to man nor beast. There was cursing and bitter laughter. And then they found the red berets. Qualifying for the maroon beret was a big deal; the men of the seaborne RASC component were certainly extremely proud of theirs, and they weren't even in Arnhem. In the inventory for delivery to Arnhem were clothing items, crowns and pips, badges of rank for officers too. These supply scales had been drawn up long before Market Garden had been a twinkle in Montgomery's beady eye. So many of the orders for their op referred to previous aborted operations, if only to save on the colossal paperwork and bureaucratic fuss that went into their planning. Powell himself could see the reasoning behind the red berets being sent – in North Africa they had been a morale booster. The men who wore these berets were reputedly held in high regard by the enemy. Powell understood all of this even as he cursed the things, and he had, of course, ordered his men to cut off their rank badges.

Geoffrey Powell wasn't the only man to run into red berets. Padre Pare met some cooks wearing bright brand-new berets, which they'd found 'in a container full of them' when looking for food.[14] Allan Samm from the Recce Squadron also found red berets and cap badges: 'socks I could have understood, shirts I could have understood, but badges and red berets were beyond me'.[15]

Airborne warfare was still in its infancy in 1944. Aerial resupply, which was being used to such regular effect in Burma and the Assam Hills for General Slim's 14th Army, was younger still. The novelty of these operations, the rush in which Market Garden had been planned, and the way the Battle quickly distorted out of its expected shape, all served up berets meant to be symbolic of one thing – the dash and elan of airborne troops and their operational impact – but which quickly became symbolic of something else, hubris. The men joked they were for the victory parade through Arnhem when the time came. On Tuesday 19 September, maybe that would be tomorrow.

In the Woods, 4th Parachute Brigade had been in full flight, and Powell's concern with his company was bringing about some semblance of order. At the same time the men returning from the Town in the east were retreating as best they could, harried by the enemy. Perhaps at the Oude Kerk, the Old Church, lay their salvation?

22

THE VILLAGE: THE CHURCH

It was distressing to see this flash of panic which could have been contagious.

Roy Urquhart, Arnhem[1]

AS THE AFTERNOON WORE ON, only three miles away from the Woods the trickle of men coming back from the Town, which had started around noon, had become a torrent. In twos and threes, disorganized, disoriented and – for now – defeated, the men who had been fighting in the Town started to stream back into the Village on the lower road. 1st, 3rd and 11th Parachute Battalions and the South Staffords, or rather what was left of them, were heading back to join the rest of the Division. All of these battalions had lost their commanding officers: Dobie of the 1st Battalion had been captured; Fitch of the 3rd was dead on the river road; Lea of the 11th was wounded and also in the bag; and McCardie of the South Staffs had been taken prisoner too. Their men had come under the railway line, in Jeeps, the walking wounded too, anyone who could get away from the intense rain of fire from mortars, self-propelled guns, tanks and cannon. It was clear they had had enough, and that no one was in charge.

As officers had tried to hold on and organize their men, the pressure from the enemy had been too much. But where to go if you're an airborne soldier, and there is no rear? If you are, in effect, surrounded? Back towards where you arrived from: the Drop Zones and Landing Zones to the west, and the seemingly secure area through which the battalions had passed in the previous days. The trap at the Bottleneck into the Town had been too much for the four battalions which had given their all in their attempt to get to the Bridge. The efforts at The Monastery, on the embankment and beside the hospital were over. The offensive battle had reached its high-water mark. Johnny Frost and his men at the Bridge were on their own; they were going to have to wait for 2nd Army to arrive.

At 3 Battery's position by the Old Church, the guns dug into pits connected by a zigzag of trenches, Lieutenant Colonel Thompson saw the moment of danger clearly. Up to this point he had relied on men from the Glider Pilot Regiment, under Major Robert Croot, to offer defence; but if the battle in the Town was over, and a rout was underway, he would need to both reorganize and bolster his defences in anticipation of the Germans arriving. The men were clearly not planning to stop at the guns, they were being harried by an increasingly confident enemy and, with no officers to take command, had no orders. The bulk of the officers who had led the attacks into the Town with such determination and decision had been left behind, killed, injured, cut off or captured; those that remained were simply unable to take control of their men in the pell-mell retreat. Thompson's guns couldn't be the last line of defence on the lower road. There needed to be an infantry screen, and quickly, if they were going to stop the Germans pressing on along the lower road, cutting the Division off from the river and the possibility of relief from across it. The Division's rear, such as it existed, was now around this western end of the Village, in a thumb shape. Even as the supply flights were coming in over the Woods, a potential disaster was unfolding right here minute by minute.

Grabbing his Sten gun, and wearing his red beret rather than his helmet, Thompson set off up the hill and started cajoling, ordering, organizing. Men from 11th Battalion and the South Staffords were on the high ground by the railway embankment, and while panic hadn't set in exactly, they were for the moment completely lost. Major Robert Cain, the senior officer present, was, Thompson remembered 'a mess', and there was a sense of relief that someone was issuing orders. A sergeant from 11th Battalion said as much: 'Thank God someone at last has given us some orders.'[2]

It didn't matter whether Thompson knew exactly what had happened at The Monastery, or how the South Staffords had pushed as far as they could on the higher road, or when the PIAT ammunition had run out, or how the men had been surrounded and burned out. Right now all that mattered was trying to bring about some semblance of order. Thompson told Cain to 'pull himself together' and get his men into a defensive posture. He ordered a roadblock of Jeeps at the church to stem the flow of men heading west. Their 'morale was very low' and he had to be forceful. Troop Sergeant Major Tom Kent from 3 Battery wondered what Thompson might have done if they hadn't complied, 'such was the mood of the man at the moment'.

Gathering together equipment, a Bren carrier, machine guns and mortars, Thompson set about organizing a defence of the south of the Village, to the east of the church. He got the men to the ammunition dump by the church, made sure they had ammunition and cigarettes, and had them digging in around the church and up the incline towards Arnhem as soon as possible. In the meantime, the glider pilots who had been assisting with the defence of the guns went about hunting for German armour, keeping up the defences in the midst of the reorganization.

The men responded to Thompson taking charge, and with some orders discipline returned and they dug in: 'Thompson Force' came into being, for now at least. Cain had about 100 men from the South Staffords with him, Lieutenant John Williams had 120 men from 1st Battalion, 46 men from 3rd Battalion under Captain Dorrien-Smith (of the 'I wouldn't do that if I were you' exchange with Lieutenant Colonel Dobie of 1st Battalion only a few hours ago in the morning), and 150 men from 11th Battalion commanded by Major Peter Milo. They had anti-tank guns, they had orders. And they didn't have to go forward any more. That ordeal was over at least.

On Tuesday afternoon at the church, 'Sheriff' Thompson saved 1st Airborne Division with his prompt and forceful action.

In the Village, at his headquarters in the Hartenstein Hotel, half a mile to the north, Roy Urquhart witnessed something similar and was also compelled to intervene. With fighting all around the Village, knowing that the battle in the Woods had failed, that the supply drop had gone tragically awry, and with a more concerted effort from German mortars landing in the Divisional area, rumours began to spread. The sense of calm and confidence that Padre Pare had savoured on Tuesday morning in the Village had evaporated completely.

The lawn outside the Hartenstein, pockmarked with mortar blasts and littered with slit trenches, saw groups of men heading west, back towards the Drop and Landing Zones. Urquhart couldn't believe his eyes:

> There were small parties of hurrying soldiers, obviously uncontrolled, and then twenty or more, under a young officer, dashed across the lawn in front of the Hartenstein shouting, 'The Germans are coming!'[3]

Urquhart felt compelled to act and was joined by his chief of staff, Charles Mackenzie. Disgusted at a 'tall young officer' who was at the head of this fleeing party, he resorted to threats 'and I had to intervene physically'. His day may have started in the loft at Zwarteweg 14, but now Urquhart was physically restraining men on the lawn outside his own headquarters. Could a major general have had a stranger, more peculiar day?

He knew these men were, for now, unable to compose themselves, and as much as he detested it – Urquhart was an emollient fellow after all – he knew he would have to, like Thompson at the church, be forceful in getting them back into line. With threats and physical force, he succeeded. He had a 'special word' with the tall young officer, 'who in his panic had set such a disgraceful example', and whom for the sake of everyone's reputations he kept anonymous when writing about it years later. What did 'intervene physically' mean? At six foot one Roy Urquhart was an imposing fellow, and a flash of anger from a man otherwise regarded as easy-going might have done the trick. Maybe he reached for his revolver. That he wrote about this moment fifteen years later is striking in itself. But at the time Roy Urquhart had an insight that he felt went some way to explaining what had happened, how these men, for all their elite selection, eagerness to go into battle, or even confidence *that very morning*, might suddenly break. It was an insight born of his experience fighting in the North African desert and Italy.

Urquhart considered one of the critical differences between regular line soldiers and airborne men: that the latter were plunged into battle immediately, rather than brought forward and acclimatized to the distant sound of guns and the notion of tangling with the enemy. For all his training and the undoubted benefits of bonding with men through the shared peril and subsequent release of a parachute or a glider landing, the airborne soldier could find himself dealing with the enemy within moments of entering theatre, the possibility of death or injury accelerating from an abstract notion back home at base to a concrete reality within moments. Urquhart felt that this placed his men at a singular disadvantage, and went some way to explain the panic there on the lawn in front of the Hartenstein Hotel.

Urquhart also knew the truth of combat in the Second World War: 'Contact with the enemy means that men are up against not so much an obvious, visual problem as the unknown, the unexpected and the unsuspected.' Certainly his men may have had a blasé attitude towards the expected German resistance, as a result of a Battalion intelligence report that had percolated down to them that the Germans were merely line-of-communication troops, ear and stomach men (German invalids), old men and kids. By Tuesday afternoon, everyone had been well and truly disabused of this notion. Four battalions had been thwarted in the Town, German self-propelled guns were prowling the streets, unexpected and unsuspected – so it's little wonder that dismay caught hold. After all, the impression was that the war was almost over, even the padre thought so. As Urquhart put it:

> Airborne soldiers . . . are in it up to the neck right away. I had no doubt that many of these jittery men who now faced us would behave quite differently once they had settled down and would turn out to be as resolute as the best. It was, however, interesting to note that they came from certain units which were weaker than others as regards their state of training, morale and leadership. Nevertheless, it was distressing to see this flash of panic which could have been contagious.[4]

The Division was his command. He was where the buck should and did stop, yet he felt comfortable enough to publish this view only fourteen years later in 1958. What is striking is that Urquhart says his men had 'deserted' their positions, a word with considerable weight in 1944 and an aspect that Urquhart felt the need to dwell on. The action he was forced to take that afternoon doubtless felt like an affront. He knew all too well that open expressions of fear, of panic, whatever it might be called, were contagious and that training, morale and leadership were the key to maintaining courage in the face of the enemy, rather than any civilian notion of 'guts'. In this Urquhart's thinking is completely conventional for the time, and while he doesn't name names, it is striking that the GOC of 1st Airborne Division should have included this in his memoir.

He wasn't the only one who thought it. Lieutenant Edmund Scrivener, fighting with A Company, 1st Battalion the Border Regiment, felt the same. A Londoner, Scrivener had come through the ranks; he had been a gunner on coastal invasion watch, manning super-heavy railway guns 'bored out of our tiny minds'. In 1943 his commanding officer put him forward for OCTU (Officer Cadet Training Unit), in response to a call for suitable men. He passed and was assigned to retrain as a gunnery officer, commanding anti-tank guns. He was then seconded to the infantry, to become an airborne soldier with 1st Battalion the Border Regiment. Scrivener also felt keenly what Urquhart had observed:

> . . . worst of all, we were totally unprepared both mentally and physically for what we were to face. It's quite a shock to be ensconced in the comfort and security of a billet in England one moment, and then, a few hours later, find yourself in a foreign country where nasty men are shooting bullets at you. For some the shock was too great and they took refuge in a half-mad world of their own where they just sat and shivered . . . I had no idea what to expect, and how I managed to avoid the consequences of my ignorance I'll never know.[5]

Conventional wisdom around fear, courage, nerve, discipline, morale had been best summed up by Lord Moran (formerly Doctor Charles Wilson); indeed, Urquhart went so far in his memoir as to paraphrase him, saying that, as Moran rightly observed, willpower was the key moral component in battle. Moran's classic musing on men in battle, *The Anatomy of Courage*, was published in 1945, but it is an excellent summary of the thinking that prevailed at the time. Between the wars, Moran had lectured at the Staff College on the subject of 'The Mind in War', and *The Anatomy of Courage* was based on these talks; his thinking was well known and respected within the Army. He drew on people he knew, things he'd seen himself, his impressions as a medical officer, anecdotes and indeed trench lore. War had changed, and a man who might deal well enough with an afternoon facing the threat of dying at spear point as the sum total of his combat experience, as in the past, might not be able to face the impersonal random hellscape of the endless days of modern warfare. Moran wrote about men who went through everything unscathed, men with luck, men who suddenly cracked, officers who knew how to work the balance of courage, fear and morale with their men, and the simple blind chance of combat and death.

Moran was, famously, also Winston Churchill's personal physician. (He saved Churchill's life over Christmas of 1943 when the Prime Minister had caught pneumonia. As well as his duties looking after Churchill, Moran was involved in much of the wartime debate about the foundation of the National Health Service. After the war he published what was seen as an indiscreet memoir of tending to Churchill, which introduced the idea of the 'Black Dog'.) He had been a doctor in the trenches on the Western Front during the Great War. There he had observed the carnage of trench warfare up close, men of every class and background, how they had coped under the relentless pressure of the improbability and danger of modern warfare. Most famously he said that:

> . . . courage is will-power, whereof no man has an unlimited stock; and when in war it is used up, he is finished, a man's courage is his capital and he is always spending.

Later, in *The Anatomy of Courage*, he pointed out that 'if a soldier is always using up his capital he may from time to time add to it. There is a paying in as well as a paying out.'[6] As the Army tried once more to cope with a huge influx of civilians, volunteers and conscripts, it needed to formulate how it dealt with the issue of courage, and work out how to shape morale. Moran's language and tone is very much of its time, and for that reason is an excellent primer on attitudes within the British establishment: 'Conscription when it came hustled to arms a lot of quivering creatures who would never have gone to war of their own free will.'

At the heart of the problem was the citizen soldier. Like so many of his contemporaries, Moran lamented that the men the Army was drawing from were no longer the stout yokels of yesteryear, whose distinctive quality was 'Phlegm', whose 'courage seems to have had its roots in a vacant mind. Their imagination played no tricks.'[7]

Instead, the civilian soldier needed not to be treated with kid gloves, nor over-burdened with 'bullshit'. Moran was no fan of the Guards' obsession with drill. What he did appreciate, however, was their undoubted *esprit de corps*. This was harder to engender in wartime:

> This citizen soldier conforms to no single type; in a national army there are many who will only respond to the rigid discipline of the past, but there are others who find this hourly bludgeoning irksome. They must have a reason for what they do.[8]

This thinking was echoed by Montgomery, who said that he felt if the British soldier knew what he was fighting for, then he could achieve anything.

That afternoon in Arnhem, these rules seemed not to apply, or only briefly. As Urquhart's plans unravelled, so some of his men's faith in what they were there to do wavered. Away from worrying about where his battalions were and what they were doing, and what he could get his brigadiers to do, his strength of character and personal leadership were put sorely to the test on the lawn of the Hartenstein.

Strikingly, though, Urquhart's shrewd insight that airborne men don't get time to acclimatize themselves to being plunged straight into battle could also be applied to him. The thirty-six hours he had been absent from his headquarters could explain his excitement, disorientation and not being psychologically prepared for the command situation in which he found himself. And Brigadier Lathbury's giddy enjoyment at going forward is maybe also a mark of the effect of being suddenly behind enemy lines – in action at last after so many false starts. And Hackett's decision-making in committing 4th Parachute Brigade to the cataclysmic battle in the Woods also seems redolent of the disorientation of arriving smack in the middle of an operation, delivered from the sky. Cool heads had been required ever since Sunday, but they had not always prevailed.

Having shaped their wayward men back into their positions, Urquhart and Mackenzie took further action, passing on word that there was too much errant firing: ammunition was short and was only going to get shorter. Mackenzie toured the defensive positions around the Hartenstein Hotel, finding at least one weapons pit, complete with an abandoned Bren and ammunition. Divisional Headquarters, which had been a safe haven that morning, was fast becoming somewhere that would need to be defended. Having finally steadied the ship at the centre, Urquhart knew there was no good news from his outposts. The wounded alone were telling their own story of the Battle of Arnhem.

Throughout the day, under fire, amid the constant rattle of small-arms, the medical organisation worked to full capacity as the casualties came in; unconscious men carried on jeeps, their camouflaged smocks stained with great smudges of dark blood; still, white-faced bodies lying on the stretchers; and the limping but inevitably cheery walking wounded.

Lieutenant Colonel Howard N. Cole[1]

EVENING

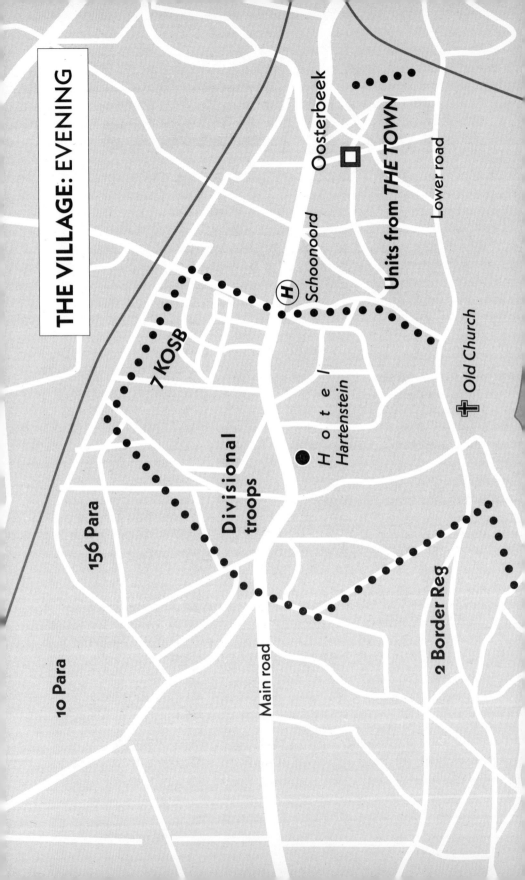

THE VILLAGE: EVENING

Oosterbeek

Units from *THE TOWN*

Lower road

Schoonoord

H

7 KOSB

Old Church

Hotel
Hartenstein

Divisional
troops

156 Para

2 Border Reg

10 Para

Main road

23

THE VILLAGE: LIFE AND DEATH
AT THE CROSSROADS

I cannot speak too highly of the extreme bravery and
self-control shown by the wounded under these most
appalling conditions; even when mortaring was at its height,
when glass and plaster were falling in profusion and when
bombshell fragments were whistling through the windows,
there was never a murmur or sign of hysteria from the
wounded.

Colonel G. M. Warrack DSO OBE ADMS,
1st Airborne Division[1]

ON TUESDAY AFTERNOON CASUALTIES were streaming in relentlessly from the Town and the Woods, swelling the numbers already
in the village. By the end of Monday, as many as 250 men were
receiving medical attention in the dressing station at Wolfheze, men
who had been defending the Drop and Landing Zones as well as
men from 4th Parachute Brigade's contested arrival in the afternoon. And the fighting in the Woods hadn't yet begun.

More buildings were repurposed as hospitals, draped with red
crosses. Getting men back to the Divisional area was becoming
increasingly difficult as more and more transport vehicles were
destroyed. On paper the three field ambulances had brought twenty-
eight Jeeps with them, but Bren carriers and any other Jeeps around
were also being used to ferry the wounded. At a school 100 yards
from the Schoonoord Hotel, a station was set up under Captain
Doyle with the Reserve Section of 181 Field Ambulance. By 1100 hrs
he was dealing with 300 casualties. A call went out to centralize the

medical effort: medics who were detached were to head for the Divisional area. More staff arrived. Men were patched up by their
comrades; some were beyond that kind of help. The padres were on
hand to offer consolation, to hear men's final words.

Captain Stuart Mawson, who had run for his life when the
German counter-attack on 11th Battalion had showered his aid post
with mortars, had made it back to the barn where earlier in the
morning Major General Urquhart had told him there was a dressing
station.

Despite his panic, arriving at the barn had brought Mawson to his
senses: to his surprise and relief the sergeant running things there
took him at face value, as an officer who knew what he was doing.
The sergeant's Regimental Medical Officer, Captain Lawson, whom
Mawson had chatted with earlier, had gone to St Elisabeth Hospital,
and now they were running a shuttle service back to the Schoonoord
Hotel. Helping the sergeant was a Dutch woman. Captain Lawson
had tried to dissuade her from joining in, but she had stayed since
early morning and was invaluable in assisting with the wounded. In
the barn it was strangely peaceful. Mawson felt detached from the
bump and crack of the mortars he had fled. But even he could see
that the situation here, for all its relative safety, was deteriorating.
The Germans were starting to snipe at the Jeeps loading up casualties. It was no longer safe to park them outside, and the doors of the
barn were kept closed because sniper rounds had come into the
building. This made Mawson furious.

Even so, he went on with his work, helped by the unperturbable
Dutch woman. He warned her it was not safe, to which she replied
it was safer in the barn than outdoors. Then she added:

> Why should I not be here? Your men have been wounded for
> my country. I'm glad to be able to help them. In any case this
> is Holland where I belong.

Mawson, humbled by this, replied, 'Thank you nurse. Quick, more gauze.'[2]

The civilians of Arnhem had greeted the landings with flowers, drink and cheers. The city had spent four long years under occupation, its spirit gradually crushed and dimmed by the German presence there. Oosterbeek had been a rather well-to-do destination for weekenders, hence the large number of hotels and guest houses. The rolling hills and parkland that surrounded it were a tourist attraction. As the fighting had gone sour, the prospects of immediate liberation dimmed, and caught in the whirlwind of battle the civilians found different ways to cope. Many took to their cellars, others even took to their beds. Still others put themselves at 1st Airborne's disposal even as their homes and city were destroyed. Mawson's respect and humility in the face of the Dutch woman's assistance was a common reaction among the men of 1st Airborne.

Meanwhile, the rest of Mawson's party had caught up with him, behaving as though it was the most natural thing in the world for him to have fled when he did. Gradually they worked through the injured men in the barn, getting them in good enough shape to be evacuated back to the Schoonoord Hotel, the barn doors opening to the revving engine of a Jeep, the stretchers held on frames welded to the Jeep's body. Every time the doors opened, the cacophony of approaching battle would burst into the haven of the barn. The afternoon wore on, and the drivers were reporting Jerries darting between the houses outside. Mawson knew it was time to go. Loading up the Jeep with the wounded, his orderlies Dwyer and Adams, and the Dutch woman, whom he knew he could not leave behind, Mawson told the driver to get them out of there. The Jeep raced out of the barn, swerving hard on to the pavement opposite and then dashing west, jinking and dodging debris on the road. Mawson had his arm around the Dutch woman to prevent her falling from the Jeep as it tore through the debris of battle. They came up over the hill on the lower road and down to the church where 3 Battery were dug in, swinging right and slowing down as they took the last few hundred yards to the Schoonoord, the driver reassuring them that they were in the Divisional area now, and safe. Mawson and his crew arrived at the Schoonoord in the early afternoon – though as ever with the Battle of Arnhem the various histories seem to disagree with his timings.

It was plain that every pair of hands that could help was needed, with the casualties mounting. But what were they dealing with? What was it that was killing and wounding the men at Arnhem?

A common refrain when writing about airborne troops is that one of the great handicaps they possessed was that they were lightly armed. And that the thing they feared the most was an opponent more amply tooled up. This was the airborne trade-off: getting men somewhere they shouldn't be – sixty miles behind enemy lines – came with the inevitable question of just what a man was able to carry, and what his battalion or regiment could transport into battle with him. Thus lightly armed soldiers were weighed down by the burden of not just their predicament but the stuff they needed to be able to fight. Conventional British infantry fighting in North-West Europe would expect to park their heavy kit before an attack. Being able to be as fleet of foot as possible could be the difference between life and death. But if a soldier was in a mortar platoon, carrying bombs forward for the platoon would take the spring out of his step. Yet in every other sense – tiny Welbike motorcycles aside – the men at Arnhem were conventionally armed. What had they brought with them?

The standard rifleman's weapon at Arnhem was the Rifle No. 4, the latest evolution of the Short Magazine Lee-Enfield (SMLE) rifle that the British Army had used in the Great War. This weapon with its .303 round offered the British infantryman accuracy and range and power. Its origins may have been at the end of the nineteenth century and as a result of a tussle between the various factions in the British Imperial military establishment – the British Army, the Indian Army and the Royal Navy – but when it came to procuring a new rifle, there were lots of considerations. Being able to use the rifle on horseback was important, as well as how much smoke the round gave off, and the question of range and power. Accuracy mattered most to the British Army, which was keen on making sure that its soldiers hit their target every time they fired a rifle: bullets were expensive after all, and in peacetime there was plenty of opportunity to perfect musketry. The Navy, however, which had the most money to spend, wanted a compact weapon that would be easier to store on ships, while the Indian Army, policing the Hindu Kush, were concerned with being able to drop a horse at 500 yards.

Compromise, as well as it being the Indian Army's 'turn', delivered the SMLE. On its introduction in the wake of the Second Boer War it was on the receiving end of a bad press, but the Army toughed it out and got used to the new equipment. With it came a new approach to musketry, and the possibility of rapid repeated fire, if not automatic. With a bolt-action that was a shorter pull than its German equivalent, the Mauser Kar98k, a well-practised rifleman could on a good day get away twenty to thirty rounds in what was called a 'mad minute'. Given it had a ten-round magazine, this certainly took some doing. The British military had come to love the SMLE and its variants, and was loath to have to replace the ammunition of which it had bought a vast amount during the Great War. These were industrial-age weapons, simple, easy to use, and while not cheap, were not expensive either. In 1943 the rifle cost £7 15s[3] to make; as the numbers increased, the quality of manufacture suffered somewhat, undermining the rifle as an accurate infantryman's weapon. Nevertheless, over seventeen million of the different varieties were produced.

The .303 round's muzzle velocity – the speed at which it left the end of the barrel – was 744 metres per second and it was effective to about 500 metres; the round would strike its target 500 metres away in under a second. The rifle had been adjusted and perfected since the Great War, but it remained essentially the same in its capability, and what it asked of the soldier. Its recoil firmly kicked its user in the shoulder, so he was better off firing it when prone or kneeling. To shoot it accurately – and airborne soldiers were trained to be adept marksmen, for ammunition was precious and had to be conserved if at all possible – took time. If a soldier was breathing hard from his exertions, it was all the more difficult. In the attack, particularly in the streets around the Bottleneck, the rifle was very much suited to something else: defence. With the power of its round and its accuracy, the Rifle No. 4 was a good enough weapon, its bolt-operated action allowing at least the possibility of making every round count. But for keeping the enemy's head down by sheer weight of fire – a weight of fire that airborne soldiers conserving their ammunition did not really possess – it was something of a relic.

Other armies had already addressed the problem of the bolt-action non-automatic rifle. The Americans had opted for the M1 Garand, a gas-operated automatic rifle, which used the gas propelling the bullet to re-load and re-cock. The Garand employed a similar size round to the Rifle No. 4, so it had considerable stopping power, but it had only come into American soldiers' hands after much controversy. The American martial self-image revolved around the frontiersman and marksmanship – conventional wisdom about the American War of Independence crediting rebel marksmanship as a deciding tactical factor – and the worry was that the Garand might encourage American soldiers not to take careful aim and simply plaster their opponents, or worse, their opponents' general direction. But as an infantryman's weapon it was one up on the Lee-Enfield.

The Germans had also found that as the war progressed and pressure increased on both industry and armies, standards in rifle training were slipping, and rifles were slow to manufacture. As a result, by the time of Arnhem they had developed the MP44 or *Sturmgewehr* 44 (it goes by both names, and it's too late to correct the confusion), which was made of pressed-steel components, though with a great deal more finesse than the Sten gun. The MP44 also fired a larger round than the standard sub-machine gun – its ammunition was 7.92mm (not much larger than a .303) but with a shorter 'pistol' cartridge. The MP44 really acknowledged the reality of the infantryman's lot – the chances he would have to shoot someone 500 metres away were slight, while knocking someone down much closer was more likely. An MP44 cost 70 Reichsmarks[4] to make, more expensive than the standard bolt-action Mauser Kar98k with its wooden body, but a conceptual leap ahead. The MP44 is often dubbed the first assault rifle, and with its curved magazine and wooden stock it very closely resembles, or rather is resembled by, the paradigmatic assault rifle, the AK-47. The MP44 was the state of the infantryman's art in terms of small arms, doing away with the need for the sub-machine gun and the rifle. The British weren't even close yet, and the rifles 1st Airborne had with them reflected that.

The fact remained that while paratroopers and glider soldiers were arriving on the battlefield by means of the very latest technology, guided in by Eureka and Rebecca radio guidance systems, the rifle that the majority brought with them in a valise, if landing by parachute, was from the turn of the century. They might be state-of-the-art elite soldiers, but as so often happens, art was not reflecting real life. For in the kind of fast-moving urban battle that was playing out on this Tuesday, a rifle with a bolt action good for killing or wounding a man on the opposite hillside in the Hindu Kush from the saddle of a pony was a long way from ideal. Certainly many of the men who arrived in the area in the south of the Village around the guns during the afternoon had initially thrown their rifles away and made do with Sten guns instead. Now they were in a defensive attitude they might need those rifles again.

The Sten gun, the 9mm sub-machine gun that airborne forces possessed, was as typical a piece of British wartime ordnance as there could be. Unlike the Rifle No. 4, this was an automatic weapon, light, portable and designed to be mass-produced cheaply in vast numbers quickly and easily. During the months after the fall of France in the summer of 1940, it became clear that the handful of Thompson sub-machine guns that had been purchased from the

United States weren't enough, and that buying more would be an expensive business. Pre-mass production Tommy guns cost a couple of hundred dollars; the Sten gun (named after Major Reginald Shepherd, Harold Turpin and the Enfield factory) cost just eleven dollars. Simplicity of design and austerity of manufacture were the hallmarks of the Sten gun, and the classic skeletal sub-machine gun, the Mark III, could be made in five hours. A later airborne model, the Mark V, had a wooden stock-and-pistol grip: sheet metal, stamped into shape and only two moving parts and a fixed firing pin, the perfect weapon for unskilled labour. The manual pointed out that:

> The Sten Machine Carbine is a small and compact automatic weapon, it is a British invention, and can be likened to the Thompson Machine Carbine in many respects.
>
> It has, however, neither the finish nor the complicated mechanism of the Thompson Machine Carbine.
>
> It is simple to produce, there is little about it that can go wrong, and it is very simple in operation. In spite of this, it is very hardy and will stand up to a good deal of usage.[5]

In the hands of the men it quickly gained a reputation. Or rather notoriety.

That notoriety was for going off unexpectedly, as Roy Urquhart and Gerald Lathbury could attest. Early models had a rudimentary safety catch, which was modified in later marks that meant soldiers had to be trained in how they cocked; experienced Sten users would carry the gun with their hand in the way of the bolt to prevent a negligent discharge. Its muzzle velocity reflected the shorter barrel and the weaker charge in its ammunition, a 9mm pistol round; the Sten threw its bullet at 365 metres per second, and its effective range was 100 metres. It offered the infantryman an automatic close-quarters weapon, light and easy to handle, with ammunition – in 32-round magazines – that was far lighter than the rifle ammo. Around four and a half million Sten guns were made; the Germans even copied it, which, given that its design owed a debt to their MP28, suggested the British had got something right.

The airborne establishment couldn't get enough of Sten guns in spite of the problems the safety catch caused when parachuting. At Bône airfield in eastern Algeria on 12 November 1942, the only man killed when 3rd Battalion the Parachute Regiment landed there was shot by his own Sten. Four days later at Béja in Tunisia, a Sten went off during the drop and wounded four men. Perhaps unsurprisingly, the practice of landing with a disassembled Sten emerged. Alternatively, some men kept theirs in their leg bag. For an airborne establishment of 12,500 men there were plenty of Stens, enough for every other man, as well as 7,000 rifles. Coming in by glider and less concerned with how bulky a rifle might be, the airlanding battalions had a higher proportion of rifles. But while the Sten may have offered the men a lightweight automatic weapon, what was clear was that its stopping power left something to be desired unless used at very close range. And automatic fire burned through ammunition.

Clearly the weapons that the British had brought with them had their limitations, but compromise is the essence of all practical design. The small arms that they were using were roughly analogous to their enemy's weapons, rifles and sub-machine guns. In the realm of light and heavy machine guns, however, the Germans had made considerable innovations and the differences were apparent. The section's light machine gun in the British Army was the Bren gun, with its distinctive curved magazine which sat atop the gun itself, firing the same round of ammunition as the .303 rifle and therefore offering the same kind of stopping power. The Bren was a fearsome piece of kit, but its German counterparts, the MG34 and MG42, were eagerly snapped up by men of 1st Airborne when they could get their hands on them. Although that brought its own problems. In Normandy, using the enemy's weapons had been the surest way to find oneself on the end of fire from one's own side. Men who were well acquainted with the sound of battle could tell a Bren from an MG34 or MG42. The problem persisted throughout the fighting in North-West Europe. Peter White, who was with the 52nd Lowland Division fighting in Holland later that year, remembered:

> The Germans had left a Spandau and an MG 34 in our billet in their hurried retreat from the village before the bayonets of the Royal Scots. These we used to bolster up our potential firepower in case of an emergency, though it was not a good practice to use enemy weapons as a rule, for their distinctive noise could lead to confusion and battle accidents. The Spandau was put with the sentry on look-out duty, gazing over the snow to the ribbon of dark woods containing the enemy. Several false alarms were caused by the sharp, zip-like crackle of this weapon which the innocent sentry always claimed went off on its own.[6]

'Battle accident' is quite the euphemism. In Arnhem, with ammunition a pressing need and with the advantage offered by automatic fire, a captured MG34 or MG42 was a welcome addition to a section's firepower. But wrapped up with these weapons and discussions of what they offered the men using them was a set of assumptions that were only just being challenged: how effective were rifles and machine guns anyway? What was it that was killing and injuring men on the battlefield? And how?

It may seem extraordinary to suggest this, in the midst of an unimaginably vast war and orgy of killing, but the science of lethality was relatively new in 1944. Or at least a fresh look was being taken at the subject by Solly Zuckerman – later Baron Zuckerman – a zoologist and research scientist, and, when the war came, a man who offered his considerable intellect in service to the British government. As soon as the war began, Zuckerman had turned his mind and its peculiar attitude to the question of lethality, or as he called it 'The Science of Killing'. He was unhappy with the assumptions around how and why bullets did what they did. It was grisly and complex work:

> A more effective approach to investigating the cause of death clearly involved the direct examination of cadavers. However, no systematic casualty surveys had been undertaken during the First World War. Consequently, the data available before the Second World War was sporadic and fragmentary and pre-1939 explanations of wounding tended to focus on experimental data produced from shooting animals. The alternative was to shoot human cadavers, which were not always readily available. At the same time, it was unclear what inferences could be drawn from making use of dead tissues.[7]

By virtue of being the only person doing this kind of research in Britain, Zuckerman quickly became the preeminent expert, attracting admirers and, inevitably, detractors. But he pressed on with his research, almost in a vacuum, relying on his knowledge of anatomy to challenge the existing assumptions around lethality and blast.

Kinetic energy was seen as the central question of lethality, delivering that energy to a target and its consequent effects. Convention said that a blast wave of air went through the respiratory system and blew out the lungs, rather than simply the force of the blast wave hitting and shattering them. Zuckerman's understanding of the anatomy of birds, with their denser musculature, led him to experiments that proved it was the force of the blast hitting a body that did the damage, not air waves. With the Blitz concentrating everyone's attention on these questions, as well as a peculiarly British early-war framing of how to get the most bang for their buck, Zuckerman and his team began to revolutionize the study of lethality. Examining corpses from France in 1940:

> His analysis, which was based on autopsies carried out on 220 service fatalities, revealed that small shell splinters caused

'dangerous, and even fatal, wounds out of all proportion to their size'. What made this interesting was that, of the 985 splinters found in the bodies of the personnel concerned, for every splinter between 2cm and 4cm there were approximately four splinters of between 1cm and 2cm, seven between 0.5 and 1cm and forty-three below 0.5cm.[8]

A great deal of what had been surmised about blast and its effectiveness was at best guesswork, at worst pure assertion. In a brickworks in Stewartby, outside Bedford, Zuckerman and his team did blast experiments on birds and rabbits, rabbits which often ended up on his staff's dinner tables. Even the most grisly work offered perks.

As the war progressed, advocates of strategic bombing took Zuckerman's work very seriously, reading into it what they needed, and it took him all over the world. In North Africa he crunched the numbers for the air-power-only offensive on Pantelleria near Sicily, which was a success that others were determined to qualify. But Zuckerman and his team arrived at the conclusion that there were so many random factors in play regarding lethality that the best you could hope for were probabilities. The received wisdom was that being struck by a certain amount of force, quantified by American studies at 58 foot-pounds (ftlbs), would kill you. But tiny things going very, very fast could also kill you, and large things moving more slowly might not, so contingency could upend these rules.

Zuckerman came to realize that this depended on where on your body you were hit, what you were wearing (clothing, a helmet and so on), the angle at which the projectile struck you, how dense the body tissue was, and so on, and that therefore it was almost impossible to say for certain what would cause death. Furthermore, when faced with a dead body for examination (and there was naturally a shortage of combat autopsies), Zuckerman and his team found it hard to determine which wound had delivered the fatal blow – a man with multiple wounds offered too many possibilities and (of course) couldn't tell you what had happened to him in what order.

Attempts to define and refine any hard and fast laws that could be applied to weapons became more and more theoretical. After all, how best to test this?

What Zuckerman's research had made clear was that the modern battlefield of the mid-1940s was a random place, one of endless and incalculable probabilities, and that while putting a rifle in a man's hand – a rifle in this instance that was simple, reliable and accurate, a reflection of what you hoped your soldiers were – might give the impression of bringing order to the chaos for the ordinary infantry-man, shooting bullets was of limited effect. You might succeed in keeping the other guy's head down, but were you doing much more than that with a bolt-action rifle or an underpowered sub-machine gun in a street fight? In September 1944 it was actually mortars that were doing the lion's share of the work.

In the close quarters of the Town, it was clear that mortars, with their ability to lob their rounds – or bombs – at steep angles, were ideal for catching men in the open and even when they were dug in. Light and portable, compared to artillery, both sides in Arnhem were keen to bring their mortars to bear, but the Germans had the advantages of transport and a more plentiful supply of ammunition working for them. An indirect weapon but one that works at close range, mortars offered the Germans a localized and immediate response to British attack; they are also relatively simple to operate, to reposition, and to alter the line and rate of fire. The Germans had developed several mortar types, of increasing levels of sophistica-tion, going way beyond the simple tube with a firing pin and a base plate. Some were heavier, others more complex, such as the M19 5cm automatic mortar.

Perhaps the best known is the notorious Nebelwerfer, or 'Moan-ing Minnie'. A five-barrelled multiple-projectile firing monster, the NbW35 could lob a 7.3-kilo bomb some three kilometres, a range that suited the situation in Arnhem entirely. It had bigger and heav-ier cousins too. The 120mm-calibre Gr.W42 threw a 15.65-kilo high-explosive bomb six kilometres. Whether airborne soldiers themselves were lightly armed or not was a moot point against well-organized and well-directed mortars like these. As we have seen in the Town, at the Bridge and in the Woods, what 1st Airborne lacked was the overarching power of British artillery, deployed as it had been at Corps level on occasion in Normandy, as well as the resources of a conventional Division's artillery. As a result 1st Airborne Division were in a sense fighting with one hand behind their back.

Mortar fire was a known quantity. The figures speak for themselves. The British Army's tally of battle wounds over the whole war stated that 75 per cent were caused by 'Mortar, grenade, aerial bomb, shell', with bullets and anti-tank shells accounting for a mere 10 per cent, landmines a further 10 per cent, blast and 'crush' another 2 per cent, chemical phosphorous 2 per cent, and the mysterious 'Other' the remaining 1 per cent.

In the North African theatre it was estimated that 75 per cent of casualties were caused by mortar and artillery fire. In their published findings from 1945, 21st Army Group's No. 2 Operational Research Section, looking back at the Normandy campaign, made it clear what a serious threat mortars were:

> The casualties in the present campaign from mortars have been very heavy, heavier in fact than from all the other weapons put together, at least as far as the infantry are concerned.
>
> This is due to a number of causes –
>
> (a) The Germans have a large number of mortars and nebelwerfers, and use them widely, while they have relatively little artillery:
>
> (b) Counter mortar methods are only partially developed and have not reached the degree of efficiency achieved by CS.[9]

No. 2 Operational Research Section was instrumental in developing countermeasures that used sound location to deal with German mortars. This was extremely challenging given that they are much quieter than artillery, owing to the low velocity of the round, and the shorter tube and distances involved. Radar was needed to detect them, heavy, truck-borne radar, a 10-ton set, technology that was being perfected in Normandy but had not found its way to 1st Airborne Division. Bringing such heavy and precious equipment into battle by glider would have meant leaving something else behind and been fraught with the question of failure. But the real problem was that, well deployed, mortars were deadly and extremely difficult to counteract:

> Exact figures for mortar casualties are hard to get. Medical records only show the weapon causing the casualty in a few cases. A number of Infantry battalion MO's, from four different Divisions all agreed in placing the proportion of mortar casualties to total casualties among their own troops as above 70%. This figure is widely accepted among Infantrymen, and it is thought if anything to be an underestimate . . . it is safe, therefore, to say that the Casualties due to mortars and nebelwerfers among British and Canadian troops in the first 7 weeks of the fighting, have been over 25,000.[10]

The problem was well known, the solutions elusive.

Because they didn't have to throw a round as far as a howitzer or gun, mortars in addition could fit more explosive power into their bombs. In an artillery shell, propellant would be 90 per cent of its weight. Not so the mortar bomb, which in general would carry twice as much explosive charge, giving it extra force to fire red-hot pieces of tiny metal at great speed at soft, fleshy people. And a mortar with a high-explosive bomb would also deliver a powerful concussive blast – taking us back to Zuckerman's range of fatal probabilities. If the red-hot flaming metal didn't get you, the blast might knock you down, crush your chest, wrench your helmet and snap your neck. Soldierly lore told you to keep your mouth open during a mortar stonk, to avoid the effects of pressure, also to cover your ears rather than putting your fingers in them when faced with a loud bang. These loud bangs were random and unpredictable of course. Some soldiers also preferred to wear berets or not to do up the chin straps on their helmets on the understanding that this would prevent your neck from being broken if your head was struck. (Zuckerman had become very interested in helmets and body armour as part of his work, and there were men at Arnhem who wore the body armour some of them had been issued with, the so-called MRC – Medical Research Council – Body Armour.) Digging in was your best and perhaps only option. In the Woods, mortars would shatter trees and send splinters flying into Solly Zuckerman's maelstrom of probable death or maiming.

In the Town, mortars would smash roofs to pieces. At the Bridge, mortar fire made British gun and weapons pits inaccessible. In the Village, Jeeps, so precious in keeping the Division moving, rearmed and in tending to the wounded, were especially vulnerable. B Company of the Borders lost all but one of their Jeeps to mortar fire. Captain Arvian Llewellyn-Jones at the Bridge described men stood still as if talking, unmarked but dead, a whole slit trench of gunners outside Brigade HQ killed simply by a blast, not a mark on them: 'the absence of blood making the method of death macabre and sinister'. It seemed that at times the German mortars held the fate of 1st Airborne Division in their hands. It was a mortar bomb striking Roy Urquhart's Jeep on Sunday and destroying his radio set that had sent him haring off away from his headquarters and up into the loft at Zwarteweg 14. And on Tuesday morning in his dash into the Town to take control of the Battle there, Colonel Hilaro Barlow, second-in-command of 1st Airlanding Brigade, was obliterated by a mortar, the command opportunity lost seemingly at random.

Elite soldiers, well motivated, and as well equipped as they could be, alert to the dangers of battle, keen on watching their flanks and their corners, faced the same random surreal dangers as anyone else. Being on the move and in the open, pressing home an attack as 4th Parachute Brigade had been that morning, meant they were vulnerable to whatever deadly mortar and flak-gun fire the Germans had in store for them, and with little chance of reply. As terrifying as panzers might be, it was mortars that dominated the Battle on the Tuesday. They had broken up and destroyed 11th Battalion as they'd formed up in the Town. And it was mortars that had mostly contributed to the stream of men pouring into the Schoonoord and Tafelberg hotels in the Village, men with shattered limbs, guts pierced, heads crushed, who would fill the field ambulances and stretch them to their limit.

On arrival at the Schoonoord Hotel, Mawson checked in at the improvised hospital reception in the hotel lobby. The Dutch woman was welcomed with a cheerful 'the more the merrier' and he set about acquainting himself with the hospital and the rest of the Divisional medical staff. The two-storey building was already transformed into a hospital, with one hundred men being looked after. A room with a grand piano and chandelier – the former hotel lounge – was now laid out with stretchers and the next room was a resuscitation ward being run by the blood-transfusion officer. Mawson noted an air of hygiene, of cleanliness, order and quiet calm. The hospital itself was being run by Lieutenant Colonel Arthur Marrable, who debriefed Mawson about the barn. They debated how best to get the rest of the wounded and the RAMC staff back from this outpost. Marrable was keen to return Mawson to his Battalion. He sent him upstairs to clean himself up and shave. Then came the news that Divisional HQ could not get hold of 11th Battalion Headquarters, and so it was decided that Mawson should stay at the Schoonoord. 'Go and have some food in the kitchen and then report to reception.'[11]

Around 1930 hrs the Schoonoord received a visit from Major General Urquhart. Everyone agreed that a visit from the GOC – about whom there had been no end of rumours – did the wounded men's morale a power of good. Banter from the wounded about being knocked out in the first half of the match, easy laughter, and the reassurance that the major general was, after all, in one piece. Arriving that evening also were 133 Field Ambulance from 4th Parachute Brigade, relocating from Wolfheze, forty more medical staff, and of course more and more casualties. It was relentless.

Padre Pare was also there, talking to as many men as he could. They had bedded down for the night before he could complete his rounds. They all asked him about 2nd Army. He claimed to find exhilaration in the Holy Spirit among the wounded.

In the nearby Tafelberg Hotel with 181 Field Ambulance was Captain Christopher James. He had come to 181 that spring, slightly shocked to have been selected for airlanding duties. As a surgeon he had a full team assigned to him, each with their allotted roles, plaster, prepping the patients for surgery; his batman, Bannister, made the tea but also ensured theatre lights were working. There was a nursing orderly, first class, who assisted James in all of his operations. With them also was Captain Barry Scott, their anaesthetist, whom James knew from medical school. James's team was designated No. 2 Team in 181 Field Ambulance. Like Stuart Mawson, James regarded himself as a:

> . . . very unwarlike Surgeon. Although I had been trained, I had no idea what things really were like in war, and that antique adage about ignorance being bliss was proved to be absolutely true for me in the days to come. As a first example of my ignorance, I instructed everyone to eat part of their haversack ration while we waited for the jeep to come and tow us.[12]

As the wounded began to arrive at the first of the Main Dressing Stations, Captain James amused himself with the fact that his pay would now finally kick in properly as a specialist.

Early on Monday morning, in the hospital they had set up in the lunatic asylum, James had performed his first operation in which he knew the patient would die, and yet he had neither the experience nor the confidence to stop going ahead with the surgery. Two moves later he was in the Village:

> The move from Wolfheze to Oosterbeek was a triumphal procession ... The whole Dutch population seemed to have turned out to greet us. The houses were decked with British and Dutch flags and with great lengths of orange streamers ... The Dutch enthusiasm gave one the feeling almost of a crusader. Here were these people being held down by the abominable 'Boche' and here we had arrived in a tremendously propagandised battle to free them.[13]

On arrival at the Schoonoord, his initial assessment was that it wasn't suitable for setting up a hospital, so James went on to the Tafelberg Hotel, where there was already a Dutch emergency-aid station. On Monday, with the fighting still distant, this must have seemed convenient. Operations at the Tafelberg began at ten that evening.

The following day fifty patients were already being treated by four officers and twelve men working together. When not in surgery James had ventured out to the church, where some men had been wounded by strafing Messerschmitts. Four had been killed and seven men wounded – he treated the injured men. He had taken a moment to examine the dead, his professional curiosity outstripping his desire for personal safety. 'On quick examination of three of the dead I could find no hole in the clothes to show where a bullet had entered, it is usually so small that one would easily miss it.'[14] Zuckerman's tiny random particles striking again.

On return to the Tafelberg (having wandered far enough east to catch sight of the collapsed and demolished railway bridge), he watched the supply run coming in. At 1800 hrs he returned to surgical duty, the plan being for his team to work on through until 0500 hrs the following morning. He had to amputate the foot of a twelve-year-old local boy with a serious ankle wound, with the help of the Dutch doctor who had brought him in.

Stuart Mawson had been fortunate to have arrived at the Schoonoord Hotel unscathed. With 1st Parachute Brigade was Corporal Geoffrey Stanners, a member of 16 Field Ambulance, who during the fighting in the Town had set up shop in the basement of a dentist's office. Stanners didn't believe in wearing a Red Cross armband; his experience in North Africa had made him of the view that he was more of a target that way. Along with all his medical kit, he carried a .45 pistol, dressings and two pints of blood. He made his way back to another dressing station at a warehouse. Stanners' father was a veteran of the Great War who had been blinded. The warehouse was hit by mortars and they were plunged into darkness. He thought, 'Christ, two blind men in one family.'[15] Some of the wounded had been killed. Stanners helped pack the survivors off to the Schoonoord, then walked back there himself. On arrival he was asked if he wanted his wounds tended to. Even though he thought he hadn't been hit, Stanners had thirty-three pieces of shrapnel in his back and some masonry stuck in his head for good measure. Adrenaline is clearly an effective painkiller. He was patched up and sent to the Vreewijk, another hotel, where he was looked after and where more Dutch people were helping. He remembered a woman called Jannie van Leuven, who had brought in injured men in a horse-drawn cart. Just as it is touching that Stuart Mawson's helper remains anonymous – he never knew her name – it is equally poignant that Geoffrey Stanners remembered Jannie.

In the time it had taken Mawson to shave and eat, some of the empty stretchers in the main ward had been filled, and the casualties kept coming. Amputations, blood transfusions, every manner of emergency surgical procedure. At the reception, men were triaged. Everything was noted down. Working together with his team on checking men's wounds and re-dressing them, the hours began to fly. With nothing to do but immerse himself in medical procedures, the stress of being in the heat of battle began to subside, and he worried much less about being separated from the Battalion and feeling isolated and useless. Here, with the other men of the RAMC,

Mawson could at least fulfil his role. As the afternoon turned to evening, the sounds of battle subsided and he and his team were granted a meal break. The anonymous Dutch woman said she had to go home; her parents were expecting her. He protested and told her it was too dangerous. She disagreed and, making to leave, her parting words were: 'Look out for me tomorrow.'[16]

Visibly exhausted, Mawson was ordered to bed by Lieutenant Colonel Marrable. He could sleep until 0200 hrs and then take the shift until reveille. It was too good an offer to refuse. Before he went to bed, they asked each other the question on everyone's minds. When would 2nd Army arrive? Marrable 'was good enough to give me the benefit of an answer in a small shrug of the shoulders and an agreed "perhaps"'. Mawson pulled off his boots, his gaiters and his tie, and went straight to sleep. Captain James worked on. The medical effort couldn't pause for the night as the fighting might.

And the fighting and the danger were getting closer to the Schoonoord. Lieutenant Bob Glover and Gunner Len Clarke from E Troop, 2nd (Oban) Airlanding Anti-tank Battery, who had been fighting with their 6-pounder in the Town, had been part of the retreat to the church that afternoon. They were now doing freelance anti-tank work, taking their gun hitched up behind a Jeep and cutting in and out of the side streets between the Divisional area and the rest of Oosterbeek.

A call went up that Tiger tanks were in the vicinity. Glover asked for volunteers: there were none, so Clarke went with him. They fired a round and scared off the tank, and then retreated to the crossroads at the Schoonoord and set up there. Glover and Clarke saw off another tank coming down the road from the station. It was good work – but by the end of the day the enemy was at the crossroads.

24

THE WOODS: FINAL DECISION

*I saw nothing to be gained out of recce parties in the dark
and it was agreed in the end that I should move the Brigade
at first light.*

Brigadier Hackett's account

BY NIGHTFALL THE RETREAT FROM the abortive attack in the Woods
had stabilized. Men had made their way across the level crossing,
had scrambled over the embankment or escaped through the culvert, some of them fighting as they went, some of them simply
fleeing. The Germans, it seemed, were not pressing their advantage.
Not that they needed to: 4th Brigade had been stopped from getting
into Arnhem, job done. With the bulk of the Division's supplies
being dropped behind enemy lines, the Germans could pick their
battles now. Brigadier Hackett would need to rally his men, once
they were over the railway line, but the immediate emergency was
over. They were still some distance, though, from the Divisional
area, the north-west corner of the Village, the men scattered and disorganized. Pulling things together would have to come first. His
Brigade Headquarters had been acting as infantry since the retreat
began – any semblance of normal order had had to be abandoned.
This improvised group saw off a German attack that threatened the
traffic at the culvert.

On hearing the roar of engines, Major Geoffrey Powell was drawn
to the scene of vehicles coming out from under the railway line and
through the culvert. In his curiosity he climbed the embankment

again and looked down at Hackett supervising the effort to get the Brigade's transport out of the trap it had made for itself, north of the railway line.

Heartened by this scene of organized effort, Powell took a moment to pause, then set out to find what was left of his company. One third of A Company hadn't made it back across. There were no mortars, no machine guns, a whole platoon was gone. The Battalion was down to 270 in all, from a total of 620 who had set off from their base in Melton Mowbray. Powell himself was still yet to fire his Sten gun.

Hackett decided to dig in there and then, south of the railway line, and not make his move to the Divisional area. 10th Battalion, numbering about 250 men now – down from the 528 who had left for Arnhem the day before – were further to the west, 200 yards south of the level crossing, themselves digging in and laagering for the night. By radio Hackett had consulted with Divisional Head-quarters about what to do and decided that a move during the night was too difficult. With men still missing and some who might return to the Brigade, he could be able to gather strength overnight. Any further moves would be problematic. His men were exhausted, and at some point the retreat would have to stop. Hackett's account sug-gests that Division advised him to stay where he was. Drawing his Brigade together for a move into the Village would be for the morn-ing. Powell summed up what he felt the morning held:

> Tomorrow at first light the Brigade would move into Ooster-beek to join the rest of the Division. But unless ammunition, together with air and artillery support, was forthcoming, the prospects were far from good.[1]

Major Pott of A Company lay in the Woods near Koppel, his leg broken, unable to move, his wrist shot through, wrapped in the smocks his men had covered him with.

By the time mechanic Albert Blockwell had reached the culvert it

was blocked – a Jeep had got stuck – so he made his way to Wolfheze as fast as he could, bullets pinging around, the trailer behind
him full of explosives bouncing, throwing up a huge cloud of
dust. He saw one Jeep turn the wrong way, right towards Wolfheze,
in the opposite direction from the rest of the Brigade and safety.
Blockwell joined the queue of fleeing traffic. He'd got away.

7th King's Own Scottish Borderers were massively depleted in
strength, having lost the whole of their A Company in the retreat.
The Scots returned to the command of 1st Airlanding Brigade and
crucially had resettled in the Village, rather than be isolated on their
own like the elements of 4th Brigade. They moved in after dark and
took the top of the right-hand corner of the perimeter, settling in
alongside the men of 21st Independent Parachute Company.

It had been a day of unmitigated disaster for the officers and men of
4th Parachute Brigade. Their attempt to take the high ground and
open another route into Arnhem had been an abject failure. When
the Brigade had arrived in the delayed Second Lift on Monday afternoon, it represented 1st Airborne's freshest asset, but within
twenty-four hours it had been eviscerated trying to take the high
ground it needed to hold before it could advance into the Town.
Reeling from a day of calamity and defeat, what would now happen
to the remaining 500 men of 4th Parachute Brigade holed up in the
trees between Wolfheze and the Divisional area?

Half-tracks prowled in the dark, but the men held firm. At first
light in the morning, Hackett decided, they would move on, and
rejoin the rest of the Division.

25

THE VILLAGE: LAST BATTALION LEFT

'Come on out, you lousy German bastards, and give us a fight!'

The men of C Company, 1st Battalion the Border Regiment[1]

THERE WAS ONE RIFLE BATTALION left intact. 1st Battalion the Border Regiment, who unlike the South Staffords and the KOSB had not been caught up in the tumult of manoeuvres and retreats of the day. In their new positions holding the western side of the Divisional area, defences had been dug during the night, so that when the Battalion was strafed in the afternoon after lunch no one was hurt, avoiding a repeat of Monday's deaths and injuries. The Battalion HQ organized patrols – there were no attacks to put in, no advances to make. The War Diary doesn't give much away either. The afternoon passed relatively quietly. Although there had been a concern that a division-sized attack was coming from the northwest, a concern that had prompted the disastrous withdrawal of 4th Parachute Brigade, no such attack crops up in the War Diary. Tuesday 19 September did not see this Battalion being filleted by German armour or mortar attack, instead it was a day of watchful waiting.

Like everyone else in the Division, they watched the supply run come in at 1500 hrs. Some stray supplies landed around the Battalion's positions and they did what they could to recover them, cursing 17 Platoon's poor luck in losing its handcart earlier in the

day. Among the containers recovered was another one bearing red
berets. There would certainly be no shortage of fresh berets come a
victory parade – the logistics people had seen to that. At 1730 hrs
Battalion Headquarters had moved into an imposing house on a
lane that ducked south of the main road and then ran parallel to it,
into the parkland, No. 3 Van Lennepweg. This building stood three
storeys tall, with a sloping roof, and high fences around its garden.
These grounds would serve to channel any German attacks around
the house and the trees surrounding it.

The day may have been calm but, with the attacks in the Town
and the Woods over, the Germans seemed to be finally turning their
attention to the men in the west of the Village. The defensive perimeter now forming around the Hartenstein Hotel was on its central
east–west axis no more than 1,300 metres wide, so any concerted
push down the main road would effectively cut the Division in half.
The perimeter's very shallowness posed the Germans the problem
of overshooting with artillery and mortars on to their own men.

By Tuesday evening the Border Regiment were the most intact
and coherent of the rifle battalions left at Major General Urquhart's
disposal: indeed, they were the only one left. Of the nine battalions
he had brought to Arnhem, one was hanging on at the Bridge, four
had been destroyed in the Town, three more demolished in the Woods.
The Polish battalions he was expecting simply hadn't arrived. Only
1st Battalion the Border Regiment had so far been spared.

At 1900 hrs the enemy started having a sniff around the Battalion, not just nibbling at the centre of the perimeter near Lennepweg,
but attacking all four companies. These attacks were seen off, as
noted by Major William Neill commanding C Company:

> Late that afternoon the Germans put in their first attack. We
> saw them assembling on both sides of the road, and as they
> crept closer we could hear them yelling to us in English 'Come
> on, Tommy, surrender!' My boys shouted back at them, 'Come
> on out, you lousy German bastards, and give us a fight!'[2]

Neill made his men hold off until the Germans were almost on top of their slit trenches, and when they were 50 yards away he ordered the men to open fire:

> The Germans faltered, then halted. I jumped out of my trench and called to my men to counter-attack, and we raced forward, firing from the hip and using the bayonet when we came close enough. The Jerries broke and ran, but we killed about 40 in all. That night the Germans sneaked out and dragged their wounded away, all the while keeping a stream of bullets pouring over the heads of their own men.[3]

Covering the approach along the main road were mortars and three 6-pounder guns. Running south from the main road was a track that continued all the way down to the river road, where the companies had occupied a house and had set up fields of fire to cover the open meadows and woods across from them. By virtue of being the last and largest coherent formation left, the Battalion was responsible for the single largest stretch of the Divisional area. It was decided to shorten the lines, to tighten up. The Battalion was now covering almost the entirety of the western side, stretched out over two kilometres, with B Company, yet again, off on their own. They had taken a significant piece of high ground at a place called Westerbouwing, on a hill right by the river, where a ferry to Driel on the other side of the river operated, exactly where the Poles should have landed that morning. There was a restaurant overlooking the approaches to the Village, which offered panoramic views. In different circumstances, it could have offered an ideal position as a lynchpin in the defence of the Division, but, as it was, B Company could only afford a single platoon to dig in by the restaurant, while the rest of the company had to cover the approaches. Again, as in their misadventures in Renkum, B Company were beyond the rest of the Battalion's orbit. Westerbouwing was essential ground to hold, but if the Germans gave it the attention they had given the brickworks on Monday, B Company might be in trouble.

With a Regimental Aid Post set up in a house near the Battalion's HQ, casualties could be taken care of and run over to the Schoonoord or Tafelberg hotels. Communication lines were laid, weapons cleaned, ammunition tallied, mortars sited on potential targets, patrols sent. The War Diary reported:

> Remainder of night active patrols were carried out with noth-
> ing to report.[4]

For the last remaining rifle Battalion in Arnhem, what would the morning bring?

In the south around the church, 'Sheriff' Thompson's improvised defence of the bottom of the Divisional area had stopped the rout and prevented the Division from being cut off at the river and sur- rounded. His prompt and firm action – unaware of the dramas playing themselves out in the Woods a couple of miles to the north – meant that the Division could dig in for the night and reorganize, and give the men who had escaped the battle in Town some respite.

Thompson reported to Division, and Brigadier Hicks sent Major 'Dickie' Lonsdale to the church to take charge; there is some debate as to when or even whether it became 'Lonsdale Force'. Either way, the Germans had been stopped, and the Division remained close to the river and in control of the southernmost road. The guns from the Light Regiment were all now dug in among the fields and mead- ows around the Church, zigzags of slit trenches connecting them with the music hall and the church. An aid post nearby had begun to take in more and more wounded, with a Dutch family, the Ter Horsts, providing their house as a hospital.

Other units of 1st Airborne were now maintaining a defensive and soldierly position, their previous roles fulfilled or at least no longer possible. 21st Independent Company were now fighting purely as infantry. There were no more manned lifts coming in except for the Poles, whenever they might leave England. And there was no chance of the men of the Independent Company getting across the river with their Eureka radio sets to guide them in.

Companies, battalions, brigades were the things of yesterday in the Oosterbeek redoubt. The men of 1st Airborne, soldiers, cooks and clerks alike, were going to have to fight in the best traditions of the British Army – and hope that 2nd Army would arrive on Wednesday. Almost inevitably, the Royal Artillery HQ Diary recorded another 'quiet night', even though there were anti-tank guns now defending the Schoonoord Hotel only a few hundred yards away. Tomorrow the fight would surely come to the Divisional area.

26

THE BRIDGE: ALL AFIRE

We didn't speak much but I remember saying, 'I wonder
what it's going to be like to die!' To which one of the
veterans replied with a grin, 'Don't know Kid, never tried it!'

James Sims[1]

Just before dark a Tiger tank drove down the lines of houses
1, 2, 3, 5, and 6 firing two or three shells into each house.

Major Digby Tatham-Warter's personal account[2]

As EVENING APPROACHED, THERE WAS no respite at the Bridge. The
Germans had repulsed the British in the Town and in the Woods,
and while they could not be sure of their next move, clearing the
Bridge now had their full attention. Although as the day wore on
their armoured attacks had been aggressively resisted, by the evening they were able to bring more and heavier metal to the Battle.

Because now there were two Tiger tanks. The roaring engines and
clanking and squealing of tracks on the tarmac signalled their
arrival. These behemoths, which had stalked Allied soldiers' imagi-
nations since their debut in Tunisia, were not invincible. With the
right weapons, a Tiger tank was one round away from being 56 tons
of scrap metal. The 17-pounder had been designed with exactly this
kind of threat in mind, and included for that reason in 1st Airborne's

inventory. But no 17-pounder had made it to the Bridge, and even if it had, they were nothing like as manoeuvrable as the 6-pounders. With the 6-pounders' gun detachments unable to get into the open, and the PIAT ammunition expended, there was little the men in Lieutenant Colonel Frost's holdout could do. The pair of Tiger tanks could drive right up to the already shattered buildings and fire into them at will.

At first, Private James Sims, perhaps inevitably, wondered whether the approaching tanks were from 2nd Army, and if finally the promise of relief was coming true. Instead, these were two Tiger tanks, forcing their way through the debris of yesterday morning's attack, with self-propelled guns in their wake. His feelings of disappointment and anger quickly followed.

The Tiger tank held a particular fascination for the British soldier. It was said that every tank encountered in Normandy was a Tiger – an impossibility given that only 1,354 had been built and they were spread to all four corners of the Nazi war effort – and 'Tiger Fever' was a very real phenomenon. The British hadn't helped themselves in this regard. When the Tiger – Panzer Mark VI – was first encountered in early 1943, the British press had gone to town describing the monster tanks and their arrival in North Africa. The *Daily Mail* called them 'land battleships' – an echo of the original Great War conception of the tank – and incorrectly reckoned they had a truly fantastical seven inches of armour plating. Not quite right but hardly something to inspire the Tommies in Tunisia, who would face them soon enough. Bigger and certainly more powerfully armed than any Allied equivalent, the first Tiger captured, No. 131, was displayed on Horse Guards Parade in November 1943, which again can hardly have served to inspire British soldiers training that winter for the invasion of Europe. But the Tiger's high-velocity 88mm gun – effective on the steppe against Soviet T-34s as far as a mile away – was now being used to blast out the paratroopers.

The tank's turret traversed and it raked the building with tracer – a prelude the men interpreted as a warning of imminent shelling. They were right. The tank fired two shells. The second one blew out the walls and brought the roof down. Six men had been ordered to hold on to the house, the rest told to go out into the garden and dig in. Private Sims had grabbed a pick and was about to start digging when another shell struck. Six men were killed outright. Sims was hit, an Irish soldier with him too. He passed out and woke up screaming in a cellar among the wounded, stuck to the floor by another man's blood, another man out of the Battle, another defender needing attention.

Major Peter 'Pongo' Lewis of C Company of 3rd Battalion, the only other infantry element of 1st Parachute Brigade that had got to the Bridge on Sunday, found a way to protect his men:

> In the evening, we were attacked by two Mark VI Tiger tanks which fired solid shot through our house at 30 yards' range. I cleared the top part of the house and as they were unable to depress their guns enough, they could not clear us from the bottom.

Lewis's men had joined Captain Mackay in the school. Despite the arrival of these huge panzers, the men's morale held. Against the flames of the burning houses the German infantry that followed the Tigers were easy to spot and to shoot. The cries of 'Whoa Mahomet!' from the remains of the shattered buildings let everyone know that they were far from done.

Nevertheless, the Germans still asked for Frost's surrender. One of Mackay's men, Lance Sergeant Stanley Halliwell, twenty-five, had been fighting in the school without rest. On Monday morning he had been trying to bash a new loophole in a wall with a sledgehammer, but had misjudged his swing and knocked Sapper Ashworth's front teeth out. Halliwell had been captured by the Germans on Tuesday afternoon, after he had rushed a tank he thought had been abandoned. The panzer had turned its guns on him and killed his mate, Sapper Terrence Hicks. As Hicks fell, Halliwell scrambled underneath the tank, reasoning it the best place to hide from the crew. He could hear them on their radio:

> Then he opened up with his main armament and nearly blew my eardrums. As if that wasn't enough, he began to start the tank. Then one of our lads hit it with a PIAT. I thought 'Christ, I've had enough of this!' I crawled out and put my hands up and was taken prisoner.[3]

Halliwell was frogmarched over the Bridge and a German officer put it to him that he should return under truce to tell his commander that the Germans wanted to meet him under the Bridge to discuss the British surrender. Halliwell was escorted back across the Bridge, but the men defending it opened fire on him and his escort – there was no truce in evidence. He ran for it, shouting at them not to be so stupid. Or words to that effect. Halliwell then spent ten minutes looking for Frost, running from building to building as mortars crumped and rounds zipped around him.

On finding Frost, he passed on the German officer's proposal – a 'big noise', in Halliwell's estimation – that Frost should meet him to discuss a surrender under a truce. Halliwell had been asked to give his word as a gentleman that he would return with his CO's reply. Frost takes up the story, saying:

> 'Tell them to go to hell.' Sergeant Halliwell, the sapper, replied, 'Do I really have to go back to tell them?' I answered, 'No. It is up to you. If you would like to stay and continue fighting, they will get the message anyway.'[4]

In Halliwell's words:

> So I thought, 'I'm not going back to tell them that', so I stayed. From then on we were just being chased from building to building, hiding where we could.[5]

But there would be no surrender at the Bridge on Tuesday.

Father Bernard Egan had already had one near miss that afternoon. He had been moved out of Battalion Headquarters, which were on fire. The radio equipment was moved to the cellar. Just as 'the Battalion comic', Sergeant 'Jack' Spratt, had said 'well, padre they've thrown everything at us but the kitchen stove',⁶ a direct hit brought the floor down on top of them, complete with kitchen stove. Spratt took the tag line that fate had so kindly offered him without hesitation: 'I knew the bastards were close, but I didn't believe they could hear us!'

Later a tank came to attack the house, and in the commotion to escape Padre Egan was hit on the staircase as he urged another man to get a move on. They fell to the ground floor. The other man was mortally wounded, and Egan had just crawled over to him when another shell struck. Coming to, he found the whole house on fire, his clothes burning, his leg broken, the pain 'excruciating'. He shouted for help, he yelled his name. The intelligence officer Lieutenant Buchanan came into the inferno, dragged him out and took him to the aid post, where all the padre could do was lie on his belly.

In the school, Captain Mackay turned on the radio at 1800 hrs and discovered that according to the BBC they had been relieved. Listening to the Battle raging around him, he drew his own conclusions. 'The sound of guns to the south was not getting any nearer. It looked like being a sticky night.'⁷ Mackay assessed his situation. He couldn't see how they would last the night – ever the sapper, he had tasked the wounded to work on improvised explosives – but with more than half the men he'd started with now wounded, and several killed, he was far from optimistic. The Tiger tanks' appearance didn't do much for his morale.

In Mackay's account the Tigers came up the ramp and started shelling the west side of the street, working in tandem, spraying the street with machine-gun fire to keep infantry at bay:

> When the leader got within thirty yards of the school it turned
> its enormous gun deliberately on us. There were two appall-
> ing explosions, and the whole north-west corner of the school
> was blown away.

Mackay hurried the wounded down to the cellar and then went up into the attic to watch out for an infantry attack. Instead of high explosive the Tigers fired two armour-piercing rounds right through the first floor of the school – a small mercy – but the whole build-ing still shook. Mackay was thinking that it would collapse: 'two more shots would have finished us'. The German infantry couldn't get by. Lit up by the burning buildings, and indeed by the burning school, they were easy targets. Mackay's assessment of the damage was, again, that of a sapper. The Tiger had left them new loopholes to defend themselves from, and as long as the fires burned the Ger-mans would not be able to evict him and his men. He ruled out using the home-made bombs on the Tigers, which had by now beat a retreat.

While they had not been forced out of the school, fires raged and smoke hung heavy over the redoubt. Mackay issued Benzedrine to his men. Fatigue had everyone in its grip; men were seeing double. But they were all hanging on, whether they were sappers, gunners, storemen, infantrymen or chaplains. At around 2300 hrs the Ger-mans attacked the school again, firing mortars and rifle grenades through the windows. Tanks could be heard grinding in nearby streets. Mackay weighed up the gruesome butcher's bill:

> The casualties were now four killed and twenty-seven wounded
> out of fifty. So ended the third day.[8]

Patrols continued, the houses burned, but incredibly the Bridge was still in British hands.

The gunners at the Bridge – Major Dennis Munford, Bombardier

Leo Hall and the rest of the crew – nursed their 'Dags', their radio batteries, in the rubble of the OP and hoped they would be able to call in fire tomorrow. They had had a good day as FOOs (Forward Observation Officers). But Hall considered 'we were in the centre of a circle of blazing buildings, our turn must come soon'.[9]

Not far from the Bridge, Major Anthony Deane-Drummond was still hiding in the toilet in the house he had broken into on Monday. The fighting in the Town had passed, but he dared not leave. He was as close as anyone had managed to get to the Bridge from the effort to push through the Town.

Peter Stainforth lay delirious on the floor of the cellar of the old people's home where he'd been taken. His wounds, morphia dreams and the nurses' kindness were the only impressions he could summon.

As midnight approached, through the cloud of sleeplessness and three days of battle Johnny Frost gathered his thoughts and surveyed his position. His men were in good spirits and miraculously didn't seem to be flagging. Within the limitations of the aid post in the cellar, the wounded were being well tended for, though, like everything else, medical supplies were running out. The Germans kept pressing their advantage, and night gave them a chance to resupply, refit, re-arm, and bring in fresh men and equipment.

As the buildings around the Bridge burned, ammunition cooking off in the flames, Frost's men were still putting out fires while his riflemen peered into the darkness around them for signs of movement from the three German approaches – west towards where the battle to break into the Town had ended in the afternoon; east along the riverfront, vehicles moving beyond the warehouses; and north into the Town itself, where 1st Parachute Brigade's original planned deployment lay. With less than a third of the Brigade's strength left, Frost had held on to his end of the Arnhem road bridge for as long as the Division had been ordered.

The buildings burning around him were an ominous sign that

Frost's position was desperate. The Battalion Diary did what it could to put a shine on the day:

> The most serious deficiency was in PIAT bombs, of which we now had none left, and so had no method of dealing with tanks which shelled our houses at very close range. The 6 Pounders still kept the Bridge and Western approaches covered, but could not maintain positions east of the Bridge.

The men at the Bridge had fought like lions, but they were out of anti-tank ammunition. The cellars were heaving with the wounded. The men who weren't watching for the enemy were putting out fires. The much-cursed 2nd Army had still not arrived, despite the slender hope offered that morning.

What would tomorrow bring?

27

POSTSCRIPT

It wasn't until late on Wednesday 20 September that the Bridge itself finally fell to the Germans. The remaining pockets of men attempted to break out from the houses now reduced to rubble, leaving them nowhere left to fight from. Lieutenant Colonel Frost was among the wounded, his leg smashed up by a mortar bomb. During the day a two-hour truce had been called to remove the wounded. The Germans were reported as congratulating the British on such a good battle, handing out the chocolate and cigarettes they'd taken from the failed supply drops. Some men carried on fighting, some with nothing but knives, until 0500 hrs on Thursday morning. By now, accounts are confused and contradictory. Frost's scratch force, 1st Airborne Division, had held the Bridge for four days, having been tasked with holding it for only two until relieved by 2nd Army. A victory of sorts, perhaps, but not the kind that was going to win you a war. Nevertheless, despite being a defeat, Arnhem is without doubt the Parachute Regiment's proudest battle honour.

Brigadier Hackett's decision to keep what was left of 4th Parachute Brigade where it had got to was yet another misstep. Surrounded by the Germans in a hollow in the trees 400 yards from the Divisional perimeter were the remnants of 156 Battalion, reduced to 150 men by late Wednesday afternoon. Hackett led a bayonet charge that finally reunited his shattered Brigade with the rest of 1st Airborne. They fed into what was now called 'the Perimeter'. By the end of the week, the Germans had a different name for it: 'der Kessel' ('the Cauldron').

Hackett's men were repositioned on the eastern side of the

Perimeter, near the crossroads at the centre of the Village, a short walk from the Hartenstein Hotel. Hackett displayed phenomenal bravery – as witnessed on Wednesday by Geoffrey Powell – rescuing a wounded officer from a burning Jeep. Hackett was injured later in the siege at Oosterbeek, receiving mortar fragments in his stomach. His life was saved by the surgical expertise of Captain Lipmann Kessel, but his Brigade had been destroyed.

Major General Urquhart, now present in his HQ, and with the rump of his Division close by, reorganized his lines and fought a defensive battle in hopeful expectation of relief. Nijmegen Bridge had been taken on Wednesday by the men of the Guards Armoured Division in tandem with a spectacularly bold daylight river assault by 3rd Battalion, 504th Parachute Infantry Regiment, who paddled their way across in boats. Facing attacks in the south that threatened to cut off the entire salient, 30 Corps were unable to press on convincingly to Arnhem. They did, however, bring something that 1st Airborne had needed from day one – firepower. Once radio contact had been made, German attacks were broken up by the medium guns of the 64th Medium Regiment, RA.

The Polish Parachute Brigade landed south of the river at Driel on Wednesday – without their anti-tank guns – and did what they could to get men across the river by boat to join 1st Airborne. Major General Stanislaw Sosabowski found himself given some of the blame for how the Battle had played out south of the river, as the British top brass closed ranks in the face of the Allied failure to relieve Urquhart and his men. Once again, the Poles were short-changed by 'Boy' Browning, who after doing so much campaigning to get them under his control now dropped them like a hot brick.

The days after Wednesday fell into a pattern – mortaring in the morning, 'the Daily Hate' – probing attacks by the Germans, broken up by the British guns south of the river, the steady accumulation of the wounded, as the men became increasingly exhausted. Promises of relief coming to nothing day after day.

At the Old Church where Lieutenant Colonel William 'Sheriff'

Thompson had saved the Division, a force under the command of Major 'Dickie' Lonsdale fought to keep the lower road in British hands and a route open across the polder to the river itself. Great acts of bravery followed in this lower sector. Lance Sergeant John Baskeyfield fended off German armour with a pair of 6-pounders, fighting on even as he was injured and the men with him were killed. He died at the gun, one of the five Victoria Crosses awarded after the Battle, along with Captain Lionel Queripel, Flight Lieutenant David Lord, Lieutenant Jack Grayburn and Major Robert Cain, the only VC winner from Arnhem not to receive his award posthumously.

Supply drops continued, some reaching the open ground beside the Hartenstein Hotel, in the centre of the Perimeter, but plenty of planes still vectoring on the old, wrong supply zone, delivering materiel to the enemy. More aircrews were lost in the shooting gallery, more precious cargo planes damaged.

On Sunday night an attempt to send 300 men of 4th Battalion the Dorsets, 43rd Wessex Division, came to nothing. Boats, DUKWs (amphibious vehicles) and men were scattered along the river, only a few making it to the guns near the Old Church, the rest being captured.

The wounded were caught in the middle of the Battle at the Schoonoord Hotel, the building repeatedly shelled and mortared, many men in their beds wounded afresh. In the south near the Old Church an aid station in the house belonging to the Ter Horst family was established, but this too was bombarded and shot up. A truce was called on Sunday, as Colonel Warrack RAMC convinced Urquhart that he should arrange a proper ceasefire to get the worst of the wounded out. The Germans agreed, and for two hours men were ferried out of Oosterbeek and to St Elisabeth Hospital. Then the fighting resumed.

Evacuation finally came on the night of Monday 25 September, not a moment too soon. The Germans had pushed hard with Tiger tanks in the south and threatened to surround the Division completely and cut it off from access to the river. In an earlier life

Urquhart had made a study of the withdrawal at Gallipoli during the Great War and now drew on what he had learned; another defeat that shared an underestimation of the enemy. The men followed tape lines down to the river, queueing in the rain as German machine guns swept the ground between the Old Church and the river. Urquhart, rather than wait and be the last man out, joined the queue with everyone else. Some swam, but many drowned. The wounded were left behind, and with them medics, whose work continued, but now as prisoners of war.

Two thousand or so got out and across the river. Some 1,984 men lost their lives, 6,854 were taken prisoner. Louis Hagen got out, Geoffrey Powell became a prisoner of war. Eric Mackay went on the run, and returned to British lines in October. Anthony Deane-Drummond spent three days hiding in a toilet, then another thirteen in a cupboard, evading the enemy. 'Shan' Hackett, disguised as deaf, was smuggled out of hospital and hidden by the underground, until he was able to escape.

Arnhem remained in German hands. They evacuated the city and the Bridge was destroyed by Allied bombing in October. Arnhem was not liberated until 16 April 1945 in Operation Anger, by the Canadians.

A disaster, and one that by noon on Black Tuesday was set in stone. Roy Urquhart, however, remained convinced that it had all been worth it and, echoing Montgomery, said:

> The operation was not one hundred per cent successful and did not end quite as we intended. The losses were heavy but all ranks appreciate that the risks involved were reasonable. There is no doubt that all would willingly undertake another operation under similar conditions in the future. We have no regrets.

Walking around the Perimeter the year before last with a group of podcast listeners, many of them new to the Battle, I was struck once more by how small the battlefield is at Arnhem. Even though so much was happening in so many different places at once, nothing is too far away. In the shade of the trees by the Old Church in the south of Oosterbeek, where the Light Regiment's guns were dug in, it is hard to imagine the men clinging on for so many days after they expected to be relieved. Similarly, the leafy parkland around the Hartenstein Hotel (now a superlative museum and archive), and the grand houses on the other side of the crossroads, suggest nothing of the struggles of eighty years ago; it is like imagining war coming to the smarter parts of Cheltenham or Harrogate. There is some spang, scarring from shrapnel and projectiles, but not so much as to dominate. At Zwarteweg 14 there is a flag marking Roy Urquhart's misfortune. The Schoonoord Hotel at the crossroads, where so many men's lives were saved, is a fine spot for a drink or a meal. At the Bridge, there is not a trace of the buildings where Frost and the men with him fought such a desperate last stand. The places can only tell you so much of the story – the Woods and fields around Johanna Hoeve are completely changed – time cannot be expected to stand still, nor a city.

Yet the Dutch remember, and in a different way perhaps to the way we remember in the United Kingdom. To visit Arnhem and Oosterbeek in September is to visit a place where remembrance of another country's sacrifice takes centre stage. Maroon and sky-blue flags, the colours of the British Airborne Divisions, depicting Bellerophon astride his winged steed Pegasus, flutter everywhere; sometimes rather chunky and frankly too old-looking airborne re-enactors zip around the streets on Jeeps and no one bats an eyelid. While the Battle of Arnhem led directly to the Hunger Winter of 1944–5, the Germans taking out their displeasure on the population which had so fervently greeted the British and Americans in September 1944, there seems to be no animus in Arnhem. As one veteran, Private Steven Morgan, who was with Lieutenant Jack Grayburn at the Bridge when he was killed, put it in 2014: 'We came here to liberate them, but we smashed their city up. It makes me wonder how they can forgive us, but they always have.'[1]

In the years that followed, veterans of the Battle were taken under the wing of residents in Arnhem and Oosterbeek, and in the most extraordinary gesture of commemoration, primary schoolchildren take on a role of personal remembrance, each adopting a grave for a year and learning and writing about the life of the man lying therein. The Commonwealth War Graves Commission cemetery at Oosterbeek, where 1,528 men lie, is situated next to the site of the Supply Drop Zone where on Black Tuesday things 'went awry'. Like so many CWGC graveyards, it is a place of almost unbearable poignancy. The names of the soldiers, their regiments, their ages, the dedications, all demanding reflection and contemplation. Some of the names are familiar to those who have read about the Battle, but the vast majority are not, even in a battle as brief and self-contained as this.

On the Sunday of the weekend's commemoration, the children place flowers on the individual grave they have been taking care of and hand over responsibility to the next year of children. It is a ceremony of unique tenderness, and a perfect response to the endurance and sacrifice of the men who fought in the Woods, the Town, the Village and at the Bridge.

Marching into the Town to join the effort to get through to the Bridge, men of 2nd Battalion the South Staffords bring their equipment with them in trolleys. They may have arrived sixty miles behind enemy lines by glider, but they had to do the remaining six miles on foot, with the enemy ever-present.

APPENDIX:

ARNHEM ORDER OF BATTLE FOR OPERATION MARKET GARDEN

THIS IS AN ABRIDGED ORDER OF BATTLE, based on the work of Mark Hickman at the Pegasus Archive.

Figures are calculated as follows:

'Went in' figures indicate the total unit strength present in Arnhem, but may not represent their full operational strength as some elements were not air-transportable.

'Died' includes all those killed in action until the Brigade was withdrawn from the area after the battle, deaths as a result of atrocities or escape attempts, and anyone who died from their wounds up until the end of 1944.

'Wounded' are those evacuated safely to the Allied rear.

'Missing' represents those taken prisoner during the battle, though a number of these men may have subsequently escaped.

1ST AIRBORNE DIVISION

Divisional HQ and Defence Platoon
Major General Roy Urquhart
GSO 1 (Operations): Lieutenant Colonel Charles Mackenzie
GSO 1 (Air): Lieutenant Colonel Eric Henry Steele-Baume (attached to IX Troop Carrier Command during the Battle)
GSO 2 (Air): Major David Madden
GSO 2 (Intelligence): Major Hugh Maguire
Commander Royal Artillery: Colonel Robert Loder-Symonds
Commander Royal Engineers: Lieutenant Colonel Eddie Myers
Commander Royal Electrical and Mechanical Engineers: Captain A. F. Ewens
Commander Royal Army Service Corps: Lieutenant Colonel Michael Packe
Assistant Adjutant and Quartermaster General: Lieutenant Colonel Henry Preston
Assistant Director of Medical Services: Colonel Graeme Warrack
Assistant Director of Ordnance Services: Lieutenant Colonel Gerald Mobbs
Assistant Provost Marshal: Major O. P. Haig
Defence Platoon: Lieutenant A. D. Butterworth
Based at Fulbeck Hall. Flew in 7 C-47s from Barkston Heath and Saltby, and 29 Horsas from Fairford, Down Ampney and Manston.

Went in: 142 men	Died: 14	Evacuated: 70	Missing: 58

1ST PARACHUTE BRIGADE

Brigadier Gerald Lathbury
Brigade HQ and Defence Platoon
Brigade Major: Major Tony Hibbert

Based at Syston Old Hall. Flew in 9 C-47s from Barkston Heath and (believed) 8 Horsas from Blakehill Farm.			
Went in: 82 men	**Died:** 5	**Evacuated:** 3	**Missing:** 74

1ST PARACHUTE BATTALION

Lieutenant Colonel David Dobie
Battalion HQ
HQ/Support Company: Captain J. A. E. Davies
Signals Platoon
Assault Platoon
Mortar Platoon
Medium Machine-Gun Platoon
R Company: Major John Timothy
S Company: Major Ronnie Stark
T Company: Major Chris Perrin-Brown
(Each rifle company had three platoons)
Based at Grimsthorpe Castle and Bourne. Flew in 34 C-47s from Barkston Heath, vehicles in 7 Horsas from Keevil and a Hamilcar from Tarrant Rushton.

Went in: 548 men	**Died:** 84	**Evacuated:** 89 or 108 (reports differ)	**Missing:** 377 or 358

2ND PARACHUTE BATTALION

Lieutenant-Colonel John Frost
Battalion HQ
Support Company
Assault Platoon
Mortar Platoon
Medium Machine-Gun Platoon
A Company: Major Digby Tatham Warter

B Company: Major Douglas Crawley
C Company: Major Victor Dover

Based at Stoke Rochford and Grantham. Flew in 34 C-47s from Saltby, vehicles in 7 Horsas from Keevil and a Hamilcar from Tarrant Rushton.

Went in: 525 men	Died: 57	Evacuated: 16	Missing: 452

3RD PARACHUTE BATTALION

Lieutenant Colonel John Fitch
Battalion HQ
HQ Company
Signals Platoon
Assault/Pioneer Platoon
Mortar Platoon
Medium Machine-Gun Platoon
A Company: Major Mervyn Dennison
B Company: Major Peter Waddy
C Company: Major Peter Lewis
(Each rifle company had three platoons)

Based at Spalding. Flew in 34 C-47s from Saltby, vehicles in 7 Horsas from Keevil and a Hamilcar from Tarrant Rushton.

Went in: 588 men	Died: 65	Evacuated: 28	Missing: 495

1ST AIRLANDING ANTI-TANK BATTERY, RA

Major Bill Arnold
Battery HQ
A Troop
B Troop
C Troop
D Troop
P Troop
Z Troop

Based at Heckington and Helpringham, with P Troop at Tarrant Rushton. Flew in 30 Horsas from Manston (mostly) and Blakehill Farm, P Troop in 8 Hamilcars from Tarrant Rushton.			
Went in: 191 men	**Died:** 24	**Evacuated:** 52	**Missing:** 115

1ST PARACHUTE SQUADRON, RE

Major Douglas Murray			
Squadron HQ			
A Troop: Captain Eric Mackay			
B Troop			
C Troop			
Based at Donington. Flew in 9 C-47s from Barkston Heath and 4 Horsas from Keevil.			
Went in: 143 men	**Died:** 20	**Evacuated:** 13	**Missing:** 110

16 PARACHUTE FIELD AMBULANCE, RAMC

Lieutenant Colonel E. Townsend			
Based at Culverthorpe. Flew in 6 C-47s from Barkston Heath and Saltby, and 6 Horsas from Keevil.			
Went in: 135 men	**Died:** 6	**Evacuated:** 0	**Missing:** 129

4TH PARACHUTE BRIGADE

Brigadier John Hackett			
Brigade HQ and Defence Platoon			
Brigade Major: Major Charles Dawson			
Based at Knossington Grange. Flew in 8 C-47s from Spanhoe and 1 C-47 with Advance Party from Barkston Heath, and 8 Horsas from Keevil.			
Went in: 86 men	**Died:** 12	**Evacuated:** 43	**Missing:** 31

156 PARACHUTE BATTALION

Lieutenant Colonel Sir Richard Des Voeux
Battalion HQ
HQ Company
Signals Platoon
Support Company
Anti-Tank Platoon
Mortar Platoon
Medium Machine-Gun Platoon
A Company: Major John Pott
B Company: Major John Waddy
C Company: Major Geoffrey Powell
(Each rifle company had three platoons)

Based in and around Melton Mowbray. Flew in 33 C-47s from Saltby and 1 C-47 with Advance Party from Barkston Heath, vehicles in 7 Horsas from Keevil and 1 Hamilcar from Tarrant Rushton.

Went in: 621–5 men	Died: 98	Evacuated: 68	Missing: 455–9

10TH PARACHUTE BATTALION

Lieutenant Colonel Ken Smyth
Battalion HQ
HQ Company
Signals Platoon
Support Company
Assault Platoon
Mortar Platoon
Medium Machine-Gun Platoon
A Company: Major Pat Anson
B Company: Major Peter Warr
D Company: Major Cedric Horsfall

Based at Somerby, Thorpe Satchville, Burrough on the Hill and Twyford. Flew in 33 C-47s from Spanhoe and 1 C-47 with Advance Party from Barkston Heath, vehicles in 7 Horsas from Keevil and a Hamilcar from Tarrant Rushton.

| Went in: 582 men | Died: 92 | Evacuated: 86 | Missing: 404 |

11TH PARACHUTE BATTALION

Lieutenant Colonel George Lea
Battalion HQ
HQ Company
Signals Platoon
Support Company
Assault Platoon
Mortar Platoon
Medium Machine-Gun Platoon
A Company: Major David Gilchrist
B Company: Major Guy Blacklidge
C Company: Major Peter Milo

Based at Melton Mowbray. Flew in 33 C-47s from Saltby and 1 C-47 with Advance Party from Barkston Heath, vehicles in 7 Horsas from Keevil and 1 Hamilcar from Tarrant Rushton.

| Went in: 571 men | Died: 99 | Evacuated: 72 | Missing: 407 |

2ND (OBAN) AIRLANDING ANTI-TANK BATTERY, RA

Major A. Haynes
Battery HQ
E Troop
F Troop
G Troop
H Troop
X Troop

Based at Harrowby. Flew in 24 Horsas from Blakehill Farm and 8 Hamilcars from Tarrant Rushton.			
Went in: 168 men	**Died:** 25	**Evacuated:** 37	**Missing:** 106

4TH PARACHUTE SQUADRON, RE

Major Aeneas Perkins
Squadron HQ
No. 1 Troop
No. 2 Troop
No. 3 Troop

Based at Uppingham. Flew in 9 C-47s from Spanhoe and 4 Horsas from Keevil.			
Went in: 155 men	**Died:** 19	**Evacuated:** 64	**Missing:** 72

133 PARACHUTE FIELD AMBULANCE, RAMC

Lieutenant Colonel W. Alford

Based at Barleythorpe Hall. Flew in 6 C-47s from Spanhoe and Saltby and 6 Horsas from Keevil.			
Went in: 129 men	**Died:** 6 (not including one officer in the sea tail)	**Evacuated:** 3	**Missing:** 120

1ST AIRLANDING BRIGADE

Brigadier Philip Hicks
Brigade HQ and Defence Platoon
Deputy Commander: Colonel Hilaro Barlow
Brigade Major: Major Charles Anthony Howell Bruce Blake

Based at Woodhall Spa. Flew in 11 Horsas from Broadwell.			
Went in: 69 men	**Died:** 7	**Evacuated:** 39	**Missing:** 23

1ST BATTALION THE BORDER REGIMENT

Lieutenant Colonel Tommy Haddon
Battalion HQ
HQ Company
Signals Platoon
Pioneer Platoon
Support Company
Mortar Group
Anti-Tank Group
Medium Machine-Gun Group
A Company: Major Thomas Montgomery
B Company: Major Tommy Armstrong
C Company: Major William Neill
D Company: Major Charles Breese
(Each rifle company had four platoons)
Based at Woodhall Spa, with B Company at Bardney. Flew in 56 Horsas from Broadwell and Blakehill Farm and a Hamilcar from Tarrant Rushton.

Went in: 788 men	Died: 121	Evacuated: 235	Missing: 432

2ND BATTALION THE SOUTH STAFFORDSHIRE REGIMENT

Lieutenant Colonel Derek McCardie
Battalion HQ
HQ Company: Major John Simonds
Signals Platoon
Pioneer Platoon
Support Company
Mortar Group
Medium Machine-Gun Group
Anti-Tank Group

A Company: Major T. B. Lane
B Company: Major Robert Cain
C Company: Major Philip Wright
D Company: Major J. E. Phillp
(Each rifle company had four platoons)
Based at Woodhall Spa. Flew to Arnhem over two days in 62 Horsas from Manston and Broadwell, and a Hamilcar from Tarrant Rushton.

Went in: 767 men	Died: 85	Evacuated: 124	Missing: 558

7TH (GALLOWAY) BATTALION THE KING'S OWN SCOTTISH BORDERERS

Lieutenant Colonel Robert Payton-Reid
HQ Company: Major Alexander Cochran
Signals Platoon
Pioneer Platoon
Support Company: Major Henry Hill
Mortar Group
Medium Machine-Gun Group
Anti-Tank Group
A Company: Major Robert Buchanan
B Company: Major M. B. Forman
C Company: Major G. M. Dinwiddie
D Company: Major Gordon Sherriff
(Each rifle company had four platoons)
Based at Woodhall Spa. Flew in 56 Horsas from Down Ampney and Blakehill Farm, and a Hamilcar from Tarrant Rushton.

Went in: 765 men	Died: 112	Evacuated: 76	Missing: 577

181 AIRLANDING FIELD AMBULANCE, RAMC

Lieutenant Colonel Arthur Marrable
Based at Stenigot House and Martin. Flew in 12 Horsas from Down Ampney.

Went in: 137 men	Died: 5	Evacuated: 10	Missing: 122

DIVISIONAL UNITS

1ST AIRLANDING LIGHT REGIMENT, RA

Lieutenant Colonel 'Sheriff' Thompson

Regimental HQ

1st Airlanding Light Battery: Major Arthur Norman-Walker

A Troop: Captain J. H. D. Lee (Forward Observation Officer, 1st Border)

A Troop: Captain John Walker (Forward Observation Officer, 7th KOSB)

2nd Airlanding Light Battery: Major James Linton

C Troop: Captain Peter Chard (Forward Observation Officer, 156 Battalion)

D Troop: Captain Percy Taylor (Forward Observation Officer, 11th Battalion)

3rd Airlanding Light Battery: Major Dennis Munford

E Troop: Captain Tony Harrison (Forward Observation Officer, 2nd Battalion)

F Troop: Captain Tudor Griffiths (Forward Observation Officer, 3rd Battalion)

Based at Boston. Flew in 57 Horsas from Fairford, Blakehill Farm, Down Ampney, Manston and Keevil on the First Lift; No. 2 Battery and the remainder flew in 33 Horsas from Manston on the Second Lift.

| Went in: 372 men | Died: 36 | Evacuated: 136 | Missing: 200 |

1 FORWARD (AIRBORNE) OBSERVATION UNIT, RA

Major Denys Wight-Boycott (1st Sea Tail)

Second-in-Command (Acting Commanding Officer): Captain Arthur Edgar O'Grady (in Arnhem)

Based at Harlaxton Hall. Flew on the First Lift in 3 Horsas from Keevil, chalk numbers 456–458, piloted by No. 21 Flight, 'D' Squadron The Glider Pilot Regiment. Further parachute parties flew in aircraft attached to their assigned units.

| Went in: 73 men | Died: 7 | Evacuated: 13 | Ditched and Rescued: 4 | Missing: 49 |

1ST AIRBORNE DIVISIONAL SIGNALS

Lieutenant Colonel Tom Stephenson
Regimental HQ
Second-in-Command: Major Anthony Deane-Drummond
No. 1 Company – Divisional HQ Signals
No. 2 Company – Brigade and Artillery Signals
E-Section (with 1st Airlanding Light Regiment): Lieutenant Robert Gregg
F-Section (with HQ Royal Artillery)
J-Section (with 1st Parachute Brigade)
K-Section (with 4th Parachute Brigade)
L-Section (with 1st Airlanding Brigade)
1st Polish Independent Parachute Brigade Group
1st Airborne Corps Signals (based at Nijmegen)
Based at Caythorpe. Flew in C-47s and Horsas from several airfields, as much of the unit had been split up among the Division to provide signals for brigade and artillery HQs.

Went in: 348 men	Died: 28	Evacuated: 149	Missing: 171

1ST AIRBORNE RECONNAISSANCE SQUADRON

Major Freddie Gough
HQ Troop
Support Troop
A Troop
C Troop
D Troop
Based at Ruskington. Flew in 8 C-47s from Barkston Heath and 22 Horsas from Tarrant Rushton.

Went in: 181 men	Died: 30	Evacuated: 73	Missing: 78

21ST INDEPENDENT PARACHUTE COMPANY

Major 'Boy' Wilson

> No. 1 Platoon

> No. 2 Platoon

> No. 3 Platoon

Based at Newark. Flew in 12 Stirlings from Fairford and a Horsa (believed from Fairford).

Went in: 186 men	Died: 20	Evacuated: 120	Missing: 46

9TH (AIRBORNE) FIELD COMPANY, RE

Major John Winchester

> No. 1 Platoon

> No. 2 Platoon

> No. 3 Platoon

Based at Tattershall and Coningsby. Flew in 22 Horsas over two lifts from Keevil.

Went in: 194 men	Died: 44	Evacuated: 71	Missing: 79

261 (AIRBORNE) FIELD PARK COMPANY, RE

Lieutenant W. Skinner

Flew in 3 Horsas and a Hamilcar, all believed to be from Tarrant Rushton.

Went in: 13 men	Died: 2	Evacuated: 5	Missing: 6

250 (AIRBORNE) LIGHT COMPOSITE COMPANY, RASC

No. 1 Para Platoon and 1st Para Jeep Section (1st Para Brigade)

No. 2 Para Platoon and 2nd Para Jeep Section (4th Para Brigade)

No. 3 Para Platoon and 3rd Para Jeep Section (1st Airlanding Brigade)

Based at Longhills Hall, Branston and Lincoln. Flew in 4 C-47s from Barkston Heath and Saltby, and 34 Horsas and 3 Hamilcars from Keevil, Harwell and Tarrant Rushton.

Went in: 226 men	Died: 29	Evacuated: 75	Missing: 122

1ST (AIRBORNE) DIVISIONAL ORDNANCE FIELD PARK, RAOC

Captain Bill Chidgey

Based at Grantham. Flew in a shared C-47 from Barkston Heath and a Horsa from Keevil.

| Went in: 19 men | Died: 2 | Evacuated: 2 | Missing: 15 |

1ST (AIRBORNE) DIVISIONAL WORKSHOPS, REME

Advanced Workshop Detachment

　1st Para Brigade Light Aid Detachment

　4th Para Brigade Light Aid Detachment

Based at Sleaford. Flew in 4 Horsas from Fairford and Down Ampney, with other men flying in with various units.

| Went in: 61 men | Died: 6 | Evacuated: 29 | Missing: 26 |

1ST (AIRBORNE) DIVISIONAL PROVOST COMPANY, CMP

Captain Bill Gray

　No. 1 Provost Section (1st Para Brigade)

　No. 2 Provost Section (4th Para Brigade)

　No. 3 Provost Section (1st Airlanding Brigade)

　No. 4 Provost Section (Divisional HQ)

Based at Stubton Hall and Newark, with sections at Divisional and Brigade HQs. Company HQ flew in a Horsa from Down Ampney, sections in C-47s and Horsas with other units.

| Went in: 69 men | Died: 7 | Evacuated: 13 | Missing: 49 |

89TH (PARACHUTE) FIELD SECURITY SECTION, INTELLIGENCE CORPS

Captain J. Killick

Based at Wellingore. HQ flew in shared Horsa from Fairford, with other men flying in with various units.

| Went in: 16 men | Died: 2 | Evacuated: 4 | Missing: 10 |

UNITS ATTACHED TO THE DIVISION

THE GLIDER PILOT REGIMENT

Colonel George Chatterton (flew to Nijmegen)
No. 1 Wing
Lieutenant Colonel Iain Murray
A Squadron: Major H. T. Bartlett
No. 1 Flight
No. 17 Flight
B Squadron: Major T. I. J. Toler
No. 3 Flight
No. 4 Flight
No. 19 Flight
No. 20 Flight
D Squadron: Captain James Ogilvie
No. 5 Flight
No. 8 Flight
No. 13 Flight
No. 21 Flight
No. 22 Flight: Captain Iain Muir
G Squadron: Major Robert Croot
No. 9 Flight
No. 10 Flight
No. 23 Flight
No. 24 Flight

NO. 2 WING

Lieutenant Colonel John Place
C Squadron: Major J. A. C. Dale
No. 6 Flight
No. 7 Flight

E Squadron: Major B. P. H. Jackson
No. 11 Flight
No. 12 Flight
No. 25 Flight
F Squadron: Major F. A. S. Murray
No. 14 Flight
No. 15 Flight
No. 16 Flight

No. 1 Wing HQ based at Harwell. A Squadron based at and flew from Harwell. B Squadron based at Brize Norton, but flew from Manston. D Squadron based at and flew from Keevil. G Squadron based at and flew from Fairford.

No. 2 Wing HQ based at Broadwell. C Squadron based at and flew from Tarrant Rushton. E Squadron based at and flew from Down Ampney. F Squadron based at and flew from Broadwell and Blakehill Farm.

Went in: 1,262 men	Died: 219	Evacuated: 532	Missing: 511

Figures do not include Regimental HQ and part of A Squadron, who flew Airborne Corps HQ to Nijmegen without sustaining any serious casualties.

DUTCH LIAISON MISSION – NO. 2 (DUTCH) TROOP OF NO. 10 (INTER-ALLIED) COMMANDO

Lieutenant M. J. Knottenbelt

Flew in with various units.

Went in: 12 men	Died: 1	Evacuated: 9	Missing: 2

6080 AND 6341 LIGHT WARNING UNITS, RAF

Flew in 4 Horsas with the Second Lift.

Went in: 45 men	Died: 9	Evacuated: 4	Missing: 32

US AIR SUPPORT SIGNALS TEAM – 306TH FIGHTER CONTROL SQUADRON

Flew in 4 Wacos from Manston.

Went in: 10 men	Died: 0	Evacuated/	Missing: Unknown

GHQ SIGNAL LIAISON REGIMENT DETACHMENT – 'PHANTOM'

Went in: 10 men	Died: 0	Evacuated: Unknown	Missing: Unknown

JEDBURGH TEAM

Went in: 3 men	Died: 1	Evacuated: 1	Missing: 1

PUBLIC RELATIONS TEAM

Went in: 15 men	Died: 0	Evacuated: 14 (unconfirmed)	Missing: 1

1. SAMODZIELNA BRYGADA SPADOCHRONOWA

Major-General Stanislaw Sosabowski

Brigade HQ

Based at Rock House, Stamford.

Went in: 104 men and 9 British liaison officers	Died: 5	Wounded: 16	Missing: 15

1ST BATTALION

Major M. Tonn

Based at Easton-on-the-Hill.

Went in: 354 men	Died: 11	Wounded: 28	Missing: 4

2ND BATTALION

Major W. Ploszewski

Based at Wansford.

| Went in: 351 men | Died: 11 | Wounded: 33 | Missing: 7 |

3RD BATTALION

Captain W. Sobocinski

Based at Peterborough.

| Went in: 374 men | Died: 30 | Wounded: 48 | Missing: 39 |

ANTI-TANK BATTERY

Captain J. Wardzala

Based at Blatherwyche.

| Went in: 132 men | Died: 30 | Wounded: 30 | Missing: 29 |

ENGINEER COMPANY

Captain P. Budziszewski

Based at Wansford.

| Went in: 133 men | Died: 2 | Wounded: 20 | Missing: 1 |

SIGNALS COMPANY

Captain J. Burzawa

Based at Easton-on-the-Hill.

| Went in: 93 men | Died: 7 or 8 | Wounded: 16 | Missing: 10 |

MEDICAL COMPANY

Lieutenant J. Mozdzierz

Based at Stamford and Blatherwyche.

| Went in: 90 men | Died: 2 | Wounded: 13 | Missing: 7 |

TRANSPORT AND SUPPLY COMPANY
Captain A. Siudzinski

Went in: 43 men	Died: 8	Wounded: 13	Missing: 8

LIGHT ARTILLERY BATTERY
Major J. Bielecki

Went in: 6 men	Died: 0	Wounded: 2	Missing: 0

Men get to grips with a supply pannier. An airborne division ran on fumes at the best of times.

NOTES

INTRODUCTION

1   Dominions-United Kingdom-Empire and Exile.

1. THE BRIDGE: THE BESIEGED

1   2nd Battalion Parachute Regiment Diary for 16 September.
2   An improvised battle group commanded by Leutnant General Kurt Chill.
3   Numbers of the dead are taken from the Arnhem Roll of Honour. What this doesn't tell the reader is the number of wounded, but it offers a rule of thumb regarding how the day went in terms of contact with the enemy.
4   Ibid.
5   Frost, *A Drop Too Many*, p. 281.
6   Pegasus Archive: Lance Corporal Arthur S. Hendy's account.
7   Eric Mackay's account, *The Royal Engineers Journal*, vol. lxviii, no. 4 (December 1954).

2. THE TOWN: THE EMBATTLED

1   Eric Davies's account | ParaData.

3. THE VILLAGE: A QUIET NIGHT?

1   1st Battalion the Border Regiment War Diary entry for 1900 hrs on 18 September, Pegasus Archive.
2   Haddon had been the Duty Officer at No. 10 Downing Street the night of Pearl Harbor, 7 December 1941.

5. THE TOWN: THE GENERAL

1   Personal account of Brigadier James Hill's experiences in Normandy | ParaData.
2   Viscount Montgomery of Alamein, *The Memoirs of Field Marshal Montgomery*.
3   Ibid.

4   G. T. Gilchrist, *Malta Strikes Back*, quoted in John Baynes, *Urquhart of Arnhem*.
5   Baynes, *Urquhart of Arnhem*. Letter to John Baynes from James Cleminson.
6   Lathbury was taken to St Elisabeth Hospital over the road later in the day.
7   Urquhart, *Arnhem*, pp. 118–19.
8   Cleminson in conversation with the author, 2004.

6. THE VILLAGE: DIVISIONAL HEADQUARTERS – THE BRIGADIERS

1   Preston quoted in Urquhart, *Arnhem*, p. 117.
2   Urquhart quoted in Hibbert, *The Battle of Arnhem*, p. 94.
3   Hicks's citation for the Military | ParaData.
4   Urquhart, *Arnhem*, p. 116.
5   Frost, *A Drop Too Many*, p. 248.
6   Henniker quoted in Baynes, *Urquhart of Arnhem*, pp. 72–3.
7   Mackenzie, Ryan Archive.
8   Ibid.
9   Hackett quoted in Julian Thompson, *Ready for Anything*.

7. THE VILLAGE AND THE WOODS: THE GUNS. 1ST LIGHT AIRLANDING REGIMENT, RA

1   6th Airborne Overlord report, part 2 | ParaData.
2   Bombardier Leo Hall, 'Memories of Arnhem', Pegasus Archive. Hall very much felt he needed to put the record straight regarding communications at Arnhem, as well as some of the accounts that he felt didn't add up.
3   It's remarkable that he admits this.

8. THE TOWN: THE COLONELS ON THE RIVER ROAD

1   Alan Bush's account | ParaData.
2   Ibid.
3   3rd Battalion War Diary.
4   Ibid.
5   Alan Bush's account | ParaData.
6   Heaps, *Escape From Arnhem*, p. 35.
7   Ibid, p. 56.

MORNING

1   Mawson, *Arnhem Doctor*, p. 46.

9. THE BRIDGE: TOTTERING ABOVE THE BOILING TIDE

1   Frost, *A Drop Too Many*, p. 318.
2   Richie, *Arnhem*, p. 208.
3   Mackay's account.
4   Ibid.
5   Frost, *A Drop Too Many*, p. 283.
6   Ibid, p. 282.
7   Account of Arvian Llewellyn-Jones | ParaData.
8   Bernard Egan's account, Cornelius Ryan WWII papers, box 110, folder 40: Bernard Egan.
9   Account of Robert Bolton 1st Airborne Recce Accounts mentioning Trooper Bolton | ParaData.
10 Ronald Brooker's personal account of his experiences during Operation Market Garden | ParaData.
11 Sims, *Arnhem Spearhead*, p. 17.
12 Ibid, p. 20.
13 5 stones, 31.75 kilograms.
14 These are the names Sims gives us in his memoir.
15 His memoir, *A Drop Too Many*, punning on this perhaps?
16 Frost, *A Drop Too Many*, p. 42.
17 11½ stone, 72.5 kilograms.
18 *Parachutists* by Major Harry Pozner, M.C., Royal Army Medical Corps. First published in the *Journal of the Royal Army Medical Corps*, April 1946, Homepage | BMJ Military Health.
19 Frost, *A Drop Too Many*, p. 47.
20 Ibid.

10. THE TOWN: THE DOCTOR

1   Fleming, *Penicillin*, p. 163.
2   Around 20 per cent of wounds were abdominal. The rule of thumb that applied is that 20 per cent of your body area is the abdomen, and in the random environment of hot flying projectiles and shocks, 20 per cent of the body took 20 per cent of the wounds. Numbers notwithstanding, these were the hardest wounds to deal with and shaped British medical policy.
3   Lipmann Kessel, *Surgeon at Arms*, p. 51.
4   Cole, *On Wings of Healing*, p. 8.
5   Lipmann Kessel, *Surgeon at Arms*, p. 27.
6   Ibid, pp. 13–14.
7   Ibid, p. 27.
8   Stainforth, *Wings of the Wind*, p. 277.
9   Ibid, p. 283.

10   Text taken from IWM, first field dressing pack | Imperial War Museums (iwm.org.uk).
11   Stainforth, *Wings of the Wind*, p. 320.
12   Mawson, *Arnhem Doctor*, p. 46.
13   Ben Lockett's account, The Battle of Arnhem Archive, Pegasus Archive.
14   Mawson, *Arnhem Doctor*, p. 52.
15   His title is vaguely misleading; he was in charge.
16   Cole, *On Wings of Healing*, p. 116.

11. THE TOWN: THE BATTALION

1   Renumbering and renaming as part of Operation Cascade was an ongoing deception plan masterminded by the extraordinary Dudley Clarke. This granular effort confused the Germans to Clarke's satisfaction, as well as Winston Churchill.
2   'Fighting in Built Up Areas' – Military Training Pamphlet No. 55, published in 1943.
3   Ibid.
4   Ibid.
5   British Parachute Rifle Company (1944–49) (battleorder.org).

12. THE TOWN: THE MONASTERY

1   In the 1945 summary of airborne operations entitled 'Airborne Airtransported Operations', in a paper peppered with epigrams, the author glumly quoted Hamlet's 'What a piece of work is man' speech: 'this most excellent canopy, the air, look you, this brave o'erhanging firmament, this majestical roof fretted with golden fire, – why, it appears no other thing to me than a foul and pestilent congregation of vapours'.
2   Ernest M. Wyss | ParaData, quoting from the almost unobtainable *By Land, Sea and Air*, pp. 107–8.
3   Captain Ernest Mariel Wyss, citation in the Pegasus Archive. He had been nominated for the Victoria Cross.
4   Ernest M. Wyss | ParaData, letter from Norman Howes.
5   Lt Col Russell's personal account of the Battle of Arnhem from the Parachute 2 Club Newsletter, 1990. | ParaData.
6   Although the War Diary ruefully noted: 'Unfortunately most of those with stories to tell failed to get back.'
7   South Staffords War Diary.

13. THE VILLAGE: DIVISIONAL HQ AND ELSEWHERE

1   Rev. G. A. Pare's account, Cornelius Ryan WWII papers, box 117, folder 01: G. A. Pare – Cornelius Ryan Collection of World War II Papers, Ohio University Libraries, Digital Archival Collections.

2   Ibid.
3   Ibid. Fascinatingly, this exchange in the original typed-up copy of
     Pare's account is crossed out with a pencil.
4   Hagen, *Arnhem Lift*, p. 18.
5   Joe Roberts's memoir, *With Spanners Descending*, probably has the
     best Arnhem book title, and is a glimpse into the mechanics of the
     Division in both senses.
6   Major Ernest Watkins, *Arnhem: 1 Airborne Division*. First published by
     the Army Bureau of Current Affairs, 9 December 1944. Kindle edition.
     Books Ulster, 2016.
7   These extraordinary, indeed mind-boggling, artificial ports were
     assembled in the fortnight that followed D-Day. Two were built: one
     at the American beach named Omaha, the other at the British harbour
     known as 'Mulberry B', at Arromanches-les-Bains north of Bayeux. The
     American Mulberry was abandoned after the storm of 19–20 July. Two
     and a half million men were brought in through 'Mulberry B' before it
     was shut down in March 1945. The remains of the gigantic concrete
     breakwaters called Phoenixes still line the bay at Arromanches.

14. THE VILLAGE: ALARUMS AND EXCURSIONS IN THE WEST

1   Joe Harvey, Pegasus Archive.
2   Lieutenant Ted Newport quoted in Eastwood, Gray and Green, *When
     Dragons Flew*, p. 118.
3   Armour piercing CRA report, Pegasus Archive.
4   Godefroy, 'For Queen, King and Empire', p. 13.

15. THE WOODS: THE BRIGADE

1   John Waddy | ParaData Archive interview.
2   Powell, *Men at Arnhem*, p. 63.
3   Blockwell, *Diary of a Red Devil*, p. 158.
4   Muir was a captain in the Glider Pilot Regiment, a veteran of
     Normandy, but given the improvised nature of things and the
     intensity of what happened it is perhaps an understandable detail for
     Hagen to have mistaken. The 156 Diary, written well after the event,
     also mentioned that Muir had been killed in this assault: he wasn't.
5   Hagen, *Arnhem Lift*, p. 35.
6   Ibid, p. 37.
7   Robert Laslett, John Pott, Pegasus Archive.
8   John Waddy | ParaData.
9   Ibid.
10   4th Parachute Brigade War Diary, Hackett's appendix.
11   Peters and Cherry with Howes and Francis, *Desert Rise*, p. 137.
12   Ibid, p. 138.

AFTERNOON

1   Quoted in *The Devil's Birthday* by Geoffrey Powell.

16. THE TOWN: ON THE BRINK

1   Jack Reynolds, IWM interview (Oral history) | Imperial War Museums (iwm.org.uk).
2   Ibid.
3   Ibid.
4   Ben Lockett's account, The Battle of Arnhem Archive, Pegasus Archive.
5   Phillip Hart Turner, Pegasus Archive.
6   Mawson, *Arnhem Doctor*, p. 54.
7   Ibid, p. 61.

17. THE BRIDGE: NO RELIEF

1   US Silver Star citation, Pegasus Archive, Frank's page.
2   Tony Frank's account, Antony M. Frank | ParaData.
3   1st Parachute Brigade Diary, entry for 0800 hrs: other accounts, and the peculiar chronology in the Diary, suggest it was at 1000 hrs rather than 0800 hrs as stated.
4   Eric Mackay's account, *Blackwood's Magazine*, 1945, reprinted in https://t.co/bMiPF9LBC9.
5   Ibid.
6   Ibid.
7   Ibid.
8   Robert Lygo | ParaData.
9   'command' for 'kamerad!': Neil Thornton, *Arnhem Umbrella*, p. 220.
10 When consulting on the film *A Bridge Too Far*, Frost insisted to an incredulous Anthony Hopkins, who was playing him, that he should not run between buildings.
11 Actions at Arnhem, account by Pte R. Janovsky | ParaData.
12 Stanley C. Panter | ParaData.
13 Ibid.
14 Sims, *Arnhem Spearhead*, p. 99.
15 Ibid, p. 102.
16 Arvian Llewellyn-Jones | ParaData.
17 Frost, *A Drop Too Many*, pp. 318–19.
18 Mackay's account.

18. THE WOODS: DISENGAGE

1   Powell, *Men at Arnhem*.
2   Urquhart, *Arnhem*, p. 125.

3   1st Airborne Division HQ War Diary.
4   Peters, Cherry, Howes and Francis, *Desert Rise*, p. 150.
5   Ibid, p. 155.
6   Powell, *Men at Arnhem*, p. 68.
7   Ibid, p. 71.
8   Ibid, p. 75.

19. 1500 HRS: SKIES OVER ARNHEM

1   Steer, *Arnhem – The Fight to Sustain*, p. 66.
2   RASC Headquarters War Diary, Pegasus Archive.
3   These boggling figures are found in Steer, *Arnhem – The Fight to Sustain*.
4   Wright, *The Wooden Sword*, p. 218.
5   Ibid.
6   Ibid.
7   Ibid.
8   Air Chief Marshal Leslie Hollingsworth DSO, AOC of 38 Group.
9   Steer, *Arnhem – The Fight to Sustain*, p. 57.
10   Urquhart, *Arnhem*, pp. 127–8.
11   Harold Bruce | ParaData.
12   Hagen, *Arnhem Lift*, p. 39.
13   John Stanleigh, recording supplied to the author by his grandson.
14   Christopher James | ParaData.
15   Stanley Holden | ParaData.
16   Lord later received a posthumous VC for his efforts and doubtless courage – but the men on board KG374 who died with him got nothing.
17   190 Squadron Diary, Pegasus Archive.
18   Warrant Officer Keith Prowd (pegasusarchive.org).
19   Stanley Maxted, https://open.spotify.com/track/5foDTOMqjvpSmb1a16IxyY?si=49d763eba9714f7b.

20. ENGLAND AND THE WOODS: THE POLES

1   Sosabowski, *Freely I Served*, p. 152.
2   Ibid, p. 188.
3   Ibid, p. 194.
4   Ibid, p. 197.
5   Ibid, p. 201.
6   Swiecicki, *With the Red Devils at Arnhem*, p. 54.
7   Ibid, p. 56.
8   Peters and Buist, *Glider Pilots at Arnhem*, pp. 413–14.

21. THE WOODS TO THE VILLAGE: CRUMBS OF COMFORT?

1   Urquhart, *Arnhem*, p. 130.
2   Blockwell, *Diary of a Red Devil*, p. 114.
3   Hackett's personal account.
4   Sapper Alan Gauntlet | ParaData.
5   Joe Sunley in Peters, Cherry, Howes and Francis, *Desert Rise*, p. 174.
6   Cornelius Ryan WWII papers, box 112, folder 29: Thomas C. Bentley –
    Cornelius Ryan Collection of World War II Papers – Ohio University
    Libraries – Digital Archival Collections.
7   Powell, *Men at Arnhem*, p. 93.
8   Steer, *Arnhem – The Fight to Sustain*, p. 162.
9   But there are no figures to support this estimation: ibid, p. 322.
10 Ibid, p. 177.
11 Ibid, pp. 180-1.
12 Ibid, p. 182.
13 https://www.paradata.org.uk/article/extracts-days-gone-richard-adams-
    detailing-events-december-1943-january-1945.
14 Cornelius Ryan WWII papers, box 117, folder 01: G. A. Pare –
    Cornelius Ryan Collection of World War II Papers – Ohio University
    Libraries – Digital Archival Collections.
15 Samm, *Traitor of Arnhem*, reproduced in 'Freddie Gough's Specials at
    Arnhem', chapter 8.

22. THE VILLAGE: THE CHURCH

1   Urquhart, *Arnhem*, p. 127.
2   Cornelius Ryan WWII papers, box 114, folder 01: W. K. F. Thompson –
    Cornelius Ryan Collection of World War II Papers – Ohio University
    Libraries – Digital Archival Collections.
3   Urquhart, *Arnhem*, pp. 126-7.
4   Ibid.
5   Edmund Scrivener, Pegasus Archive.
6   Moran, *The Anatomy of Courage*, p. 70.
7   Ibid, p. 6.
8   Ibid, p. 178.

EVENING

1   Cole, *On Wings of Healing*, p. 118.

23. THE VILLAGE: LIFE AND DEATH AT THE CROSSROADS

1   Warrack, 'The RAMC at Arnhem', after-action report.
2   Mawson, *Arnhem Doctor*, pp. 64-5.

3   £275.52 in today's money according to the National Archive currency index. The modern British Army rifle, the SA80, costs around £1,000 with a £4,000 combat upgrade. The British Army's purse strings were tight when it came to small arms – reflecting perhaps what they thought of their riflemen.

4   Converting Reichsmarks to Sterling is tricky given the German economy had been running hot for years.

5   The Manual of the Sten Gun machine carbine, in Thompson, *The Sten Gun*, p. 30.

6   White, *With the Jocks*, p. 197.

7   Ford, *Weapon of Choice*, p. 80.

8   Ibid, p. 82.

9   Among its number another research scientist, the molecular biologist Captain Michael Swann (later The Lord Swann).

10   Operational Research in Northwest Europe, the Work of No. 2 Operational Research Section with 21 Army Group (dtic.mil).

11   Mawson, *Arnhem Doctor*, p. 72.

12   Christopher James | ParaData.

13   Ibid.

14   Ibid.

15   Cornelius Ryan WWII papers, box 110, folder 24: Geoffrey Stanners – Cornelius Ryan Collection of World War II Papers – Ohio University Libraries – Digital Archival Collections.

16   Mawson, *Arnhem Doctor*, p. 75.

24. THE WOODS: FINAL DECISION

1   Powell, *Men at Arnhem*, p. 99.

25. THE VILLAGE: LAST BATTALION LEFT

1   Major William Neil account. Major William Neill, Pegasus Archive.

2   Ibid.

3   Ibid.

4   1st Battalion the Border regiment War Diary. 1st Battalion The Border Regiment, Pegasus Archive.

26. THE BRIDGE: ALL AFIRE

1   Sims, *Arnhem Spearhead*, p. 104.

2   Tatham-Warter quoted in Thornton, *Arnhem Umbrella*, p. 505 (e-book edition).

3   Halliwell quoted in Arthur, *Men of the Red Beret*, p. 199.

4   Frost, *A Drop Too Many*, p. 311.

5   Halliwell quoted in Arthur, *Men of the Red Beret*, p. 200.

6   Cornelius Ryan WWII papers, box 110, folder 40: Bernard Egan – Cornelius Ryan Collection of World War II Papers – Ohio University Libraries – Digital Archival Collections. In accounts it is the kitchen sink/kitchen stove wisecrack that pops up again and again.
7   Mackay's account.
8   Ibid.
9   Leo Hall, Pegasus Archive.

27. POSTSCRIPT

1   Dutch children laid flowers at graves in tribute to Arnhem soldiers | UK | News | Express.co.uk

BIBLIOGRAPHY AND SOURCES

If you want to know about the rest of the campaign as well as the events in Arnhem following Black Tuesday:

William Buckingham, *Arnhem 1944*. Temps Publishing, 2002. Buckingham has little time for 'Boy' Browning. A refreshing and manageable account of the whole Market Garden campaign.

Christopher Hibbert, *The Battle of Arnhem*. Batsford, 1962. A straight-bat telling of the 1st Airborne's battle.

Robert Kershaw, *It Never Snows in September*. Ian Allan Publishing, 1990. Kershaw's breakthrough account, using German sources, to try to understand the Battle from the German perspective.

Martin Middlebrook, *Arnhem 1944: The Airborne Battle*. Viking, 1994. A classic account of the Battle. Comprehensive, though some of it is disputed!

Cornelius Ryan, *A Bridge Too Far*, 1974.

A NOTE ON SOURCES

A by-product of the Battle of Arnhem's fame, or notoriety, is that it has had more ink spilt about it than perhaps any other British battle of the Second World War. Excellent books have been written drawing on personal accounts, memoirs and the War Diaries. There is a mountain of stuff online too, poring over exact locations and photographs, then and now. So here's the conundrum: little of this was written down on 19 September, when there wasn't much time for personal diaries, and the Battalion War Diaries are by their very nature fragmented and incomplete.

One of the richest sources, ironically perhaps, is the Cornelius Ryan Archive at Ohio University. His interviews for his research for *A Bridge Too Far* are available online, in the form of digital copies and transcriptions thereof. The strength of these wide-ranging interviews, questionnaire responses, recollections, and in some cases unpublished personal accounts, is that they were made before *A Bridge Too Far* was published, before the film was a twinkle in the eyes of producers Joseph E. Levine and Richard P. Levine. Therefore, they come uncoloured by a great deal of the narrative that has since been laid down and that has determined how the Battle is looked at. Even now, more than fifty years later, they feel fresh.

PEGASUSARCHIVE.ORG

War Diaries, order of battle, accounts and biographies. A completely essential starting point for anyone interested in British Airborne Forces and the Battle of Arnhem.

PARADATA.ORG.UK

ParaData offers anyone interested in British Airborne Forces information about individual names, units and personal accounts.

THE RYAN ARCHIVE

Cornelius Ryan's archive at Ohio University Libraries is simply fantastic. It offers interviews from *A Bridge Too Far*, *The Longest Day* and *The Last Battle*.

IWM.ORG.UK

Operational Research in Northwest Europe, the Work of No. 2 Operational Research Section with 21 Army Group (dtic.mil).

BATTLEORDER.ORG

This site offers a comprehensive inventory of the British army's working parts, as well as a wealth of contemporary information.

PUBLISHED SOURCES

Max Arthur, *Men of the Red Beret: Airborne Forces 1940–1990*. Sphere, 1992.
John Baynes, *Urquhart of Arnhem: The Life of Major General R. E. Urquhart, CB, DSO*. Brassey's, 1993.
Albert Blockwell, *Diary of a Red Devil: By Glider to Arnhem with the 7th King's Own Scottish Borderers*. Helion, 2005.
Howard N. Cole, *On Wings of Healing: The Story of the Airborne Medical Services, 1940–1960*. Naval & Military Press, 1963.

Stuart Eastwood, Charles Gray and Alan Green, *When Dragons Flew: An Illustrated History of The 1st Battalion The Border Regiment 1939–45.* Silver Link Publishing, 2009.

Alexander Fleming, *Penicillin: Its Practical Application.* Butterworth, 1946.

Matthew Ford, *Weapon of Choice: Small Arms and the Culture of Military Innovation.* Oxford University Press, 2017. Kindle Edition.

John Frost, *A Drop Too Many.* Pen & Sword Books, 2002. Kindle Edition.

Andrew B. Godefroy, 'For Queen, King and Empire: Canadians Recruited into the British Army, 1858–1944', *Journal of the Society for Army Historical Research*, vol. 87, no. 350 (Summer 2009), pp. 135–49.

Louis Hagen, *Arnhem Lift: A German Jew in the Glider Pilot Regiment.* The History Press, 2012. Kindle Edition.

Leo Heaps, *Escape From Arnhem: A Canadian Among the Lost Paratroops.* Sapere Books, 2023. Kindle Edition.

Robert Hilton, *Freddie Gough's Specials at Arnhem. An illustrated history of the 1st Airborne Reconnaissance Squadron from official records and personal accounts of members of the Squadron.* R. N. Sigmond Publishing, 2017.

Alexander Lipmann Kessel, *Surgeon at Arms: Parachuting into Arnhem with the First Airbornes.* Pen & Sword Books, 2011. Kindle Edition.

Stuart Mawson, *Arnhem Doctor.* Spellmount, 1981.

Eric Mackay, *The Royal Engineers Journal*, vol. lxviii, no. 4, pp. 305–25 (December 1954).

Richard Mead, *General 'Boy': The Life of Lieutenant General Sir Frederick Browning.* Pen & Sword Books, 2011. Kindle Edition.

Viscount Montgomery of Alamein, *The Memoirs of Field Marshal Montgomery.* Pen & Sword Books, 1958. Kindle Edition.

Lord Moran, *The Anatomy of Courage: The Classic WWI Study of the Psychological Effects of War.* Little, Brown, 2007. Kindle Edition.

Martin Peters and Niall Cherry with John Howes and Graham Francis, *Desert Rise – Arnhem Descent: The 10th Parachute Battalion in the Second World War.* Brendon Publishing, 2016.

Mike Peters and Luuk Buist, *Glider Pilots at Arnhem.* Pen & Sword Books, 2010. Kindle Edition.

Geoffrey Powell, *Men at Arnhem.* Pen & Sword Books, 2010. Kindle Edition.

Sebastian Richie, *Arnhem – Myth and Reality: Airborne Warfare, Air Power and the Failure of Operation Market Garden.* Robert Hale, 2019.

Joe Roberts, *With Spanners Descending: A History of the Royal Electrical and Mechanical Engineers with 1st Airborne Division, 1942–1945.* The Bluecoat Press, 1996.

Allan Samm, *Traitor of Arnhem.* Minerva Press, 1996.

James Sims, *Arnhem Spearhead: A Private Soldier's Story.* Imperial War Museum, 1978.

Stanislaw Sosabowski, *Freely I Served: The Memoir of the Commander, the 1st Polish Independent Parachute Brigade 1941–1944*. Pen & Sword Books, 2013. Kindle Edition.

Peter Stainforth, *Wings of the Wind*. Grafton Books, 1985/Falcon Press, 1952.

Frank Steer, *Arnhem – The Fight to Sustain: The Untold Story of the Airborne Logisticians*. Pen & Sword Books, 2000. Kindle Edition.

Marek Swiecicki, *With the Red Devils at Arnhem: Personal Experiences with the 1st Polish Parachute Brigade 1944*. Helion and Company, 2012. Kindle Edition.

Julian Thompson, *Ready for Anything: The Parachute Regiment at War*. Weidenfeld & Nicolson, 1989.

Leroy Thompson, *The Sten Gun* (Weapon Book 22). Bloomsbury Publishing, 2012. Kindle Edition.

Neil Thornton, *Arnhem Umbrella: Major Digby Tatham Warter DSO*. Fonthill Media, 2022. Kindle Edition.

Will Townend and Frank Baldwin, *Gunners in Normandy: The History of the Royal Artillery in North-West Europe, January 1942 to August 1944*. The History Press, 2020. Kindle Edition.

R. E. Urquhart, *Arnhem* (Pen & Sword Military Classics). Pen & Sword Books, 2008. Kindle Edition.

Major Ernest Watkins, *Arnhem: 1 Airborne Division* (Annotated). Books Ulster, 2016. Kindle Edition.

Peter White, *With the Jocks: A Soldier's Struggle for Europe 1944–45*. Sutton Publishing, 2001.

Lawrence Wright, *The Wooden Sword: The Untold Story of the Gliders in WWII*. ELEK Books, 1967.

OTHER

John Stanleigh, recording supplied to the author by his grandson.

ACKNOWLEDGEMENTS

THIS BOOK HAS ONLY BEEN POSSIBLE with the help of an array of brilliant, helpful and insightful people. Which isn't my way of saying that if you don't like it you know who to blame: the buck stops here with this. But in being able to write *Arnhem: Black Tuesday*, and to try to locate another way of writing about the Battle of Arnhem, I have been incredibly fortunate.

When I write a stand-up show I always say that I write it with the audience. You come up with what you think will work, and then the audience help you to edit, adjust, refine over the weeks of try-outs (a huge thanks to anyone who has come to see one of my shows where there's a sheet of paper perched on the bar stool). Writing a book isn't quite the same; there's more sitting on your backside looking at a blank page, but using other people as a sounding board and as stimulus has been essential.

The first thank you is to my father, Ingram Murray; there'd be no book without him. If anyone has sent me in this direction, it is Dad. And of course my mother, Juliet, who has put up with him and then with the apple falling not that far from the tree. Their love of history and their encouragement of my interest in it, as well as their enjoyment of the way in which *We Have Ways of Making You Talk* has come to be a part of all our lives, has been a delightful family thing.

James Holland, whom I speak to an inordinate amount, and who flatters me with his time and generosity of intellect, is also up to his neck in how this book came about, trying to find other ways of looking at things; his deep knowledge, understanding and sympathy for the history of the Second World War is the most extraordinary resource to have at one's disposal. The last few years with the podcast, the growth of the Festival that accompanies it, the Independent Company community that has grown up around it, all entirely spontaneously and out of a fascination with the subject, continues to stagger me. So thank you to the listeners, the contributors, the enthusiasts.

This brings me to people who have directly helped with sources and research. Niall Cherry is the don of Arnhem scholarship. Having published multiple times with exhaustively researched and detailed accounts, he serves as the link with a great deal of witness testimony. I am in a sense dreading him reading this! The Arnhem Fellowship – in which a new member is greeted with the question 'please tell us something about your interest in the Battle of Arnhem' – is a friendly and bottomless pit of Arnhem-related stuff, keeping tabs on family connections as well as commemoration. Niall pointed me in the right direction for several accounts I might need in trying to cover a couple of parts of the Battle that can get overlooked.

Online there is the Pegasus Archive run by Mark Hickman, who also provided me with copies of the War Diaries. Mark's site covers all British airborne operations during the Second World War and is a comprehensive source of Army and RAF accounts of the Battle of Arnhem. Going through the damage to every aircraft in the Third Lift on Black Tuesday makes for an absorbing afternoon. In tandem with this is the ParaData website, where one can search names, units and accounts for all the history of British Airborne Forces. Together these are a treasure trove of accounts that tell the story of the experiences of the men from the ground up, and they are essential for it.

ParaData is part of the Air Assault Museum in Duxford, which allowed Merryn Walters to engage in research for me. Merryn sniffed out several excellent leads and has a sound approach to viewing sources that this scattergun author appreciated immensely. Similarly John Tregonning, who upon hearing that I was interested in the medical side of the Battle took himself off to the Wellcome Archive and in the process has become an expert on airborne medical provision in 1944. Keith Brigstock of the Garrison Artillery

Volunteers helped with questions on firepower and the 75mm howitzer drills. The Garrison's role is to keep alive the techniques used in the British Army for gunnery, and what he doesn't know isn't worth asking about.

And then there are the people who've been sounding boards. My eldest daughter Scarlett Murray has been reading drafts since I began, redirecting her dad where necessary. It's also gratifying that another generation of this family has been exposed to the Arnhem story. Willow for the distraction of having another project to occupy myself with when not doing this . . . Paul Davies has been similarly helpful reviewing an early halfway draft. And Andy Aitcheson, former sapper and crap hat, has been tremendously helpful when I have a chapter done and need eyes on it. Andy's work around 52nd Lowland Division, who had a narrow escape at Arnhem when scheduled to arrive by plane, then very temporarily by glider, God help them, is fascinating and faintly obsessive. These people are my tribe!

Thanks to the team at Goalhanger podcasts, who make *We Have Ways of Making You Talk*, and Tony Pastor, whose idea it was in the first place. Also to Joey McCarthy, who produces the podcast, as well as Jon, Laura, Izzy, Harry and the rest of the team.

Thank you to my manager Richard Allen Turner and the rest of the team at Avalon. Twenty years ago Richard rang me just before I parachuted on to Ginkelse Heide in Arnhem for a TV programme, telling me I didn't have to do it if I didn't want to. Yeah, well, sometimes you have to say no to your manager. Jon Thoday, Dan Lloyd, Steve O'Connor and Mary Grace Brunker, thank you.

Bill Scott Kerr and the team at Transworld, Phil Lord, Barbara Thompson, Richard Mason, Katrina Whone, Tony Maddock and Nicole Witmer, thank you for taking on the idea and making it dazzle.

And my wife Eleanor, who one day will get dragged around the battlefield, but not just yet. Thank you for the encouragement, listening to me witter on about 'Shan' Hackett on a French hillside, and the endless cups of tea that materialize on my desk.

Parachuting required intense training: men joining the Parachute Regiment underwent rigorous physical training as well as psychological screening. Jumping in 'sticks', these men exit their Dakotas as fast as they can. But arriving suddenly in battle brought its own pressures.

PICTURE ACKNOWLEDGEMENTS

Principal characters

All courtesy of the author with the exception of:

Captain Stuart Mawson, RAMC: courtesy of the author/ParaData. org.uk

Padre Bernard Egan, Lieutenant Colonel John Frost, Brigadier 'Shan' Hackett, Brigadier Philip Hicks, Brigadier Gerald 'Legs' Lathbury, Captain Eric Mackay, Major Geoffrey Powell, Captain Lionel Queripel: courtesy of the author/pegasusarchive.org

Captain Alexander Lipmann Kessel, RAMC: National Library of Medicine/Kessel family.

Part-opener pictures

Imperial War Museum.

Integrated pictures

Page xvi
Gliders on Landing Zone 'L' around Wolfheze: Imperial War Museum.

Pages xxviii–xxix, top
Cross section of the terrain in the town: courtesy of the author.

Pages xxx–xxxi
An aerial view of the vital bridge at Arnhem: courtesy of the author.

Page 330
Marching into the Town to join the effort: courtesy of the author.

Page 350
Men get to grips with a supply pannier: courtesy of the author.

Page 368
Parachuting required intense training: courtesy of the author.

Pages 386–7
Bombardier J. Buckley: courtesy of the author.

Pages 388–9
Prisoners of War – a mixed bag: courtesy of the author.

Pages 390–1
In the morning 1st Airborne Division was on the attack: courtesy of the author.

Plate section pictures

All courtesy of the author with the exception of:

Page 16, bottom
Jacobsen/Bundesarchiv, bild 101I-497-3531A-34.

Endpapers

Lance corporal battle kit of the 1st Parachute Brigade, 1st Airborne Division, 1944: photograph © Thom Atkinson, inventory supplied by Alan Looke of The Devils in Red.

INDEX

artillery transport, 257; view of
Drop Zones, 257; waiting in
England, 14–15, 241–2, 261
Special Operations Executive (SOE),
97, 177, 252
Spratt, Sergeant 'Jack', 320
Stainforth, Captain Peter, 117–20,
204, 322
Stanleigh, Private John, 246
Stanners, Corporal Geoffrey, 306
Stark, Major Ronald, 79
Sunley, Sergeant Joe, 227, 266–7
supplies: ammunition, 19–20, 25–6,
75, 87, 91–2, 174, 203, 218, 229,
232–3, 236–8, 250, 266, 269, 272,
276, 323; berets, 272–3, 312;
cigarettes, 114, 194, 276, 324;
delivery, 243–50; food, 26, 174, 194,
203, 218, 229, 232–3, 250, 269–70,
272; medicine and medical
equipment, 107–8, 114–15, 232–3,
238, 269, 322; radio sets and
batteries, 67, 229, 238, 322; water,
25–6, 100, 203, 218, 229, 234
Swiecicki, Marek, 259–60

Tatham-Warter, Major Digby, 23, 87,
212, 216–17, 316
Taylor, Captain P. A., 137, 153
Taylor, Captain Willie, 45, 46–7
Taylor, Private George, 195
Ter Horst family, 314, 326
Theirs Is The Glory (movie), 2
Thomas, Lieutenant Colonel Micky,
130–1
Thompson, Lieutenant Colonel
William 'Sheriff', 70, 275–7,
314, 325–6
Todd, Lieutenant Harvey, 179
Totalize, Operation, 254
Transfigure, Operation, 13, 233–5, 257, 272
Tunisia campaign: 1st Parachute
Brigade, 38, 256; 2nd Parachute
Battalion, 96; 4th Parachute
Brigade, 129; casualties, 38, 96; Sten
problems, 295; Tiger tanks, 316, 317;
veterans, 186

Turner, Artificer Quartermaster
Sergeant, 166
Turner, Lieutenant Philip, 205

Urquhart, Major General Roy: 1st
Airborne Division appointment,
43–4, 256; absence from Divisional
HQ, 33–4, 46, 47–8, 50–1, 55, 120,
138; accompanying 3rd Parachute
Brigade to the front, 27, 44–5, 46–7,
77–8, 302; air plan, 167–8, 171–2;
appointment of Barlow, 157;
Arnhem glider landing, 36, 158;
batman, 156; briefing on return to
Divisional HQ, 156; career, 36,
39–43; ceasefire (Sunday 24th
September), 326; changes decisions
made in his absence, 137–8, 155;
character, 39, 42–3, 53, 57, 277–8;
escape from loft (Tuesday
morning), 117, 123–4, 160–1, 204,
288; expecting relief (Wednesday),
325; instructions to Divisional HQ,
82; 'Jedburgh' team intelligence,
179; Landing and Drop Zones
choice, 239–41, 243; meeting
Hackett (Tuesday afternoon), 179,
222–5; message to Hackett
(Tuesday morning), 158, 222;
Operation Transfigure plans, 233,
257; radio communications
difficulties, 243; preventing
panicked retreat, 277–80, 282–3;
relationship with Sosabowski,
257–8; replacement during
absence, 50–3, 55–7, 157; return to
Divisional HQ, 123–4, 125, 155, 156;
rifle battalions, 312; trapped in loft,
28, 36, 40, 43, 45, 47–8, 144, 159,
302, 328; Tuesday morning
timetable, 167; view of Arnhem
Battle, 326; view of his own
decisions, 156; view of Gough, 95;
view of Sten guns, 294; view of
Tuesday afternoon, 232, 274;
visiting wounded (Tuesday
evening), 303–4; watching supply

ABOUT THE AUTHOR

Al Murray's alter ego, The Pub Landlord, is one of the most recognizable and successful comic creations of the past twenty years, and Murray, who has won numerous awards and accolades, continues to fill arenas and theatres around the world.

He is also the author of many successful books including *Watching War Films with My Dad* and *Command*, a sharply entertaining analysis of the key allied military leaders in the Second World War. He is well known for co-hosting the hugely popular Second World War history podcast *We Have Ways of Making You Talk* with fellow bestselling military author James Holland.

Arnhem: Black Tuesday is his first history book about a single campaign.

Field dressing on his left shoulder, Bombardier J. Buckley of 1 Battery fires his 75mm pack howitzer.

Prisoners of War – a mixed bag. The man on the left is a Dutch fifth columnist captured by Dutch police; the others are men pressed into German service. The shorter man is a Tatar from the Soviet Union; the other two are Poles.

In the morning 1st Airborne Division
was on the attack; by nightfall defence
was its only option.

KEY TO THE ENDPAPERS

The kit shown in the endpapers was issued to a Lance Corporal, Parachute Brigade, Battle of Arnhem in 1944.

1   Parachute, Personnel, GQ X-Type Statichute and Harness
2   Denison Smock and over (jump) smock
3   Toggle rope
4   Battledress blouse, Pattern 37, with wrist watch and dog tags placed on sleeves
5   Individual Soldier's Service/Pay Book
6   Braces, trousers, pair
7   Gators, web, pair
8   Socks, pair
9   Ammunition boots, pair
10 Gloves, wool, pair
11 Wallet, leather
12 Shield (veil), face, camouflaged (scarf)
13 Battledress trousers, Pattern 37 (Airborne modified), colourless shirt, undervest, underpants
14 Haversack, Pattern 37, with mess tin, mug, water bottle, two 24-hour ration kits
15 Kitbag, Parachutist, Mk II, with handling line and sleeve
16 Shovel (in kitbag)
17 Cutlery, 'Housewife', spare boot laces, wash towel
18 Entrenching tool head
19 Haft (handle) for entrenching tool
20 Ammunition pouches, universal, Pattern 37, pair
21 Web belt and braces, Pattern 37
22 9mm Machine Carbine, Sten MkV and cleaning kit (below)
23 Bayonet, No. 4 Mk II, with scabbard (and Frog, web, airborne)
24 Pocket loading tool for Sten
25 Magazine, Sten, 32 rounds of 9mm ammunition (28 rds usually loaded)
26 Bandoleer, web, with 7 magazines for Sten
27 Cigarettes, matches, playing cards

28 Haversack, Respirator, Lightweight, Mk II
29 Grenades, Hand, No. 36M Mk I and No. 69
30 Fighting knife, Fairbairn-Sykes, with scabbard
31 Cape, gas, in roll
32 Respirator (gas mask), Lightweight No. 5 Mk I
33 Ointment, anti-gas
34 Hood, anti-gas
35 Eye shield, anti-gas
36 Ground cloth, with sewing kit/thimble from 'Housewife' on top
37 Beret, maroon ('Red'), Airborne Forces, with Parachute Regiment cap badge
38 Torch (flashlight)
39 First field dressing
40 Helmet, steel, Airborne, Troops (HSAT) Mk I, leather harness/chin cup, camouflaged netting

References: Norton, Maj G. G. (personal correspondence), Airborne Forces Museum, Altershot, Hants., 6 April 1974.

KIT ISSUED TO A LANCE CORPORAL, PARACHUTE BRIGADE, ARNHEM 1944 (See key on pages 395–6)